THE AIR DEFENSE OF THE UNITED STATES

A STUDY OF THE WORK OF THE AIR DEFENSE COMMAND AND ITS PREDECESSORS THROUGH JUNE 1951

The air defense of the United States, a
study of the work of ADC and its
predecessors through June 1951. Air
Defense Command. (Feb 52)

Prepared By
THE DIRECTORATE OF HISTORICAL SERVICES
OFFICE OF THE AIR ADJUTANT GENERAL
HEADQUARTERS, AIR DEFENSE COMMAND

HEADQUARTERS
AIR DEFENSE COMMAND
ENT AIR FORCE BASE
COLORADO SPRINGS, COLORADO

4 April 1952

ADAHS 314.7

SUBJECT: Air Defense Command Historical Study

TO: Commandant
    Command and General
      Staff College
    Fort Leavenworth, Kansas

    1. The Commanding General of the Army Antiaircraft Command has requested that your headquarters be furnished the attached copy of the Air Defense Command Historical Study titled, The Air Defense of the United States. As noted in the preface, the attempt was made in this study to trace the evolution of the air defense system in this country from approximately the end of WW II through June 1951. The study was printed for dissemination because it was felt the data contained in it would be of value for orientation and reference purposes.

    2. The study is the work of the Directorate of Historical Services, Headquarters, Air Defense Command, and full responsibility for the factual and analytical accuracy of the volume is assumed by that office.

    FOR THE COMMANDING GENERAL:

                                   Donald C. Morris

1 Attachment
  ADC Hist.

This Document Contains Information Affecting the National Defense of the United States Within the Meaning of the Espionage Laws, Title 18 U.S.C., Sections 793 and 794. Its Transmission or the Revelation of Its Contents in any Manner to an Unauthorized Person is Prohibited by Law.

DO NOT DESTROY. RETURN TO AAG.

This Document Contains
435 pages and 19 Charts.

No. __61__ of 200 Copies.

PREFACE

The present volume is a history of the evolution of an air defense system in the United States from approximately the end of World War II through June 1951. The decision to include in the present work an account of the pioneer air defense efforts of its predecessors as well as major developments within the Air Defense Command for the first half of 1951 was prompted by certain important historiographical considerations. Foremost of these was the necessity for placing the present Air Defense Command's air defense effort in its proper historical setting. Unfortunately, there was a year and one half period (June 1947-December 1948) when no history of air defense was written. And while Continental Air Command histories for the period January 1949-June 1950 contained much information of value, the diversity of missions of that command had the effect of obscuring its air defense contributions as revealed in its official history.

It is frankly admitted that a great wealth of data on certain of the subjects treated herein remains to be exploited. It is also acknowledged that several subjects deserving of treatment were not presented, either for lack of time or because of a paucity of reference data. It is felt, however, that the considerations necessary to an historical appreciation of the complex subject of air defense have been revealed in the present work. In future semi-annual histories and historical monographs any omissions appearing in this volume will be corrected.

The greatest of care was exercised to substantiate all facts and analyses in the history with pertinent documentation. Also, the officers of the headquarters were solicited to read and comment freely on those chapters the subject matter of which was most familiar to them. If, in spite of these precautions, inaccuracies of fact or misleading interpretations are subsequently revealed, immediate correction will be made in all outstanding copies.

Credit for whatever merits the history may have is shared with the historians of the lower echelons and with the many officers of the headquarters who gave so freely of their time to discussions with the historians and to the reading of drafts. Appreciation is extended also to Major General Charles T. Myers, Vice Commander, and Colonel Walter W. Robinson, Air Adjutant General, without whose administrative and supervisory support preparation of the history would have been impossible. Finally, to the clerical staff of the historical office - Mr. Albert Fuquay, Editor; S/Sgt Monroe Buehring, Chief Clerk; and Mesdames Marietta Polly and Betty Terry, Clerk Stenographers - acknowledgement is due for the consistency of form and legibility of the manuscript.

    Thomas A. Sturm
    Denys Volan
    George Billias
    Howard Stevens

TABLE OF CONTENTS

PREFACE

LIST OF CHARTS AND MAPS

PART I: THE BACKGROUND

    Chapter One: The Growth of Air Defense Consciousness, 1933 – 1945 1
    Chapter Two: ADC and the Air Defense Mission 30

PART II: THE GROWTH OF AN AC&W SYSTEM

    Chapter Three: The Year of Decision – 1948 55
    Chapter Four: LASHUP 75
    Chapter Five: The Permanent AC&W System 95

PART III: FIGHTER AIRCRAFT IN AIR DEFENSE

    Chapter Six: Units and Bases 116
    Chapter Seven: Aircraft for Air Defense 140
    Chapter Eight: Fighter Crews and their Training 177

PART IV: ORGANIZATION FOR AIR DEFENSE

    Chapter Nine: The Evolving Pattern of Air Defense Organization 197

PART V: A NATIONAL AIR DEFENSE IN THE MAKING

    Chapter Ten: The Army and Air Defense 217
    Chapter Eleven: The Role of the Navy in Air Defense 237
    Chapter Twelve: The Ground Observer Corps 251
    Chapter Thirteen: Air Raid Warning Systems 288
    Chapter Fourteen: Air Traffic Control 311
    Chapter Fifteen: Toward a Hemispheric Defense: Canada . . . 338

PART VI: THE AIR DEFENSE SYSTEM IN OPERATION

    Chapter Sixteen: Early Warning 360
    Chapter Seventeen: Identification 372
    Chapter Eighteen: Operating the Interim Air Defense System 407

INDEX 436

Vol. I -	Supporting Documents*	Nos.	1 to 56
Vol. II -	Supporting Documents	Nos.	57 to 122
Vol. III -	Supporting Documents	Nos.	123 to 176
Vol. IV -	Supporting Documents	Nos.	177 to 236
Vol. V -	Supporting Documents	Nos.	237 to 328

* Footnotes are numbered consecutively within chapters. Supporting documents are numbered consecutively throughout the history for ease of reference. Each volume of supporting documents is prefaced with an index of the documents contained therein.

CHARTS AND MAPS

	Facing Page
Deployment of Air Defense Radar (April - June 1948)	76
Deployment of Air Defense Radar - LASHUP (April 1950)	80
The Permanent AC&W Radar System and Mobile Deployment and Adjacent Canadian Radars	112
Fighter - Interceptor Squadron Deployment (January 1951)	130
Fighter - Interceptor Squadron Deployment (June 1951)	136
Re-equipping Schedules for Air Defense Command Fighter - Interceptor Squadrons	154
Combat Crews in Air Defense Command	186
Organization Chart - Air Defense Command	214
Communications Facilities for Transmission of Ground Observer Information	260
Transmission of Ground Observer Information	262
Implementation of GOC Plan Phase I and Phase II	278
Facilities for Alerting Civilian Defense Organizations	294
Key Point Civil Air Raid Warning Centers (15 July 1951)	302
Military Air Raid Warning Multi-Point Private Line Telephone Network and Private Toll Terminals (15 July 1951)	310
Regions and Regional Offices of the CAA	318
Corridors and Reporting Points for Aircraft	328
Canadian Radar Extension Plan	344
AC&W Program Chart - Canadian Radar Sites (June 1951)	346
Air Defense Identification Zones (15 January 1951)	376

CHAPTER ONE

THE GROWTH OF AIR DEFENSE CONSCIOUSNESS
1933 - 1945

I

The history of the air defenses of the continental United States covers barely two decades. Since 1933 much has been accomplished in establishing a system of military air defense and in integrating into that system the defense capabilities of the entire nation. The progress has not been smooth, being impeded by interservice rivalries and misunderstandings, by national complacency, by constitutional barriers and historical traditions making for lack of inter-agency rapport, and by the maladjustments caused by a second World War and its bewildering aftermath.

That the theory and practice of national air defense is so recent may be attributed in great part to the newness of strategic bombardment aviation in the last two decades and to the parallel growth of bomb-power. If we were to seek an arbitrary date to begin our narrative, perhaps the most persuasive date which would come to mind is the year 1933. That year is significant not only because of the fact that during its course the military planners for the first time considered air defense from a continental point of view, but also because it serves as an historic date in the development of American foreign policy and in the growth of air power, both of which factors played a most significant role in the history of air defense.

1933 and the years immediately following saw the birth of an irrational force in power politics, Nazi Germany, before which no nation could rest in confidence of international peace. Although much of the United States still reposed in the illusion of geographical isolation, the effect of Nazi saber-rattling was to make substantial inroads on the defense consciousness of American military leaders. Perhaps not entirely without coincidence, the Nazi political resurgence developed apace with the spectacular growth of striking power in military aviation. The appearance of these two forces on the international scene - a hostile nation and a new weapon of disquieting potentiality - combined with their effect on our military preparedness, may be considered a logical starting-point for the story of American air defense.

II

As early as 1932 the rise of fascist militarism centered the attention of the United States on the need for an increase of military readiness to meet any national emergency. To this end the War Department General Staff reorganized its establishment in order to weld its military units into an "integrated machine

capable of instantaneous response to the orders of the President."
A major aspect of this process of girding for battle was the consolidation of Army tactical units into four continental field armies. Elaborate defense plans were drawn up; and for the first time in the planning process the air arm of the Army, having been asked to formulate its concept of air defense, proposed for itself a defense role unprecedented in its history.

The plan, submitted in June 1933 by the Chief of the Air Corps, denied that all air force operations must tie in with ground operations and laid great emphasis on the initial air defense of the coast to a distance of 200 to 300 miles offshore.[2] As protection for seven designated critical defense areas the plan recommended the detail of planes to operate as a coastal defense unit, controlled by a GHQ Air Force and coordinated with a radio communication and alarm system along the coast. Upon the approach of an enemy by land, sea or in the air, proper notice would be given to Air Headquarters ashore. In the meantime, the striking part of the Air Force, consisting of bombardment and/or attack planes, would be held in a state of constant readiness to be used as the situation might demand. Though the plan would distribute portions of the Air Force among the most critical areas at the

---

1. Memo for CGs of the Four Field Armies by Gen. Douglas MacArthur, Chief of Staff, 22 Oct 1932, cited in AAF Historical Study No. 25, "Organization of Military Aeronautics, 1907-1935," p. 89 fn 10.

2. AAF Historical Study No. 25, pp. 89-92. This study is invaluable for its information on early air defense planning to 1935, and has been used extensively in this chapter in paraphrase.

beginning of or just prior to a war, it was not intended that the distribution would be a permanent one. It was to be used until the location of the main enemy effort was determined, and then was to be concentrated where the main enemy threat was being made.

The plan submitted by the Air Corps was reviewed subsequently by a board appointed by the Secretary of War, and headed by Major General Hugh Drum, the Deputy Chief of Staff. It was a typical General Staff board, completely dominated by ground officers. The only member representing the Air Corps was its chief, Major General B. D. Foulois. The report of the Drum Board, issued in October 1933, minimized the importance of air power and branded as unsound and fallacious the claims that land-based enemy air forces presented a danger to the defense of the United States.[3]

Shortly after the Drum Board report, a second board, headed by Newton D. Baker, was appointed in the spring of 1934. The purpose of this board was to make a constructive study of the operation, flying equipment and training of the Army Air Corps and to determine its adequacy and efficiency in the performance of its missions "in peace and war."[4] As on the preceding commission, the air officers were outnumbered by the ground men. Like previous boards, the Baker Board stressed the principle of unity of command and disapproved the separation of the air arm

---

3. Ibid., 91.

4. Ibid., 93-4.

from Army operations as violating that principle. Though admitting that aviation had increased the power of the offense where the belligerent countries bordered upon one another and the power of defense where the warring powers were widely separated, the Baker Board pointed out what it deemed to be the "vital limitations and inherent weaknesses of military aviation." These it conceived to be the necessity of either land or floating bases, dependency upon weather conditions, expense and load-capacity of airplanes. In answer to the oft-repeated contention that the United States was vulnerable to air attack, the report declared:[5]

> The "air invasion of the United States" and the "air defense of the United States" are conceptions of those who fail adequately to consider the effect of ocean barriers and other limitations. Aircraft in sufficient numbers to threaten serious damage can be brought against us only in conjunction with sea forces or with land forces which must be met by forces identical in nature and equally capable of prolonged effort.

In spite of pronouncements and decisions such as those of the Drum and Baker boards, the impact of increasing international crisis and the growth of air power in the succeeding months did much to change military opinion in favor of a more positive role for military aviation. Japanese and Italian aggression against China and Abyssinia and the growing belligerency of Nazi Germany made it clear that America's status in international affairs

---

5. *Ibid.*, 94.

was to be commensurate with her military and industrial strength. The civil war in Spain and the large role of air power in that conflict brought home the message sharply that henceforth civilians as well as the military would be subject to enemy attack. Long range flights of aircraft, both civil and military, were made with greater regularity, safety, and load-capacity to distant points. Even the two poles fell before the progress of aviation.

III

In 1935 the Joint Board of the Army and the Navy made the Army responsible for seeing to it that its air component was provided with all types of aircraft primarily designed for ". . . direct defense of the land and coastal frontiers of the continental United States and its overseas possessions, or in repelling air raids against shore objectives, or at shipping within our harbors."[6] In 1936, research in the detection of hostile aircraft was begun and given priority over all other items.[7]

Having assigned the Army the duty of providing the means of air defense, the Joint Board of the Army and the Navy awarded

---

6. The Joint Board of the Army and the Navy, Joint Action of the Army and the Navy, ch. iv, 1935. (DOC 1   )

7. United States Air Force Office of Air Force History, The Army Air Forces in World War II, Vol. I, Plans and Early Operations, Jan 1939 to Aug 1942, (Chicago, 1948) 287. Hereafter cited as USAF, I. See also, Watson, Mark S., Chief of Staff: Prewar Plans and Preparations, (Wash. D.C., 1950) pp. 43,50.

to the air arm of the Army the primary function of operating

> . . . as an arm of the mobile Army, both in the conduct of air operations over the land in support of land operations and in the conduct of air operations over the sea in direct defense of the coast.

As a secondary function, the air arm was to be responsible for[9]

> . . . air operations in connection with the defense of important industrial centers and military and naval installations.

Although a clear cut award of responsibility for air defense of continental facilities and installations was high time in coming, the doctrinal pronouncement of the Joint Board in 1935 was also the starting point of a long and sometimes bitter controversy over the extent of the responsibility of the air forces and the degree of authority necessary to perform effectively the assigned function of air defense. Since this controversy will occupy an important part of the present history, it would be well to set the stage at this point by giving a brief description of the status of the air arm within the War Department during the pre-war era.[10]

---

8. *Joint Action*, ch. iv.

9. *Ibid.*

10. On the organizational history of the Air Corps, see: USAF, I; Watson; AAF Historical Study No. 25, "Organization of Military Aeronautics, 1907-1935" (1944); AAF Historical Study No. 10, "Organization of the Army Air Arm, 1935-1945" (Revised, 1947); AAF Historical Study No. 46, "Organization of Military Aeronautics, 1935-1945" (1946).

The position of the Army air arm as a component of the U. S. Army in 1935 was a far cry from the exalted status of that organization during the later war years.[11] At the time of the assignment of the air defense mission to the Army in 1935, the Air Corps had recently been reorganized with the purpose of giving the air arm greater freedom in the operational control of its own units. The General Headquarters (GHQ) Air Force had been created as the combat command of Army aviation, directly responsible to the Chief of Staff. The Office of the Chief of the Air Corps (OCAC) was organized to supply and service the combat units, being directly responsible also to the Chief of Staff. Both offices were thus on the same level of command, with neither exercising authority over the other. Prior to this time, the tactical units of the Air Corps had been responsible to the commanding generals of the Army Corps areas, with the Air Corps office itself serving

---

11. Military aviation commenced in the United States with the establishment of the Aeronautical Division of the Office of the Chief Signal Officer in 1907. In 1914 the designation of this office was changed to that of Aviation Section of the Signal Corps. In 1926 military aviation was incorporated into the Air Corps, given sectional representation in the General Staff, and allotted an Assistant Secretary of War for Air. In 1934 the Baker Board, mentioned in the text, recommended the dropping of the Assistant Secretaryship and the division of the Air Corps into two parts, one for combat, the other for service and supply activities. These recommendations were carried out by the creation of the GHQ Air Force and the Office of the Chief of the Air Corps. In 1939 these branches of the air arm were united, but in November 1940 they were separated again. In June 1941, the two offices were reunited under the new office of the Chief, AAF. In March 1942, the AAF was placed on a coequal status within the WD with the AGF and the ASF.

as a specialized supply arm. In the new structure, the authority of the Commanding General, GHQ Air Force, was increased over his tactical units; but his control over supply was nonexistent, while command of air bases remained with the Army corps area commanders.

Nowadays, a situation such as that just described would be startling. In those days, however, when there existed neither aircraft warning service nor ground control of interception, and when the striking power of aircraft, though growing at an alarming rate, was relatively puerile, the question of air defense was academic. The realities of existing principles of warfare under which the War Department operated in 1935 pointed to the greater advantages of an organization of air power under the field forces, whereby America's striking forces could be kept intact by maximum air defense resources, and in which all capabilities for air defense could be united. Very shortly, indeed, the air forces were to upset these doctrines via the great readjustments of World War II, and were to win their battle to elevate air power in warfare to a co-equal status with the ground forces.[12]

Between 1935 and 1941, as the potentialities of air power became increasingly apparent, a correspondingly grave concern was felt about continental air defenses. In 1936, the War Department

---

12. As late as 1939 the air forces were smaller in numbers than the field artillery and less than one-eighth of the whole army. Watson, 279.

ranked research in the detection of hostile aircraft first in its research program, and thenceforward, under the aegis of the Signal Corps in its laboratories at Fort Monmouth, an intensive program of radar research was developed.[13] In spite of these increasing evidences of concern, the first overt step towards a national military air defense system was not taken until November, 1939. At that time Major General Henry H. Arnold, then Chief of the Air Corps, called the attention of the War Department to the complete absence of national air defenses and urged that a unit be established to study the problem.[14]

---

13. Watson, 43, 50; USAF, I, 287. The first field radar erected by the Signal Corps was located in Panama, 7 Oct 1940. The true origin of modern radar dates from 1935 when practical microwave sets were developed.

14. USAF, I, 289. OCAC and GHQ Air Force were united under the Chief of the Air Corps in Mar 1939, but only to be separated again in Nov 1940. General Arnold's suggestion, therefore, was on behalf of the entire Army air arm.

IV

The result of General Arnold's admonition was the establishment of the Air Defense Command on 26 February 1940.[15] This command, first in the line of three Air Defense Commands,[16] undertook to study the special capabilities of pursuit aviation, anti-aircraft artillery, radio equipment, and passive defense measures, and to formulate the most effective combination of the several means of defense. Under a strict interpretation of air defense the new organization was not concerned with air striking units, which were designed to seek out and destroy hostile aircraft great distances away, but was concerned only with the problems of attacking planes over the U. S. Since ADC was only a planning body, pursuit aviation remained under the jurisdiction of the GHQ Air Force.

The Battle of Britain provided ADC with an excellent laboratory of air defense operations for its study. Observers returned from England with enthusiastic reports of the effectiveness of

---

15. Headed by Brig. Gen. James E. Chaney and located at Mitchel Field, N.Y., ADC was primarily a planning agency, limited in size to a staff of only 10 officers, and under the administrative authority of the CG First Army. See: *History of the Air Defense Command, 26 Feb 1940 to 2 Jun 1941*, also USAF, I, 152-3, 289 ff.

16. The sequence and chronology of the Air Defense Commands is as follows: (1) 26 Feb 1940 to 2 Jul 1941 (2) Mar 1946 to Jul 1950 (From Dec 1948 to Jul 1950 ADC functioned as an operational headquarters under the Continental Air Command) (3) 1 Jan 1951 to date.

British radar devices against the Luftwaffe. In May 1940 the War Department accordingly directed that commanders of armies and overseas departments prepare or revise plans for an aircraft warning service which would include provision for the use of radar detectors.

In its studies, ADC received excellent cooperation from the British, and the friendly relations and common interests of the two countries prompted the mutual exchange of technical equipment and information. Before the end of 1940 the United States began to receive information on airborne interception equipment and early in 1941 was given the prototype of the British VHF radio set. Similarly, the IFF device developed in England was copied by the Signal Corps and was adopted in August 1941 as the standard American equipment.

V

The experience of the Battle of Britain clearly demonstrated one fact to American observers: If the United States were to embark on the creation of a similarly effective air defense system, responsibility for its operation would have to be defined within the military structure. The functions of local air defense, it has been mentioned, were assigned to the Army air arm as early as 1935, but the air arm's disorganized condition in 1940 precluded the award of responsibility to it of the operation of a continent-wide system of air defenses. It will be recalled that the Joint Board had given the air forces the primary function of operating "as an arm of the mobile Army." The mission of air defense would inevitably be in direct conflict with this primary assignment. And yet, the air forces were manifestly the logical choice to manage the country's air defenses.

Although the air force organizational structure was weakened by the separation of GHQ Air Force from OCAC in November 1940, in another manner it was strengthened for the burden it was about to undertake. In November 1940 four air districts were created to correspond in territory to the four continental land armies, the purpose of which was to decentralize the GHQ Air Force activities, which were becoming more complex as the rearmament program progressed. Although the air district structure could well serve the purposes of management of the proposed continental air defense system, the absence of unity of command within the air forces was a glaring anomaly, and the missions carried a strong possibility of becoming mutually contradictory. Nevertheless, "time was of the essence" and the choice was made.

In March 1941 the Commanding General, GHQ Air Force, received the mission of organizing, training for, and operating the air defenses of the continental United States.[17] Simultaneously, the War Department created four defense commands, corresponding to the four Army areas as "territorial agencies . . . designed

---

17. WD Ltr AG 320.2 (3-6-41): "Air Defense," 7 Mar 1941.
(DOC 2)

to coordinate or prepare and to initiate the execution of all plans for the employment of Army Forces and installations in defense against enemy action in that portion of the United States lying within the command boundaries."[18] In wartime, it was announced, the defense commanders were to be responsible for all defense operations. The responsibilities of the CG, GHQ Air Force were indicated as follows:[19]

> The Commanding General, GHQ Air Force, under GHQ is responsible for the peace time organization and training for air operations and defense against air attack in the continental United States except:
>
> 1. Operation of aviation attached to ground units.
>
> 2. Operation of antiaircraft artillery assigned or attached to mobile ground units, and technical training of all antiaircraft artillery.
>
> 3. Measures against low flying aircraft with organic means available to ground troops.
>
> 4. Passive defense measures (except those pertaining to GHQ Air Force units and installations.)

At the same time, the four air districts were abolished and replaced by four continental air forces, corresponding in territory to the four defense command areas. To the new air forces were assigned ". . . for the purpose of defense organization and planning, primary responsibilities under the Commanding

---

18. WD Ltr AG 320.2 (2-28-41): "Defense Plans - Continental United States," 17 Mar 1941. (DOC 3)

19. Ibid.

General, GHQ Air Force."[20]

The arrangements of March 1941 clearly awarded air defense responsibilities to the GHQ Air Force – so long as peace prevailed. At the danger point, GHQ's responsibilities were to cease. The critical moment was to arrive, however, much sooner than was expected. Meanwhile, plans for air defense and construction of the first radar network received first priority in War Department considerations.[21]

Because much radar siting activity was soon underway, and many WD agencies were actively engaged in the birth of the air defense system, the War Department deemed it wise to avoid the risk of the Defense Commands' tampering with these activities under their overall planning authority by issuing the following supplementary instructions:[22]

> Current plans and projects for the organization of the means for air defense, to include the location

---

20. Ibid.

21. The plan of air defense was officially summarized in: Major Gordon P. Saville, Air Defense Doctrine, 27 Oct 1941. It goes without saying that the decision to adopt the British technique of ground controlled interception was not accompanied by plans to copy British strategic defense organization and deployment of radar and aircraft. The great extent of United States territory precluded a perimeter defense such as existed in the United Kingdom. Of necessity, the Air Defense Command recommended that a system of defense of "strategic areas" be adopted for the United States, on a priority basis.

22. WD Ltr AG 320.2: "Defense Plans – Continental United States," 25 Mar 1941 (DOC 4)

of detector stations and ~~communications~~ and ~~other~~ systems will be transferred from the Army and other Commanders to the Commanding General, GHQ Air Force or his designated representatives.

For the purpose of ground organization for Air Defense and the allocation of additional responsibilities to Air Force Commanders, boundaries will be prescribed by the Commanding General, GHQ Air Force. These boundaries will not necessarily conform to the boundaries of the Defense Command.

There is no doubt, of course, that GHQ Air Force's mission was awarded to it in the best of faith. Repeated utterances of the Secretary of War in 1941 stated that henceforward it would be WD policy to grant the air forces as much autonomy as possible.[23] If war had not begun so shortly afterward, it is possible that the Army air arm might have established itself in the air defense "business" and acquired the authority commensurate with its extended operations. In the space of time allotted to it, however, the air forces could do little more than initiate action on an air defense system. Meanwhile, air defense capabilities were limited to existing fighter aircraft and antiaircraft artillery. The possibilities of interception without early warning were practically non-existent, while the great areas to be covered in air defense limited the effectiveness of antiaircraft artillery.

The directives of March 1941 revealed a situation replete with troublesome illogicalities. GHQ Air Force was to organize and operate the nation's first air defense system, but

---

23. AAF Historical ~~Studies~~ 10, ~~p.~~ 73

on the verge of war it was told to release its prerogatives to the defense commanders. Under the theory of unified command this was not inconsistent, but when coupled with the mandate given to GHQ Air Force to deploy its radars as it saw fit and to redelineate its boundaries in a like manner, the possibility was present that the defense commanders would be faced with an accomplished fact which they could do little to alter under pressure of crisis.

On the other hand, in spite of the increased emphasis on defense planning, the entire question of air defense was still generally considered to be an academic one in 1941, as it was to be later, in 1946-1947. Even the air forces themselves were determined to take the developments in stride, as is testified by the apparent lack of controversy over the matter of conflicting defense responsibilities. In truth, the air forces throughout 1941 were too preoccupied with their great expansion program to be overly concerned in this matter. As General Arnold indicated when sympathizers continued to press for air force independence during the early war years, the air force needed the support of the Army's facilities and services in its armament program and the existing crisis was deemed inopportune for such polemics.

In June 1941, meanwhile, the War Department, belatedly recognizing the incongruity of split Air Corps authorities, reunited the Office of the Chief of Air Corps with the GHQ Air

Force (now renamed the Air Force Combat Command) under the new office of the Chief of the Army Air Forces. The new AAF also inherited GHQ Air Force's mission of air defense.

VI

The warning network planned for the United States in the spring of 1941 represented a compromise with the ideal. A perfect arrangement would have depended primarily upon a series of radar stations sufficient in number to assure mechanical detection of any hostile force.[24] But there were not enough radar sets or technicians qualified to man them for coverage of the entire area of the country; and radar had not reached a stage of development which permitted it to operate over land with the same effectiveness it showed over the ocean. No radar equipment in existence in 1941, outside the laboratories, could locate low-flying airplanes without detecting as "permanent echoes" the images of prominent landmarks.[25] Accordingly, the War Department planned to recruit civilians to serve as ground observers to report on the identity and movements of aircraft over land and to use radar to provide a seaward extension of the

---

24. The author is indebted for the material in this section to the account of early World War II air defenses in USAF, I, 290-298, and also to the Fourth Air Force Historical Study No. III-2, "Defense Plans and Operations in the Fourth Air Force, 1942-1945," Vol. I, 146-226. Footnote references in this section are those appearing in USAF, I, 290-298.

25. Report of R. A. Watson-Watt on the Air Defense System of the Pacific Coast of the U. S., Jan 1942, Doc. 40 in 4AF Historical Study III-1.

warning network.

Organization for air defense was strengthened in the spring of 1941 by the creation within each of the new continental air forces of interceptor commands which were charged in their areas with control for air defense purposes of air warning equipment, fighters, antiaircraft artillery, and barrage balloons. These so-called active agents of defense were supplemented by such passive measures as provision for civilian air raid warning and blackouts, which were made the responsibility of organizations working under the supervision of an Office of Civilian Defense.

In the six months which immediately preceded Pearl Harbor, the four interceptor commands worked feverishly to create a coastal radar net and a supporting ground observer corps as components of the air defense system. When war came, sites had been picked for thirteen radar stations along the East Coast, and eight of the stations were approaching completion.[26] On the West Coast, there were ten radars to guard the 1,200 miles from Seattle to San Diego.[27] This radar coverage was supplemented on the East Coast by approximately 4,000 ground observer stations and along the Pacific by an additional 2,400. Reports from ground observers had to be processed through filter and

---

26. History, I Fighter Command, 1941-1944, p. 104 ff.
27. 4AF Historical Study II-2, p. 146 ff.

information centers, both of which required the services of large numbers of volunteer workers. The interceptor commands had managed to expedite the construction of the basic elements of this complex system, but there had not been time to recruit and train all the personnel required to operate it. Moreover, the network, even when placed in perfect readiness, could have met only the primary need of early warning. The effective control of fighter planes at night or during bad weather would have required the addition of mobile units equipped with the newer radar aids developed in Britain. But in December 1941 the United States had no radar equipment comparable to the GCI set of Great Britain, and fighter planes in this country were still using high frequency - rather than VHF - radio sets. Airborne radar for night fighters was lacking, as was IFF equipment.

In providing a remedy for the recognized deficiencies of the American warning service, the War Department once again was able to draw on the experience of Britain. Immediately after Pearl Harbor, at the suggestion of the U. S. military mission in London, the RAF offered the services of Robert Watson-Watt, Scientific Advisor on Telecommunications to the Air Ministry. Watson-Watt arrived in the United States before the end of December 1941 for the purpose of undertaking a detailed analysis of the peculiar problems of American air defense.

Any vestiges of complacency as to the adequacy of the

American aircraft warning service which may have remained in War Department circles were destroyed by the severely critical report of the air defenses of the West Coast made by Watson-Watt in January 1942. Dangerously unsatisfactory conditions were said to exist, reflecting "insufficient organization applied to technically inadequate equipment used in exceptionally difficult conditions."[28] The British expert found our seaward reconnaissance grossly inefficient because of the total lack of anti-submarine detection equipment and because of the limited number of patrol aircraft of suitable range. The radar screen along the West Coast was based on too few stations, and the equipment itself had inherent defects which made it "gravely unsuitable." Dependable employment of this radar had been made even more unlikely because of mistakes in the selection of sites for its installation. Personnel to operate the radars had not been carefully selected and were inadequate, both in numbers and in training. The United States was found to have repeated an early error of Britain in failing to provide for the training of large numbers of skilled radar technicians.

Officials in Washington accepted the report in the constructive spirit in which it was offered. The director of air defense at AAF Headquarters, Colonel Gordon P. Saville, concurred in every detail with the findings and called the study "a damning

---

28. Watson-Watt Report in *4AF Historical Study III-1*.

indictment of our whole warning service." He also expressed the view that the situation on the East Coast was even worse than the conditions reported along the Pacific. Independent analyses by American officials bore out the general verdict rendered by Watson-Watt.

The hard fact was that many of the measures required for an operationally dependable air defense system could not be improvised. It was not until late 1943 that the continental air defenses were generally equipped with VHF radio and a workable system for controlling interceptions at night.

Helpful to an immediate improvement of continental air defenses were organizational changes which served to clarify responsibilities. The Western Defense Command had been designated a theater of operations on 11 December 1941. With headquarters in San Francisco, the command included an extensive area of nine western states, Alaska, and the Aleutians, and to it three air forces were initially assigned - the Fourth and Second Air Forces along the Pacific Coast and, in addition, the Alaskan Air Force. A similar situation existed on the other side of the continent, where on 20 December the Eastern Theater of Operations was established with headquarters in New York City and with units in the Eastern Seaboard states and in Newfoundland and Bermuda. Two air forces, the First and the Third, were assigned to this theater. Thus, all four of the domestic air forces, which had been created early in 1941 and had been operating under the Air Force Combat Command, were removed from AAF control and placed under theater commanders. It is not surprising that this arrangement pleased no one: the defense commands found it confusing to have more than one subordinate air force commander, while the AAF felt that its combat training program would be jeopardized if it had no direct control of any of the continental air forces. A compromise was accordingly worked out and announced on 30 December 1941. The essential element of the new plan was a provision which called for moving two of the continental air forces to inland stations and assigning them to the AAF as training air forces. To effect this arrangement, the Second Air Force relinquished its coastal stations and was removed from assignment to the Western Defense Command, and air defense duties for the entire Pacific Coast were thereupon assigned to the Fourth Air Force. A similar move within the Eastern Defense Command made the Third Air Force a training unit under the AAF, while the First Air Force took over responsibility for air defense operations along the entire extent of the Atlantic Coast. This arrangement lasted until the fall of 1943, when the danger of air attack had greatly decreased and the First and Fourth Air Forces were reassigned to the AAF.

After the organizational adjustments had been made in the winter of 1941, a defense zone of approximately 150 miles in depth

and extending 200 miles seaward was created along the Pacific Coast
by the Western Defense Command. A similar zone was established by
the Eastern Defense Command along the Atlantic Coast. Air operations within the western zone were directed by the Fourth Air Force
through its subordinate interceptor and bomber commands. The air
force provided planes to defend vital targets and to conduct offshore patrols, supplied an aircraft warning service to alert both
military and civilian agencies, and through regional commanders
integrated all elements of air defense, including units of the
Fourth Antiaircraft Command.[29] On the East Coast a similar pattern established the First Air Force as the air arm of the Eastern
Defense Command, although its primary concern was in anti-submarine
operations along the coast. Radar siting and construction continued at a feverish pace in 1942 only to slow down in 1943 as danger
decreased. All told, 65 stations were placed in operation along
the West Coast, where defense activity was mostly concentrated,
and 34 stations were established on the East Coast at war's end.[30]

VII

Perhaps the most significant steps taken during the war
years in the matter of air defense doctrines and responsibilities

---

29. See: History of the Fourth Antiaircraft Command.
30. 4AF Historical Study III-2, p. 146.

came as a result of the overseas experiences of the AAF combat units. The close proximity of these units to hostile air operations made the matter of air defense far more urgent than air defense considerations at home. In almost all overseas theaters, interceptor commands or defense commands or both were established. These overseas experiences in defense organization were to have significant repercussions on future air defense organization and doctrine in the Zone of the Interior.

In April 1942 Field Manual 1-15 was issued by the War Department. This pamphlet, entitled "Tactics and Techniques of Air Fighting," had some very pertinent statements to make about air defense. For the first time under such an authoritative imprimatur, radar detection was given a positive role in military doctrine.[31]

> An aircraft warning service is essential for the employment of interceptor units, force or aviation in local defense. The effectiveness of this defense is vitally dependent upon the nature and extent of the information provided by the warning service and the rapidity with which it can be transmitted to the interceptor units, force or aviation. To assure interceptions, an accurate, timely and continuous flow of information of the approach of hostile air forces must be furnished to the pursuit commander both prior to and after the pursuit leaves the ground to effect interception.

Of much significance for the future relations between

---

31. WD FM 1-15, Tactics and Techniques of Air Fighting, 10 Apr 1942, pp. 19-20.

the AAF and the Army Ground Forces was the statement that

> The interceptor command must have operational control over all antiaircraft artillery, searchlights and barrage balloons in the defense area.

Although these statements did much to blaze a path for AAF control of air defense operations, it should be borne in mind that, as yet, no statement had been made placing air power on a co-equal basis with land power, or defining the prerogatives of air power in an integrated combat effort. This deficiency was supplied in July 1943.

Although in March 1942 a War Department reorganization had placed the AAF, AGF and Army Service Forces on a par within the War Department, no doctrinal statement had placed their three _functions_ on a co-equal basis. This condition was altered in Field Manual 100-20, issued in July 1943. Besides the historic announcement that "Land Power and Air Power are co-equal and interdependent forces" and that "neither is auxiliary of the other," this document had important bearings on the question of air defense. Organizationally,[33]

> ... the normal composition of an air force includes a strategic air force, a tactical air force, an air defense command and an air service command.

Having prescribed an air defense command for theaters of

---

32. _Ibid._, p. 20.

33. WD FM 100-20, _Command and Employment of Air Power_, 21 Jul 1943, p. 4.

operation, the manual went on to define air defense.[34]

> Air defense is the direct defense against hostile air operations as distinguished from the indirect defense afforded by counter air force operations. Air defense comprises all other methods designed to prevent, to interfere with, or reduce the effectiveness of hostile air action.
>
> Air defense is divided into active air defense and passive air defense.
>
>> (1) Active air defense comprises all measures aimed to destroy or to threaten destruction of hostile aircraft and their crews in the air. Active air defense is provided by fighter aircraft, antiaircraft artillery, and small arms fire; and by obstacles, principally barrage balloons.
>
> The active air defense means for any area may include fighter aviation, antiaircraft artillery, searchlights, barrage balloons and aircraft warning service.
>
> When antiaircraft artillery, searchlights, and barrage balloons operate in the air defense of the same area with aviation, the efficient exploitation of the special capabilities of each, and the avoidance of unnecessary losses to friendly aviation, demand that all be placed under the command of the air commander responsible for the area. This must be done.

The effect of these two statements was to confirm the air defense responsibilities of the air forces, even under a unified command structure such as existed in the combat theaters. It was inevitable that these doctrines, although primarily directed to overseas theaters, should have important effects at home.

---

34. Ibid., pp. 12-13.

Late in 1943 the Fourth Air Force, tired of its subordinate relationship to the Western Defense Commander, asked that antiaircraft artillery within its boundaries be placed under its operational control.[35] Under FM 100-20 and FM 1-15 the request appeared to be justified, but the conditions obtaining in the Zone of the Interior were different from those existing overseas. The theater concept in the ZI had been abandoned in the fall of 1943; consequently, no unified command existed at home.

The alternative to this dilemma, which occasioned some bitter controversy between AGF and AAF, was found by resorting to the dormant statement in the March 1941 air defense directive which had given overall planning authority in peace-time to the defense commanders, and in making direct allusions therein to the employment of air force units in planning.[36]

> The general mission of Commanding Generals of Defense Commands is redefined as indicated below:
>
> To plan for all measures for defense against external attack by land, sea or air of that portion of United States territory included in the Command boundaries and such adjacent territories or offshore bases as may be specified by the War Department.
>
> To coordinate plans for the employment of units of the Army Air Forces stationed within the limits of the Command or designated to provide air defense when required.

---

35. See: AAF Historical Study III-2, pp. 295-346, and History of the Fourth Antiaircraft Command.

36. WD Ltr AG 381 OB-S-E: "Defense of the Continental United States - Defense Commands," 23 Mar 1944 (DOC 5)

The inclusion in the redefined mission of the defense commands of the last paragraph apparently provided the assurance the Ground Forces needed. The road was now paved for the award to the Fourth Air Force of operational control of antiaircraft artillery.

On 1 May 1944 the Fourth Antiaircraft Artillery Command was assigned to the Fourth Air Force. Simultaneously, the CG, Western Defense Command, was relieved of the responsibility of providing active air defense of his territory and the mission was given to the Fourth Air Force. However,[37]

> Responsibility for planning all measures for defense against external attack, including air, remains with the Commanding General, Western Defense Command.

This highly intricate scheme of command relationships between the Fourth Air Force and Western Defense Command served in reality to keep the air defense mission in a state of suspension between AAF and AGF. Informally, the two organizations had succeeded in reaching a _modus operandi_. Legally, however, little had been settled toward a clear-cut definition of air defense responsibilities for the continental United States. Here matters rested until the momentous reorganization of the War Department at war's end.

---

37. 2d Ind. 15 Apr 1944 to WD AG 353 OB-S-E: "Combined Air Defense Training, Fourth Air Force," 14 Feb 1944 (DOC 6)

CHAPTER TWO

ADC AND THE AIR DEFENSE MISSION[1]

1946 - 1948

I

With the end of the Second World War, it was inevitable that the great forward strides in air power made during the war years be given formal cognizance in a restatement of air doctrine. After the tempo of occupational activity and demobilization had slackened, the War Department began a reshuffling of its component parts and their responsibilities. In 1945 and 1946 considerable discussion and debate took place within the War Department leading to many changes in its organizational structure. Because of the pressure of time to reorganize the WD mansion to house the peace-time establishment, many of the changes were made without immediate doctrinal restatement.

Within the AAF the pattern of reorganization was based upon the experiences of combat unit organization. Essentially, the new AAF command structure followed the theory of air organization established in July 1943 in FM 100-20. In that document

---

1. This chapter owes much to the excellent account of air defense written by Mr. Milton Klein in History of the Air Defense Command, Mar 1946 - Mar 1947, Vol. 1, "The Evolution of the Mission."

> The Air Defense Command will organize and administer the integrated air defense system of the Continental United States; will exercise direct control of all active measures and coordinate all passive means of air defense; will be prepared to operate either independently or in cooperation with Naval forces against hostile surface and undersurface vessels and in the protection of coastwise shipping; ... to train units and personnel in the operation of the most advanced methods and means designed to nullify hostile aerial weapons; ... to train units and personnel for the maintenance of the air defense mission in any part of the world.

In at least three instances the ADC interim mission broke ground in air defense doctrine. The first was the statement that ADC "will organize and administer the integrated air defense system of the Continental United States." General Stratemeyer's interpretation of this aspect of his air defense mission was broadly expressed in April as follows:[4]

> The Air Defense Command with its subordinate Air Forces will have primary interest in the repelling of an air attack, and we should therefore have at our command all air, ground, and sea forces which may be necessary to repel such an attack.

In short, the word "integrated" was pregnant with future controversy in that it presaged an AAF campaign to reach far and wide, possibly beyond its historic sphere of action, in order to carry out its air defense responsibilities.

Secondly, the phrase "will exercise direct control of all

---

4. Gen. Stratemeyer to CG's, ADC air forces, 26 Apr 1946. Cited in "The Evolution of the Mission," p. 8.

> The Air Defense Command will organize and administer the integrated air defense system of the Continental United States; will exercise direct control of all active measures and coordinate all passive means of air defense; will be prepared to operate either independently or in cooperation with Naval forces against hostile surface and undersurface vessels and in the protection of coastwise shipping; ... to train units and personnel in the operation of the most advanced methods and means designed to nullify hostile aerial weapons; ... to train units and personnel for the maintenance of the air defense mission in any part of the world.

In at least three instances the ADC interim mission broke ground in air defense doctrine. The first was the statement that ADC "will organize and administer the integrated air defense system of the Continental United States." General Stratemeyer's interpretation of this aspect of his air defense mission was broadly expressed in April as follows:[4]

> The Air Defense Command with its subordinate Air Forces will have primary interest in the repelling of an air attack, and we should therefore have at our command all air, ground, and sea forces which may be necessary to repel such an attack.

In short, the word "integrated" was pregnant with future controversy in that it presaged an AAF campaign to reach far and wide, possibly beyond its historic sphere of action, in order to carry out its air defense responsibilities.

Secondly, the phrase "will exercise direct control of all

---

4. Gen. Stratemeyer to CG's, ADC air forces, 26 Apr 1946. Cited in "The Evolution of the Mission," p. 8.

active measures . . ." although ensconced in FM 100-20 and FM 1-15, was likely to be considered out of place when applied to the static conditions of ZI organization as compared to the fluid command relationships in the combat theaters. It will be recalled that the Fourth Air Force, endeavoring to duplicate the overseas air forces' operational control of antiaircraft artillery within the ZI, had experienced much resistance on the part of the Ground Forces, and had won out only at the expense of increasing the Ground Forces authority in air defense matters. The question of control of "all active measures" presaged a battle royal between the AAF and AGF over control of antiaircraft artillery. As will be seen, AGF was not slow to take up the challenge.

Thirdly, the phrase "will coordinate all passive means of air defense" was novel in its entirety to air defense theory and practice. Although FM 100-20 had defined passive air defense as being provided by "dispersion, camouflage, blackouts, and other measures which minimize the effect of hostile air attack," it had left control over passive measures undetermined. On the other hand, the directive of 17 March 1941 which had initially allotted the air defense mission to GHQ Air Force had specifically exempted all passive air defense measures from air force control, with the exception of those measures pertaining strictly to GHQ Air Force units and installations. Subsequent official correspondence had either consciously or unconsciously differentiated the terms "active" and "passive" air defense so that in reality AAF was without precedent in its desire to encompass both active and passive air defense authority.

The creation of ADC and the assignment to it of such an ambitious mission was an auspicious step towards greater national security. Unfortunately, these inherent promises remained unfulfilled for several years. Eager to begin its work, ADC sought to prepare for the task ahead by obtaining clear-cut delineation of its authority and the means with which its plans might be implemented, only to be disappointed in both.

II

From the outset it was clear that the execution of the air defense mission of ADC was to be complicated by the intention of Headquarters, AAF, to limit the air defense capabilities of the new command, and, at the same time, to expend its functions in a decidedly different direction - that of training the AAF's civilian components.

The limitation on ADC's role in active air defense arose from the early assignment of the bulk of the existing forces to the Strategic and Tactical Air Commands. Thus, if ADC were to execute the task it publicly announced, that of meeting the first phase of any future hostilities - "to thwart any attempt by an enemy to attack our homeland" - it had to be by means other than the regular units assigned to it. A natural inference was the view that ADC's tactical strength would flow from the Air National Guard and Air Reserve units, for which training responsibility had also been vested in the Air Defense Command.[6] The assumption that "the means available to the Air Defense Command for the purpose of implementing the mission of that Command are the Air National Guard and the Air Reserve programs" developed from the coupling of tactical defense and reserve training in the interim mission. It seemed clear to General Stratemeyer that because of the shortage of regular AAF combat units within the United States, it followed that the task of air national security – and the air defense mission of ADC – would be discharged in large measure through the Air National Guard, and less directly through the Air Reserve.

Clarification from AAF resulted in the realization that the air units of both the National Guard and the Organized Reserves constituted a total AAF reserve; that personnel of these units might well be utilized as fillers for all types of regular AAF units; and that the civilian components would be utilized in an emergency to support the entire AAF, even though air defense would be the paramount concern in national security during an

---

5. From an Army Day address by Maj. Gen. Charles B. Stone, C/S ADC, Apr 1946. Cited in "Evolution of the Mission," p. 5 fn 6.

6. "Interim Mission," 12 Mar 1946 (DOC 7)

emergency. Considerations other than those of air defense had apparently entered into the assignment of training responsibilities for the Air Force's civilian components, and ADC's preparations for air defense operations had to be viewed accordingly in this new light. It was patent that the command had received a tactical mission - air defense - without the wherewithal with which to accomplish it, either in the form of regular or reserve forces. Accordingly, the air defense task actually undertaken by ADC became essentially a planning one: the preparation of air defense plans contemplating the reception and utilization by ADC of forces of other AAF commands for utilization in an emergency. Long range plans would go beyond the confines of existing AAF organization in establishing the over-all requirements of the air defense system of the United States in the future. More specific preparations for active air defense, such as unit training, maneuvers, and the development of techniques and tactics, had to remain outside the sphere of ADC activity pending the allocation to the command, either temporarily or permanently, of the forces required to conduct active defense preparations.

Within this broad limitation, the tactical mission of ADC became further circumscribed as active measures were undertaken to prepare plans for the air defense of the United States. From the outset, ADC planning was restricted by the vexing problem of limited authority and control over the forces, personnel, and weapons it considered vital to a single, integrated air defense system. Further, ADC planning was bound, initially, by an organizational structure of six "air defense areas," imposed by War Department direction,[7] which did not correspond exactly to the requirements of the most effective air defense system. In the process of preparing plans for an air defense providing security in case of air attack in the immediate future, these problems of limited control and territorial organization proved intensely frustrating to ADC personnel.

In spite of the limitations imposed upon the Air Defense Command, General Stratemeyer found himself and his command pitched headlong into two struggles to assert ADC's concept of an "integrated" system both within the AAF structure itself and as the AAF agency in the AAF controversy with the Ground Forces over the operational control of antiaircraft artillery.

In the absence of assigned tactical units, ADC, in its plan for defense in the immediate future, necessarily assumed that regular AAF units, irrespective of command assignments, would be placed at the disposal of ADC air forces for operational purposes. This assumption was in recognition, also, of the non-availability of combat effective reserve units prior to 1948 at the earliest. Although this assumption seemed valid enough from any realistic

---

7. WD Circular 138, 14 May 1946, par. 7d.

consideration of ADC's own combat strength, official approval of the plan was not forthcoming until 17 December 1947, almost two years after ADC had been awarded the air defense mission. The delay occurred in spite of repeated admonitions by ADC to AAF that ADC had neither the means of its own to accomplish its mission, nor the authority to use the means belonging to its sister commands in an emergency. As early as 10 June 1946, AAF had stated that:[8]

> The Joint Chiefs of Staff, in the event of a sustained attack against this country and under existing command and operational procedures, would most probably assess the situation, declare a theater of operations, appoint a theater commander, assign him a mission and allocate suitable forces. It is not likely under present joint procedures, that the Air Defense Commander would be appointed to function as a theater commander and, as such be held responsible for the conduct of theater operations concurrently with the conduct of all air defense measures in protection of the continental United States.

In the ADC commander's opinion, however, this should not have prevented AAF itself from awarding ADC the operational control of the Air Force's air defense capabilities in time of emergency. Indeed, this inference seemed justified because in the same message AAF had stated as follows:[9]

> It is the opinion of this Headquarters that effective coordination can only be achieved through the

---

8. AAF to ADC: "Investment of Command Responsibilities of the Land, Sea and Air Forces in Event of an Air Invasion," 10 Jun 1946. (DOC 8)

9. Ibid.

assignment of operational control of such units of other services to the Commanding General, Air Defense Command, during periods of emergency.

However, even in such a realistic proposal as that of placing AAF air defense resources under ADC during an emergency, ADC ran into frustrating opposition.

General Stratemeyer reported as follows in regard to a conference held at the Headquarters of the Tactical Air Command on 10 August 1946:[10]

> ... it became apparent that the Commanding General, Tactical Air Command and myself differ in our understanding of my responsibilities for the provision of the air defense of the continental United States. You have indicated that a theater commander is expected to be appointed in any area of the United States which is attacked or threatened with attack. My concern is for the period between the time hostile action occurs or is first expected to occur, and the time a theater commander has actually been appointed and assumes responsibility in the area. During this period I believe a unified air command in any one area is essential.

It was not until 17 December 1947 that this matter was resolved to the satisfaction of ADC. At that time USAF announced:[11]

> Upon directive from this or higher headquarters, or in the event of the detection of potentially hostile forces, the Commanding General, Air Defense Command, will provide for the defense of the United States against hostile air attack. He will initially be

---

10. Gen. Stratemeyer to CG AAF: "Responsibility of the Air Defense Command," 13 Sep 1946. (DOC 9)

11. USAF to ADC: "Coordination of Air Defense Command, Strategic Air Command, and Tactical Air Command Operations under Emergency Conditions," 17 Dec 1947. (DOC 10)

assigned operational control of such specific units of the Tactical Air Command and Strategic Air Command as have been designated for employment in defense against hostile air attack, such operational control to be terminated by direction of the Chief of Staff, Air Force, or higher authority. For present planning purposes these units will include all fighter units and all aircraft warning units, with their supporting services and such antiaircraft units as may be assigned or attached to the USAF.

Until such time as an air commander for the United States is appointed by the Chief of Staff, Air Force, or the Joint Chiefs of Staff, the Commanding General, Air Defense Command will additionally provide the overall direction of a United States Air Force coordinated defense against enemy attacks, other than air with such units of the three USAF combat commands as are made available for this purpose. The USAF combat commands will be responsible for the provision, operation, and training of the above forces.

The Commanding General of the Air Defense Command in coordination with the Commanding Generals, Tactical Air Command and Strategic Air Command will prepare, and maintain current, integrated plans for the defense of the United States in conformity with the above principles.

III

The limitations within which ADC's air defense mission was to be accomplished were further evidenced in AAF-AGF relations. A basic conflict concerning defense responsibility arose from the simultaneous assignment by the War Department to AAF of responsibility for the air defense of the United States, and to AGF of responsibility for continental defense "in conjunction with designated air and naval commanders."

A peculiar condition affecting the assignment of the air defense mission to ADC in March 1946 was the fact that, officially, the AAF did not have the mission to delegate to ADC. The WD reorganization was effected in great part without prior resort to doctrinal modifications. AAF, however, proceeded confidently in its assurance that the air defense mission, which up until that time reposed in the hands of the defense commanders, would pass to itself. For ADC, however, the assignment of the broadly worded air defense mission without tangible assurances that AAF possessed authority to provide ADC with the teeth it needed, did not arouse commensurate optimism. ADC felt acutely the absence of clearly defined jurisdictions among the components of the War Department in the matter of air defense responsibilities.

The first official indication that air defense doctrine was in the process of redefinition, and that the air defense mission was to be reassigned, was a WD directive of 8 April 1946 addressed to the Army Ground Forces. After rescinding previous instructions to AGF with respect to the latter's defense responsibilities, the War Department announced the defense mission of the AGF to be as follows:[12]

> Under the general plans of the War Department, and in conjunction with designated air and naval commanders, prepare for, and on order, or in imminent

---

12. WD to CG AGF: "Defense Missions of Army Ground Forces," 8 Apr 1946. (DOC 11)

emergency, execute planned operations for the defense of the United States.

Coordination. Coordinate ground plans, including coastal defense and antiaircraft projects, with designated air and naval commanders.

The new mission of AGF was greeted with mixed feelings by AAF and particularly by ADC. In one way, the War Department had decided to give AAF the air defense mission, but in a fashion which was extremely galling to AAF it left the ground open for intra-War Department controversy by failing to clarify the manner in which plans would be prepared in conjunction with the AAF, or the manner in which antiaircraft plans would be coordinated by AGF.

ADC's reaction to this anomalous situation was expressed by its A-5, Colonel R. E. Beebe, in a letter to Major General Lauris Norstad of AAF Headquarters.[13]

> As far as the record here, ADC is still supporting AGF under the old missions of the Eastern and Western Defense Commands and conducting planning under Army supervision. Actually, we know that this has been rescinded by WD letter 8 April 1946 . . . . Apparently no directive has been issued to AAF or WD as to coordinate or conjunctive planning with specific Naval commanders . . . . The primary mission of ADC in air defense is to operate independently or in cooperation with Naval forces. This leaves our relationship with the Armies unstated . . . . Can we be informed of the following: Has the WD issued the AF a mission similar to that given AGF? Do you plan to direct us to support the Army in its mission of defense, or is there any hope of getting this reversed?

---

13. Col. Beebe to Maj. Gen. Norstad: "Air Defense of the United States," 3 May 1946. (DOC 12)

General Norstad's reply was indicative of the dilemma in which AAF found itself at the time in its relations with the Ground Forces and the Navy.[14]

> Clarification of responsibilities of Air, Army and Navy commanders as to coordination of defense efforts is at this time inseparable from the questions of unification of the armed forces and the missions of the land, naval and air forces. Recommendations for the establishment of clear-cut command and operational responsibilities for employment of joint forces in the defense of the continental United States are now under study by the War Department.
>
> As indicated . . . the AAF will have its air defense activities coordinated with the defense activities of other services under the terms of directives yet to be issued by the War Department.

In May 1946, the War Department had cast a measure of oil on the troubled waters by the issuance of Circular No. 138, which was designed to lend official sanction to the general shakeup of the spring of 1946. The circular was intended to present a tentative doctrine and was scheduled for revision at the earliest possible date. Of special significance to the question of air defense were these functions specifically assigned to the Air Defense Command therein:[15]

> (1) Provides for the air defense of the United States.

---

14. Maj. Gen. Norstad to Col. Beebe: "Air Defense of the United States," 3 May 1946. (DOC 13)

15. WD Circular No. 138, 14 May 1946.

(2) Controls and trains antiaircraft units as may be assigned to this command.

In the more general field of air defense cooperation, the circular directed that the AAF and the AGF cooperate [16] "in the development and determination of such special tactics as are necessary ... for the use of arms by the Army Air Forces, especially antiaircraft artillery.

> Cooperate with the Commanding General, AGF in the development and determination of the technique of fire at aerial targets, in prescribing military characteristics of weapons and equipment, and in preparation of Tables of Organization and Equipment for units of antiaircraft artillery.
>
> Recommend to the War Department the means, including the necessary antiaircraft artillery units, required for air defense.

During June 1946 the AAF Board met in Washington to attempt a clarification of the thorny problems posed by the division of air defense responsibilities between AAF and AGF. The views of the AAF on Air Defense and Security were placed on record as follows:[17]

> The Army Air Force is charged with the mission of air defense. The Army Air Force has no officially adopted policies with respect to the personnel and organization of air defense. War Department thinking is not crystallized to the point that we know what they will favor. As a result we have drawn up ten proposals. The first involved integration of the antiaircraft into the Air Forces. The

---

16. Ibid.

17. ADC Staff Study No. 17: "Responsibilities for Air Defense," Jul 1946, p. 2. (DOC 14)

other nine proposals attempt to attain all the
other advantages of integration without that
integration and they will require no change if
the antiaircraft is ever integrated into the
Air Forces.

In this dilemma, General Stratemeyer took a positive position on the matter of prior responsibilities in air defense. The ADC commander was emphatic in his contention that "continuing and primary responsibility . . . for . . . provision of the Air Defense of the Continental United States . . ." rested with the Air Forces, and that no air defense plan prepared under his jurisdiction would subordinate the air force to either ground or naval commanders, except in a theater or similar combat establishment.[18]

The interpretation of War Department directives was more than a matter of semantics. It involved the very meaning of the term "air defense," and it bore directly upon the question of which agency, AAF or AGF, would exercise control of antiaircraft artillery. General Jacob L. Devers, Commanding General of AGF, was quick to assert his command's views. He proposed, on 14 June 1946, an interpretation of his own defense responsibilities that would retain under ground control the employment of AAA units engaged in air defense, and that would limit the definition of air defense to "defense by air." The intent of his suggestion was clearly to revise existing War Department regulations in order to

---

18. Lecture, Gen. Stratemeyer to Air War College, 15 Oct 1946, in ADC A-5 Proj. 28.

remove AA units entirely from AAF control.   Implicit in the issue raised was also the broader question of future control of ground-to-air guided missiles.

ADC and AAF challenged the Ground Forces' interpretation, reiterating the principle of single command control of all forces, weapons and means engaged in air defense, including AA, under a single commander. However, it was left to the War Department to resolve the question; and this it did, in somewhat diplomatic fashion, by refusing to modify the definition of air defense enunciated in WD Circular 138, and, in effect, by sustaining the AAF contention that AA should not revert to exclusive Ground Forces control. At most, however, this hedged upon the broader issue involved, and retained the dual assignment of antiaircraft artillery to AAF and AGF previously announced by the War Department. This was hardly the decision necessary to implement the AAF contention of integrated air defense, but the matter was not pressed by AAF, which was apparently looking toward unification of the services to provide a more propitious opportunity to reopen the question.

IV

The most serious restriction encountered by ADC was the shortage of personnel, forces, and weapons with which to accomplish its air defense mission. This situation was not at all

---

19. Gen. Devers to Gen. Spaatz, "Responsibilities for Air Defense," 14 June 1946. (DOC 15)

unknown to AAF, which apparently was reconciled to a limited regular air defense establishment in peacetime, with considerable dependence placed upon the civilian components for "practically all our air defense" in an emergency.[20] ADC planning, however, was based upon less sanguine expectations of the reserve components. Short term plans discounted the ANG as a combat effective force before 1948, while plans for an active air defense in being were based on the utilization of regular units and personnel exclusively.[21] In recognition of the inadequacy of available air units within the United States for utilization in air defense, ADC's "Short Term" plan contemplated the active defense of only one of the five priority areas selected to be defended from air attack. The potentialities of the command with respect to the

---

20. Second Interim Report of the Air Board, 4-6 Jun 1946.

21. ADC initially possessed two night fighter squadrons, the 425th located at McChord, and the 427th at Mitchel Field. The former was equipped with P-61's and the latter with P-47 aircraft. Shortly thereafter there were formed the 14th and 325th Fighter Groups, both stationed in the East, to act as headquarters for the two squadrons. Until May 1947 this was the sum total of the air defense capability assigned to the ADC. In July 1947, the fighter strength was increased on paper by the assignment at records strength of the 52nd and 78th Fighter Groups. It was not until late in 1948 that these two groups received personnel and equipment to permit active operations. On 31 March 1947 the assigned strength of the 14th Fighter Group was about 50% of authorized; that of the 425th, less than 10%. The operational effectiveness of the units mentioned were estimated at 20-29% and 0-19% respectively. See "ADC Strength" and "Monthly Unit Operational Effectiveness Report," 31 Mar 1947.

operation of an adequate control and warning system were no better than its tactical effectiveness, with no AC&W units assigned, and with only one such group earmarked for allocation to ADC in the near future.[22]

V

It was within the above-mentioned limitations and restrictions that ADC undertook the preparation of plans for the air defense of the United States. Within the first twelve month period of its existence, ADC prepared three plans: the first, essentially a capability study embodying the decision of the command as to its action in case of hostile air attack in the immediate future; the other two in the nature of requirement studies, projecting, and recommending to AAF, the forces, the resources, and the organization required for the air defense of the United States in the future.

In the preparation of the first of these plans,[23] the difficulties engendered by existing interservice relationships, and by command alignments within the AAF itself, were most clearly revealed. Necessarily, in the absence of assigned forces and the non-effectiveness of the reserve components for a period of years, a basic assumption in this short term plan was the

---

22. In May 1947 the 505th Aircraft Control and Warning Group was assigned to ADC with personnel of base units hitherto assigned to the Fourth Air Force.

23. ADC, "Air Defense Plan (Short Term)" 18 Oct 1946.

utilization by ADC air force commanders of tactical units of other AAF commands, the ground armies and the Navy to conduct any type of effective air defense operation. This concept of unified command under the air force area commander loomed large throughout the entire plan, and yet, a month after the plan's appearance, ADC admitted that it "states many things as fact which have not been approved by Army Air Forces or agreed upon between the services."[24]

The completion of the short term plan demonstrated convincingly to ADC the "inability of the AAF to provide an adequate air defense for this country under present conditions, particularly if a surprise attack . . . were to occur."[25] The recommendation of the command to remedy this ineffectiveness came in the form of a requirement study, projecting the permanent assignment to ADC of a sufficient number of regular, tactical air and ground units, together with supporting services, to provide "the framework necessary in any air defense system, and to give the minimum acceptable degree of protection from a surprise attack."[26] With the forces thus available, an effective air defense for five priority areas could be provided in place of the one contemplated in the short

---

24. Gen. Stratemeyer to Gen. Douglass, 18 Nov 1946. Cited in "The Evolution of the Mission," p. 23.

25. Gen. Stratemeyer to AAF: "Air Defense Plan (Long Term)" 8 Apr 1947, in ADC A-5 Proj. 56.

26. Ibid.

term plan. This plan for "An Air Defense in Being" contemplated the permanent assignment to ADC of some twelve fighter groups, two VHB and eight AC&W groups, 140 AAA units, and corresponding service and supporting units for "normal garrison" permitting deployment and operation of the air defense system within 24 hours. The organizational pattern suggested was three air forces: the First, to defend the entire East Coast; the Second, the Mid-west; and the Fourth, the West Coast.

The third ADC air defense plan attempted to[27]

> ... forecast the character of war which may occur in the future ... establish the methods of defense against that type of warfare ... determine in quality and quantity the resources required for that defense, and ... establish a date by which these resources must have been brought into existence.

The requirements of the plan were all-inclusive, if only general in nature.[28] The priority areas to be defended were more extensive than those contained in the "In Being" plan, but were limited to five. Organizationally, the envisaged air defense structure comprised four air defense air forces, covering respectively the Northeast and industrial Mid-west; the South and Gulf Coast area; the West Coast; and the North Central Plains area; all under an overall headquarters, not necessarily the existing Air

---

27. A-5 Presentation at ADC Air Force Commanders' Meeting, Offutt Field, Neb., 3 Oct 1946, in A-5 Proj. 30.

28. Gen. Stratemeyer to AAF: "Air Defense Plan (Long Term)" 8 Apr 1947, in ADC A-5 Proj. 56.

Defense Command, located preferably in the Mid-west. Forces allocated for air defense would be further organized under subordinate divisions and wings. A reorganization of ground and naval commands to correspond with the air force areas was suggested. In recognition of the requirement of supplementing continental United States organization by the inclusion of troops and installations in Canada, creation of a United States Arctic Theater was proposed as an essential element of the air defense organization.

Lacking the forces to effectively perform its defense mission independently, it was inevitable that ADC should indulge in the very broad assumption that units of other services should be made available for air defense operations. Both its short term plan and "In Being" plan were restricted by the necessity of planning for an air defense system within the framework of existing realities. In its long range planning, however, ADC could more validly engage in speculations, and in this respect it envisaged a pattern of air defense freed from direct dependence on ground and sea forces and fulfilling completely the airmen's vision of air power at its best.

That an effective air defense should not have been brought into existence by ADC is not surprising. That ADC should even have initiated and carried through to completion a comprehensive air defense plan in the face of archaic operational doctrines, legislative restrictions, organizational reservations, and its own limited combat potential, is remarkable. The plans drawn represented accomodations, from the short-range point of view, to the limitations placed upon the Air Forces and ADC by the existing military and naval structure and the command's inadequate combat potential. In compensation a future pattern of air defense was drawn permitting full application of the concepts of air power that past experience and future developments appeared to make realizable.

VI

The nature of the air defense problem was such that "unification" of the Armed Services in the summer of 1947 could do little to alleviate the difficulties inherent in it. In one way, however, unification did much to ease the conscience of the protagonists in the air defense controversy. The arbiter of air defense doctrine in the future was not to be an inflexible Field Manual, but the Joint Chiefs of Staff themselves. No matter how preferable a permanent statement of USAF's prerogatives in air defense operations might be, the creation of the JCS as final arbiters in the controversies between the services was perhaps the next best thing.[29] Here at any rate lay the responsibility for making the crucial decisions in the light of the immediate circumstances of an emergency.

---

29. The paramount position awarded to the JCS at Key West was not received with universal optimism as to its efficacy in reconciling inter-service disagreements. See Memo to Gen. Stratemeyer by Col. R. C. Candee.

The Key West Conference of March 1948, which defined the military responsibilities of the three services, allowed USAF to retain its air defense mission without important modification "subject to the policies and doctrines established by the Joint Chiefs of Staff."[30] Of greater importance to the air defense mission, however, was the stimulus which "independence" gave to the Air Force in streamlining its own organization. The anomalous position of ADC within the USAF command structure had caused concern both to the personnel of ADC and to USAF. Almost at once steps were taken to reorganize ADC for a more effective performance of its air defense mission, but although the urgency of clearing ADC's mission-laden decks was recognized in many official statements, little was done until the formation of the Continental Air Command in December 1948.[31]

---

30. Functional Agreement of the Key West Conference, Mar 1948. (DOC 16)

31. In October 1947, USAF established a committee headed by Major General Reuben C. Hood to examine the missions of ADC. It was recommended that the assorted training missions of ADC be assigned to the Air Training Command. None of the recommendations of the Hood Committee bore fruit, however. On 19 December 1947 USAF directed ADC to submit a plan for its own reorganization, to be guided by the "paramount importance of your responsibilities in connection with the defense of the Continental United States." On 29 January 1948 ADC submitted its plan. The primary features of the reorganization were to be the reduction of the numbered air forces from six to four. Although Gen. Stratemeyer believed this would leave ADC well-suited to the accomplishment of its mission so far as the air forces were concerned, he considered additional organizational preparations as essential before ADC could effectively execute its assignment.

(Cont'd on next page)

The pressing question of a greater combat potential for ADC was rather unsatisfactorily answered by earmarking the ANG for the Air Defense Command.[32]

> In performing The Air Defense Mission, the Air National Guard will constitute your major source of Air Defense units . . . . In the event of war or national emergency, initially, all Air National Guard units will be available to the Air Defense Commander, and until other requirements develop which necessitate their employment elsewhere, you will have full use thereof.

In the long run it was the pressure of international crisis which was to break the jam in which the air defense of the United States was tightly locked.

> One of these preparations is the construction of command posts especially suited to meet the requirements of commanders charged with defense against air attack by known and foreseeable weapons. Such installations must be constructed in peace-time at or near the administrative headquarters of Air Defense Command air forces.

The reduction in the number of air forces was accomplished soon thereafter, but the recommendation to construct command posts met a quiet demise.

32. USAF to ADC: "Air Defense," 17 Dec 1947 (DOC 17) At the same time, USAF provided for ADC emergency use of units assigned to TAC and SAC. See p. 39.

CHAPTER THREE

RADAR: THE YEAR OF DECISION - 1948

I

Although the Air Defense Command had labored long to establish an air defense in being, at the beginning of 1948 ADC was still without adequate capabilities to set up even a token air defense system. The insistent demands by ADC and by key officers in USAF Headquarters that concrete action be taken in behalf of air defense had an inevitable cumulative effect, however. These admonitions, plus the increased freedom of action which "unification" brought to USAF and the growing popular reaction to Russian aggression, brought more vigorous action toward the setting up of an air defense system.

In the summer of 1947 it was determined by USAF that, though a comprehensive air defense system of fighters, radar stations and other necessary facilities might be a long time in coming, a good start might well be made by the establishment of a network of ground radar stations. As a result of renewed vigor in planning and the increased sense of urgency which imbued the entire Air Force establishment at this time, a plan for an extensive radar network was drawn up and approved by the Chief of Staff, USAF, in November 1947 and turned over to the Air Defense Command for its

This radar plan, given the code name SUPREMACY, was dependent for implementation, however, upon Congressional action in making the necessary funds available to USAF for construction of sites. After certain delays caused by the necessity of obtaining concurrence from the other services, the plan was introduced in the 80th Congress in April 1948. There it died, without any action being taken by the legislature.[2]

Although SUPREMACY was abortive, it acted as a catalyst upon both USAF and ADC. On 19 January 1948 ADC was officially apprised of the plan and notified that it had been chosen as the implementing agency.[3] The news of SUPREMACY had an electric effect on ADC. Immediately, ADC began fervently to prepare for the moment when Congress would give the Air Force the green-light. Being writ large in the manner habitually employed by ADC in its own air defense thinking, SUPREMACY was greeted enthusiastically.

As finally determined through an exchange of ideas between USAF and ADC, SUPREMACY was to be implemented in three phases over a period of five years, with a proposed deployment of 374 basic

---

1. For the background of these decisions see Maj. Gen. Gordon P. Saville's presentation on the Interim AC&W system to Secretary Forrestal, 9 Sep 1948. (DOC 18)

2. The history of Plan SUPREMACY is described in the presentation cited in fn 1 above.

3. USAF to ADC: "Aircraft Control and Warning Plan for the United States," 19 Jan 1948. (DOC 19)

radar stations and fourteen control centers manned by a total of 33,526 personnel, and with construction costs alone amounting to $316,595,000. 676 pieces of radar equipment were to be utilized, including early warning radars and height finders. Although coverage for the entire continental United States was not contemplated because of prohibitive cost, the vital industrial areas and atomic plants were covered, and the entire northern border of the United States provided for.[4]

Phase I of SUPREMACY was to result in the construction of 40 basic radars and two control centers, comprising 50 pieces of equipment to be deployed and to be operational within one year from the date of allocation of the necessary funds. The radar stations were to be manned by the two AC&W groups (the 505th and 503d) then authorized for ADC under the FY 1949, 55-group program. Both groups were to be brought up to their fully authorized manning of 2,726 persons when combined. Equipping of Phase I installation was to be achieved from radar present in depots of the Air Materiel Command, which radar was to be replaced with more modern equipment of the AN/CPS-6B and AN/FPS-3 type as that became available. ADC's recommended deployment of these Phase I installations concentrated them in the industrial northeast and in three selected target areas in the vicinity of the West Coast: Seattle-Pasco, San Francisco

---

4. ADC, Memo: "A-6 Conference. Early Warning for the Continental United States," 3 Mar 1948. (DOC 20)

and Los Alamos in New Mexico.

Phase II of SUPREMACY was to add to Phase I a total of 44 basic radar stations and six more control centers totalling 61 additional pieces of radar equipment. No time element was determined for this stage of the plan, but deployment of this equipment was earmarked for the industrial northeast, with some augmentation along the West Coast. An additional 5,514 regular troops were to be provided for this phase.

Phase III was to round out the radar system to its full strength of 374 stations and 676 pieces of radar. 11,498 regular troops were to be added for AC&W purposes, making a grand total of 19,738 regular troops in the system. However, during Phase III the total strength of the ANG AC&W units was to be integrated into the system, thus adding an estimated 13,788 personnel for an overall total of 33,526 at the end of the five year period. Deployment of Phase III sites was to fill in the blanks in the perimeter coverage of the continental United States, particularly along the northern international boundary. Radar equipment for Phases II and III of the plan was to be of the latest type, to be procured either at the inception of the plan or in the course of its implementation.

After intensive study of the proposal for Plan SUPREMACY, ADC put forth its own reactions to the plan on 8 April 1948.[5] With

---

5. 1st Ind, ADC to USAF, 8 Apr 1948, to USAF to ADC: "AC&W Plan for the United States," 19 Jan 1948. (DOC 19)

characteristic understatement ADC concluded that the plan, in general, provided "a minimum aircraft control and warning coverage for the strategic areas of the continental United States within the inherent capabilities of presently available equipment." ADC pointed out that more need be done to make this radar screen adequate for air defense purposes.

> It is desired to point out that coverage along the coasts must be extended by radar picket boats or airborne early warning stations in order to provide adequate early warning for interception before the bomb release line is reached by high-speed hostile flights. This is particularly true for single airplanes or small flights which can be detected generally only at reduced ranges.
>
> It is essential that the Air Defense Command be connected by reliable communications circuits to the Canadian Air Defense System, Hq. Alaska Air Command, and the proposed Northeast Air Command.

The great increase in manpower foreseen to man the proposed radar network posed an additional problem.

> The expansion of the troops basis for regular aircraft control and warning units in the Air Defense Command, from present actual strength of approximately 700 to a total of 19,738 presents a positive requirement for a suitable air defense training center for training air defense units.

ADC began to gird itself for the big tasks ahead even before it was provided with the funds necessary to the commencement of preparations. The first and most important job was the siting of the new radar stations according to the time-phasing of Plan SUPREMACY. Before the siting teams could be sent out into the field, theoretical deployment of the radar had to be made. The question inevitably arose of the value of the old World War II radar sites. Modern equipment possessed characteristics different from those of World War II radar, and the old sites would consequently be inadequate. In addition hostile aircraft would be high-powered jets and come from directions different from those anticipated in the earlier period. Furthermore, SUPREMACY was not deemed to be a self-sufficient system but had to fit into the Canadian, Alaskan and Greenland radar systems.[6]

Radar siting team requirements were drawn up by ADC, but no team was dispatched because of the fact that SUPREMACY was never implemented as such.[7] By the summer of 1948 it had become apparent to all concerned that Congressional procrastination had killed any chance of implementing the plan for any part of the current fiscal year.[8] The only hope remaining was that when Congress convened again in January 1949 a new start might be made on the master plan. In the meantime, the year 1948 was not a complete loss.

---

6. IRS, Col. Hobart R. Yeager to A-6: "Radar Siting Teams," 16 Apr 1948 (DOC 21) Approximately 65 radar stations had been established on the West Coast in World War II and some 34 on the East Coast. Almost all of these sites had been disposed of by the War Assets Administration.

7. ADC to 1st AF: "Radar Siting Teams," 20 Apr 1948 (DOC 22)

8. Memo, Col. H. R. Yeager, 9 Jun 1948. (DOC 23)

II

While negotiations were underway for the Congressional approval of SUPREMACY, and while ADC was making ambitious plans for implementation, several other factors entered the air defense scene which in part recouped the losses caused by the delays attending the plan. Indeed, before ADC had been given even the opportunity to record its initial reactions to SUPREMACY, the command was directed to establish an air defense in being for the Seattle-Pasco area of Washington and to operate it on a continuous 24-hour basis until notified to the contrary.

As early as the autumn of 1947, suggestions of a possible maneuver scheduled for the spring of 1948 in the New York area had led ADC to plan ahead for such an eventuality. In preparation for this exercise ADC scheduled the transfer of the 505th AC&W Group from the Northwest area to the Northeast for the spring of 1948. When the order came in March to put the air defenses in the Northwest into operation, there was little that ADC could do to establish a realistic air defense for that area. The total AC&W facilities on the West Coast included one AN/CPS-5 radar at Half Moon Bay in California for training purposes, and another at Arlington, Washington (near Bellingham).

Immediately on receipt of the order to establish defenses in the Northwest, ADC directed the Fourth Air Force to set up radar stations in the vicinity of Spokane, Hanford, Neah Bay and Portland, using AN/TPS-1B sets drawn from the McClellan AFB depot, and to put the Arlington GCI on a 24-hour operational basis.[9] The 325th Fighter Group stationed at Hamilton Field, and equipped with P-61 night fighters, was to be alerted and deployed at the discretion of the Commanding General of the Fourth Air Force.[10] In addition to the possible use of the 325th Group, the 27th Fighter Group, equipped with P-51 aircraft, was to be borrowed from the Strategic Air Command and stationed at McChord AFB until the end of April 1948 to operate under the operational control of the Fourth Air Force.

The pathetic insufficiency of these arrangements for the defense of the crucial Northwest was all too soon apparent, and the fiasco which inevitably resulted did much to add conviction at the top level of both USAF and ADC that only an intense concentration of effort could rectify the flagrant deficiency in our air defense.

Having duly received the 27th Fighter Group on loan from SAC, and having established radars at Walla Walla, Spokane, Neah Bay and Arlington in Washington, and Seaside in Oregon, the Northwest Air Defense Wing was created as the tactical agency responsible for the overall local defense, with the commanding officer of the

---

9. TWX, ADC to 4AF, 27 Mar 1948. (DOC 24)

10. ADC to 4AF: "Air Defense System," 31 Mar 1948. (DOC 25)

27th Group as the wing commander.[11] The 325th Fighter Group did not participate in the maneuver, being marooned at Hamilton Field for want of radar observers.[12] The extremely adverse weather indigenous to the Seattle area rendered the P-51 fighters of the 27th Group all but ineffective as interceptors. These developments, coupled with the fact that the 27th was neither trained in, nor equipped for, ground-controlled interception techniques, made it clear that the Fourth Air Force could make not even a pretense toward the air defense of the Northwest.[13]

The ambitious requirement imposed on the 505th AC&W Group soon led to an almost complete breakdown in its operations. On 14 April, ADC removed the requirement of 24-hour operations and allowed the Fourth Air Force to shut down one radar at all times in rotation.[14] ADC made the following observations to USAF:[15]

> Both personnel and equipment now available in the 505th Aircraft Control and Warning Group are inadequate to maintain 24-hour operation of warning

---

11. 4AF to ADC: "Protection of the Seattle-Pasco Area Against Air Attack," 12 Apr 1948. (DOC 26)

12. TWX, 4AF to ADC, 8 Apr 1948. (DOC 27)

13. ADC to USAF: "Status of Continental Air Defense," 15 Apr 1948. (DOC 28)

14. TWX, ADC to USAF, 14 Apr 1948. (DOC 29)

15. ADC to USAF: "Status of Continental Air Defense," 15 Apr 1948 (DOC 28) Some interesting documents relative to this maneuver can be found in: History of the Fourth Air Force, 1948.

sites for an indefinite period. All personnel already on hand are tired and overworked... The portable type equipment now being used also will not stand continuous operation. Sets are frequently out of commission for repairs, and the small portable power units which are the only source of power presently available frequently break down.

III

The totally inadequate air defenses revealed in the Northwest maneuver and the failure of SUPREMACY to receive approval of Congress since its adoption in November 1947 by the Chief of Staff of the Air Force prompted ADC to present the issue squarely to USAF. On 24 April, General Stratemeyer addressed a strongly worded letter to the Chief of Staff outlining his recommendations toward the establishment of an air defense in being with the least delay. With characteristic force, General Stratemeyer stated:[16]

> Adequate defense of the continental United States against air attack is not possible even though the total forces, resources, and facilities presently available to the United States Air Force were placed at my disposal.

The ADC commander went on to press that the Chief of Staff "... take a firm decision to establish an air defense system and to maintain air defense in being."

While the Northwest maneuver was continuing, and while ADC was making plans for the establishment of another token defense in being for the Northeast, USAF directed ADC on 23 April 1948 to

---

16. ADC to USAF: "Air Defense of the United States," 24 Apr 1948. (DOC 30)

"immediately implement certain portions of our defense plans."[17]

According to this directive USAF's decision to take unilateral action in establishing a continuing air defense in being apparently stemmed from the decisions reached at the Key West Conference in March 1948 which confirmed the provision that the land-based air defense of the United States was a primary function of the Air Force. It will be recalled that prior to the Key West agreement, which put paramount authority into the hands of the Joint Chiefs of Staff, the Air Force had been guided by the temporary statement of air defense authority included in WD Circular No. 138.[18] After unification in September 1947, and until the Key West Conference in March 1948, there was no clear-cut statement of the responsibilities of the Air Force, and its absence thwarted any USAF decision to take the responsibility for a far-flung, ground-based air defense system into its own hands without official authorization.

The directive of 23 April authorized the Air Defense Command to establish with current means aircraft control and warning systems in the following priority:[19]

    a. Northwestern U. S. area
    b. Northeastern U. S. area
    c. Albuquerque, New Mexico, area.

---

17. USAF to ADC: "Air Defense of the Continental United States," 23 Apr 1948. (DOC 31)

18. See above, p. 43.

19. USAF to ADC: "Air Defense of the Continental United States," 23 Apr 1948. (DOC 31).

The first step in the implementation of the Northeastern area was to be "the establishment of a model air defense system, initially in the vicinity of New York City." In addition to being an integral part of the air defenses of the area, the model system was to be "utilized to test and develop strategic and air defense tactics and techniques."

More detailed information of priorities within each of the above areas was forthcoming from USAF on 4 May 1948.[20] In the Northwest the following vital installations were listed in order of priority:

    a. Hanford Engineering Works, Pasco, Washington
    b. Seattle, Washington
    c. Renton, Washington
    d. Bonneville Hydro Electric Station, Bonneville, Oregon
    e. Tacoma, Washington.

In the Northeast the following were listed:

    a. Washington, D. C.
    b. New York-Newark-Jersey City
    c. Philadelphia
    d. Westover AFB, Chicopee Falls, Mass.
    e. McGuire AFB, Fort Dix, N. J.
    f. Hartford, Conn.
    g. Boston, Mass.
    h. Niagara Falls, N. Y.

And in the New Mexico area, these:

    a. AFSWP facility at Sandia, including Kirtland AFB
    b. AEC facility at Los Alamos
    c. Walker AFB, Roswell.

The necessary manpower to accomplish these defenses was to

---

20. USAF to ADC: "Air Defense of the Continental United States," 4 May 1948, and Incl. (DOC 32)

come from the transfer of 587 persons from the Caribbean Defense Command and the additional assignment of personnel to the two AC&W Groups to bring them to their combined, authorized strength of 2,726.[21] As for the indispensable interceptors, USAF indicated that "fighter units, currently assigned to other major commands, will be made available from time to time."[22]

IV

The directive of 23 April 1948 which authorized the Air Defense Command to establish "with current means" AC&W systems for the Northwest, Northeast and Albuquerque areas, indicated a rather desperate predicament. The maneuver in the Northwest in March showed very clearly that America was virtually defenseless against air attack. While it is true that USAF had proposed an elaborate radar system in Plan SUPREMACY, expectations that the authorization would be pushed through Congress in time to do any good in the present situation were not too sanguine. The decision to throw what was available into the breech was apparently the last resort. An indication of this compulsion was the statement in the directive mentioned to the effect that[23]

Until such time as /funds/ are made available,

---

21. USAF to ADC: "Air Defense of the Continental United States," 23 Apr 1948. (DOC 31)

22. Ibid.

23. Ibid.

however, it will be necessary to limit the air defense dispositions and operations envisaged herein to such as can be effected without them.

In reality, the process of taking radar of World War II vintage out of moth balls had been resorted to before the April decision. Token radar foundations had been laid in the Northwest in behalf of the March maneuver in that area. Radar deployment in the Northeast had been scheduled as early as the winter of 1947-48 in anticipation of a maneuver scheduled for that area in the spring of 1948. By the end of April 1948, a start had been made in the Northeast by deployment of radars at Montauk, N. Y. and Palermo, while an AN/CPS-6 radar at Twin Lights (N.J.) had been undergoing tests.[24]

Pressure to establish an air defense in being for the Northeast was increased by the arrival of a squadron of Vampire aircraft from Great Britain late in May 1948.[25] As part of the itinerary of these visitors, exercises in ground-controlled interception were

---

24. ADC to USAF: "Transfer of Radar Site and Equipment," 2 Jan 1948 (DOC 33) See also: Col. Yeager to Col. Wilson, 10 Feb 1948, for interesting information about the status of various radar projects early in 1948 (DOC 34) For radar activity in the Northeast see: ADC to 1st AF: "Preparation of Installations for Occupancy," 9 Apr 1948 (DOC 35) An excellent summary of the radar situation at this time is in ADC to 1st AF: "Air Defense Activities," 6 Apr 1948 (DOC 36); also, 1st AF to ADC: "Air Defense Activities," 12 Apr 1948 (DOC 37); and ADC to 1st AF: "Radar Siting Teams," 20 Apr 1948 (DOC 22)

25. 1st AF to ADC: "Participation of the RAF Vampire Aircraft in Local Air Defense Maneuvers," 18 Jun 1948 (DOC 38); 1st AF to ADC: "Report on Air Defense Maneuvers in the Metropolitan New York Area," 14 Oct 1948 (DOC 39)

prepared for the First Air Force area. During these exercises, held in June 1948, the First Air Force had in operation, besides the AN/CPS-6 at Twin Lights, the following equipment: at Palermo, an AN/TPS-1B radar, with an AN/CPS-5 scheduled for installation by July; at Montauk Point, an AN/TPS-1B with an AN/CPS-5 earmarked for that site. Assorted communication facilities at the designated control center at Roslyn were assembled but were characterized by First Air Force as "totally inadequate." The token Northeastern radar "net" was found to be no better than the one in the Northwest.[26]

The national predicament was appreciated by ADC, but without necessary funds there was little that could be done.[27] In August 1948, General Norstad of USAF Headquarters wired General Stratemeyer that, in view of the delays encountered by SUPREMACY, USAF was struggling to obtain approval from the appropriations committees of Congress so that sufficient funds could be diverted from regular USAF appropriations for construction purposes in the Northeast.[28] ADC was asked to submit with all possible haste detailed estimates for minimum construction costs for both the Northeast and the Seattle-

---

26. For attempts to set up an air defense for the Albuquerque area see: TWX, ADC to 4AF, 6 May 1948 (DOC 40); and, ADC to SAC: "Air Defense of the Albuquerque-Roswell, New Mexico Area," 23 Jul 1948 (DOC 41) ADC planned to deploy 3 radars in this area and asked to borrow a fighter squadron from SAC for interception.

27. The strain of earlier preparations for Plan SUPREMACY had already begun to tell on ADC's limited resources. See: IRS, A-5 to AG: "ADC Air Defense Plans and Preparations," 22 Apr 1948 (DOC 42)

28. TWX, Gen. Norstad to Gen. Stratemeyer, 4 Aug 1948. (DOC 43)

Pasco areas. This time USAF was to go to Congress not to demand hundreds of millions, but to ask for a pittance in order to establish a token network. Even this was to be an unconscionably long time in coming.

V

On 9 September 1948 Major General Gordon P. Saville, one of the most aggressive supporters of an air defense in being policy in USAF, presented to Secretary Forrestal, on behalf of the Air Force, a plan to put into effect immediately an "Interim" AC&W system for the continental United States.[29]

After tracing the history of Plan SUPREMACY and indicating that the "Air Force cannot discharge its responsibilities by continued waiting . . ." General Saville recommended that "immediate and positive action . . . start at once on the establishment of a limited air defense in being - pending final approval on any overall air defense program."

General Saville had nothing but disparagement for the air defenses of the United States.

> It would be utterly impossible for me to overstate the complete inadequacy of this deployment to provide aircraft warning and control in the event of air attack. It is so wholly inadequate that it not only provides negligible air defense capability, but does not even provide a sufficient system for the development of tactics, techniques and procedures involved in any air defense system.

---

29. Maj. Gen. Gordon P. Saville, presentation to Secretary Forrestal on the Interim AC&W Program, 9 Sep 1948. (DOC 18)

General Saville spoke for both USAF and ADC when he reiterated that

> We must have a limited air defense in being if we are to solve the many and varied systems problems involved in any reasonable time. Basic radar stations, control centers, and interconnecting communications inevitably will be the skeleton upon which the whole air defense system is erected. Without that skeleton, we will have nothing to grow on . . . . We can develop new equipment but we cannot have an effective air defense unless and until we have a SYSTEM.

General Saville pointed out that at that time (September 1948) only five AC&W stations were operating. He demanded a minimum of 76 radar stations and ten control centers for a limited air defense in being. General Saville pointed out that he was asking for authorization by Congress not of funds to purchase this equipment but of funds to construct facilities so that equipment on hand or on procurement could be installed.

The extension of radar coverage from five to 76 basic radar stations was to be accomplished in two phases, according to General Saville. Since the Air Force had in its possession nineteen heavy type radars in storage and five more in the field, it was proposed that this total of 24 heavy-search equipments be deployed permanently in sites to be prepared with public works funds provided by Congress. In addition to this total of old-type radars, all the search radars of modern vintage then on procurement (twelve AN/CPS-6Bs and 25 AN/FPS-3s) were to be similarly deployed, thus making a total of 61 basic radar stations. This 61-radar program was dubbed the Interim AC&W program.

Realizing that the proposed Interim program would still be inadequate in its coverage, General Saville proposed that additional construction be undertaken to house fifteen more radars of the AN/CPS-6B type, which the Air Force would procure out of funds in its FY 1950 budget. This expansion of the Interim program was called by General Saville the "First Augmentation." The Interim program and the First Augmentation, therefore, were to provide a total of 76 basic radar stations and ten control centers. In order to begin work on this system at once, it was proposed to divert $706,000 from Air Force projects of lesser priority and assign this sum to construction.

Approval of the Joint Chiefs of Staff and the Secretary of Defense was granted to this proposal, and the Department of the Air Force then undertook to obtain an authorization bill in the 81st Congress. In this action, USAF slightly modified its construction requirements to provide for 75 sites for search radar equipment and for ten control centers.[30]

On 30 March 1949 Congress passed Public Law 30, authorizing

---

[30]. See remarks by Maj. Gen. G. P. Saville to the Committee on Armed Services, House of Representatives, 17 Mar 1949 (DOC 44); also answers to questions of the House of Representatives' Committee on Armed Services, 7 Feb 1949; also statement of Maj. Gen. Saville before the Committee on Armed Services, U. S. Senate, 17 Mar 1949.

the Secretary of the Air Force to construct aircraft control and warning facilities to the extent of $85,500,000 for both the United States and Alaska. But - it was not until 29 October 1949 that Congress saw fit to appropriate necessary funds. The predicament of having won its Congressional battle but of having failed to acquire the necessary funds was solved by USAF by the drastic measure of reprogramming $50,000,000 from the aircraft procurement funds for the radar net. Of this amount, however, only $18,800,000 was allocated to the Zone of the Interior radar program, the balance going towards the construction of an Alaskan radar net which was deemed to have first priority.[31] Enough was on hand, however, so that positive steps could be taken to begin construction. What came to be known as the Permanent System was at last on its way,[32] and with good fortune USAF anticipated that it would be in operation by sometime in 1952.

VI

The time between the end of 1948 and sometime in 1952 was

---

31. "Summary of Appropriations for the Construction and Operation of Aircraft Warning and Radar Systems," [n. d.] (DOC 45)

32. In this history only two names for radar systems will be used: the LASHUP system and the Permanent System. In reality the programs called by General Saville the Interim program and the First Augmentation when combined constituted what ADC was to call the Permanent System, in order to distinguish the system from the strictly temporary LASHUP system. LASHUP will be discussed in the following chapter.

too long a period to be without an air defense in being even though a calculated risk on a future air defense system were taken. USAF determined in September 1948 to scrape the bottom of its financial barrel and to deploy its old radar equipment at once. Not having sufficient funds to install this radar on operationally desirable sites, USAF came to the conclusion that compromise with the ideal was inevitable. If this radar equipment was to be deployed at all, it would have to be deployed on land and in buildings which would cost the Air Force an absolute minimum, and this meant installation on Government-owned land. To do this meant that in many instances the maximum operational effectiveness of the radar would have to be sacrificed. An alternative being nonexistent, the decision was made at the end of August 1948. The result was the AC&W system known as LASHUP.

CHAPTER FOUR

LASHUP

I

For almost three years from the time of its inception in the autumn of 1948 the temporary aircraft control and warning system, or LASHUP, bore the brunt of the continental air defense. The Air Force was under no illusion that in bringing World War II radar out of storage and deploying it in locations which cost the government next to nothing it would be creating a realistic air defense. So long as it existed, the temporary system more than fulfilled its primary function of providing a proving ground for air defense systems development. After Korea, though LASHUP's training function was still paramount, its role as America's only early warning and control capability was inevitably thrust forward. By that time, however, the trials and errors of almost two years of operation of LASHUP had produced a system which, although still far short of an acceptable minimum aircraft warning and control system, could still contribute greatly in any war effort involving the defense of the continental United States.

From an historical viewpoint, therefore, LASHUP, though destined to be eclipsed by the Permanent System, must not be dismissed lightly. In the growth and operation of this system there were revealed problems whose resolution helped to clear the path for the more efficient operation of the air defense system which was to follow. It was responsible for sponsoring a pattern of air defense organization which was both peculiar and indispensable to the forging of an entirely new weapon - ground-controlled interception. LASHUP's progress evoked clashes of jurisdiction between the armed services and between the Air Force and civil agencies which resulted in greater, not less, harmony among all concerned in national air defense, though much remained to be accomplished in this direction. It brought to light additional inadequacies in the organization and training of the Air National Guard and in the recruiting and training of regular Air Force personnel. It clearly revealed the necessity for the closest relationship in thought and action between the radar operator on the ground and the fighter pilot in the air, and it pointed to the need for an effective system of air traffic control.

II

The problem of setting up a temporary aircraft control and warning system was not as simple as receiving radars from AMC depots and deploying them. Appropriate locations had to be found which would conform to the criteria of negligible cost and maximum operational efficiency. In this siting effort the factors of speed and cost resulted in a compromise with the factor of efficiency.

The announcement by USAF that it intended to deploy its

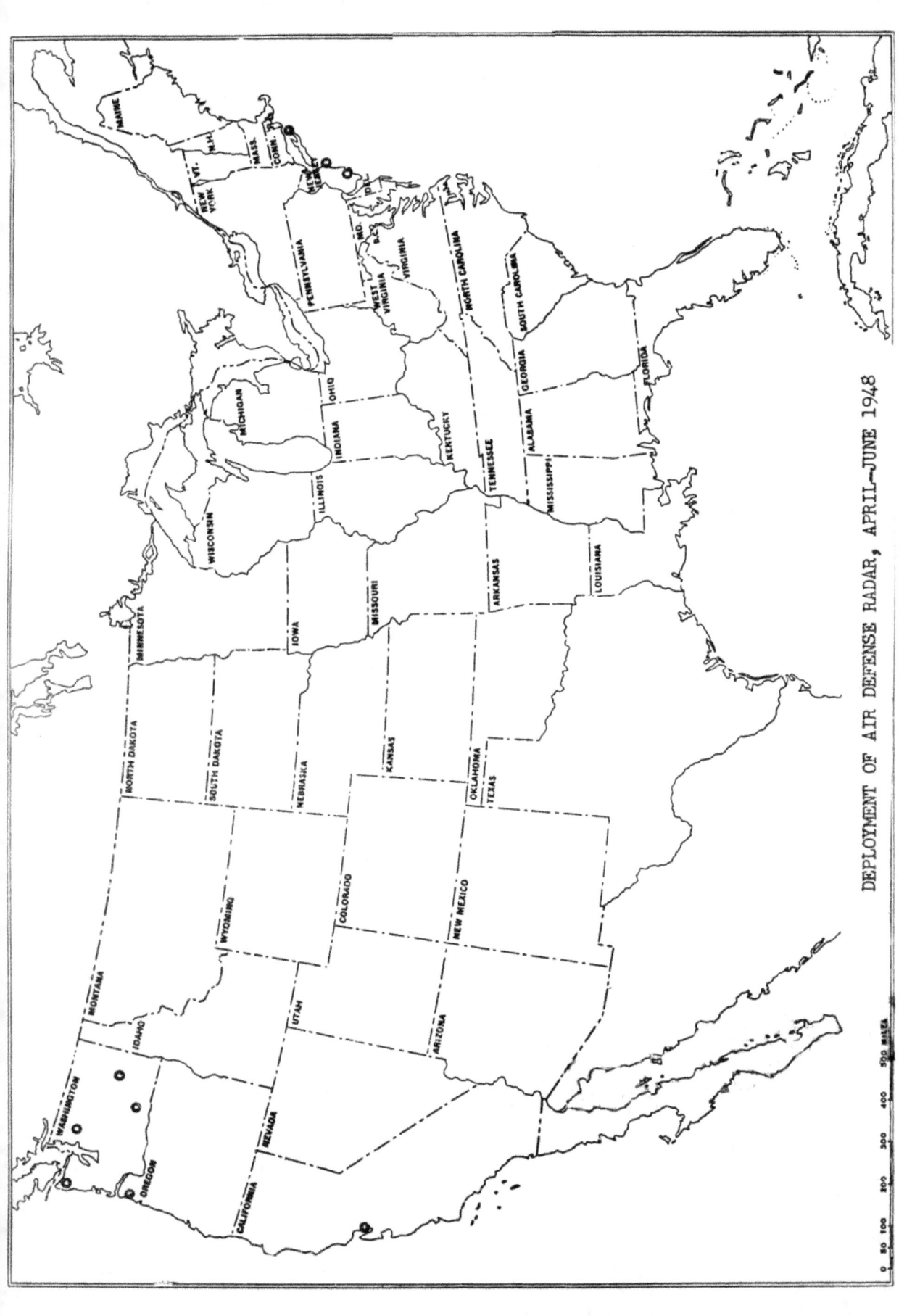

DEPLOYMENT OF AIR DEFENSE RADAR, APRIL–JUNE 1948

available ground radars temporarily was followed immediately by an authorization to ADC in September 1948 to expand the Northeastern radar system by the addition of thirteen more stations.[1] For this purpose the sum of $152,000 was earmarked for construction.[2] By the end of September, thirteen sites had been chosen by the First Air Force to supplement the three stations already in existence at Twin Lights, Palermo and Montauk.[3] For the whole network, a control center was chosen at Roslyn in Long Island, in close proximity to Mitchel Air Force Base.[4]

Although a target date of 15 March 1949 was imposed by USAF for completion of the Northeastern system, delays caused by the failure of speedy fund allocation forced the extension of that deadline on several occasions.[5] By June 1949, however, First Air Force was able to announce that its radar had been deployed and the system was operational. The accomplishment of this deployment was accelerated by the announcement by USAF of a scheduled exercise for the

---

1. IRS, Air Defense to DO, 13 Sep 1948 (DOC 46)

2. Ibid.

3. IRS, DCE to AirD: "Radar Sites," 14 Sep 1948 (DOC 47); ADC to USAF: "Establishment and Operation of Thirteen Radar Sites for the 503d Aircraft Control and Warning Group," 23 Sep 1948 (DOC 48); TWX, ADC to USAF, 30 Sep 1948 (listing sites) (DOC 49)

4. For sites in operation at end of 1948 and plans for future deployments see: ConAC to AMC: "Logistic Support for Project 'AC&W Defense Plan'" 4 Nov 1948. (DOC 50)

5. TWX, ADC to USAF, 19 Nov 1948 (DOC 51)

Northeastern system to be held in May. When deployment of the radar was delayed, however, the date for this exercise was postponed until the following month.

The exercise which was held for the new Northeastern radar net in June 1949 was known as operation BLACKJACK.[6] Although calibration of the newly installed radar equipment was still in progress, the system was tested in this operation by a series of missions performed in part by SAC heavy bombers and in part by ConAC's own B-26s. A total of eighteen operational radars in the Northeast was divided among five provisional air divisions with control centers operating at Roslyn, Pine Camp, Grenier, Selfridge and Washington, all responsible to an organization established for the period of the exercise and called the Eastern Air Defenses. Results of BLACKJACK were highly informative. Performance of the radars varied considerably, some being just barely operational and others picking up aircraft and tracking them in from surprisingly long ranges. Radar capability at the AN/CPS-6 at Twin Lights, for example, was practically zero, while the AN/CPS-5 at Selfridge, Michigan, after some experimentation in the course of the exercise, gratified observers by painting aircraft solid out to 210 miles.

Another exercise of the Northeastern system was held in

---

6. Report of Air Defense Exercise BLACKJACK, 1 - 30 Jun 1949. (DOC 52)

September 1949. A feature of this maneuver, called LOOKOUT, was the testing of the newly-formed Ground Observer Corps in this area, whose purpose was to extend early warning capability by providing the low coverage needed to supplement the limited coverage of the radar. In this test, three divisions were established, with control centers at Pine Camp, Grenier and Roslyn under the supervision of the newly-established Eastern Air Defense Force Headquarters. Radar performance was characterized as "below the equipments' maximum capability due to location of equipment and state of training of the operating personnel." An important and encouraging result observed, however, was the increased cooperation between pilots and controllers. Techniques of radar maintenance came in for severe criticism, reflecting the acute shortage of skilled technicians in the new system.

Deployment of radar in the Northeast was matched during 1949, although in not so ambitious a scale, by the establishment of a Northwestern radar network and by the provisions of token radar coverage for the important atomic installations in New Mexico. By the end of 1949 emphasis on integrating the radar system shifted from the Northeast, where two exercises had already been held, to the Northwest. By the end of October 1949 radars had been deployed at Whidbey Island (a naval installation),

---

7. Report of Air Defense Exercise LOOKOUT, 10 - 16 Sep 1949 (DOC 53); 26th AD to EADF: "Final Report and Overall Evaluation for LOOKOUT," 19 Sep 1949. (DOC 54)

Olympia, Pacific Beach, Neah Bay, Sequim, Moses Lake and Spokane — a total of seven radars. Headquarters of the 25th Air Division was established at the control center for the network at Silver Lake, Everett, Washington.

During the period 4 - 14 November 1949 an exercise called DRUMMERBOY was held in the Northwest under the supervision of the 25th Air Division and the newly-established Western Air Defense Force.[8] Reaction to this test indicated that the Northwestern radar system performed considerably better than had been anticipated. Primary obstacles revealed in the exercise were not so much concerned with radar performance, however, as with the organizational confusion which prevailed in the West, and also with deployment of aircraft in the troublesome Cascade mountain area.

By April 1950, LASHUP deployment in the Northwest included the following stations: Spokane, Moses Lake, Pasco, Paine Field, McChord AFB, Vancouver, Neah Bay, Pacific Beach, Seaside (Oregon) and Whidbey Island.[9]

The progress of radar deployment which followed the three maneuvers of 1949 saw the extension of radar into areas hitherto neglected in favor of the Northwest and Northeast. In 1950 major emphasis in deployment of radar was placed upon the establishment

---

8. USAF to ConAC: "Special Report of Observation on Exercise DRUMMERBOY," 2 Dec 1949 (DOC 55)

9. "List of Radar Stations, Continental United States," 30 Apr 1950.

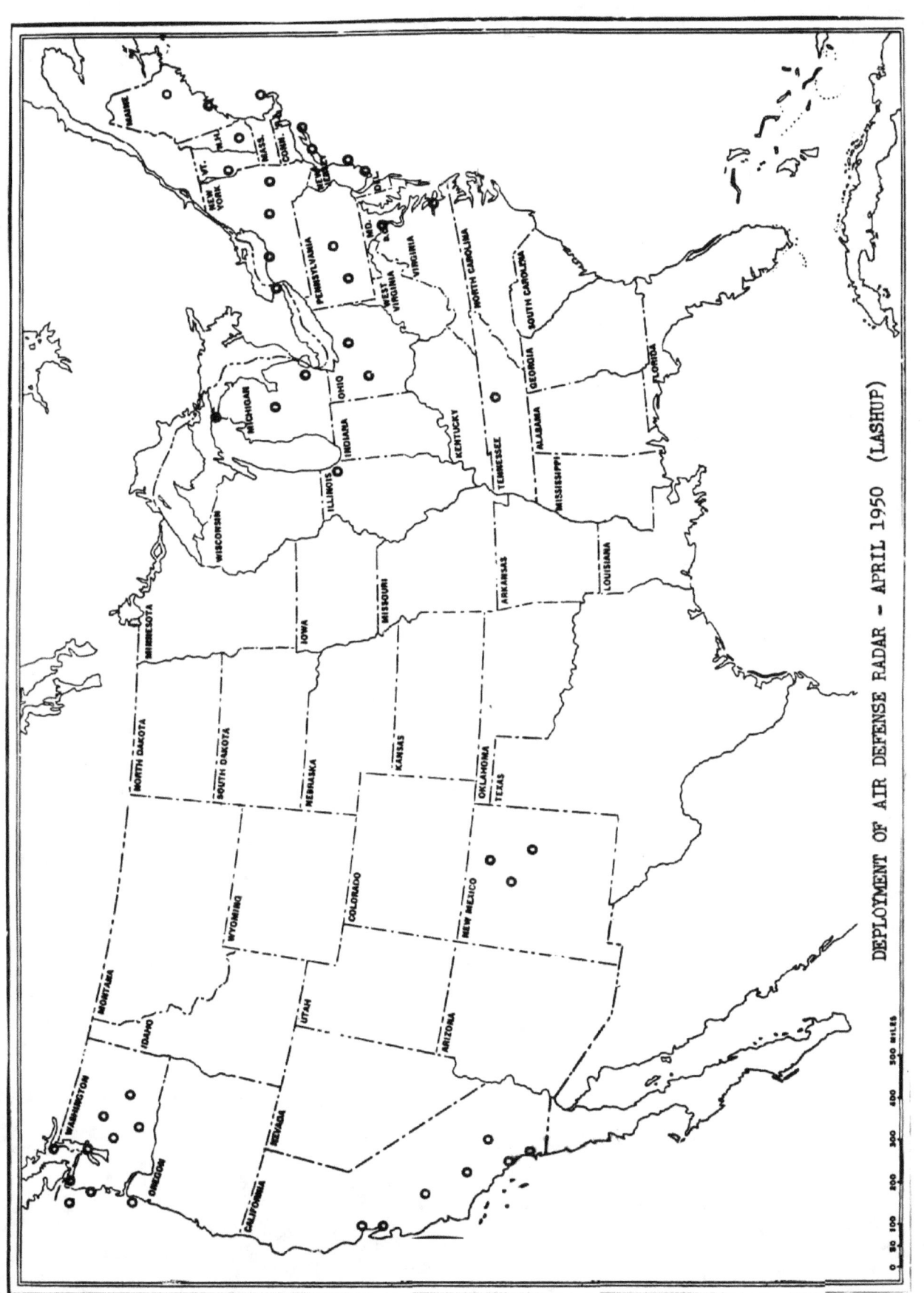

DEPLOYMENT OF AIR DEFENSE RADAR - APRIL 1950 (LASHUP)

of air defense capabilities in the California area. Prior to 1950 the only radar in the area was that operating at Half Moon Bay. Soon thereafter, radars near Mount Tamalpais, Taft, Muroc, Point Conception, Van Nuys and Fort MacArthur were added.[10] The New Mexico area, hitherto guarded by a solitary radar at Kirtland Air Force Base, was reinforced during 1950 by radars near Los Alamos and Roswell. A single radar at McGhee-Tyson Airport, Tennessee, was set up to provide the nucleus for the future protection of the important atomic project at Oak Ridge. By June 1950, 44 radar stations had been established in the temporary network, and LASHUP was deemed to have been completed so far as deployment of radar was concerned.

The only major test of the AC&W system in 1950 took place in the Northwest. Operation WHIPSTOCK, held during 18 - 24 June, was featured by the extension of early warning by the use of a naval radar picket ship and the use of one Canadian Ames II radar station for the duration of the maneuver.[11] A complete overhaul of the Northwestern radar by AMC prior to the exercise and some changes in deployment of equipment did much to improve radar coverage over the November 1949 exercise. In this, the increasing

---

10. Ibid.

11. For a complete collection of documentary material relating to Operation WHIPSTOCK, see: WADF, "History of Operation WHIPSTOCK, 18 - 24 Jun 1950," a special study which may be consulted in USAF Historical Archives. Annex III of the Report of the 25th Division is included in the Appendix as (DOC 56)

experience of operating personnel was clearly evident. Within its inherent capability, the LASHUP radar did as well as could be expected. Major problems revealed by the test were in the realm of GCI operational procedures and in the organization of the various air defense components within the system.

III

Although research and development of radar had continued after World War II, and was stimulated by USAF's determination to set up an ambitious radar network, for practical purposes the only radar available to the Air Force for LASHUP deployment was of the World War II variety. Of this equipment, three types of early warning radar and two types of height-finding equipment were used. Early warning radar included the AN/CPS-5, the AN/CPS-1, the AN/CPS-6 and the AN/TPS-1B sets. The two height-finders were the AN/CPS-4 and the AN/TPS-10A.

The AN/CPS-5, workhorse of the LASHUP system, was an air-transportable, long-range ground radar designed for both early warning and solid search.[12] This set could be employed as a ground control station when coupled with an adequate height-finder such as the AN/CPS-4. The maximum range of the set was in the neighborhood of 150 miles, while for solid search it could

---

12. For a description of the AN/CPS-5 see: ADC <u>Communications and Electronics Digest</u>, Apr 1951; also, Watson Laboratories, <u>Survey of Major USAF Ground Radars for Interim Air Defense System</u>, 15 Jun 1949.

perform at a maximum of 60 miles. Although this equipment was susceptible to permanent echoes which cluttered up the scope when sited in mountainous terrain, modification of the set by the addition of the AN/GPA-7A Moving Target Indicator made possible tracking of targets through cluttered areas of the scope screen. So modified, and coupled with the AN/CPS-4 height-finder, the AN/CPS-5 had a reasonably good GCI capability. In early plans for the Permanent System, use of the CPS-5 set was included for gap-filling purposes.

The AN/CPS-1, generally considered the best of the LASHUP radar, was an air-transportable, early warning radar with a range somewhat similar to that of the CPS-5. The equipment had the advantage of having a high traffic handling capacity and was relatively free from siting difficulties. The internal operational capabilities of the set were similar to those of the AN/CPS-6B, although it did not possess the built-in height-finder which was the characteristic of the latter.[13]

With the CPS-5, the AN/TPS-1B radar bore the brunt of LASHUP deployment.[14] A long-range portable radar with a maximum early warning capability of 150 miles, the set had the disadvantage, like the CPS-5, of being very sensitive to siting difficulties. For best results this set required a level reflecting

---

13. Watson Laboratories, Survey of Major USAF Ground Radars for Interim Air Defense System. 15 Jun 1949.

14. Ibid.

surface of at least 1000 feet radius and had to be sited at low altitudes. The special disadvantage of the TPS-1B was the fact that it was not built for sustained operation.

Perhaps the most troublesome equipment problem which LASHUP faced in its career was the matter of height-finders. Not that this problem was unforeseen. As early as in the fall of 1948 General Saville had made it clear to the Secretary of Defense that there would be serious deficiencies of height-finding radar.

The importance of height-finders to a radar network employing World War II equipment and scheduled for ground control operations could not be overemphasized. With the exception of the experimental AN/CPS-6 radar at Twin Lights, and at Ft. Meade, Md., no radar set in LASHUP possessed GCI capability unless the search radar was coupled with a height-finder. The importance of the problem is made clear when it is observed that of height-finding equipment only the AN/CPS-4 set, of which fifteen sets in all were available to the Continental Air Command and its successor, ADC, was adequate.

The AN/CPS-4 radar, although limited in range for use with the new equipment destined for the future AC&W system, was adequate for use in the LASHUP GCI network. The AN/TPS-10A, another height-finder of which eleven were available for use, was deemed thoroughly unsatisfactory. Maximum possible range of this equipment was no more than 60 miles with a maximum height indication of only

35,000 feet, and numerous design shortcomings and maintenance difficulties made the set a constant source of worry to the user. Reports from AC&W detachments in the field were unanimous in their condemnation of the set.[15] However, since it was a premise of the LASHUP system that expenditures on its behalf would be drastically restricted in favor of the projected Permanent System, the TPS-10A was perforce retained.

IV

As soon as the radar equipment of LASHUP was deployed, the anticipated problems of operation and maintenance inevitably arose. The primary obstacle in this respect was the insufficiency of skilled personnel. Drastic post-war demobilization had released the vast majority of trained electronics personnel from armed service, and the resulting shortage was acutely felt by the Air Force. In view of the existing shortage and the failure of recruiting methods to induce skilled technicians to return, the only normal recourse available to ConAC and ADC was to make the best of what they had by the use of demonstration-instruction techniques and reliance upon the Air Training Command to provide them with basically skilled personnel. Neither of these measures could alleviate the almost complete absence of skilled instructors and operators, and

---

15. ConAC to Watson Labs: "Unsatisfactory Performance of TPS-10 and TPS-10A Radar Sets," 6 May 1950; also 1st AF to ConAC: "Inadequacies of AN/TPS-10A . . . ." 23 May 1950 (DOCs 57, 58)

experts in systems operation. Drastic measures were called for.

The only source of skilled electronics personnel available to USAF in an emergency was the civilian public, and to this source the Air Force turned.[16] In the AC&W system established in the postwar Far East Air Force, the experiment of employing civilian technicians to instruct in radar operations and maintenance had been tried with much success. Both General Ennis C. Whitehead and Colonel Hobart R. Yeager, ADC's Director of Communications and Electronics, had served with the Far East Air Force and it was only natural that they would turn to this prior experience as a temporary solution to the personnel problem which now concerned them. In March 1948, consequently, nine civilian electronics engineers were obtained by contract with the Philco Corporation. Three of these technical representatives were assigned for service with the 505th AC&W Group, three with the 503d AC&W Group and three with the Alaska-bound 531st AC&W Group.

With the coming of the Korean War and the consequent expansion of the air defense system, the number of civilian technicians was greatly increased. By the summer of 1951, approximately 300 Philco field engineers were on duty within the ADC AC&W system. An additional feature of the expansion was the increasing need for communications personnel. The answer to this

---

16. Information about the civilian technical representatives was obtained by interview with Mr. G. L. Ashby, Philco Supervisor, Hq. ADC.

problem was solved temporarily by recourse to the same expedient which brought electronics personnel into the system. A contract with the Radio Corporation of America resulted in ADC's acquisition of 150 communications specialists who took their places beside the Philco representatives in the field.

By the beginning of 1951 ADC's requirements for skilled technicians had increased to such an extent that it was estimated that an additional levy of civilian technicians was necessary to bring the total of field engineers to 648 through FY 1953.[17] Requesting a total of $4,680,234 for FY 1952, ADC was disappointed to learn that USAF saw fit to allot only $2,600,000. An immediate protest by ADC noted that[18]

> It is inconceivable that any consideration would be given toward curtailing the Contractor-Technician program to the extent that the present available funds would dictate. The importance of the uninterrupted functioning of this program in the present stage of development of the AC&W network is heightened by the low level of experience prevalent in the electronic field. The operator type personnel presently available to this command must be trained in the operation and maintenance of the highly technical and expensive electronics equipment if the AC&W program is to function properly. Any retarding of the Contractor-Technician program at this time would prove financially as well as operationally unsound from the standpoint of resultant breakdowns necessitating costly replacement of equipment.

---

17. TWX, ConAC to USAF, 5 Jul 1950 (DOC 59)

18. USAF to ADC: "Contracts for Technicians," 16 Aug 1951 and Ind (DOC 60)

By mid-1951 ADC was determined to leave no stone unturned in order to ensure the continued expansion of the program of civilian technicians in the AC&W system. This determination was prompted by the failure of measures available within the military establishment to make provisions for adequate personnel.

V

One of the primary reasons for the difficulties which both ConAC and ADC experienced in obtaining skilled military personnel for the AC&W system was the paramount emphasis given during 1948 - 1949 by USAF to the manning of SAC units and overseas units. So long as this overriding priority prevailed within USAF, air defense had to be content with getting what personnel was left, if any. Early in 1950, however, emphasis on the air defense mission increased to the point where air defense was awarded equal precedence with SAC in manning schedules.[19] As SAC manning reached the saturation point, new sources were made available to ADC and the personnel problem was considerably alleviated. By the end of 1951, it was estimated, the entire AC&W system would achieve 100% manning. But this was considerably different from the ideal goal of 100% _effective_ manning. As General Whitehead pointed out to the Air Defense Forces, full manning did not mean that the system would function any better. A continuous training program was

---

19. Gen. Whitehead to Gen. Barcus, 4 Mar 1950, quoted in: History of the 26th Air Division, 1 Sep - 31 Dec 1950, p. 1.

indispensable in order to achieve that goal.[20]

As soon as LASHUP was determined upon, plans were drawn up for an extensive training program in the basic principles of radar operation and air defense procedures.[21] Early in February 1949, and again in March 1949, conferences at Mitchel AFB and at Orlando, Florida, were held to prepare training standards and SOPs and to clarify basic doctrines of training and operation. As concluded in these meetings, the requirements of both the present and projected radar systems called not so much for individual training as for team training. The plan decided upon was to train radar teams and control squadrons in a precise schedule geared to the expected production of equipment and to the rate of construction of sites in the radar system. Early in 1949, consequently, plans were made to establish an AC&W systems training school at Orlando.[22] The function of this school would be to receive trained technicians from the Air Training Command and basic trainees from other sources and to organize them into teams for training. Lack of funds and jurisdictional problems involving the Air Training Command prevented the accomplishment of this worthwhile project. Meanwhile, team training had to be provided by the actual operation

---

20. ConAC to WADF: "Airmen Manning of AC&W Units," 25 Oct 1950 (DOC 61)

21. History of the Continental Air Command, 1 Dec 1948 – 31 Dec 1949, III, 61-65.

22. Ibid., p. 64.

of LASHUP.

To ensure that the specialized component parts of the air defense system might be harmonized into an effective air defense, unit commanders were instructed at an early date to arrange for exchange of personnel visits. Though this fraternization helped somewhat to break the psychological barrier between the ground personnel and the fighter pilots, it did not take the place of actual systems training. That training was hindered by the inexperience of the radar personnel. The result was that it was not until late in 1949 that regular systems training could be begun and adhered to. In this training program, the exercises held to test the system helped considerably, although some commanders protested that preparations for these exercises retarded rather than accelerated the training effort. Nevertheless, few begrudged the importance or the necessity of the exercises in view of the important experiments involved in them for determining the proper relationships between controller, pilot and commander and in revealing flaws in radar coverage.

VI

The decision to create an air defense in being by the deployment of radar in temporary locations decreed that steps be taken simultaneously to adopt a procedure for the calibration of the ground radar. The experience of the air forces during World War II had made it sharply clear that no matter how efficient radar equipment was, unless that equipment was calibrated with accuracy to correspond to that of the rest of a radar network, confusion would inevitably result which would mean loss of precious time in the relay and synthesis of vital information. In June 1948, consequently, steps were taken to activate the 12th and 7th Radar Calibration Units at Mitchel Air Force Base and at Hamilton Air Force Base, respectively. Early in 1949 the 11th Radar Calibration Unit was also established at Hamilton AFB on the West Coast. The reorganization of 1 December 1948 which placed TAC under the Continental Air Command permitted also a limited use of the 5th Radar Calibration Unit of TAC for LASHUP calibration. In late 1949 the 7th Radar Calibration Unit was established at Griffis AFB, New York. In spite of the fact that there were three such units under ADC, the 7th, 11th and 12th, the total number of B-29 aircraft assigned to the three units was eight, a number which was woefully inadequate considering the vast expanse of territory they had to cover in calibrating the LASHUP radar. Another problem was the fact that maintenance and housing for these units was

---

23. The following sources give a good account of the calibration effort: History of the 7th Calibration Unit, 1 Oct - 31 Dec 1950; History of the 7th Radar Calibration Squadron, 1 Jan - 31 Mar 1951; and 1 Apr - 30 Jun 1951; History of the 11th Calibration Squadron, 1 Jan - 31 Mar 1951; and 1 Apr - 30 Jun 1951; also, History of the 12th Radar Calibration Units, 1 Oct 1950 - 31 Jan 1951.

provided generally at TAC bases, by TAC personnel and facilities which were not prepared for B-29 maintenance. A third important problem was that AMC support capability for B-29s was limited so that the flying hours of the calibration B-29s were restricted far below the total flying time required for air defense calibration.[24]

In June 1950 the calibration requirements of the Air Defense Forces reached the point where drastic action had to be taken soon. General Whitehead demanded of USAF that the three calibration units be integrated into two full squadrons totalling twenty B-29 aircraft and that, in addition, a ground calibration team be established in each AC&W Group within the command.[25] Not until January and February 1951 was the desired action taken by USAF. The results were gratifying. Two squadrons, the 7th and 11th, were created with a strength of eight planes for the 11th on the West Coast and twelve planes for the 7th on the East Coast. Furthermore, each squadron was placed under the respective Air Defense Force Commander to use as he saw fit. Fully equipped maintenance sections in the new squadrons were now self-sufficient for aircraft maintenance, which proved to decrease the AOCP rate for the aircraft. In addition, AMC was prevailed upon to increase

---

24. TWX, EADF to ADC, 21 Jun 1951; and TWX, ADC to EADF, 25 Jun 1951 (DOCs 62   63)

25. ConAC to USAF: "Radar Calibration Squadrons," 7 Jun 1950 (DOC 64)

its B-29 support capabilities so that more flying time was possible for these aircraft.

The importance of an efficient and adequate calibration system for air defense radar could not be overestimated. Constant calibration was necessary because of the urgency of faultless continuous tracking of aircraft from sector to sector and for accurate interceptor control. Until the Permanent System was fully calibrated, its capability would be small and LASHUP would be prevented from demobilizing and merging its potentialities with the new system.

VII

By the end of 1950 progress on the construction of the Permanent AC&W System had reached the point where plans for the disposition of LASHUP equipment had to be made. Early in December, a meeting between General Whitehead and General Edwards of USAF Headquarters resulted in a decision to leave the redeployment of lightweight LASHUP equipment in the hands of ADC.[26]

As concerned search radar, ADC deemed it feasible to retain only the lightweight AN/TPS-1B set in the Permanent System as backup equipment for the AN/FPS-3 at the lower priority sites. It was thought that by speeding up the delivery schedules for the new prime search radar it would be unnecessary to rely on the heavier AN/CPS-5 and AN/CPS-1 sets for use in the Permanent System. Where

---

26. Memo. Gen. Edwards to Gen. Whitehead, 15 Dec 1950 (DOC 65)

height-finders were concerned, however, the Air Defense Command could not afford to be so optimistic. Both the scarcity of and tardy delivery dates on new equipment demanded that the AN/CPS-4 height-finder be dispatched to first priority AN/FPS-3 sites, but unforeseen logistical problems delayed this transfer. As for the AN/TPS-10A height-finder, ADC was glad to let that equipment revert to control of USAF.[27]

The phasing-out of the LASHUP radar network was geared to the development of the Permanent System. Primary consideration in this conversion program was the premise of continuity in air defense capability. Only when the new Permanent sites were fully calibrated and their capabilities were fully known was LASHUP to cease operations. The process inevitably was to be a gradual one with individual LASHUP sites being decommissioned one by one until the whole network disappeared. It was estimated that the conversion would be complete sometime late in 1952.

---

27. Ibid.

CHAPTER FIVE

THE PERMANENT AIRCRAFT CONTROL and WARNING SYSTEM

I

The decision to create the Permanent radar system was the outcome of a year of alternating expectancy and disappointment. As told in Chapter Three, USAF, in January 1948, gave its indorsement to Plan SUPREMACY, which was to create an extensive network of ground radar stations. That plan did not materialize because of the failure of Congress to concur in the necessity for such an elaborate system at the time. While action was pending in Congress on SUPREMACY, USAF made a feeble effort to set up a token air defense system by deploying its existing radar equipment, but the shortage of construction funds proved the effort abortive. In September 1948, USAF broached the suggestion that enough public works funds be allocated to deploy "permanent type" radars on hand and on order. This suggestion, then called the Interim program, was to be supplemented by the permanent installation of additional modern radar equipment. The Interim program and the First Augmentation program just alluded to, were to result in the establishment on permanently constructed sites, chosen for maximum operating effectiveness, of a total of 75 basic radar stations and ten control centers. In time this program was popularly referred to as the Permanent AC&W program to distinguish it from the temporary LASHUP program.

Having received the approval of the Joint Chiefs of Staff, USAF began work on the Permanent program immediately, in anticipation that Congress would provide the necessary funds.[1] In October 1948 ADC presented to USAF its recommendation for deployment of the radar in the Permanent System and made provisions for the assembly of radar siting teams to choose the actual locations for the equipment.[2] By the beginning of 1949 two siting teams had been chosen and were on their way.

The problems incident to selecting site locations for the Permanent System may be illustrated by the experiences of the Western siting team headed by Colonel James R. McNitt.[3] This team was instructed to select the best possible locations within a 25 to 30 mile radius of geographical points already selected by ConAC.[4]

---

1. USAF to ADC: "Interim Program for Employment of Aircraft Control and Warning Radar," 20 Oct 1948 (DOC 66); also, "Brief Fiscal History of the AC&W Facilities Construction Program," 26 Jun 1950 (DOC 67)

2. ADC to USAF: "Recommended Final Deployment of Radars for the Interim Plan Plus First Augmentation," 26 Oct 1948 (DOC 68)

3. ConAC to 4AF: "Radar and Control Center Sites," 22 Oct 1949, and Inds (DOC 69)

4. USAF to ConAC: "Detailed Cost Data on Programmed Aircraft Control and Warning Systems in Continental United States and Alaska," 23 Dec 1948 (DOC 70) This document contains a list of approximate locations which were to guide the siting teams. See Tab E.

Verbal instructions were given this team to select high sites wherever possible.

Supporting criteria for the selection of high sites for radar stations were established as follows: (1) selected sites were to be capable of low angle coverage; (2) the Moving Target Indicator (MTI) destined for auxiliary use with the proposed radar equipment was assumed to be successful, thus permitting the siting team to disregard permanent echoes and clutter and consequently to select high locations, and (3) it was assumed that improvements in free-space radar beam performance would negate the need for a ground reflecting surface.

Cost of installation was another factor in the selection of sites. Many possible locations were disregarded by the siting team because of excessive access road building construction cost estimates. In selecting locations for the proposed control centers, the availability of communications was a factor of prime importance. The availability of communications, though desirable for the radar stations also, was a consideration which did not enter frequently into the selection process, because much of the Western area was sparsely populated and cities were far apart.

Another siting problem which was to cause considerable difficulty in a later period arose from the decision to ignore the proximity of living accomodations as a siting factor. In one instance, at least (at Colville, in northeastern Washington), this resulted in the locating of a living site three airline miles distant from the radar equipment.

Unlike the selection of LASHUP sites, maximum utilization of existing permanent Air Force facilities was not a high factor on the list of criteria. However, in the case of the control centers, all were recommended for location on permanent military installations.

The selection of sites by either siting team did not always result in a permanent choice being made at first try. In several instances, re-study made it advisable to relocate chosen sites. In this matter, the original instructions to choose high sites came in for discussion. The controversy which resulted was based on the value of MTI and the need for a reflecting surface for some ground radars. With the experience gained in the operation of LASHUP radars in 1949, it was confirmed that the need for reflecting surfaces was obviated in certain sets then in use, e. g., the AN/CPS-1. A test conducted at the Neah Bay site in August 1949 revealed that MTI did much to eliminate tracking difficulties through scope clutter caused by permanent echoes, but not sufficiently to warrant disregarding fixed echoes entirely, especially in landed areas.[5]

The difficulty of establishing fixed criteria for siting was inherent in the dependency of ground radar equipment upon its

---

5. ConAC to USAF: "Additional AN/CPS-5 MTI Equipment Kits," 8 Dec 1949 (DOC 71)

topographical locations. Compromise with the ideal was inevitable. For instance, the site at El Vado in the north central area of New Mexico at an elevation of 8,000 feet and well below the surrounding terrain, was selected to give warning to the important Albuquerque area. Many considerations precluded the selection of a higher site, even though many were available. MTI sub-clutter visibility, the fact that radar equipment was not designed to operate at altitudes above 8,000 feet, the high cost of construction, unstable weather conditions, and maintenance and morale problems contributed to the compromise which resulted in the locating of this station at a site which kept the ground clutter down to an average of 20 or 30 miles without excessive screening and which was yet in a fairly livable location.[6]

The problem of siting sensitive radar equipment was heightened by the fact that more than one agency was concerned with the end product. The Corps of Engineers of the Army (OCE) was to supervise actual construction, and the Air Materiel Command was to install the equipment.[7] Unilateral action by any one of the three agencies was very likely to result in a conflict with one or both of the other participants in the work on the Permanent System —

---

6. Speech, Col. Haskell Neal, at ADC Commanders meeting, 26 Jan 1951.

7. Gen. Chidlaw to Gen. Whitehead, 5 Apr 1950, and 3 Incls (DOC 72)

and frequently did. In August 1950 the problem was resolved by the decision of USAF to have AMC's prior approval before any site plans were submitted to USAF.[9] In 1950, when ConAC was engaged in the effort of siting the Canadian radar net, USAF made it mandatory that the OCE be represented on all siting teams.[10] Although much of the confusion over siting was in time straightened out, suggestions were voiced that a siting board composed of experienced experts in electronics, communications and engineering might well be the best insurance against future acrimony.[11]

The construction of 85 permanent sites, having an overall deadline of 1 July 1952 for completion, made it necessary to allot construction priorities to the separate projects. In October 1949 it was decided at a conference between OCE and ADC to establish a first priority group of 24 stations.[12] These stations were slated for early construction because of their strategic position in the target areas and the high traffic density in those locations. In

---

8. USAF to ConAC: "Air Installations Support for Communications Projects," 20 Mar 1950 (DOC 73)

9. ConAC to EADF and WADF: "AMC Approval of AC&W Preliminary Site Layout Plans," 16 Aug 1950 (DOC 74); and, ConAC to USAF: "AMC Review of AC&W Site Layout Plans," 15 Sep 1950 (DOC 75)

10. TWX, USAF to ConAC, 9 Sep 1950.

11. TWX, Col. Stinson to Col. Yeager, 20 Sep 1949 (DOC 76)

12. ConAC to USAF: "Initial Priorities for Engineering Construction, Permanent Air Defense Plan," 2 Nov 1949 (DOC 77)

January 1950 ConAC informed OCE of the locations of sites of two additional priority groups.[13] General Whitehead made it entirely clear, however, that priorities were established as a guide to the OCE in cases where there was a conflict because of shortages of materiel or other reasons, and that the target date of July 1952 was still firm for the entire system.[14] For the most part, construction dates were met, although some delays extended the estimated target date several months.

Actual construction on the Permanent System began in March 1950 after a preliminary period in which siting was completed, real estate requests forwarded to USAF, rights of entry obtained, leases secured, preliminary site plans approved, construction directives issued, bids advertised and contracts awarded.

By the end of June 1951 construction had been completed on nineteen of the 85 sites. Most of the other sites were more than 90% completed, and only five sites were less than 90% completed.[15] All in all, the construction program adhered reasonably well to the target dates imposed in 1949, and completion of the last site contract was anticipated by 1 August 1951.

Even though construction was not entirely completed in all

---

13. ConAC to USAF: "Construction Priorities, Permanent Air Control and Warning System," 4 Jan 1950 (DOC 78)

14. Col. Bowman to Gen. Whitehead, 16 Mar 1950 (DOC 79)

15. ADC, *Command Data Book*, 30 Jun 1951.

85 sites, the ADC was enabled to move in AC&W personnel in "beneficial occupancy" of the sites to ensure security and utilities maintenance. By the end of June 1951, 76 of these sites were thus occupied by ADC, with the command personnel assisting in the installation of the communications and electronics equipment and thereby familiarizing themselves with their new tools. By the end of June, seventeen sites were reported by AMC as having reached technically equipped status.[16]

The pending completion of the Permanent System resulted in the decision in 1951 to occupy those sites whose locations would duplicate LASHUP coverage and to phase out the superfluous LASHUP sites. However, in view of the fact that in many such cases new equipment was not as yet installed, and that in all cases calibration had not taken place, it was decided to move some LASHUP radar equipment to certain permanent sites. The result was the emergence of a hybrid radar station known as an LP (LASHUP-Permanent) site. By the end of June the following LP sites were in operation:[17]

```
45 - Camp Hero, N. Y.          33 - Klamath, Calif.
 9 - Navesink, N. R., N. J.    37 - Hill Peak Rd., Calif.
54 - Palermo, N. J.            40 - Saddle Mt., Wash.
56 - Ft. Custis, Va.           51 - Moriarty, N. Mex.
20 - Selfridge AFB, Mich.      60 - Colville, Wash.
66 - Sault Ste Marie, Mich.    74 - Madera, Calif.
31 - Elkhorn, Wisc.            69 - Finland, Minn.
```

---

16. Ibid.

17. Ibid.

80 - Caswell, Me. 2 - Cambria, Calif.
67 - Ft. Custer, Mich. 8 - El Vado, N. Mex.
 6 - Mt. Bonaparte, Wash. 16 - Keweenaw, Mich.
 7 - Gonzales, N. Mex. 32 - Condon, Ore.
   61 - Port Austin, Mich.

II

The AN/CPS-6B, the ground radar set which was scheduled to bear the brunt of the GCI effort in the Permanent System, was in the process of development long before the decision was made by USAF to implement the Interim radar plan.[18] During the later stages of World War II, radar development had reached the point where a practical method of combining early warning and height-finding radar in one set had been evolved. These advances were incorporated in a set known as the AN/CPS-6, of which about a half dozen were in actual operation at war's end, three of them in the Zone of the Interior. The CPS-6, however, was never deemed to be a piece of equipment in a finished form, ready to take its place in prolonged operations. Work in improving the model continued immediately after the war, and in time many improvements over the existing models were blueprinted. These improvements consisted in the addition of MTI, better reception, an increased scanning rate,

---

18. On radar development during and after World War II see: AAF, Scientific Advisory Report on Radar and Communications, May 1946; Watson Laboratories, Survey of Major USAF Ground Radars for Interim Air Defense System, 15 Jun 1949; Air Proving Ground, Projects Summaries, 1941 through 1948. On recent post-war trends in ground radar research and development see: Watson Laboratories, New Developments of Defense Radar Equipments, 16 Oct 1950.

the addition of video mapping, improved scope performance, and a radome to house the antenna for the latter's protection.[19] In 1947 a joint development-production contract was let with the General Electric Company, and sixteen of the new AN/CPS-6Bs were ordered, with complete delivery scheduled by the end of June 1950.

The proposal for the Interim radar system, made in September 1948, envisioned twelve of these sets for that system within the continental United States.[20] The First Augmentation plan, which supplemented the Interim program, earmarked another fourteen sets for the Zone of the Interior, thus resulting in a total of 26 AN/CPS-6Bs destined for continental defense.[21]

The unique characteristic of the AN/CPS-6B was not only an increased search performance, but the combination of early warning and height-finding capabilities.[22] This combination, plus the elaborate internal operational facilities which enabled it to have a large traffic handling capability, made it theoretically ideal for operation as a GCI station. It was discovered,

---

19. Watson Laboratories, Survey of Major USAF Ground Radars for Interim Air Defense System, 15 Jun 1949, p. 32.

20. Maj. Gen. G. P. Saville, presentation on the Interim AC&W System to Secretary Forrestal, 9 Sep 1948 (DOC 18)

21. Ibid.

22. ADC, Communications and Electronics Digest, Jun 1951 (see article on the AN/CPS-6B)

however, as a result of the experience gained in LASHUP operations by ConAC personnel, that the use of MTI seriously limited the early warning capability of search radars, but that, on the other hand, for solid and meticulous close-in search operations, so necessary to GCI work, MTI was indispensable in mountainous terrain. This realization prompted ConAC to request of USAF and AMC in February 1950 that modifications be introduced in production so that the conflict between early warning and GCI be eliminated, thus enabling the set to operate both as an early warning station and as a GCI station simultaneously.[23] Although USAF was loath to impede production schedules for this sorely-needed equipment, a development project was undertaken at General Electric Laboratories in Syracuse, New York, in this matter. The result of this work was the decision to modify the set by the introduction of an auxiliary early warning search set, to the existing production model of the 6B, which would work independently of the other components.[24] This modification involved the addition of a third antenna solely concerned with early warning transmission, the other two antennas being concerned with solid search and height-finding.

An additional modification of the 6B resulted when the

---

23. ConAC to USAF: "Requirement for Simultaneous GCI with MTI and Long Range Early Warning Using AN/CPS-6B and AN/FPS-3 Radars," 3 Feb 1950 (DOC 80)

24. ADC, *Communications and Electronics Digest*, "Auxiliary Search Set for the AN/CPS-6B," Jun 1951.

decision was made to retain the large version of the model for areas where traffic was dense and where enemy intrusion was most likely. For areas of lesser traffic density, a reduced-scale version of this set, with fewer controller positions, was determined upon and dubbed the AN/CPS-6B(M) and later the AN/FPS-10.

By the end of 1950 it appeared that the original delivery schedules would slip considerably. By that time fourteen of the 6B sets had been delivered into the hands of AMC for eventual installation in the permanent sites. Completion of the total delivery schedule was anticipated by the end of June 1951.[25]

Although the AN/CPS-6B was theoretically the last word in ground radar development, there were some who were quite skeptical as to the ability of the set to continuously operate in the face of anticipated parts shortages and inexperience of maintenance personnel. In June 1951, Major General Frederic H. Smith Jr., Commanding General of the Eastern Air Defense Force, expressed his misgivings on this score and recommended that LASHUP equipment be redeployed to sites utilizing the AN/CPS-6B and the AN/FPS-3 as backup equipment to insure continuous operation in case of breakdown of the prime radar.[26] Unfortunately, world-wide shortages of radar equipment made this solution impossible, according to ADC, especially in view of the requirements of the

---

25. Speech, Col. Haskell Neal, at ADC Commanders meeting, 15 Feb 1951.

26. Gen. Smith to Gen. Whitehead, 29 Jun 1951, and Ind.

expanded ANG program.[27] Late plans, however, anticipated that sufficient quantities of a lightweight search radar, the AN/TPS-1D, would be available for backup in view of the relative inexpensiveness of this lightweight portable equipment as compared to the heavier AN/CPS-5. For height-finding backup it was anticipated that the AN/TPS-10D would also be available for similar reasons.[28]

The following locations in the Permanent System were scheduled to receive the AN/CPS-6B equipment:[29]

    P-1A at McChord AFB, Wash.
    P-9 at Navesink, N. J.
    P-10 at North Truro, Mass.
    P-13 at Brunswick Naval Air Station, Me.
    P-14 at Bellevue Hill, Vt.
    P-20 at Selfridge AFB, Mich.
    P-21 at Shawnee, N. Y.
    P-30 at Mud Pond, Pa.
    P-31 at Elkhorn, Wisc.
    P-35 at East Farmington, Wisc.
    P-38 at Mt Tamalpais, Cal.
    P-34 at Empire, Mich.

The following fourteen stations were scheduled to receive the smaller version of the 6B, the AN/FPS-10:[30]

---

27. Ibid.

28. Speech, Col. Haskell Neal, at ADC Commanders meeting, 15 Feb 1951.

29. ADC, "Air Defense AC&W System," Jun 1951. This is part of a series of detailed charts issued monthly by ADC Hq and an excellent source of information on the status of the AC&W program.

30. Ibid.

        P-15 Santa Rosa I., Cal.
        P-42 Cross Mt. Tenn.
        P-46 Birch Bay, Wash.
        P-47 Hutchinson NAS, Kans.
        P-52 Tinker AFB, Okla.
        P-53 Rockville, Ind.
        P-58 Mather AFB, Cal.
        P-59 Atolia, Cal.
        P-64 Sublette, Mo.
        P-77 Bartlesville, Okla.
        P-78 Duncansville, Tex.
        P-79 Ellington, Tex.
        P-80 Caswell, Me.
        P-81 Waverley, Iowa

The distribution of the AN/CPS-6B, as indicated on the map on page 114, reveals the bulk of the deployment as falling in the industrial northeastern section of the United States, with the smaller version of this equipment occupying the central belt, with some concentration in the localities of the Seattle and California areas.

Another radar equipment which was well on the development road in the immediate post-war period was the AN/FPS-3.[31] This set was originally developed as an improvement of the AN/CPS-5, which was in extensive use during the end of the war and which was redeployed as the basic search radar in the LASHUP system. Ultimately, however, development progressed to the point where the basic system was extensively altered so that it bore little

---

    31. On the AN/FPS-3 radar set, see: ADC, Communications and Electronics Digest, May 1951; and, Watson Laboratories, Survey of Major USAF Ground Radars for Interim Air Defense System, 15 Jun 1949.

resemblance to the CPS-5 radar. Like the CPS-6B, the FPS-3 incorporated post-war improvements such as accelerated scanning rate, video mapping, MTI, and antenna radome as well as increase in the effective radiated power over the CPS-5.[32] Unlike the CPS-6B, however, the FPS-3 was designed as a basic early warning search radar, without the built-in height-finder which characterized the 6B set. Consequently, in order to operate as a GCI station, the FPS-3 required an auxiliary height-finding radar. A joint development-production contract with the Bendix Corporation promised production of this set for sometime in the spring of 1950, but delays in production extended this target date well into 1951. A separate contract with Airborne Instruments Laboratory provided for production of the antenna.

Originally it was anticipated that 24 FPS-3 radars would be deployed in the Permanent System, but in August 1950 USAF informed ConAC that additional quantities of this set were scheduled for the Air Force, and that ultimately 49 sets would be available for air defense purposes.[33] This news occasioned a change in ConAC's plans for radar deployment. It had been planned that the CPS-5 set would be deployed on 23 Permanent sites, but the increase

---

32. Ibid.

33. ConAC to USAF: "Equipments for the Permanent Aircraft Control and Warning Program," 25 Sep 1950, and Ind.

in FPS-3 procurement made this unnecessary since it was now possible to use the FPS-3 for this purpose. The tardy delivery schedule for the FPS-3, however, made it necessary to consider the use of some CPS-5 sets, to be deployed on those sites destined later to receive the FPS-3, as an interim measure. As in the earlier proposal to employ the CPS-5 pending installation of the CPS-6B, this proposal was frowned upon by USAF, although in several instances exceptions to the rule were permitted.[34]

The FPS-3 promised to be of much value to the AC&W capability because of its long range characteristics. At a distance of 300 nautical miles it was anticipated that a B-29 type bomber could be spotted, while a jet fighter of the P-80 type could be picked up at 125 nautical miles, provided they were above the radar horizon. The set was also equipped with large plotting boards for tracking purposes.[35]

As planned in October 1950 the ultimate disposition of equipment in the TYPE II sites (FPS-3) of the Permanent System envisaged the use of the power FPS-6 height-finder and two backup equipments, the lightweight AN/TPS-1D and the AN/TPS-10D height-finder. Locations for these FPS-3 stations were scheduled as

---

34. USAF to ConAC: "Redeployment of LASHUP Radar Equipment," 26 Oct 1950, and Ind.

35. ADC, Communications and Electronics Digest, May 1951.

follows:[36]

P-2	Cambria, Cal.	P-50	Schuylerville, N. Y.
P-6	Mt. Bonaparte, Wash.	P-54	Palermo, N. J.
P-11	Yaak, Mont.	P-55	Quantico, Va.
P-12	Reedsport, Ore.	P-56	Ft. Custis, Va.
P-17	Leaf River, Minn.	P-57	Naselle, Wash.
P-18	Moulton, Minn.	P-60	Colville, Wash.
P-19	Antigo, Wisc.	P-61	Pt. Austin, Mich.
P-24	Del Bonita, Mont.	P-62	Brookfield, Ohio
P-25	Simpson, Mont.	P-63	Blue Knob Prk, Pa.
P-26	Opheim, Mont.	P-65	Charleston, Me.
P-27	Fortuna, ND	P-66	Sault Ste Marie, Mich.
P-28	Velva, ND	P-67	Ft. Custer, Mich.
P-29	Finlay, ND	P-68	Fordland, Mo.
P-32	Condon, Ore.	P-70	Belleville, Ill.
P-33	Klamath, Cal.	P-71	Omaha, Neb.
P-37	Pt. Arena, Cal.	P-72	Olathe NAS, Kans.
P-39	San Clemente Isle, Cal.	P-73	Bellefontaine, Ohio
P-40	Saddle Mt., Wash.	P-74	Madera, Cal.
P-43	Guthrie, W. Va.	P-75	Lackland AFB, Tex.
P-44	Bohokus Peak, Wash.	P-76	Mt. Laguna, Cal.
P-45	Montauk Pt., N. Y.	P-82	Ft. Knox, Ky.
P-49	Watertown, N. Y.	P-85	Hanna City, Ill.

The difficulties experienced with height-finding radar in the LASHUP system motivated both ConAC and ADC to take precautions that similar difficulties would not be experienced in the Permanent system. In this respect the most important problem which faced these commands was that of gearing modern type height-finder production to the estimated delivery dates of the AN/FPS-3 long-range search radar. In view of the fact that production of the new AN/FPS-6 height-finding radar was not foreseen before July 1951, there appeared a strong possibility that the many FPS-3 stations would be denied a GCI capability until FPS-6 production

---

36. ADC, Chart, "Air Defense AC&W System," Jun 1951, issued by P&R.

was well underway. Although the possibility of using LASHUP height-finders in the Permanent System as a temporary measure occurred to ConAC and ADC, the fact remained that only fifteen AN/CPS-4s were available in the LASHUP system, and to destroy LASHUP GCI capability before the Permanent System was fully calibrated was a risk that was deemed far too great. The other LASHUP height-finder, the AN/TPS-10A was totally inadequate for air defense purposes.

To counter the threat of a time lag between delivery of the FPS-3 and its companion height-finder, the FPS-6, ConAC, in May 1950, took the drastic step of suggesting that USAF intercede with the Navy in order to obtain 24 AN/MPS-4 radars in production for the Navy by Hazeltine Corporation.[37] Of this number sixteen were allotted to ConAC. By authorizing unlimited overtime for the manufacturer, it was possible to speed up delivery of this equipment so that both USAF and the Navy could be satisfied. The plans for utilization of height-finders in the Permanent System included provision for a lightweight, medium-range height-finder known as the AN/TPS-10D, of which there were 75 on order in January 1951. Plans called for the use of this radar as backup equipment at all of the sites in the Permanent System, as well as prime equipment

---

37. ConAC to USAF: "Procurement of AN/MPS-4 Height Finders for the Air Defense of the United States," 25 May 1950 (DOC 81); also, AMC to USAF: "Procurement of Height Finding Radar Equipment," 26 Jun 1950 (DOC 82)

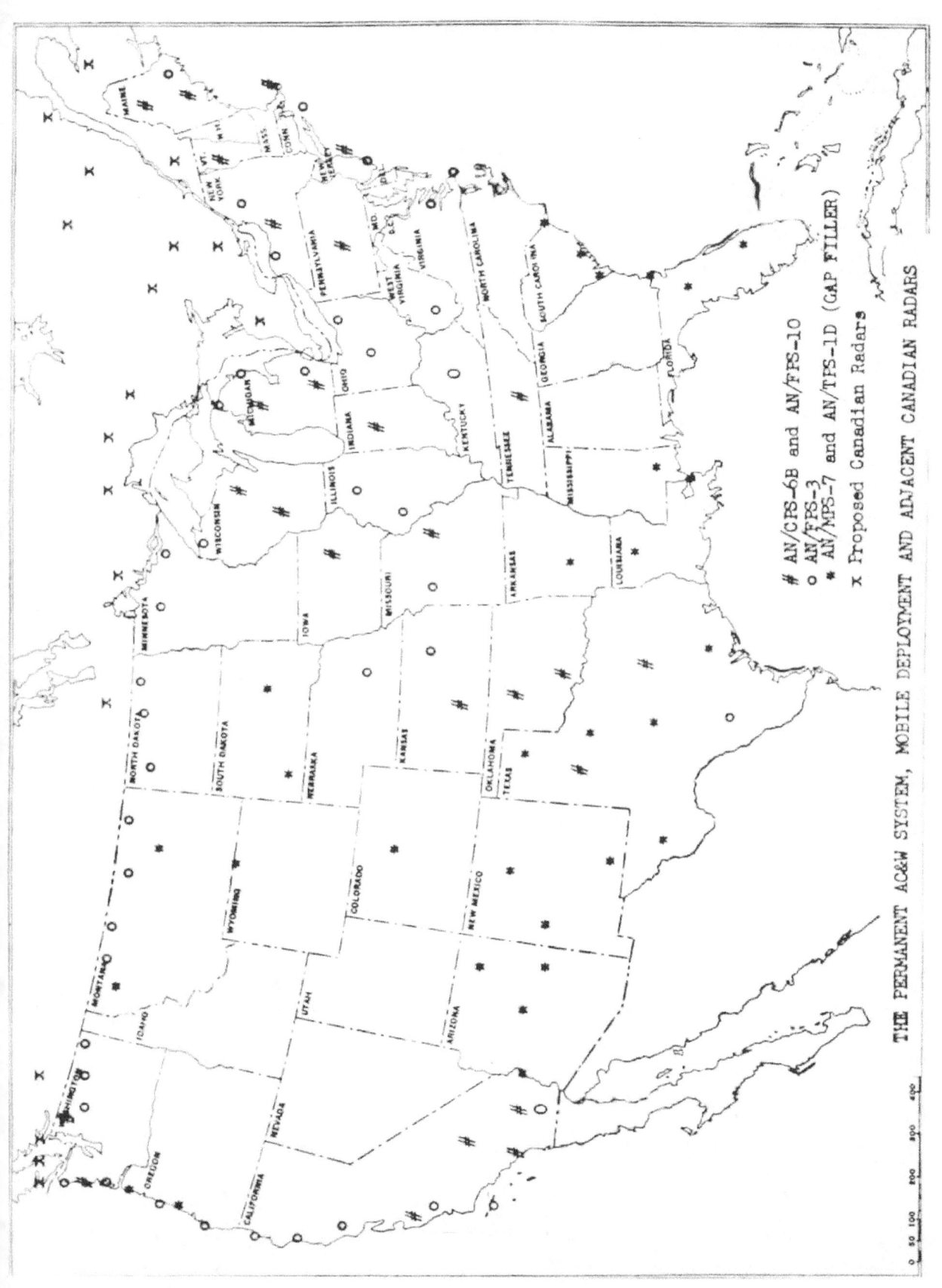

for a few sites.[38] Thus, by ensuring that height-finding equipment would be on hand to enable full calibration of the permanent stations according to schedule, a great load was lifted from the shoulders of ConAC and ADC. After delivery of the FPS-6 was completed, provision for use of the MPS-4 as height-finders for the mobile stations in the AC&W program could be made, thus endowing every station in the entire network with a GCI capability. The Permanent System was not to experience the greatest difficulty experienced by LASH-UP- the inadequacy of height-finders.

III

In his briefing to Congress on the Permanent System in early 1949, General Saville had intimated that the Permanent System would be complemented in time by a number of gap-filling ground radars.[39] Shortage of ground radar equipment, and the preoccupation with construction of the Permanent System and the deployment and operation of LASHUP delayed activity on the gap-filler program, however.

In mid-1950, a requirement to provide for the security of SAC bases prompted renewed consideration of the gap-filler program. In view of the vital importance of SAC bases for the national

---

38. Speech, Col. Haskell Neal, at ADC Commanders meeting, 15 Feb 1951.

39. Answers to questions of the House of Representatives Committee on Armed Services, 7 Feb 1950.

security, decision was made to provide each of these installations with EW ground radar and concentrated antiaircraft artillery support. In this matter, the provision of EW capability for SAC bases was fortunately well suited to ADC plans to provide coverage for those areas not provided for by the Permanent System. In most cases SAC bases were distributed in those parts of the country where population concentration was less heavy than in the Northeast and West Coast areas, especially in the Southwest and Southeast. Early warning radar on SAC bases would have the advantage not only of providing a measure of independence for those bases, but also of providing a measure of radar coverage for the exposed portions of the United States.

The decision to provide radar coverage for the SAC bases prompted reconsideration of an enlarged program of gap-filling radar to complete a perimeter coverage for the United States. To this end 44 mobile type radars were programmed for the soft "underbelly" of the United States, and for those areas in the north where a greater defense in depth was desired. This plan, however, ran into complications. To request additional public funds from Congress for site construction meant the inevitable delays which had attended the Permanent System. In view of the accelerated radar production since 1949, it was decided to circumvent the construction cost obstacle by deploying mobile ground radars in the desired areas and on SAC bases. Fortunately, a mobile version of the AN/FPS-3, the AN/MPS-7, was practicable, while the Air Force had begun procurement of a lightweight and portable set known as the AN/TPS-1D, in production for the Navy, which also was entirely adequate for gap-filler purposes. With the provision of prefabricated, movable shelters, an entirely adequate EW installation was made possible without the necessity of extensive building on the premises. By June 1951, 34 out of the 44 programmed gap-filler sites had been selected.[40] (See chart). A GCI capability was made possible for many of these mobile sites by the release of MPS-4 HFs from the Permanent System once the latter had been provided with the new FPS-6 HF.

---

40. ADC, Chart, " Air Defense AC&W System," Jun 1951, issued by P&R.

CHAPTER SIX

FIGHTER UNITS AND AIR BASES

I

The first post-war Air Defense Command gave frequent warning that there were not enough trained and equipped fighter units in the Zone of the Interior to protect the nation against air attack. Possessed of extremely limited fighter resources of its own, ADC contracted for use of the fighter units of the other major Air Commands in the event of emergency. It also strove to organize and train the fighter units of the Air National Guard for an air defense role. But these arrangements lacked realism; the fighter units of the other major commands were too occupied with training in their primary missions to engage to any great extent in air defense training; and the ANG units were, for the most part, too poorly equipped and organized and, oftentimes, too affected by politics to inculcate confidence in the Air Defense Command concerning their M-Day capabilities.

The extent of the weakness of fighter resources for air defense in the United States during the period the air defense mission was invested in the first post-war ADC was sharply revealed by the Northwest maneuver of April 1948.[1] To insure

---

1. See above, Chapter Three

against as poor a display of fighter protection against enemy bombers as had been made against friendly attacking aircraft in the maneuver, the ADC Commander, following the maneuver, pressed the Chief of Staff to "take a firm decision to establish an air defense system and to maintain air defense in being" by assigning to ADC three of SAC's and two of TAC's fighter wings and the 36th Fighter Wing of the Caribbean Defense Command to supplement ADC's meager fighter resources.[2] In the event a direct assignment of these wings was not possible, it was recommended that they be given the secondary mission of air defense and deployed to stations whose locations would serve air defense requirements.[3]

It was late in 1948 before additional fighter resources were provided the major Air Force command charged with the air defense mission. In December of that year, USAF Headquarters elected to increase the fighter strength of the air defense system from within its own resources, as had been suggested earlier by General Stratemeyer. This _fait accompli_ was brought about in a slightly different manner, however, from that envisaged by the ADC Commander. A new major Air Force command, the Continental Air Command, was formed, and the Air Defense and Tactical Air Commands were reduced from major command status to operational air commands

---

2. ADC to USAF: "Air Defense of the United States," 24 Apr 1948 (DOC 30)

3. Ibid.

subordinate to this organization. The fighter units formerly possessed by ADC and TAC were reassigned to ConAC. At the same time, three of SAC's four fighter wings were reassigned to the new command.

Following the above reorganization, practically all of USAF's fighter resources in the Zone of the Interior were pooled in ConAC. Of the ten fighter wings assigned ConAC, four were the units formerly possessed by the Air Defense Command: the 14th and 78th Fighter Wings and the 52d and 325th Fighter All-weather Wings.[4] The 14th and 78th Fighter Wings each had three squadrons, and both the 52d and 325th Fighter All-weather Wings had two squadrons. With the exception of one squadron of the 325th, the squadrons of each of these units were stationed on the same base as their parent headquarters.[5] All the former ADC units retained air defense as their primary mission and were assigned fighter-escort as a secondary mission.[6]

The three fighter wings transferred from TAC to ConAC were

---

4. For purposes of convenience fighter units will be discussed in terms of wing and squadron throughout this section of the history. The fighter wing is composed of four groups: air base group, maintenance and supply group, medical group, and tactical group.

5. The third squadrons of both the 52d and 325th Fighter All-weather Wings were on overseas assignment.

6. See: History of the Continental Air Command, Vol. III, "Operations and Training," 1 Dec 48 - 31 Dec 49.

the 1st, 20th, and 31st. The 1st was assigned the primary mission of air defense and the secondary mission of fighter-escort. This wing was composed of three squadrons, all of them located on the same base as the wing headquarters. The other two units retained the primary mission of tactical support and were scheduled to enter into air defense operations and training when commitments to the Army were such as to free them for such activities, which, as events proved, was very seldom.

From SAC the Continental Air Command obtained the 56th, 4th, and 33d Fighter Wings. Each of these units consisted of three squadrons, all of which were stationed on the same base as their wing headquarters. The former primary mission of these units, bomber-escort, was made a secondary mission and operations and training for air defense became their primary duties.

Thus, the fighter force assigned the air defense system was more than doubled in December 1948, expanding from four wings, ten squadrons, to eight wings, 22 squadrons (excluding the 20th and 31st Fighter Wings from consideration as air defense units). This was a force considerably less than the one the Air Defense Command had asked for in 1947 to provide defense for what it called the five "most vital areas" in the nation.[8] Yet, this

---

7. Certain additional units equipped with fighter type aircraft were transferred from TAC to ConAC at this time. These units never figured into the air defense structure, however.

8. ADC Staff Study, "Establishment of an Air Defense in Being," 22 Nov 46. See above, Chapter Two.

was more fighter strength than had ever before been available in the postwar period for air defense. Possession of these units, events were to prove, enabled ConAC to embark on the program of building a fighter-interceptor force equipped with aircraft suited to air defense operations, and deployed on bases from which it could best defend critical target areas.

The above resources constituted, for the most part, ConAC's fighter strength during the two year period that command was charged with the air defense mission.[9] By making air defense the primary mission of the majority of these units, USAF served notice of its support of the thesis broached by the first Air Defense Command that in the event of hostilities air defense would be the first role the fighters stationed in the ZI would be called on to perform. At the same time, by assigning secondary missions to these same fighter units, USAF made clear that it was not ignoring fighter requirements for other combat purposes. Until additional fighter resources could be provided, the ZI fighter force was to assume the appearance of an all-purpose organization. At a later date, when aircraft especially designed for air defense operations appeared, this all-purpose fighter force concept would be abandoned. But so long as

---

9. On 2 Oct 1949 the 14th Fighter Wing was deactivated. In Jul 1949, the 81st Fighter Wing was received from PAC. The 1st Fighter Wing, following its assignment to ConAC from TAC, was, in Mar 1949, reassigned to SAC. In early 1950, this unit returned to the air defense fold. The 82d Fighter Wing was reassigned from SAC to ConAC in Aug 1949 but was inactivated in October of the same year.

an aircraft could perform fighter duties in addition to its primary duty, the crew of that aircraft was expected to be conversant with the talents required for carrying out secondary missions of either fighter-escort or fighter-bomber.

II

During the period the air defense mission resided in the Air Defense Command (March 1946-December 1948), deployment of fighters to bases from which they could best protect the nation's most critical targets was limited. The reason for this was that there were too few fighter units assigned the air defense mission to permit ADC to initiate any sort of deployment program on a large scale. In November 1948, elements of the 325th Fighter All-weather Wing were moved from Hamilton Air Force Base in California to Moses Lake Air Force Base to:[10]

> . . . plug the blind spot in the aerial defenses in the Northwestern United States and to further the protection of the Atomic Energy Commission's plants located on the outskirts of Richland and Pasco, Washington, the Boeing Airplane Factory at Seattle, plus that of the many power dams (Grand Coulee, Rock Island, etc) providing electricity for industry and irrigation for reclamation and farming in this state.

The need for all-weather fighters in the Northwest had been revealed by the April 1948 maneuver in that area. Following that exercise ADC had recommended to USAF that the ADC "be given the

---

10. See: *History of Fourth Air Force, 1 Jan - 30 Nov 1948*, Part 2, p. 25.

right of entry into Moses Lake Air Force Base on a tenancy basis . . . " to permit immediate movement of the 325th Fighter All-weather Wing to that base.[11] USAF, however, rejected this request on the ground that "utilization of Moses Lake Air Force Base [could not be effected at that time] due to the lack of jet fuel and to the inability of the Air Materiel Command to provide the necessary base services."[12] A storm of protest greeted this reply when it arrived in ADC Headquarters. "We cannot accept [this] reply as a final answer. To do so would be to accept that a defense in being is not possible of achievement . . ." the Deputy of Operations of ADC Headquarters stated.[13] As noted above, ADC finally succeeded in placing the 325th on the Moses Lake Base, but it took six months to accomplish the move.[14]

Concurrent with the move of the 325th to Moses Lake, the 78th Fighter Wing then at record strength was transferred from Mitchel Field to Hamilton Field in California and there equipped to three squadron strength to fill the void created by the departure of the 325th. That left the 14th Fighter Wing at Dow Field,

---

11. ADC to USAF: "Status of Continental Air Defense," 15 Apr 1948 (DOC 28)

12. Ibid., 1st Ind, USAF to ADC (DOC 28)

13. IRS, DO to DAD, 13 May 1948 (DOC 28)

14. The wing headquarters and one squadron were located at Moses Lake AFB. At the same time, the 318th Squadron of the 325th Wing was located at McChord Field.

Maine, and the 52d Fighter All-weather Wing on Mitchel Field on Long Island to provide fighter protection for the East Coast. While ADC made plans for extensive deployment of __all__ fighter units in the ZI, regular as well as reserve, in the event of hostilities,[15] the above moves constituted the extent of actual deployment of fighter units for air defense during ADC's two and one-half years of existence.

Under ConAC, deployment of fighter units for greater air defense protection commenced slowly. In November 1949, ConAC, perturbed over the difficulty the 25th Air Division was having meeting its responsibilities for intercepting unidentified aircraft over the Northwest area,[16] informed USAF Headquarters that it was "essential to Northwest Air Defense . . . that fighter units be disposed both east and west of the Cascade Range."[17] With USAF's permission, ConAC set out to rectify this problem. In April 1950, the 81st Fighter Wing at Kirtland Air Force Base in New Mexico was moved to Moses Lake. To ensure the continued protection of atomic energy installations in New Mexico, the 81st left one of its squadrons behind at Kirtland. At the same time,

---

15. ADC to C/S USAF: "Survey of Naval Air Stations for Possible Location of Air Defense Units," 31 Mar 1948 (DOC 83)

16. WADF to ConAC: "Jet Aircraft for the 25th Air Division Area," 27 Dec 1949 (DOC 84)

17. ConAC to C/S USAF: "Realignment of the Northwest Air Defense System," 2 Nov 1949 (DOC 85)

the 325th Wing Headquarters and one of its squadrons was moved from Moses Lake to McChord. The 319th squadron of the 325th, which had returned from overseas in July 1949, remained at Moses Lake to afford all-weather protection for the area east of the Cascade Mountains.

Separation of squadrons from their parent wing headquarters in this manner complicated somewhat the logistical support of the squadrons.[18] However, this type of deployment procedure enabled ConAC to strengthen the Northwest defenses and, at the same time, did not deprive the atomic energy installations in New Mexico of fighter protection. Deployment by squadron was soon destined to become the rule rather than the exception.

III

In April 1950 the Commanding General of the Eastern Air Defense Force, Major General R. M. Webster, requested permission to move the Fourth Fighter Wing up from Andrews Field in Washington D. C. to either Rome or Pine Camp airdromes in New York to strengthen EADF's defenses in the Northeast area.[19] ConAC refused this request but at the same time made known that it had a plan before USAF which, if "bought" by the latter headquarters, would permit ConAC to deploy fighter squadrons on a large scale

---

18. USAF to ConAC: "Planned Organization of the 93d Fighter-Interceptor Squadron," 1 Mar 1950, and 1st Ind, ConAC to USAF, 16 Mar 1950 (DOC 86)

19. EADF to ConAC: "Effective Employment of the 4th Fighter Wing in Active Defense," Apr 1950 (DOC 87)

to bases separate from the stations on which their wing headquarters were located. The intent of the plan was to plug just such gaps in the continental air defenses as existed in the EADF area.[20]

The above proposal called for the immediate deployment of the 23 squadrons which ConAC possessed over the following fourteen bases: McChord, Larson, Kirtland, McGuire, Otis, Selfridge, Hamilton, George, Griffis, Westover, O'Hare, Andrews, New Castle, and Dover. Additionally, it made provisions for the further deployment of ConAC's 23 squadrons to Suffolk County, Niagara, and Greater Pittsburgh, and McGhee-Tyson Municipal Airports and Paine Field and Oxnard Flight Strip as soon as arrangements could be made and facilities rehabilitated to permit occupation of these sites by jet fighter aircraft units.[21]

The plan also made provisions for the deployment of the fighter squadrons ConAC had been informed it would receive as a result of the USAF expansion programs. Under the terms of the 58-wing Air Force, ConAC was to receive four additional fighter wings, or twelve squadrons, which added to the 23 squadrons already assigned ConAC would make for a total of 35 squadrons in the air defense system. These squadrons ConAC planned to deploy onto 30 bases. Under the 69-wing Air Force plan, the fighter-interceptor

---

20. Ibid., 1st Ind, ConAC to EADF, 28 Apr 1950 (DOC 87)

21. ConAC to C/S USAF: "Plan for Separate Deployment of Interceptor Forces," 6 Jul 1950.

force was to consist of 48 squadrons. ConAC listed 40 bases onto which these 48 squadrons would be deployed. Finally, when the USAF reached 95-wing strength, scheduled for sometime in 1953, the air defense fighter force was to total 61 squadrons deployed onto 52 bases.

The 61-squadron, 52-base structure was established as the final fighter-interceptor force expansion and deployment figure in the "Package Plan," the program for ConAC's phased establishment of radar and fighter facilities for air defense.

By mid-1950, the 23 squadron portion of the above deployment plan had been concurred in by USAF, with minor modification,[22] and higher headquarters had informed that action was underway to secure the sanction of the Joint Chiefs of Staff on the 61-squadron, 52-base program which ConAC had recommended be the fighter plan for air defense under the 95-wing Air Force.[23]

IV

Shortly after USAF confirmed ConAC's plan to deploy its 23 squadrons to fourteen bases and gave the go-ahead signal on that project, war broke out in Korea. Immediately, ConAC recommended that the fighter-interceptor force be strengthened beyond the 23 squadron figure. According to the time-schedule of the

---

22. TWX, USAF to SAC, MATS, and Hq CMD, Jul 1950 (DOC 88)

23. ConAC to C/S USAF: "Immediate Redeployment of Interceptor Fighter Forces," 4 Jul 1950 and 1st Ind, USAF to ConAC, 17 Jul 1950 (DOC 89)

58-wing USAF expansion program, the air defense system was to have 35 squadrons by the end of June 1951. This was to be accomplished by the activation of four regular fighter-interceptor units.[24] However, this was too slow an augmentation, ConAC considered, when at any moment the war in Korea might break out into a world-wide conflict.

In a letter to the Chief of Staff, USAF, in July 1950, General Thatcher, Deputy for Operations, Headquarters ConAC, expressed the concern of ConAC over the relatively weak fighter-interceptor force assigned the air defense system and requested that higher headquarters take action to federalize twenty Air National Guard squadrons and assign them to ConAC. "The capabilities of the Continental Air Command to provide an active air defense /could/ be greatly strengthened by the call to active duty of . . . these squadrons at their home stations . . ." General Thatcher stated.[25]

Higher headquarters did not endorse this first request of ConAC for strengthening the air defense system by recalling squadrons of the ANG. USAF felt that the deployment of ConAC's 23 squadrons, and the scheduled increase of the fighter-interceptor force by four wings during fiscal year 1951 and the deployment of these squadrons to bases from which they could provide maximum

---

24. USAF to ConAC: "Air Base Requirements for FEAF Augmentation and 58 Wing Program," 7 Aug 1950 (DOC 90)

25. Gen. Thatcher to C/S USAF: "Air Defense Augmentation," 15 Jul 1950 (DOC 91)

protection to the nation were sufficient preparations at that time to ensure the maintenance of the air defense system.[26]

As the Korean conflict increased in intensity, greater demands were made on the Air Force at home in support of FEAF operations. In November 1950, the air defense system was seriously weakened in the Baltimore-Washington-Philadelphia area when the 4th Fighter-Interceptor Wing was assigned to FEAF on TDY for combat in Korea. As a consequence, ConAC reiterated its request to USAF for federalization of certain ANG fighter units to augment the air defense system until additional regular fighter resources were activated. This time, USAF was receptive to the proposal.

In December, in a letter bearing the signature of General Whitehead, ConAC forwarded USAF a roster of fifteen Air National Guard fighter squadrons which were stationed on bases listed among the stations scheduled for housing air defense fighter squadrons in the 52-base "Package Plan." ConAC requested that these units be federalized immediately since they could be fitted without delay into the fighter-interceptor defenses. An additional list was furnished of 23 ANG squadrons which were operational to the degree that they could immediately strengthen the air defense system. Since these latter squadrons were not located on bases included within the permanent fighter base plans, however, it was suggested that federalization of these units be delayed until

---

26. Ibid., 1st Ind USAF to ConAC, Aug 1950 (DOC 91)

additional permanent bases could be readied for occupancy by these units.[27]

Higher headquarters approved the above presentation and action was commenced for federalizing the fifteen ANG squadrons which were located on bases scheduled for permanent retention in the fighter-interceptor program. It was not intended that federalization of these units would take the place of regular Air Force units scheduled for activation and assignment to the air defense system under the terms of the USAF expansion program. The build-up of regular units was to continue concurrently with the training of the federalized ANG fighter units and as rapidly as possible. Activation of the ANG squadrons would "buy time" until additional regular fighter-interceptor squadrons could take their places on the line.

V

On 1 January 1951 the Air Defense Command was reestablished as a major Air Force command and the air defense mission reassigned from ConAC to the new organization. At the same time, the fighter-interceptor wings formerly assigned ConAC were transferred to ADC.

ADC inherited eight fighter-interceptor wings from ConAC, totalling 23 fighter squadrons. These were the 1st, 4th, 33d, 52a, 56th, 78th, 81st and 325th Wings. Of these units, all but the 4th

---

27. ConAC to C/S USAF: "Use of Air National Guard Units in the Air Defense of the United States" Dec 1950 (DOC 92)

were available to the ADC for air defense purposes during the first six months of 1951; that wing with its three fighter squadrons was, as has been noted, assigned to temporary duty with FEAF. Location of the remaining twenty squadrons and their wing headquarters on 1 January 1951 is shown on the map which follows.

By the end of June 1951, the ADC's fighter strength had increased to fifteen wings, or to a total of 44 squadrons. This increase was brought about by the activation in January 1951 of a new regular fighter-interceptor wing, the 23rd at Presque Isle, Maine,[28] and the federalization of 21 Air National Guard squadrons, fifteen of which were called to active duty in February and six in March.

The fifteen ANG fighter squadrons and the four ANG fighter wing headquarters federalized in February 1951 and their locations at the time of federalization were as follows:[29]

Unit	Base At Which Federalized
101st Fighter Wing, Hqs	Dow AFB, Bangor, Maine
132d Fighter Squadron	Dow AFB, Bangor, Maine
133d " "	Grenier AFB, Manchester, N.H.
134th " "	Burlington Municipal Airport, Vt.
113th Fighter Wing, Hqs	Andrews AFB, Washington D. C.
148th Fighter Squadron	Reading Municipal Airport, Penns.
121st " "	Andrews AFB, Washington D. C.
142d " "	New Castle County Airport, Del.

---

28. Hq EADF, G. O. #3, 9 Jan 1951.

29. ADC, G. O. #13, 6 Feb 1951.

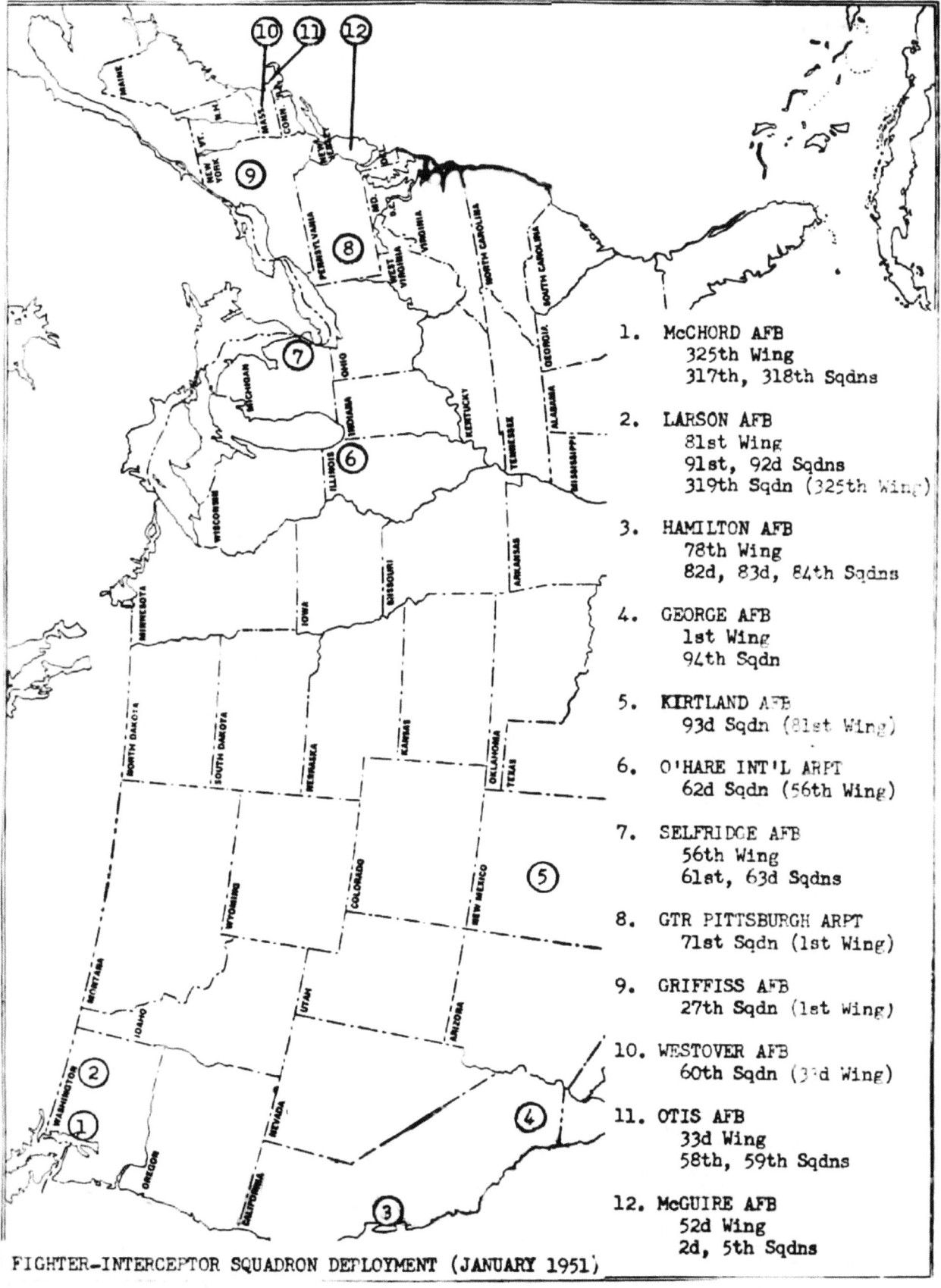

FIGHTER-INTERCEPTOR SQUADRON DEPLOYMENT (JANUARY 1951)

Unit	Base At Which Federalized
122d Fighter Wing, Hqs	Stout Fld., Indianapolis, Ind.
113th Fighter Squadron	Stout Fld., Indianapolis, Ind.
163d " "	Baer Fld., Ft. Wayne, Ind.
166th " "	Lockbourne AFB, Columbus, Ohio
128th Fighter Wing, Hqs	Gen. Mitchell Fld., Milwaukee, Wisc.
176th Fighter Squadron	Truax Fld., Madison, Wisc.
172d " "	Kellogg Fld., Battle Creek, Mich.
118th Fighter Squadron	Bradley Fld., Windsor Locks, Conn.
116th " "	Geiger Fld., Spokane, Wash.
123d " "	Portland Airport, Portland, Ore.
188th " "	Kirtland AFB, Albuquerque, N. M.

The three Air National Guard fighter wings and the six ANG squadrons federalized in March 1951 and the bases at which they were federalized were:[30]

Unit	Base At Which Federalized
103d Fighter Wing, Hqs	Brainard Fld., Hartford, Conn.
142d Fighter Wing, Hqs	Geiger Fld., Washington
133d Fighter Wing, Hqs	Holman Fld., St. Paul, Minn.
175th Fighter Squadron	Municipal Airport, Sioux Falls, S. D.
109th " "	Holman Fld., St. Paul, Minn.
179th " "	Municipal Airport, Duluth, Minn.
126th Fighter Squadron	Gen. Mitchell Fld., Milwaukee, Wisc.
105th " "	Berry Fld., Nashville, Tenn.
136th " "	Niagara Municipal Airport, N. Y.

Almost immediately after federalization of the above units, a regrouping of squadrons under wing headquarters other than the ones to which they had been assigned while under state control began. At this time a new word crept into ADC's organizational

---

30. ADC, G. O. #21, 2 Mar 1951.

vocabulary: ANG squadrons placed under regular Air Force wing headquarters and regular Air Force squadrons placed under ANG wing headquarters were considered as "attached" to those wings even though the latter wings assumed administrative, logistical, and operational control over these squadrons. In other words, while the "attached" squadron was considered an integral member of the wing under which it was grouped for air defense, that squadron was at the same time considered as remaining organically a component of the wing of which it had been a part prior to the federalization of the ANG units. To eliminate this schizophrenic situation ADC Headquarters sought permission from higher headquarters to directly assign ANG squadrons to the regular Air Force wings under which they operated for air defense and to directly assign the regular Air Force squadrons "attached" to ANG wings to those wings, but, as of the end of June 1951, this request had not been approved. The objection to ADC's carrying out this reassignment appeared to be that such action would destroy the historical continuity of World War II combat relations between certain squadrons and groups. Organization charts in Part IV illustrate the extent of the somewhat confusing organizational structure which existed in the fighter-interceptor program at the end of June 1951.

The Air National Guard squadrons federalized in the first half of 1951 did not immediately assume an air defense capability commensurate with that of the regular Air Force squadrons who for the past two years, under ConAC's tutelage, had engaged in air defense operations and training. They first ran through an intensive 120-day training and organization period. This was necessary, for the majority of the ANG pilots were not "checked out" in jet aircraft and even those units equipped with jet F-84s were not sufficiently versed in ground controlled interception procedures to permit them to assume immediately an air defense role.

With these units in its possession, however, ADC could and did proceed full-speed ahead with its programmed fighter conversion and deployment programs.

VI

In January 1951 USAF Headquarters published SEEDCORN, a document setting forth the programmed expansion of the major Air Force commands in accordance with the overall expansion of USAF. According to this program guide, ADC was scheduled to possess 45 squadrons at the end of fiscal year 1951.[31] These squadrons were to be deployed onto 39 of the permanent bases included in the 52-base "Package Plan."

The activation of the 21 ANG squadrons made it possible for ADC to reach 44 squadron strength by the end of June. However, ADC was not able to place each of these squadrons onto its

---

31. Hqs ADC, Current Planning Activities Report 1-51, 22 Jan 1951.

permanent base. ADC fighter squadrons were located on 34 bases at the end of June, but twelve squadrons were located on interim bases, some of which were temporary bases, others of which were included in permanent bases plans. It was estimated in early 1951 that work on most of the permanent bases would be completed late in that year.[32] However, planning estimates at the end of June 1951 were that it would be late in 1952 before all the fighter squadrons would be situated on a permanent base.[33]

The 39 bases scheduled in January 1951 for occupation by fighter-interceptor units at the end of June and the number of fighter elements to be stationed on each base were:[34]

Base	F-I Deployment	Base	F-I Deployment
Westover	0/1	Presque Isle	1/1
Otis	1/2	Rapid City	0/1
McGuire	1/2	Geiger	0/1
Andrews	0/1	Oscoda	0/1
Dover	0/1	Wright-Patterson	0/1
New Castle	1/1	Suffolk County	1/1
Selfridge	1/1	Youngstown	0/1
O'Hare	1/1	Burlington (Vt)	0/1
Kirtland	0/1	Hanscom	0/1
George	1/1	Langley	0/1
Niagara	0/1	Offutt	0/1

---

32. ADC to EADF: "Facilities for Federalized Air National Guard Units," 5 Jan 1951 (DOC 93)

33. Air Defense Fighter Interceptor Program, 1 Jul 1951.

34. Hqs ADC, Current Planning Activities Report, 22 Jan 1951. In explanation of the cryptic code employed under F-I Deployment: the figure in front of the slash-mark indicates the number of wing headquarters at the base; the figure behind the slash-mark indicates the number of fighter squadrons to be stationed on the base.

Base	F-I Deployment	Base	F-I Deployment
Greater Pittsburgh	1/1	Wichita	1/1
McGhee-Tyson	0/1	Oxnard	0/1
Truax	1/2	Paine	0/1
Duluth	0/1	Scott	0/1
Wold-Chamberlain	1/1	Kinross	0/1
Hamilton	1/2	NAS Hensley	0/1
McChord	1/2	Portland, Ore.	0/1
Larson	1/2	Travis	0/1
Griffis	0/1		

Several changes were made in the above plan in the six month period following its publication. In several instances, USAF suggested that bases on which facilities were already existent be substituted for bases scheduled in permanent fighter base plans at which extensive rehabilitation would have to be made in order to ensure effective fighter-interceptor operations. In other instances, certain of the bases originally selected were subsequently found to be crowded, and less crowded stations were substituted for them in the permanent base plans. During the whole of the first six months of 1951, Air Defense Command installation officers devoted unceasing study to the matter of selecting permanent fighter-interceptor bases. The tactical advantages the location of a site afforded, the ability of a base to support jet fighter operations, and the cost of construction and rehabilitation were the major criteria by which bases were considered as permanent stations for fighter-interceptor units.[35]

---

35. The best documents illustrative of these changes in the programming of bases for permanent occupancy by fighter-interceptor units were the monthly Fighter-Interceptor Program charts, prepared by Hqs ADC Operations and sent to all elements of ADC for information purposes and for planning guides.

The actual location of fighter wing headquarters and fighter squadrons at the end of June 1951 was as follows:[36]

Base	F-I Deployment	Base	F-I Deployment
McChord	1/2	Wright-Patterson	0/1
Portland, Ore.	0/1	McGuire	1/2
Larson	1/3	Nashville	0/1
Geiger	0/1	Grenier	1/1
Hamilton	1/3	Dow	0/1
George	1/1	Niagara	0/1
Kirtland	0/1	Presque Isle	1/2
Long Beach	0/1	Burlington	0/1
Baer	1/1	Otis	1/2
Lockbourne	0/1	Westover	0/1
Wold-Chamberlain	1/1	Suffolk	1/1
Sioux Falls	0/1	Griffis	0/1
Duluth	0/1	Pittsburgh	0/1
Truax	1/2	New Castle	1/1
Selfridge	1/2	Andrews	0/1
Oscoda	0/1	Dover	0/1
O'Hare	1/1	Scott	0/1

The squadrons located at Long Beach, Baer, Lockbourne, Sioux Falls, Nashville, Dow and Grenier were scheduled for ultimate redeployment to Oxnard, Grandview, Youngstown, Rapid City, McGhee-Tyson, Langley and Bedford air bases. Additionally, squadrons sharing permanent bases with other squadrons at the close of the period were to be ultimately relocated on the following bases: Paine, Travis, Kinross, and Offutt. One of the squadrons at Hamilton Field was also scheduled for eventual redeployment to Geiger, increasing the strength at the latter base to two squadrons.[37]

---

36. Air Defense Fighter Interceptor Program, 1 Jul 1951.

37. Ibid. The 449th Fighter-Interceptor Wing, assigned to the Alaskan Air Command, was scheduled for reassignment to ADC and deployment to Hensley Naval Air Station in February 1952.

ADC FIGHTER SQUADRON DEPLOYMENT AS OF 30 JUN 51

NO	F/I WING DESIGNATION LOCATION	ASSIGNED SQUADRONS NON-DEPLOYED SQUADRONS		DEPLOYED SQUADRONS NON-ATTACHED UNIT LOCATION	ATTACHED OTHER WINGS UNIT LOCATION	ATTACHED SQUADRONS LOCATED ON STATION WITH ATCH'D WG	LOCATED ON A DIFFERENT STATION UNIT LOCATION
1st	George AFB, Cal.	94th					188th Long Beach M/A, Cal
23rd	Presque Isle AFB, Me.	74th	75th				134th Burlington M/A, Vt.
33rd	Otis AFB, Mass.	58th	59th	60th Westover AFB, Mass			
52nd	McGuire AFB, NJ	2nd	5th				105th Berry Fld, Tenn.
56th	Selfridge AFB, Mich	61st		63rd Oscoda AFB, Mich.	62nd O'Hare Aprt, Ill.	172nd	
78th	Hamilton AFB, Cal.	82nd	83rd	84th			
81st	Larson AFB, Wash.	91st	92nd		93rd Kirtland AFB, NM		116th Geiger Fld, Wash.
101st	Grenier AFB, NH	133rd		132nd Dow AFB, Me. 136th Niagra Falls, NY	134th Burlington M/A, Vt		
103rd	Suffolk Co/Aprt, NY	118th					27th Griffiss AFB, NY 71st Gtr Pitt Aprt, Pa.
115th	New Castle, Del.	142nd		121st Andrews AFB, Md. 148th Dover AFB, Del.			
122nd	Baer Fld, Ind.	163rd		113th Scott AFB, Ill. 166th Lockbourne AFB, O.			
128th	Truax Fld, Wis.	126th	178th		172nd Selfridge AFB, M.		
133rd	St. Paul, Minn.	109th		175th Sioux Falls, SD 179th Duluth Aprt, Minn.			
142nd	O'Hare Aprt, Ill.					62nd	97th Wri-Patt AFB, Ohio
325th	McChord AFB, Wash.	317th	318th	319th Larson AFB, Wash.			123rd Portland M/A, Ore.
SQ'S NOT ASGD TO F/I WINGS					97th Wri-Patt AFB, O. 105th Berry Fld, Tenn. 116th Geiger Fld, Wash. 123rd Portland M/A, Ore. 188th Kirtland AFB, NM	93rd	

Air National Guard units reporting to active duty at bases other than those listed in the "Package Plan" were provided only the minimum facilities they required for operations. The facilities provided at these bases were, for the most part, those which the ANG units formerly occupied plus sufficient additional barrack space to house the men not living within reasonable driving distance, and whatever additional mess facilities they required. Air National Guard units federalized at stations included in the permanent fighter base program were provided additional barrack and mess space immediately to ensure operations. At the same time, work went forward as rapidly as possible to provide them with complete facilities.[38]

VII

The ADC's fighter base construction program during the first six months of 1951 was only a part of a tremendous USAF expansion program nation-wide. While the 61-squadron, 52-base, fighter-interceptor expansion program was the goal on which ADC had set its sights, there was really no way for ADC to know precisely what size its fighter-interceptor force would eventually attain. This was only natural since USAF itself was not certain how large it would ultimately grow. There were rumors at the end of the period that USAF would have to have 163 groups or more if

---

38. ADC to EADF: "Facilities for Federalized Air National Guard Units," 5 Jan 1951 (DOC 93)

it was to be equipped to perform the tasks that would come its way in the event of hostilities.

In consideration of the fact that it might increase in size far beyond the programmed 95-wing structure, USAF constantly stressed to its major subordinate commands the necessity for the maintenance of flexible plans for development of bases.[39] And because of the great necessity for conserving funds against the requirement for even greater expansion, it was absolutely mandatory that every precaution be taken against wastage in rehabilitation and construction programs. Consequently, during this period, "no frills, adornment, decorative refinements, elaborate recreational facilities"[40] or other non-operational construction appeared in ADC's or the other major commands' expansion programs. The replacement of existing facilities was limited to those whose retention would have resulted in making operation cumbersome or which would have created unhealthy living and working conditions and excessive maintenance costs.[41]

General Vandenberg stated clearly the problems inherent in the great expansion project the Air Force would be engaged in

---

39. USAF to ADC: "Supplemental Planning Data on Bases Included in Initial Increment of Proposed Air Force Expansion Program," 15 Jan 1951 (DOC 94)

40. TWX, ADC to Defense Forces, 1 Mar 1951, repeating a message received from USAF (DOC 95)

41. Ibid.

implementing during the remainder of 1951 and during 1952. USAF was going ahead, General Vandenberg said, with the 95-wing program as the Air Force objective. All planning and action was to be geared to this concept and any barriers that impeded the attainment of an Air Force of this size were to be immediately attacked. The following problems were those selected as contributing most to delays in the USAF construction program during the first half of 1951:[42]

> Lag in developing criteria for non-standard projects;
> Unwillingness to accept standard and preliminary plans without extensive and frequently non-essential refinements;
> Unnecessary changes in master plans to incorporate refinements;
> Delays in selecting sites;
> Placing conflicting and confusing requests on District Engineers;
> Attempting to enlarge project scopes or deviate from authorized construction programs.

Elimination of these snags from the overall USAF construction program portended to be a major task for ADC and the other major Air Force Commands in the ZI for the remainder of 1951 and until the USAF had reached combat strength.

---

42. TWX, personal from Gen. Vandenberg, 31 Mar 1951 (DOC 96)

CHAPTER SEVEN

AIRCRAFT FOR AIR DEFENSE

I

The fighter aircraft is the "mailed fist" of the air defense system. One day our scientists may evolve a pilotless projectile capable of intercepting and destroying invading enemy bombers. As to when such a lethal weapon will appear, however, no one knows. Consequently, the hopes of the United States at the present time for escaping annihilation as a result of a concerted atomic attack from the air appear to be irrevocably invested in the successful establishment of a powerful fighter-interceptor force.

The experts on strategic bombing, the Strategic Air Command, have expressed their concurrence in the thesis that the enemy will strike at night with his bombers or during periods of inclement weather.[1] At least, were SAC to be ordered on the offensive it would choose these conditions to dispatch its own bombers to minimize the extent of enemy interceptor capabilities; there is no reason to assume that the enemy will be less prepared to apply the same tactics.

---

1. Maj. Gen. Thomas S. Power, Deputy Commander, SAC, to Brig. Gen. Herbert B. Thatcher, Deputy for Operations, ConAC, 10 Nov 1949. (DOC 97)

Spurred on by the above dire prediction, the Air Force commands entrusted with the air defense of the United States in the post World War II era have pressed for arming the fighter-interceptor units with all-weather aircraft — jet aircraft equipped with adequate electronic, anti-icing, and other equipment to enable them to operate on a 24-hour schedule regardless of climatic conditions.

Until 1950 these pleas went totally unheeded so far as actual assignment of all-weather aircraft, or of even a competent night performer, to the fighter-interceptor units was concerned. This does not say that higher authority was unaware of this need or that all-weather aircraft were not in the process of development prior to this date. Sufficient funds just were not provided to permit USAF to initiate large-scale production of all-weather aircraft and to step-up research, development, and production of the intricate radar equipment so essential to all-weather fighter operations.

During the period March 1946 - October 1950, the fighter-interceptor units were equipped with (1) World War II vintage night fighters, conventional aircraft[2] outfitted with a modicum of electronic aids, and (2) non-electronic equipped jet and standard engine airplanes which could be used during hours of daylight only.

---

2. As used throughout this chapter the term "conventional aircraft" denotes propeller type airplane, in contradistinction to jet propelled aircraft.

Late in 1950, through a little technological sleight-of-hand, a jet model aircraft was rigged with radar equipment and put into use as a night fighter. By June 1951, the conventional night fighters had been displaced by the new model; by that date, also two additional squadrons had transitioned from their non-electronic equipped jet fighters to the new jet night fighter. The preponderance of the aircraft in the air defense system at the close of June 1951, however, still did not possess night fighting capabilities.

Consequently, throughout the entire post-war period the concept of a dual fighter-interceptor force, one for day and one for night and foul weather operations, obtained. Available night fighters were located in the areas where muggy weather prevailed the majority of the time and where the operational capabilities of the strictly day fighters would be reduced to a minimum in the event of an attack. Of course, experiments were made to analyse the possibilities of utilizing day fighters for night and inclement weather operations in case of an emergency. Data obtained from these tests would have undoubtedly proved beneficial had the non-electronically equipped aircraft been forced into service as night and all-weather fighters; however, the results were not conducive to an optimistic evaluation of the merit of day fighters for use at other times.³ All in all, the post-war period has been

---

3. For information on this subject see the following: ADC to WADF: "Night Interceptions by Day Fighters," /Jan/ 1951; and Memo from the 52d F-I Gp Operations Officer to his Commanding Officer: "Evaluation of Night Interception by Day Fighters." 17 Jan 1951. (DOC 98)

one of trepidation from the standpoint of the adequacy of fighter-interceptor resources.[4] Had the enemy struck with modern bombers at any time prior to the completion date of this history and at a time when the day fighter force could not have operated, there would have been little chance of turning him from his target.

II

While a truly adequate all-weather fighter-interceptor was never assigned the air defense system during the period March 1946 through June 1951, the quality of aircraft which were utilized for air defense did perceptively improve. Perhaps the best way to illustrate this favorable advance would be to recount briefly the several types of aircraft assigned the air defense system during the post-war period and the individual success of these airplanes as fighter-interceptors.

---

4. Gen. Whitehead summarized the combat readiness status of ConAC fighter units in July 1949 as follows: "As of 30 June 1949 only 10 Groups of the 53 in United States Air Force had a combat effectiveness of 80% or more. Of these 10 Groups, 5 were in FEAF, 4 were in SAC, and 1 was in Alaska. There were none in ConAC." Reasons for ConAC's poor showing were: "The two F-82 Groups have had a rough time from the supply and maintenance standpoint. The transition of all ConAC fighter groups from conventional to jet fighters before jet fighters were available in sufficient quantity to fully equip these groups has been another contributing factor. Turnover of personnel has interferred. The above for the most part were beyond the control of ConAC excepting the decisions made late in 1948 to convert to jets before they knew whether or not sufficient jet fighters would be available." /Gen. Whitehead to Maj. Gen. John E. Upston, CG 4th AF, 26 July 1949 (DOC 99)/

The 14th Fighter Wing was initially equipped with F-47 "Thunderbolts." In November 1947, this unit transitioned into F-84s, becoming the first post-war unit to be equipped with this type aircraft and the "guinea pig" of the Air Force in experimentation to learn its fighter potentialities. The 325th and 52d Fighter-All-weather Wings were equipped with P-61s initially, the twin fuselaged, propeller driven aircraft known as "Black Widows" by World War II fighter pilots. The remaining fighter wing assigned the first post-war Air Defense Command, the 78th, was equipped with F-84s at the time of its activation. These were the type fighter planes assigned the air defense mission from March 1946 through November 1948.

While the above models of airplanes, excluding the F-84, had earned staunch approbations for their performance during World War II, they were definitely not the types of airplanes to be assigned a fighter interception mission. The minimum requisites of a fighter-interceptor, air defense leaders pointed out time and again, had to be (1) a high rate of speed, particularly on the climb and in closing with the enemy, and (2) an all-weather capability. Each of the above type aircraft fell far short of satisfying these needs.

The inadequacy of the aircraft then available for air defense was well demonstrated in the Northwest maneuver in May 1948. It will be recalled that during this maneuver the 27th Fighter

Wing of SAC, flying F-51s, had participated, as had F-61s of the 325th Fighter All-weather Wing and F-80s of the 71st Fighter Squadron of the 1st Fighter Wing, then assigned to TAC.[5] In analysing this maneuver, General Upston, Commander of the 4th Air Force, reported to General Stratemeyer as follows:[6]

> The limitations of the defensive fighters in adverse weather conditions were emphasized during the maneuver. The P-61 fighter is of no practical value. Its speed and altitude limitations make it ineffective against today's bombers. Deficiencies in electronic equipment, both ground and airborne, along with the inexperience of operators and pilots, further limited the effectiveness of the P-61 under adverse weather conditions in the mountainous terrain. The P-80s were not equipped to penetrate an overcast. Replacement of instruments to relieve this limitation is in progress. The ground controller could not pick-up, track, and direct a P-80 with success . . . The operation of the P-51s was hindered by adverse weather in the mountainous terrain. These points have emphasized the need for modern all-weather fighter aircraft in this area.

Thus, the principal criticism of fighter-interceptor capabilities for air defense emanating from this maneuver was that F-61s were not fast enough for night fighter operations and that F-80s, while adequate from the standpoint of speed, were hamstrung in their operations by the fact that they had no radar equipment for night and all-weather fighter operations. This was a condition that continued unabated until late 1950; the only type of aircraft really suited for interceptor operations was the jet,

---

5. See Chapter Four, LASHUP.

6. Maj. Gen. Upston to Gen. Whitehead: "Report on Maneuvers," 27 May 1948. See: <u>History of 4th AF</u>, 1948 Part II, Appendix III.

but the jet models available were not electronically and otherwise rigged for night and all-weather flying.

The formation of ConAC witnessed the assignment of F-80s,[7] the first American jet propelled fighters to become operational, directly to the air defense system. During 1949, this airplane put in more flying hours than any other type of aircraft assigned to the command. Because of the long period this plane had been in use, most of the "bugs" had been worked out of it prior to its advent into the air defense system. It was an excellent aircraft from the standpoint of simplicity of design, ruggedness of construction, and ease of maintenance. With a speed of approximately 575 miles per hour and an extreme ceiling of 45,000 feet, it was a reliable performer. It remained, of course, strictly a day fighter because it did not carry radar equipment.[8]

The F-84 was the second most used aircraft in the air defense system during 1949. As a fighter-bomber this plane gave a good account of itself; as a fighter-interceptor, however, it had serious shortcomings. Additionally, it had many structural defects, particularly in the wing areas, which gave great maintenance

---

7. For a brief but excellent description of USAF fighter aircraft, both interceptor and fighter-bomber, see the article "Modern Weapons in Today's Air Force," by Maj. Gen. David M. Schlatter, CG Research and Development Command, which appeared in the August 1951 edition of the Army Information Digest.

8. The volumes on Supply and Maintenance in the 1949 and 1 Jan-30 Jun Histories of ConAC contain detailed information on the fighter aircraft utilized for air defense during those periods.

difficulties and restricted use of these planes on many occasions.[9]

During the latter part of 1949, the first North American F-86 Sabre Jets were assigned the fighter-interceptor units. This airplane, with a top speed of approximately 670 miles per hour, and the ability to climb rapidly and operate safely at a ceiling between 50,000 and 60,000 feet, soon proved itself the best interceptor yet developed. It was not long before it became the favorite of the interceptor units. By 30 June 1950, there were almost as many F-86s in the air defense system as there were all other types of aircraft. By the end of that year, the F-86 had come to be the workhorse of the air defense fighter-interceptor system for daylight operations.

At the close of 1950 the F-80s had been phased out of the air defense system and action was underway to get rid of the F-84s. This left the F-86 as the predominant day fighter-interceptor. At this time, plans were afoot to replace even this faithful performer. What was wanted was an airplane which could operate as successfully as the F-86 but which could work at night and in foul weather as

___

9. Of the capabilities of the F-84 ConAC had the following to say in November 1950: "The F-84D aircraft have little value as a fighter-interceptor . . . in view of the continued wing failures that have been encountered and general inherent characteristics of the airplane." /TWX, ConAC to Director of Maintenance, USAF, 6 Nov 1950. For additional information on this subject see: 78th F-I Gp to CG WADF: "Wing Failures on F-84 Aircraft," 14 Aug 1950. (DOC 100)/

well as during daylight hours.

III

In 1949, the F-82 "Twin Mustang" replaced the F-61s in the 325th and 52d Fighter All-weather Wings. A complicated conventional aircraft, the F-82 not only gave much maintenance difficulty but it was soon obvious that it did not have sufficient performance to cope with modern bombers of the B-50 type.[10] Jet propelled all-weather aircraft were in the experimental stage but the date when they were scheduled to come off the assembly lines for assignment to the fighter-interceptor units was too far in the future to meet the immediate need for them.

Late in 1949 the Lockheed Aircraft Corporation came up with an idea which portended to resolve if not the need for an all-weather aircraft at least the requirement for an adequate night fighter. It was suggested that electronic equipment be installed in the T-33, a jet trainer aircraft, and that this aircraft be put into service as a night fighter. The T-33 was the only jet aircraft then available which could be renovated in such a manner for the simple reason that it was the only two-place jet in production. USAF gave the green light to this project, the refitted T-33s were dubbed F-94As, and on October 1949 an Air Force accepting

---

10. By mid 1950 these aircraft went out of construction with the result that ConAC had much difficulty obtaining parts for those F-82s still in operation in the fighter all-weather units.

board went on record as follows concerning the completed job:

> The configuration of the F-94A airplane is not satisfactory for the procurement of more airplanes than is necessary to fill the interim need. Incorporation of features, such as thermal de-icing and improved armament installations such as, a six gun nose with automatic pneumatic gun charges, provisions for blind landing, and any other features which will contribute to making the airplane a more effective all-weather fighter, are necessary to take the airplane out of the interim class.

As revealed by the above, the Air Force was fully cognizant that the initial model of the F-94 could not be considered more than a night fighter because it lacked adequate protective devices to permit cold weather operations. However, subsequent models, it was intended, would include equipment to allow for all-weather operations. A refined model of this "makeshift" airplane, it was hoped, would fill an interim bill until production of airplanes especially designed for all-weather operations could be accelerated.

---

11. *Communications and Electronics Digest*, prepared by the Director of C&E, Hqs ADC, May 1951, pp. 5-6.

12. *Ibid*. The F-94A is powered by a single centrifugal compressor type turbo-jet engine, J-33-A-33, incorporating an afterburner to augment thrust for climb and combat. The aircraft has a limiting Mach No. of 0.80, the same as the F-80. It is equipped with an E-1 fire control system incorporating the A-1CM gun-bomb-rocket sight and computer with the AN/APG-33 radar. This fire control system allows the pilot to track and fire either visually or blind. Armament consists of four caliber .50 M3 machine guns with ammunition containers for 300 rounds per gun. A hot-mike intercommunication system is used between the radar observer and the pilot to enable them to converse without the necessity of pushing mike buttons.

In February 1950 USAF informed ConAC that it had scheduled for the shipment of 39 F-94As to the 56th Fighter Wing at Selfridge Field. After thoroughly studying its air defense requirements, ConAC recommended that these planes be assigned to the 325th Wing at Moses Lake and McChord in Washington State initially. The operations analyses of the two 1949 air defense maneuvers DRUMMER-BOY and LOOKOUT, in which the great need for all-weather fighters in the Northwest and Northeast was pointed up, played the large factor in ConAC's reaching this decision.

USAF "bought" ConAC's recommendation, and in late February the Air Materiel Command informed that the 325th's F-82s would be replaced with F-94As commencing about June 1950. The first thirteen F-94As to roll off the assembly line were to go to the 325th's squadron at Larson Air Force Base. The next thirteen were to go to the Alaskan Air Command.[13] The next 26 were then to go to the two remaining squadrons of the 325th at McChord Air Force Base.

The drastic shortage of radar observers which existed at this time was the reason for the decision to allocate only thirteen F-94As to each squadron of the 325th.[14] ConAC was in favor of an initial allocation of 25 per squadron in spite of the fact that there were not enough radar observers to man this number. ConAC

---

13. TWX, AMC to ConAC, 24 Feb 1950. (DOC 101)

14. 1st Ind, USAF to ConAC, to ConAC to DCS/O, USAF: "Composition of Certain Fighter Wings," (DOC 102)

recommended that F-94As for which there were no radar observers available be provided without radar equipment. These planes could then be operated as day fighters until additional radar observers could be trained or otherwise procured, at which time the radar equipment could be installed. USAF turned thumbs down on this proposal, however, on the grounds that it was too expensive. Too, USAF felt that the denuded F-94As would not be nearly so good for day operations as were F-86s of which there were ample numbers.

      The 325th commenced to transition into F-94As in the second quarter of 1950.[15] By June 1951, the changeover from F-82s in this unit to the new model jet night fighter had been completed. Additionally, delivery of F-94As to the 52d Fighter All-weather Wing commenced in October 1950 and by the close of June 1951 the two squadrons of that unit had completely transitioned into the new jet night fighter. Two additional squadrons, one each from the 33d and 56th Fighter Interceptor Wings, had, by the above date, exchanged their day fighter jet aircraft for F-94Bs, a

---

    15. See: History of 325th F-I Gp, April-June 1951, p. 1.

refined version of the F-94A model.

IV

The total number of fighter aircraft assigned the newly activated Air Defense Command on 1 January 1951 was 365. 236, or approximately 65 per cent of the total, were F-86s. There were 26 F-82s (used primarily for tow-target purposes), 43 F-84s, and 60 F-94s. By the end of June 1951, this aircraft inventory had more than doubled, totaling 813. The primary reason for this increase was, of course, the recalling to active duty of the ANG squadrons in the early months of 1951. The following chart indicates the numerical increase in assigned fighter aircraft which occurred

---

16. The following is from the DC&E Digest for May 1951, p. 9: "Six major changes incorporated in the F-94B over the F-94A are as follows: (1) ILS glide path and localizer receiver plus the zero reader have been installed to make possible an approach under lower weather minimums than presently /is/ possible with GCA equipment. The ILS and zero-reader equipment permits simultaneous handling of more than one aircraft on final approach, thus providing a more rapid system for the recovery of aircraft. All future interceptors will have ILS receivers and zero-readers for this purpose. (2) The cockpit pressure differential of the F-94B has been raised to 5 PSI differential. This enables the pilot to fly in an altitude environment lower than the actual altitude that the aircraft is flying. (3) Provisions have been made for windshield anti-icing equipment. (4) A high pressure oxygen system similar to the one installed in early World War II aircraft has been installed in the F-94B. By using the high pressure oxygen system, space, which is a critical item in an aircraft utilizing a large amount of electronic equipment, is saved in the aircraft. (5) The hydraulic system pressure has been increased from 1000 PSI to 1,500 PSI. This increase in pressure allows much faster action relative to landing gear, speed brake control, and aileron boost control. (6) Wing revisions provide for external fuel tanks to be center line mounted instead of previously being suspended from the wing tanks. The net gain is larger feed capacity and less aero-dynamic drag."

during the period January - June 1951:[17]

TYPE	Jan	Feb	Mar	Apr	May	Jun
Conventional Fighters						
F-47	0	54	107	102	97	96
F-51	0	133	194	176	193	213
F-82	26	29	27	26	21	19
Jet Day Fighters						
F-80	0	17	30	35	37	41
F-84	43	119	122	119	118	103
F-86	236	238	239	239	242	255
Jet All-weather Fighters						
F-86D	0	0	0	0	0	0
F-89	0	0	0	0	0	4
F-94	60	57	72	83	83	82

While additional F-94s and F-86s were on hand at the end of June 1951, the major increase in the fighter-interceptor inventory was in obsolescent F-47s and F-51s. At the same time, large numbers of F-84s and F-80s reentered the air defense system with the recalled Air National Guard units. Utilization of these out-moded fighters for air defense, ADC hoped, would last only until increased production could effect their replacement with all-weather airplanes.

Specifically, ADC's fighter-interceptor squadrons were equipped with three general types of aircraft at the end of June 1951: Jet airplanes equipped with radar to permit night and limited

---

17. *Air Defense Command Data Book, June 1951* (Compiled from Daily Combat Readiness Reports, RCS: ADC-DC-C1)

all-weather operations; jet fighters not equipped with radar and, consequently, suited for day operations only; and conventional airplanes. Five squadrons had converted to F-94As and two squadrons to F-94Bs for a total of seven squadrons capable of night and limited all-weather operations. Twenty-three squadrons were flying non-electronically equipped jets, and these comprised the major part of the actual combat capability of the fighter-interceptor force.[18] The remaining fourteen squadrons possessed F-47s and F-51s.

It was planned that by the end of 1952 and early 1953 the fighter-interceptor squadrons would _all_ be equipped with all-weather airplanes. Twelve squadrons were scheduled to be equipped with refined models of the F-94; eleven squadrons with F-89s; and fifteen with F-86Ds.[19] The chart on the following page illustrates the type of aircraft each squadron in the air defense system was equipped with at the end of June 1951, the type each was to receive in the near future to enhance its combat capabilities, and,

---

18. Fourteen squadrons were equipped with F-86s, six with F-84s, and two with F-80s. The 84th Squadron of the 78th Fighter-Interceptor Wing was in the process of converting from F-84s to the new F-89s at the close of June 1951.

19. The 81st Fighter-Interceptor Wing was scheduled for a tour of duty in England commencing in August or September 1951. The 113th Wing was scheduled to depart for reassignment to the Alaskan Air Command in February, 1952. The 449th Squadron, equipped with F-94s, was to be reassigned from the Alaskan Air Command to ADC in February, 1952. /See reference, Chapter Six, to Fighter-Interceptor Program Charts./

SECURITY INFORMATION

Squadron	Wing	Type A/C 30 June 51	Type A/C to Conv' to on These Dates
123d	325th	F-51D	F-86E on Nov 51; F-94C 4th quarter 1952
317th	"	F-94A	F-94C Nov 51
318th	"	F-94A	F-94C Jan 52
319th	"	F-94A	F-94C 2d qtr 52
91st	81st	F-86A	(overseas to England)
92d	"	F-86A	(overseas to England)
116th	"	F-86A	(overseas to England)
82d	78th	F-84D	F-89C Oct 51
83d	"	F-84D	F-89B Aug 51
84th	"	F-84D/F-89B	
94th	1st	F-86A	F-86D Dec 51
93d	"	F-86A	F-86D Jan 52
188th	"	F-51D	F-86E Oct 51; F-86D 4th qtr 52
113th	122d	F-51H	F-86E Jan 51; F-89D 3d qtr 52
163d	"	F-51D	F-86A Nov 51; F-89D 3d qtr 52
166th	"	F-84C	F-89C Dec 51
(449th)	"	F-94C	
109th	133d	F-51D	F-86A Jan 52; F-89D 3d qtr 52
175th	"	F-51D	F-84C Dec 51; F-89D 3d qtr 52
179th	"	F-51D	F-86A Dec 51; F-89D 3d qtr 52
126th	128th	F-80A	F-89C Nov 51
176th	"	F-51D	F-80A Nov 51; F-89C Jan 52
61st	56th	F-94B	F-94C Jan 52
63d	"	F-86A	F-94C Nov 51
172d	"	F-51D	F-86E Jan 52; F-94C 3d qtr 52
62d	142d	F-86A	F-86D Jan 52
97th	"	F-86E	F-86D 2d qtr 52
2d	52d	F-94A	F-94C Mar 52
5th	"	F-94A	F-94C 2d qtr 52
105th	"	F-47D	F-94C 3d qtr 52
132d	101st	F-80C	F-86D 4th qtr 52
133d	"	F-47D	F-86E Feb 52; F-86D 4th qtr 52
136th	"	F-47D	F-86E 2d qtr 52; F-86D 4th qtr 52
74th	23d	F-86E	F-86D Jan 52
75th	"	F-86E	F-86D 1st qtr 53
134th	"	F-51D	F-86E Feb 52; F-86D 1st qtr 53
58th	33d	F-86A	F-94C Jan 52
59th	"	F-94B	F-94C Feb 52
60th	"	F-86A	F-86D Jan 52
118th	163d	F-47N	F-86E 2d qtr 52; F-86D 4th qtr 52
27th	"	F-86A	F-86D Feb 52
71st	"	F-86A	F-86D Feb 52
142d	113th	F-84C	F-94B Aug 51 (scheduled for Alaska)
121st	"	F-84C	F-94B Aug 51 " " "
148th	"	F-84C	F-94B Aug 51 " " "

finally, the model each was to be assigned by early 1953.[20]

Of the two new models of all-weather aircraft scheduled for assignment to the fighter-interceptor units by 1953, the F-89 and F-86D, the former is a two-place type fighter manned by a pilot and a radar observer; the latter, however, combines pilot and radar observer in one man and is a single seater.

The decision to purchase the Northrup F-89 "Scorpion" was made late in 1948.[21] This airplane is a mid-wing type powered by two jet engines in which an after-burner is incorporated for short take-off runs and swift climbs. It was originally conceived as a night fighter only and the original specifications were drawn up according to this conception. However, the change of concept from a fighter-interceptor force consisting of day, night, and inclement weather teams as separate entities to a single all-weather force demanded a revision of these original specifications. Since

---

20. ANG squadrons equipped with standard engine airplanes at the end of June 1951 were scheduled to convert to F-86Es prior to their being equipped with all-weather aircraft. The F-86E is basically the same as the F-86A. The main change is in the control surfaces in the tail section. Movement of the stick to forward and rear position will move the horizontal stabilizer to increase or decrease the angle of attack. The elevator is always streamlined with the horizontal stabilizer. Since only small change of angle of attack is necessary when actuating the stabilizers at high speeds, this will prevent large movements of the elevators into the slipstream which at present is the main cause of elevators on the F-86As shredding at high speed. The other main change is the rerouting of the fuel venting system. /See: IRS, Dir of Tng to DO, WADF, 24 Oct 1950 (DOC 103)/

21. ADC to Numbered Air Forces: "Monthly Letter, Commanding General, Air Defense Command," 10 Nov 1948. (DOC 104)

the prototype model had already been constructed and tested at the time this decision was made, production on this model had to be delayed until the engineering changes were made and tested.[22] At a conference at Edwards Air Force Base early in 1951 the decision was made to put the F-89 into service as rapidly as possible.[23] By the end of June 1951, four of these planes had been assigned the 78th Fighter-Interceptor Wing at Hamilton.

The F-86D has been a highly controversial weapon and eventual acceptance of it as an interceptor will probably depend on its proving itself after it has been in service for awhile. Many pilots with night fighter experience are of the opinion that a pilot is unable to do the job of radar search, lock-on, and tracking in addition to his normal flying of the aircraft. The persons on the other side of the argument voice the opinion that with suitable equipment to relieve the pilot of primary flying, such as a good automatic pilot, the pilot will have ample freedom to devote himself to radar observer duties. In addition, automatic tracking after lock-on, it is estimated, will allow the pilot to fly the final attack portion of his mission to successfully make the kill.

---

22. An excellent descriptive article on the F-86D, from which this brief account was taken, is that prepared by Major D. L. Rodewald, Requirements Division of the Directorate of Plans and Requirements, Hqs ADC, in the July issue of the DC&E *Digest*, pp. 20-25.

23. Report of Headquarters ADC Staff Briefing, 17 Mar 1951. (DOC 105)

The F-86D is a low wing, 35 degrees swept wing type, very similar in configuration to the F-86A Sabre Jet. It has one feature considerably different from the latter type. Its nose is a streamlined radome, 30 inches in diameter where it connects to the fuselage. Below the radome and slightly aft is a large in-take duct for the engine.

Test models of the F-86D were received starting in March 1951, and testing was scheduled to be completed on this aircraft before the end of June 1951. ADC furnished personnel to help conduct the test. While results of the test had not been published at the time the history was completed, plans were firm for assigning this aircraft to the fighter-interceptor units.[24]

V

The demand for new aircraft to replace the battle weary jets in Korea, slowness of production of all-weather aircraft, and requirements for modifying aircraft already in use in the air defense system combined to delay the reequipping of the fighter interceptor units with aircraft better suited for the air defense mission.

In 1950 it had been planned that all the squadrons in a group would trade in their old airplanes for all-weather aircraft as the latter came off the production line. As one group completed

---

24. Ibid.

its conversion another group would commence the process. Because of the slowness of production, however, and the other factors enumerated above, ADC changed this conversion concept early in 1951. Rather than attempt to equip all squadrons of a group at one time with jet all-weather aircraft, ADC elected to spread these planes through the system by equipping single squadrons in each group with them. While this action portended to complicate materiel and personnel matters, it was considered necessary in order to spread the limited all-weather capability to the maximum number of critical areas. This explains why only one squadron each of the 33d and 56th Fighter-Interceptor Wings possessed F-94Bs at the end of June 1951.[25]

The limitation on the number of all-weather aircraft of the F-94, F-89, and F-86D models which could be initially assigned per squadron also led ADC into interim by-ways of procedure. The USAF World-wide Conversion and Equipping Program released in January 1951 informed that ADC squadrons would be limited by production to twelve jet all-weather aircraft per squadron initially.

---

25. Hqs, ADC, Current Planning Activities Report, 29 Jan 1951. These are reports of a committee composed of the Directors of Plans and Requirements, Materiel Planning, Personnel Planning and Management, and Budget. The responsibilities of this committee are to "assure improved coordination in the accomplishment of ADC missions and tasks and to assure that the objectives and procedures of the major staff divisions are harmonized to facilitate accomplishments of these missions and tasks." /ADC Staff Memo 11-23, 15 May 1951/

159

Official sanction had been given in 1950 to the proposal that fighter-interceptor squadrons be equipped to 25 jet all-weather aircraft per squadron. However, this new development required a revision of plans and the initiation of a procedure which would guarantee against the squadrons being under-equipped until they could be manned to full complement with the new aircraft.

Accordingly, ADC requested that the squadrons converting to jet all-weather aircraft be permitted to retain enough old model aircraft to keep their aircraft inventory at 25. This was necessary if proficiency training of air crews and a capability against massed raids were to be sustained. At the same time it made this request, ADC recommended that every effort be taken to accelerate the production of new aircraft.[26] USAF granted the request and promised to do all within its power to speed-up the flow of jet all-weather aircraft into the air defense system.

A requirement to reequip one squadron of the 4th Fighter-Interceptor Wing in Korea with 25 F-86Es arose late in the first six months of 1951 and portended to further delay the conversion of the ANG squadrons from standard engine aircraft to jets. In June, USAF informed that all F-86Es produced by North American during July and August and the first three produced in September

---

26. ADC to Director of Operations, USAF: "Interceptor Aircraft Inventory," 21 May 1951. (DOC 106)

would be delivered to FEAF. In turn, FEAF was to release seventeen F-86As for return shipment to meet continental United States air defense requirements.[28] These returned aircraft were to be modernized and assigned to the fighter-interceptor units. This action would obviate the necessity of ADC having to relinquish its own F-86As to the factories for renovation and ameliorate somewhat the delays resulting from the loss of the F-86Es to the Korean levy. The re-routing of F-86Es originally scheduled for assignment to the fighter-interceptor force to Korea would seriously delay the conversion program discussed previously, but it was not expected that it would alter it drastically.[29]

As a result of the change in delivery schedules of F-86Es, plans for equipping squadrons with this model airplane were changed somewhat. Instead of assigning 25 F-86Es to any one squadron at one time, as originally planned, twenty were to be provided each squadron initially. After each squadron scheduled to receive them possessed this number, ADC then planned to return

---

27. TWX, ADC to Air Defense Forces, 20 Jun 1951. (DOC 107) The "wing slats" in all F-86As bearing the production number 48-254 and below did not afford the maneuverability necessary for combat operations. It was vitally essential that the newer models of the F-86, in which this condition had been corrected, be furnished those units competing with the Russian built MIG-15s for air supremacy in Korea.

28. TWX, AMC to ADC, 22 Jun 1951. (DOC 108)

29. TWX, ADC to AMC, 27 Jun 1951. (DOC 109)

to the head of the list and make distribution of the additional five.[30]

The necessity for factory modification of F-84s threatened to reduce the combat capabilities of the 78th Fighter-Interceptor Wing to zero for a six week to two month period during the latter half of 1951. It was originally planned that the 78th would turn over all its F-84Ds to the factory in July 1951 for modernization at one time.[31] ADC objected strenuously to this for the reason that it would be mid-September or October before the first modernized aircraft would be returned for duty. Had the 78th been able to plan on receiving additional F-89s its training and other commitments would not have been too seriously prejudiced by the loss of the F-84s during this long period. But it could not count on such a contingency, and, consequently, the end result would have been the reduction of the 78th's aircraft inventory far below an acceptable level during the time the F-84s were being refitted.

ADC recommended that F-84s be released for modification on the basis of either (1) one non-modified F-84 for one which had been modified, or (2) one F-84 for one F-89, this exchange to obtain until 26 F-89s were assigned.[32] USAF in response to

---

30. Hqs ADC, Current Planning Activities Report, 9 Apr 1951.

31. Ibid.

32. Hqs ADC, Current Planning Activities Report, 17 Apr 1951.

this request, directed that the 78th deliver up its F-84s to Republic according to ADC's first recommendation. A higher priority was given at this time for modernizing the 78th's F-84s than was given to TAC's 20th Wing, whose F-84s were also scheduled for modernization.

At the end of June 1951, then, F-89s were scheduled for delivery to the air defense system as rapidly as they could be produced.[33] Delivery of F-86Es, on the other hand, was to be temporarily postponed to meet FEAF requirements. The assigned number of F-86Es was to increase as a result of the modification line turning out these aircraft without ADC having to release any of its own for modernization. And factory modification of the 78th's F-84s was to proceed on a one-for-one basis.

VI

The number of aircraft assigned a unit is a relatively meaningless figure; it is the percentage of these "on-hand" aircraft that are in a flyable condition and ready for combat[34] that is the truly vital statistic.

During the first six months of its operations, ADC set the figure of 75 per cent of assigned aircraft in-commission as

---

33. Ibid., 30 Apr 1951.

34. The following is ADC's definition of combat ready aircraft: Aircraft in commission and possessing the combat equipment allocated. The equipment must be operational.

the performance goal for unit maintenance and supply staffs to shoot toward. On the whole, the in-commission rate for the command compared quite favorably with this figure during the period 1 January through 30 June 1951. The following table indicates the monthly percentage of aircraft out of commission and the reasons therefore:[35]

CAUSES	Jan	Feb	Mar	Apr	May	Jun
Number of Aircraft On-Hand	378	610	802	800	790	811
Miscellaneous	2%	1%	2%	4%	3%	2%
Tech Order Compliance	1%	2%	1%	2%	1%	1%
Lack of Parts	7%	7%	8%	7%	9%	10%
Maintenance	13%	16%	15%	15%	14%	14%
TOTAL	23%	26%	26%	28%	27%	27%

From the foregoing statistical table it will be seen that maintenance difficulties played the major role in keeping airplanes on the ground during the first six months of 1951. Assignment of new models of aircraft with the attendant necessity for training mechanics in the skills necessary for maintaining these aircraft contributed to the maintenance workload. In certain instances, because of training and deployment requirements, units were required to perform maintenance at several sites. This also increased

---

35. *ADC Command Data Books* for months of January and June 1951, prepared by the Directorate of Programs and Costs, Office of the Comptroller, Hqs ADC.

the maintenance workload. Also, the great emphasis placed on making the fullest use possible of all available aircraft to permit ADC to carry out its tremendous training program served to increase the maintenance load.

Parts shortages played a secondary role to maintenance as a cause for grounding aircraft, but the extent of these shortages reached major proportions at times. Especially severe was the shortage of parts and ground handling equipment in the newly recalled Air National Guard Squadrons.[36] In order to ready these units for combat ADC had to reequip them as well as to effect their reorganization and increase their training.

ADC, in its efforts to overcome aircraft parts shortages, closely monitored parts and equipment programs throughout the command. Increased supply discipline was stressed and every effort was made to correct supply deficiencies. Regular staff and stock control visits were made to all units. Finally, equipment was redistributed to where it would be put to the greatest use, and firm directives on stock control, aircraft grounded for lack of parts, aircraft lacking combat equipment, and other supply procedures were published.[37]

---

36. See the following for an explicit enumeration of the items that were in particular short supply: ADC to AMC: "Shortages of Supplies Affecting Operational Effectiveness of Air Defense Command," 18 Apr 1951. (DOC 110)

37. Gen. Myers to Lt. Gen. Benjamin W. Chidlaw, CG AMC, 18 May 1951. See also: ADC to AMC, "High AOCP Rate at Larson AFB," 21 Jun 1951. (DOC 111)

The increased utilization of F-47s and F-51s plus the loss of maintenance personnel imposed a serious maintenance burden on the ANG units equipped with these aircraft. Additionally, parts for these airplanes were extremely difficult to obtain. The out of commission rate for F-47s and F-51s was on the increase at the end of June 1951 and there was every indication that an increasing number of these aircraft would be grounded during the ensuing months. While these standard engine type aircraft would be of no value as interceptors during a night attack, and of dubious value even as day interceptors, it was very necessary that they be kept in flyable shape until they could be replaced with more modern aircraft, if only to permit crews to maintain their flying proficiency.[38]

A serious maintenance problem during the first half of 1951 in the 52d Fighter-Interceptor Wing reduced ADC's already feeble all-weather potential. In January, the F-94As of that unit were knocked out of commission, except for active air defense emergencies and local visual flying, because of malfunctioning float valves in the fuel system.[39] As a consequence, these planes had to be reported as non-combat ready to be used only in the event

---

38. AMC informed ADC in January 1951 that there were no replacements available for the F-51s, F-80s, and F-84s and that parts to be obtained through reclamation and salvage of storaged aircraft for F-51s and F-47s would be available for only a maximum period of eighteen months. /Interview, Historian with R. W. Dalton, Office of Aircraft Distribution, Hqs ADC/

39. TWX, 52d FW to AMC, 6 Mar 1951. (DOC 112)

of a red or yellow alert.[40] This condition lasted into March, at
which time a complete replacement of the valves then in use was
made. This action did not "fix" the condition, however, and
trouble with fuel lines and fuel pumps continued to restrict the
usability of these aircraft. After much investigation, at the
expense of an extremely low in-commission rate, it was deduced
that the fuel in use was contaminated.[41] Consequently, in May,
use of contaminated JP-3 fuel was discontinued in favor of 100/
130 fuel. The consensus at the end of June was that all the F-94As
of the 52d would have to have their engines replaced as well as
all other parts, fuel lines, tanks, etc., which had come into contact with the contaminated fuel.

The squadrons of the 56th and 33d Fighter-Interceptor
Wings which converted to F-94Bs were also plagued by their share
of maintenance troubles. Lack of sufficient test equipment slowed
down maintenance on these airplanes. Further, after a pilot of
the 33d Wing was killed when a released tip tank smashed back
into the tail assembly of his F-94B, all F-94Bs were restricted
from further flight with tip tanks.[42] This action increased the

---

40. TWX, EADF to ADC, 20 Mar 1951. (DOC 113) There
are three types of alert: (1) RED - attack imminent; (2) YELLOW
--hostile aircraft approaching; and (3) WHITE -- all clear. See
Chapter Thirteen, Air Raid Warning Systems.

41. IRS, Dir. of Maint. to DM, Hqs ADC, 7 May 1951.
(DOC 114)

42. TWX, AMC to All Major Commands, 17 May 1951. (DOC 115)

number of flights required to conduct training and operations.

According to a 33d Fighter-Interceptor Wing Historian, continued maintenance difficulties could be expected on the F-94B.[43] The shortage of engines for this model airplane, as well as for all the new jet all-weather types, which obtained at the end of June was expected to further cripple the efforts of the mechanics to keep these planes in action.[44]

The in-commission rate of the T-33 training aircraft was at a low ebb at the beginning of 1951. Shortage of parts and the failure of commanders to place proper emphasis on the maintenance of T-33s were the major causes behind this problem. In March, General Whitehead personally directed that action be taken to increase the utilization of each T-33 from 30 hours to 60 hours per month and that greater attention be given to keeping these aircraft operational. The result of this action was a reduction in the out-of-commission rate for these airplanes from 46 per cent in January to 39 per cent at the end of June. At no time, however, was the 60 hour utilization rate achieved. Since none of the ANG

---

43. History of the 33d F-I Gp, January - March 1951, p. 4.

44. The shortage of engines for F-94s restricted their utilization throughout the first six months of 1951 as well as increased maintenance on this model airplane. /See: Command Data Books for January and June 1951/ This shortage resulted from AMC's inability to supply the necessary reserve five J-33-35 jet engines per squadron per month for the F-94s. /History of the Aircraft Supply Division, Hqs ADC, January 1951/

squadrons possessed these aircraft the rate of transfer of the training airplanes from one squadron to the other remained high during the first six months of 1951. This was a factor which contributed to the continued low utility rate of the T-33s.[45] The shortage of parts problem also remained critical throughout the period for this particular model of aircraft.[46]

In June 1951, ADC had 47 T-33s. Scheduled transfers of these aircraft from the command to support Air Training Command programs threatened to leave ADC with only 26 in the ensuing months. At the end of June USAF was reviewing T-33 requirements among the several major commands in an effort to permit ADC to retain at least 32 of them. It was hoped that eventually each fighter-interceptor squadron would be assigned one T-33.[47]

VII

During the first half of 1951, as in the past, programs were continually underway to incorporate, either in production or through retrofit, improvements to increase the combat capability

---

45. Hqs ADC, Command Data Book, March 1951.

46. Ibid., April 1951.

47. Current Planning Activities Report, Hqs ADC, 27 Jun 1951. ADC was scheduled to transfer approximately 25 T-33s, 41 F-84Bs, 23 F-86As in the latter part of 1951 and early 1952 to the Training Command to augment the fighter Combat Crew Training School to be established in the last half of 1951. Additional requirements to support that school with aircraft from production was an additional factor which threatened to retard the equipping schedule of the fighter-interceptor units

of the fighter-interceptors.

A prime defect in the F-94, the only aircraft which could possibly be developed into an all-weather fighter among those assigned the Air Defense Command in June 1951, was its lack of de-icing equipment as well as other safety features to protect the aircraft from the ravages of ice, snow and cold. The F-94As were not designed to be all-weather fighters, as was told previously, and, consequently, anti-icing and de-icing equipment was omitted on them. Future all-weather fighters were to be provided with this equipment at the factories, but so long as the Air Defense Command had to rely on the F-94A as its basic night fighter and possibly as an all-weather fighter it was vitally interested in seeing it refitted with anti-icing and de-icing equipment. AMC informed in February 1950 that it planned to equip at least a few of ADC's F-94s with this equipment before the winter of 1951.[48] But by February of the latter year this action had not been taken. At that time ADC reiterated its anxiety on this subject by recommending to AMC that, "action be initiated immediately on a research program through which a satisfactory winterization and climatizing project can be made possible for these aircraft."

---

48. TWX, AMC to USAF, 20 Dec 1950. (DOC 116)

49. ADC to AMC: "F-94A General Icing Conditions," 27 Feb 1951. (DOC 117)

Whether or not future models of the F-94 will have an all-weather capability depends upon the ability of the engineers to outfit them with de-icing equipment. The following report from AMC reveals the work that was being done on this project:[50]

> The F-94C series aircraft have been designed as all-weather aircraft provided that adequate de-icing equipment can be designed for the wings and empennage surfaces. Pneumatic boots or a thermally heated wing have been found inadequate and electrically heated blankets are currently under investigation by the airplane contractor. In the event that adequate anti-icing equipment is developed it will be provided for F-94C series aircraft to provide adequate protection for all-weather flying.

The equipping of fighter-interceptors with adequate identification and radar assist electronic equipment has been another problem which has long perturbed those in charge of establishing an air defense system. In May 1950 General Whitehead reiterated the problem as follows to General Chidlaw of AMC:[51]

> I have a serious operational problem on my hands in relation to IFF /Identification Friend or Foe/ and Radar Assist Beacons in the Air Defense System. . . . Our present radars do not "see" jet fighters very well at any distance so we cannot control fighters to interceptions or navigate them above an overcast. If we had the AN/APX-6 IFF Transpondor in operation, most of these difficulties would be overcome.

It was General Whitehead's request at this time that, "no stone . . . remain unturned in an effort to start retrofitting AN/APX-6s immediately and to speed up production of the necessary ground

---

50. 2nd Ind, Hq AMC to CO Larson AFB, 8 Nov 1950, to Larson AFB to AMC: "01-L F-94A Aircraft," 29 Aug 1950. (DOC 118) See also: 1st Ind, USAF to ADC, 12 Feb 1951 to Ltr ADC to USAF, "Supervision of Pilot Proficiency Training," 4 Jan 1951. (DOC 119)

51. Gen. Whitehead to Gen. Chidlaw, 9 May 1950. (DOC 120)

equipment."[52]

USAF as well as ConAC, and later ADC, was well aware of the necessity for this identification and radar assist equipment in the fighter-interceptors. In January 1950 that headquarters had stated:[53]

> It has been noted . . . that the operational effectiveness of jet fighter groups, both in operational readiness tests and in maneuvers, is adversely affected by the lack of a suitable airborne beacon.

USAF had then explained what the basic action was to be in providing this equipment:[54]

> In accordance with the JCS policy on IFF, the Armed Forces are committed to the Mark X System of beacon and interrogator; this system to be operational by 1 July 1952. The primary function of this system to provide beacon assist in the tracking and control of high speed aircraft. Currently /as of January 1950/ the Air Force is committed to the implementation of this program, and the procurement of beacons has been adjusted accordingly.

In reply to this pronouncement, ConAC informed that a test of the operational suitability of identification and radar assist equipment available in early 1950, of which the AN/APX-6 was one, had revealed that neither the AN/APX-6 nor the other types were truly adequate. At that time, ConAC had advised that "steps be taken at once to perfect and produce a beacon which

---

52. Ibid.

53. USAF to ConAC: "USAF Procurement Plan for IFF Beacons," 24 Jan 1950. (DOC 121)

54. Ibid.

adequately fulfills the radar assistance function necessary for fighter aircraft."[55] At the same time, ConAC had pointed up the primary difficulty which, in its opinion, was going to inhibit USAF's good intentions to supply the air defense system with adequate identification and radar assist equipment:[56]

> Since the Mark X Beaconry and IFF System will not be available as a complete facility until ground interrogator-responser units are available for ground radars, request every effort be made to obtain the delivery of ground components, test equipment and spare parts of the Mark X system concurrently with the 1950 airborne retrofit program. Without this ground equipment the APX-6s in the aircraft are useless.

ConAC then stated that while the Mark X system was deficient in many respects, there was a firm requirement that it be placed into use until a more satisfactory system had been designed and produced.

Agreed that Mark X IFF was the system toward which the air defense system was to work, ConAC and USAF set about putting it into operation. ConAC, however, at the same time, established the policy that Mark III IFF would be made operational in all combat aircraft having that system installed during the period of transition to Mark X IFF. All combat aircraft within ConAC in July 1950, with the exception of the F-80s and F-84s, were equipped with SCR 695 Mark III IFF components and could be made

---

55. Ibid., 1st Ind, ConAC to USAF, 2 Mar 1950.
56. Ibid. /underlining added/

operational by organizational and field level maintenance within Wing-Base organizations. Through the installation of AN-95C antennas, all of the F-80s and approximately 50 per cent of the F-84s could be equipped for Mark III operations. It was planned to outfit the remaining F-84s for this work by retrofitting.[57]

After the outbreak of the Korean War the seriousness of the lack of this equipment was summarized by General Whitehead:[58]

> At the present time, without airborne beacons and ground interrogators, it is not possible for GCI controllers to properly control and vector jet type interceptor aircraft. Although this deficiency has been recognized and procurement action initiated, the schedules as presented by the Director of Requirements, Headquarters, United States Air Force, indicate 1 July 1952 as completion date and are therefore unacceptable. The current world-wide situation makes imperative immediate and strenuous efforts to accelerate delivery of this essential equipment. . . . To summarize, the provision of effective beaconry through immediate retrofit of interceptor aircraft and immediate procurement of minimum essential ground interrogators with minimum associated equipment is a matter of the utmost urgency. <u>This problem, although related to the IFF requirement, is of more immediate importance.</u>

Consequently, the Mark III IFF System, even in an interim capacity, would not do, would not provide the beacon assistance absolutely necessary to permit ground radar to control the flight of the interceptors. In view of the need for an effective air

---

57. IRS, Comm to DM, O&T, DAD, DO, Hqs ConAC, "Field Conditions Existing With Regard to Airborne Components of the Mark III IFF Systems," 13 Jul 1950. (DOC 122)

58. Gen. Whitehead to Gen. Vandenberg: "Radar Equipment for Air Defense," 17 Jul 1950. (DOC 123) /underlining added/

defense system at that time, it was mandatory that corrective action be taken, not by 1952 but a year earlier.

Retrofit of the fighter-interceptors with Mark X IFF transpondor APX-6 commenced 10 September 1950 with the F-86s of the 81st Fighter-Interceptor Wing at Larson AFB in Washington.[59] It was planned that all the F-86s would be refitted with this piece of equipment first, followed by the F-84s. The F-94s were being delivered from the factory with this item already installed. A deadline date of 31 December 1950 was set by AMC for the complete retrofit of the fighter-interceptor aircraft in the air defense system. At the same time, steps were taken to attempt equipping the Lashup III radar sites with Mark X ground IFF equipment by the same date.[60]

AMC was unable to meet the above deadline, but by April 1951 approximately 80 percent of the fighter-interceptors in the air defense system were equipped with APX-6 Mark X IFF. At that time, ten per cent of the aircraft were still equipped with SCR-695 Mark III IFF. The remaining ten per cent were not equipped with any type of beacon assist, identification equipment. The ANG squadrons recently activated were not included in that estimation. The recommendation was made at that time by ADC that,

---

59. ConAC to AMC: "Supply and Maintenance of AN/APX-6," 18 Sep 1950. (DOC 124)

60. IRS, Comm to O&T, "Mark X IFF and SII System," 7 Oct 1950. (DOC 125)

since the Mark X IFF System would reasonably assure provisions for adequate beaconry coverage by the latter part of 1951, the Mark III IFF System be discontinued completely.[61] In May, it was resolved that the Mark III IFF be taken out of commission effective 1 July 1951 and that all equipment of this type which could not be converted over to Mark X IFF be dismantled.[62]

VIII

Thus, the end of June 1951 found the Air Defense Command still in search of additional fighter-interceptor aircraft, especially those equipped for all-weather operations. While firm plans had been drawn up as to where the new model aircraft would be emplaced once procured, these plans appeared destined for revision at the close of the period. The demands of the Korean War especially and the inability of production to keep pace with requirements threatened to push back the 1953 date the air defense system had hoped to keep for fully outfitting its fighter-interceptor units.

In the design of aircraft eventually scheduled for assignment to the air defense system the Air Defense Command was advocating an increase in armament and in combat radius or endurance. The latter changes would be especially necessary once the air

---

61. IRS, C&E to VC, "Staff Study," 10 Apr 1951. (DOC 126)

62. ADC to Air Defense Forces; "Mark III IFF, System Policy," 22 May 1951. (DOC 127)

defense ground system was extended in depth by the addition of ground radar, picket ships, and airborne early warning.[63] Higher headquarters affirmed that it was taking these suggested improvements into consideration and that it intended to translate into actuality as many as possible of ADC's aircraft requirements so long as these changes did not interfere with or slow down production schedules.[64]

In the meantime, the Air Defense Command was struggling along with what it had -- a few night fighters, a pretty capable day fighter-interceptor force, and a bevy of obsolescent airplanes good only for enabling pilots to keep their hands in at their trade. All in all, the fighter-interceptor picture was a bleak one at the close of June 1951. It was a better scene than ever before in the history of post-war air defense, but it was still an inadequate one for purposes of defending the nation if matters came to a showdown.

---

63. ADC to USAF: "Requirement to Increase Combat Capability of Interceptors," 17 Jul 1951. (DOC 128)

64. *Ibid.*, 1st Ind, USAF to ADC, 31 Jul 1951.

CHAPTER EIGHT

FIGHTER CREWS AND THEIR TRAINING

I

The Air Defense Command, we have seen, planned to equip each of the 45 fighter-interceptor squadrons it was scheduled to possess in early 1953 with 25 jet all-weather aircraft. Concomitant with these plans, provisions had to be made to insure that enough trained crews would be available by that date to operate these aircraft on a 24-hour combat basis. It was estimated that 1,200 pilots and an equal number of radar observers to man the F-94s and F-89s, and 1,050 pilots to operate the F-86Ds would be needed to support the 1953 fighter-interceptor program.[1] These figures were based on the assignment of two crews to each aircraft.

---

1. Gen. Fairchild, early in 1950, requested Gen. Whitehead to estimate the number of combat crews per assigned aircraft ConAC would require to operate 25 aircraft per squadron on a 24-hour combat basis. ConAC studies of this matter, prepared at Gen. Whitehead's direction, stated that to provide air defense, train, and at the same time not overwork crews to the point where their morale would be threatened, 2.8 crews per aircraft would be the minimum figure required. In December 1950, USAF scaled this figure down to 2 crews per aircraft. See the following documents: Memo, Gen. Whitehead to Gen. Thatcher, DO, Hqs ConAC: "Number of Combat Crews Required in Fighter Squadrons for Air Defense Mission," 17 Feb 1950 (DOC 129); IRS, DO to O&T, 10 Feb 1950, and attachments (DOC 130); and USAF to ConAC: "Air Defense Combat Crew Requirements," 2 Dec 1950. (DOC 131)

If the number of jet all-weather crews was to be increased from the less than one hundred assigned ADC in June 1951 to the figures given above, ADC was going to require all the procuring and training assistance USAF and the Air Training Command (ATRC) could give in the forthcoming year and one-half. The ideal arrangement for ADC would be for crews to be fully trained in the rudiments of jet all-weather operations and radar observer skills by ATRC prior to their assignment to fighter-interceptor units. In the past, the major Air Force commands invested with the air defense mission conducted the majority of this training within their own households. But the mounting complexity of crew training and the growing necessity for maintaining an active air defense required that action be taken to relieve ADC of some of its training burdens. General Whitehead expressed ADC's sentiment on this subject as follows:[2]

> In these days of complex high speed jet aircraft, the attaining of /combat crew proficiency/ is a specialized task. Aircraft must be operated with the precision of a guided missile under weather conditions beyond the capability of the average pilot. Furthermore, attacks must be pressed home with skill and determination under all circumstances. This requires specialized instruction with proper facilities. It cannot be done on a shoe-string or as an overload on resources provided to do my primary mission.

---

2. ADC to C/S USAF: "Specialized Training for Air Defense Combat Crews," 16 Apr 1951 (DOC 132). This letter was dispatched when it looked as if the ATRC all-weather crew training school would be struck from the fiscal 1952 funding program. See also: TWX, USAF to ADC, 7 Apr 1951 (DOC 133); TWX, USAF to ADC, 11 Apr 1951. (DOC 134)

The urgencies of the air defense mission require me to provide a defense of the United States right now. This presupposes an air defense system in being and combat crews in readiness 24 hours a day. Untrained crews cannot do this job. 20% of my night fighters and 10% of my all-weather fighters are now committed to this readiness condition. This figure will be increased as my all-weather resources are increased.

II

Actual plans for procuring and training the jet all-weather pilots who would be needed to support the fighter-interceptor program when it came of age in 1953 commenced at least as far back as early 1950. At that time, ConAC convinced USAF of the need for an ATRC Combat Crew Training School (CCTS) as a postgraduate course for pilots emerging from Advanced Single Engine School. As planned, this school would consist of (1) a day jet interceptor course to provide jet transition, gunnery, instrument and GCI training, and (2) a jet all-weather course to provide transition training into F-94s/F-89s, more extensive instrument training, scope work, and training in the use of airborne intercept radar.

The outbreak of the Korean war caused the abandonment of this plan and the postponement, until January 1951, of any ATRC training facilities for all-weather pilots.[3] In the latter month, an All-weather Fighter Interceptor School for training F-94/F-89

---

3. 3d Ind, ConAC to WADF, 31 Dec 1950, to 78th F-I Gp to ConAC: "Reduction of Service Requirements for School Eligibility," 24 Oct 1950. (DOC 135)

pilots was established at Tyndall Air Force Base and ADC was given a quota to this school of five per class.[4]

In March 1951, ADC recommended that the pilot output of the All-weather School be increased. One way of doing this would be for ATRC to transition newly recalled ANG pilots in jet aircraft and then assign them directly to the All-weather School. This would kill two birds with one stone: It would assist in preparing the former ANG units for receipt of jet aircraft and would increase the total number of jet all-weather pilots assigned to ADC. USAF concurred in this proposal and established 6 August 1951 as the date when this accelerated program would go into effect. On that date, a two-week (20 hours) course for transition of conventional pilots into jet aircraft would commence at Tyndall. ADC would be given a quota of four pilots per week to this course. Upon graduation from the transition course, these pilots would go directly into the All-weather Fighter-Interceptor School.[5] Commencing on 1 October, a quota of five pilots from other major Air Force commands for attendance at the All-weather School would be established. This number, plus the four ADC sent to the jet transition course, plus the jet pilots ADC sent to the All-weather

---

4. Hqs Flying Training Air Force, Course Outline - <u>All Weather Jet Aircrew Training (Interceptor)</u>, 11 Jul 1951.

5. ADC to USAF: "Quotas for Transitioning Fighter Pilots to Jet Type Aircraft," 12 Apr 1951 and 1st Ind, USAF to ADC, 17 May 1951. (DOC 136)

School would result, by 1 July 1952, in a gain of about 500 jet all-weather pilots and an overall strength increase of 160 pilots. Beginning 1 July 1952, students for this school would come from the Advanced Engine School.[6]

A plan existed, at the end of June 1951, for the establishment of an ATRC F-89 interceptor training course in December of that year. By April 1952, this course was scheduled to reach a yearly maximum production rate of approximately 400 pilots. This accelerated program was to continue until the air defense requirements for F-89 pilots had been met. At the same time, it was planned to open an F-86D crew training school within the ATRC in January 1952. By ADC's calculations, fifteen pilots per week would have to emerge from this school commencing in January 1952, if F-86D pilot requirements were to be met by 1953.[7]

The F-94/F-89 interceptor training program conducted within the ATRC, then, was designed to give maximum assistance to ADC in converting jet and conventional fighter pilots to jet all-weather aircraft. Additionally, sufficient numbers of pilots had to be graduated from this school to provide instructors for the F-89 and F-86D training schools to be opened in late 1951 and early 1952. Once ADC's jet and conventional type aircraft crews had been trained for all-weather aircraft operations, the principal

---

6. Hqs ADC, Current Planning Activities Report, 4 Jun 1951.
7. Ibid.

source of students for these schools was to be the Advanced Single Engine School.

Radar observers as well as pilots, of course, had to be procured and trained if the requirements of the 1953 fighter-interceptor program were to be met. The decision had been made in 1950 that pilots would not be trained as radar observers. In September of that year, ConAC recommended that upon the establishment of the ATRC all-weather school the Radar Observer School be discontinued and training of radar observers be made a part of the all-weather school. That ConAC's thinking on the subject was clearly along the lines of training pilots as radar observers is exemplified by the following recommendation:[8]

> . . . the course of the All-weather School /should/ be sufficiently comprehensive in all its phases so that graduates are capable of flying instruments under minimum weather conditions, day or night; that they are completely familiar with GCI control in all its aspects; that they are capable of performing all required duties of an O520; that they be qualified in aerial gunnery, visually and after "locking on" with existing radar fire control equipment.

In other words, ConAC was of the opinion that all fighter pilots should be prepared not only for performing radar observer duties in F-94s and F-89s but also for flying F-86Ds, or similar type aircraft where the pilot performs both pilot and radar observer duties.[9]

---

8. ConAC to USAF: "Fighter Pilots Career Program," 9 Sep 1950. (DOC 137)

9. Interview, the Historian with Captain R. Dingledein, Office of Personnel Plans and Management, Hqs ADC, 30 Oct 1951.

USAF, however, was not in favor of combining the two occupations at that time. Production of one-seater type all-weather aircraft of the F-86D type was not in effect and pilot shortages and training considerations dictated the inadvisability of attempting to train pilots as radar observers.[10] Consequently, the majority of the students for radar observer training, ADC knew at the time of its reactivation, were going to have to come from sources outside the command.

In January 1951, ADC's quota for furnishing students to the Radar Observer School at Keesler Air Force Base was six per class. In February, USAF informed that commencing in April of that year enrollment to the radar observer course would be increased to fifteen per class, the increased quota to be supported from ADC resources.[11]

While ADC agreed that the "proposal . . . to increase

---

10. USAF to ConAC: "Air Defense Combat Crew Requirements," 2 Dec 1950 (DOC 131). The historian of the 52d Fighter Group reported that pilots serving as radar observers in that unit were not pleased with that assignment. The 52d transitioned six radar-observer/ pilot-observers in the F-94 during the first quarter of 1951. However, that unit would have preferred to qualify them simply as all-weather pilots for the following reasons: (1) Pilots were not content to act as radar observers, resulting in lowered morale; (2) there was a group shortage of pilots; and (3) it was difficult for radar /observer/ pilots to maintain their 60-2 requirements in base aircraft and also remain proficient in their radar observer duties. 52d Fighter Group History, 1 Jan - 31 Mar 1951.

11. USAF to ADC: "Training of Radar Observers, All-Weather Fighter," 16 Feb 1951. (DOC 138)

enrollment to fifteen per class /was/ a definite requirement and should be continued on a permanent basis at least until March 1953," it also noted:[12]

> . . . if the required expansion of the Air Defense System /was/ to meet with any measure of success, it /was/ essential that a pipeline source of Radar Observer Students be established immediately, since internal sources of eligible officers for this course /were/ rapidly being depleted.

To effect an increase in radar observer students from sources other than its own units, ADC recommended that ROTC graduates who volunteered for such training be called to active duty. ADC also favored the establishment of an aviation cadet program similar to the pilot, navigator programs for the procuring and training of radar observers.[13]

USAF's thinking on this score was similar to ADC's. In April 1951, higher headquarters notified that it planned to recruit non-rated officers throughout the Air Force for radar observer training. Student officers eliminated from pilot training were to be eligible for radar observer schooling under this category. Additionally, USAF was favorably disposed toward the idea of ordering to active duty those ROTC officers who volunteered for this training. Finally, USAF planned to initiate a cadet program for radar observers. Persons selected for this training would be processed through Officer's Candidate School to guarantee their qualification

---

12. Ibid., 1st Ind, ADC to USAF, 1 Mar. 1951. (DOC 138)
13. Ibid.

for a commission. To make the program as attractive as possible, it was planned to award an aeronautical rating and permanent flying status to officers successfully completing the radar observer school.[14]

III

Statistical charts for the first six months of 1951 revealed a considerable amount of growth in the number of fighter-interceptor crews assigned ADC. In January there was a total of 380 crews assigned the command; at the end of June this figure had more than doubled, totaling 823. This large increase was due to the same reason as that for the numerical growth in units and aircraft during the same period - the federalization of the ANG squadrons. Consequently, crew increases were primarily in the F-47, F-51, F-80, and F-84 categories. Crew increases in the F-86 and F-94 classes, however, were very slight.

Of the crews assigned in January, approximately 80 per cent were combat ready. About 75 per cent of them were combat ready in June. This high figure, both at the commencement and at the end of the six month period, spoke well for the degree of training of the ANG squadrons at the time of their recall to active duty. At the same time, however, the low status of the combat potential of the air defense fighter-interceptor system throughout the period is revealed in the combat ready statistics. It will

---

14. Hqs ADC, Current Planning Activities Report, 30 Apr 1951.

be noted on the chart which follows that the lowest status of combat readiness was in the F-86 and F-94 squadrons.

Thus, in spite of the high combat readiness average reflected in the statistical summaries, the fighter-interceptor crew situation within ADC during the first six months of 1951 actually remained at an extremely low level. Levies on pilots for combat replacements in Korea, for instructors in the ATRC all-weather school, and for other permanent change of station requirements, struck where they hurt the most, at the units' experienced and combat trained all-weather or jet day interceptor pilots. A continuing high "absentee" rate of pilots temporarily assigned to schools, gunnery training, on leave, for reasons of illness, etc., contributed its share to the dangerously low combat capability which obtained in the jet fighter units, both day and night, during the first six months of 1951. These losses of experienced pilots, both permanently and temporarily, not only affected ADC's ability to maintain an active air defense, but also seriously reduced its capacity to provide instruction to the newly recalled reserve pilots, the newly graduated pilots from basic flying school, and the newly federalized ANG pilots who formed the majority of the replacements for the out-going experienced pilots.

The loss of experienced pilots since the outbreak of the Korean war was an extremely serious matter to air defense leaders,

SECURITY INFORMATION

COMBAT CREWS IN AIR DEFENSE COMMAND*
1 January - 30 June 1

Type	Jan O/H	Jan C/R	Feb O/H	Feb C/R	Mar O/H	Mar C/R	Apr O/H	Apr C/R	May O/H	May C/R	Jun O/H	Jun C/R
Conventional Fighters:												
F-47	0	0	42	34	67	63	89	55	99	77	79	69
F-51	0	0	189	139	277	173	272	218	267	217	231	195
F-82	24	18	21	18	15	15	9	9	2	2	4	4
Jet Day Fighters:												
F-80	0	0	13	0	43	14	44	28	43	19	40	35
F-84	55	44	136	89	119	87	141	90	151	109	127	95
F-86	278	219	257	213	240	198	216	154	301	177	290	174
Jet A/W Fighters:												
F-86D	0	0	0	0	0	0	0	0	0	0	0	0
F-89	0	0	0	0	0	0	0	0	0	0	0	0
F-94	23	18	28	18	38	31	28	24	45	40	52	40

O/H - - Combat Crews On Hand
C/R - - Crews Combat Ready

*Source: ADC Command Data Book, June 1951 (compiled from Daily Combat Readiness Reports: ADC-DO-C1)

**ADC's interpretation of a Combat Ready Crew:
    PILOT: A pilot possessing either SSN 1058 or 1059 may be reported as combat ready when he has accomplished the prescribed unit transition program in UE aircraft, or a pilot not possessing SSN 1058 or 1059 may be reported as combat ready when: (1) he has flown 50 hours in UE aircraft; (2) he has completed a total of 12 aerial gunnery missions, of which two will be above 20,000 feet, and has achieved a minimum of 10% hits on one or more missions; (3) he has flown three hours of night time in UE aircraft; (4) he has led three successful GCI missions; (5) he possesses a current instrument card, and has demonstrated the capability to fly instruments in UE aircraft.
    AIRCREW: An aircrew assigned to a fighter-all weather unit may be reported as combat ready when: the pilot satisfies the minimum prescribed above, has accomplished five hours of airborne intercept training and the radar observer, in the opinion of the unit commander, is capable of performing his combat mission.

as the following report from WADF in October 1950, indicates:[15]

> . . . during the last three months more qualified personnel have been transferred out of the units than have been trained within them. The recent assignment of recallees has not provided an appreciable increase of our capability due to the considerable amount of refresher and qualification training needed by each pilot. There is no apparent trend towards a greater degree of stabilization in evidence; in fact, the opposite is true. Overseas requirements and school quotas of the past have made a very unequal experience level distribution in the fighter squadrons.

For ConAC Headquarters, in late 1950, "the loss of qualified personnel . . . experienced by all tactical units of Continental Air Command /had/ been a matter of concern . . . for some time."[16]

The loss of pilots temporarily to schools and other such duty, also, was not a new experience for those who had been associated with the air defense system for any period of time. The following summary indicates the past status of this problem at the time of ADC's reactivation:[17]

> For the 7 month period ending 31 January 1951, approximately 29 per cent of the total pilot assigned strength was not available for duty or training in their parent unit. Out of an average monthly pilot strength of 625 assigned pilots . . . only 449 pilots were on hand to their parent unit at any one time. Since unit training requirements were based on assigned pilot strength, each group had to consistently over-fly all available pilots to meet the total flying hour program each month.

---

15. WADF to ConAC: "Operational Effectiveness of WADF Units," 10 Oct 1950. (DOC 139)

16. Ibid., 1st Ind, ConAC to WADF, 25 Oct 1950. (DOC 139)

17. Hqs ADC, Command Data Book, January 1951.

The discontinuance of the policy of training pilots as radar observers would serve to reduce the drain of experienced pilots from the fighter-interceptor units. Another such action, the intent of which was to reduce the number of experienced pilots lost to the units for reasons of schooling, was the reduction of pilot quotas to the controllers school, during the first six months of 1951, from 30 to 10 per class.[18] An additional effort taken by ADC to ameliorate the effect of experienced pilot losses in the units was a request to higher headquarters that the policy (AFR 36-25) whereby pilots newly graduated from flying school could not be selected for schooling for a year's period be removed in those evident instances where such schooling would definitely contribute to the career advancement of these individuals. This requirement, while it had permitted new pilots to engage in uninterrupted unit training for that period, had forced commanders to fill all quotas with their more experienced personnel.[19] USAF granted this latter request, stating:[20]

> Authority is granted to send any second lieutenant to schools which will directly contribute to the development of his pilotage qualifications. Provided the school assignment involves a permanent change of station, concurrence of this headquarters will be obtained before movement of a regular officer whose permanent grade is second lieutenant /is made/.

---

18. 1st Ind, ConAC to WADF, 25 Oct 1950. (DOC 139)

19. ADC to USAF: "Utilization of Graduates of Advanced Pilot Schools," 16 Apr 1951. (DOC 140)

20. Ibid., 1st Ind, USAF to ADC, 4 May 1951. (DOC 140)

Late in 1950 the requirement had been lifted that pilot graduates of the controller's school had to spend a year with an aircraft control and warning unit after graduation. The importance of this decision to the ability of the fighter-interceptor units to retain their experienced pilots is best revealed by a brief history of this particular program.

The program of cross-training pilots as controllers was initiated in early 1950, at ConAC's request. The intent of the program was to familiarize potential fighter-interceptor group and wing commanders with controller operations. In implementing this program, fighter wing commanders had been instructed to fill Controller School quotas with only their most highly qualified pilots. After completion of the controller course, these pilots were to serve a year with a ground radar unit. At the very outset of the program, difficulty was experienced because of the serious shortage of qualified fighter pilots. Commanders felt that the loss of these pilots for the period of time required for the school would not materially affect their operational readiness; however, their loss for a period of one year following graduation threatened the ability of these pilots to retain their flying proficiency. Because of the latter effect of this program, unit commanders were opposed to it.[21]

---

21. Hqs ADC, Current Planning Activities Report, 14 Feb 1951. For further information on this subject see: ConAC to WADF: "Pilots in the AC&W System," 10 Nov 1950 (DOC 141); and WADF to ConAC: "Controller Experience for Fighter Pilots," 13 Dec 1950. (DOC 142)

Accordingly, in order that the plan could be carried out to a limited extent, the authority to waive the provisions of AFR 35-570, thereby permitting the return of fighter pilots trained as controllers (SSN 1014) to their parent fighter organizations prior to the completion of their one year tour as controllers, was requested and obtained from higher headquarters. This authority was then delegated to the air defense force commanders.[22]

Aside from pressing for release from certain school and reassignment quotas, as discussed above, however, ADC was not able to do much to reduce the losses of combat trained jet pilots. All in all, the probability of ADC's being able to resolve this problem in the near future was slight at the close of June 1951. Headquarters ADC's planning committee expressed its feelings on this subject as follows:[23]

> The constant drain of experienced pilots out of this command is aggravating an already serious shortage of trained pilots. It appears that the situation will become worse during the next six to eight months until relief is obtained by crew production of the Air Training Command.

IV

Crew proficiency training in the Regular Air Force fighter-interceptor units during the first six months of 1951 was conducted under training directives and standards prepared by ConAC in 1950.

---

22. Hqs ADC, *Current Planning Activities Report*, 14 Feb 1951.
23. Hqs ADC, *Current Planning Activities Report*, 16 Jul 1951.

ConAC Training Directive 10-9 established the minimum training requirements for all-weather crews. The F-86 pilots trained in consonance with the provisions of ConAC Training Standard 10-10. In June and early July 1951, these directives were rewritten and published under the imprimatur of Headquarters ADC.[24]

The federalized ANG squadrons, immediately upon their assignment to ADC, were placed on an extensive 60 to 90 day training schedule, dependent upon their degree of training at the time of their recall to active duty. Later this period was extended to 120 days. Training of the ANG squadrons during this period was conducted in accordance with ADC Training Program Number 1, published expressly for the purpose of bringing ANG pilots and ground personnel up to date on overall Air Force policies as well as on air defense operational standards.[25]

The major problems affecting training during the first six months of 1951 were, as was told previously, (1) the loss of experienced pilots to Korea and their replacement with inexperienced

---

24. See the following: (1) ADC Unit Proficiency Directive 10-1, "Fighter Interceptor Unit (AI Equipped)," 11 June 1951 (DOC 143); (2) ADC Unit Proficiency Directive 10-2, "Fighter Interceptor Unit (Non AI Equipped)," 11 June 1951 (DOC 144); and (3) ADC Training Standards, 10-1 thru 10-7, 2 July 1951 (DOC 145). These documents indicate the training and proficiency required of ADC pilots in the several types of fighter aircraft assigned the air defense system. Statistics contained in the ADC Command Data Book for June 1951 reveal the extent and degree of accomplishment of flying training during the first six months of 1951 by unit.

25. ADC Training Program No. 1, "Fighter Interceptor Unit (Accelerated)," Jan 1951. (DOC 146)

pilots who required extensive training before they could be qualified as fighter-interceptor pilots, (2) the conversion of units from conventional aircraft to jet day and night fighters, and (3) the shortage of T-33 aircraft. Other major factors which served to retard training programs were: lack of adequate training facilities and equipment; adverse weather during the early months of the year; and flying hour restrictions (because of engine shortages) on the F-94s.[26]

An outstanding training problem not previously discussed was the continued shortage of adequate gunnery facilities which obtained during the first six months of 1951. The requirement for additional ranges, an old problem, persisted, as did the need for improved tow targets and tow aircraft.[27]

The reassignment of air-to-ground gunnery to fighter-interceptor units in late 1950[28] plus the need for improving the air-to-air gunnery skill of the interceptor pilots (training which pilots did not receive in ATRC schools) pointed up the continuing lack of adequate gunnery ranges. In March 1951, representatives from ADC, TAC, and SAC met with USAF officials at ADC Headquarters

---

26. See the following for information on flying hour allocations: ADC to EADF: "Aircraft and Flying Hour Allocations for Fiscal Year 1951," 23 Feb 1951. (DOC 147)

27. Hqs ADC, Command Data Books, Jan-Jun 1951.

28. USAF to ConAC: "Air-to-Ground Gunnery Training," 20 Nov 1950 (DOC 148); Also: ConAC to Air Defense Forces: "Air-to-Ground Gunnery Training," 21 Dec 1950. (DOC 149)

to study this problem and to attempt to establish working policies on use of present ranges and on the reopening of new ones.[29] A spirit of cooperativeness on this problem was the keynote of the conference.[30] At the end of June, higher headquarters and the major tactical Air Force commands were cooperating closely on ways and means of resolving this problem.

Unsatisfactory performance in gunnery training during the first half of 1951 also resulted from the continued lack of suitable tow targets and tow aircraft. Targets used had to be dragged behind the tow aircraft, with the result that both the aircraft and target were frequently damaged on the take-off. Also, the limited endurance of the jet fighters used as tow aircraft greatly reduced the time available for firing on the ranges. AMC informed that an improved polyethylene banner target suitable for towing at high altitudes and speeds was under development and would be available by July 1951. A carrier for launching targets after the tow aircraft was airborne was also being devised. It was expected that these improvements would greatly improve ADC's actual aerial gunnery training programs.[31]

---

29. Minutes, Bombing and Gunnery Range Conference, Hqs ADC, 22 Mar 1951. (DOC 150)

30. Interview, the Historian with Maj. G. W. Engel, Directorate of Operations and Training, Hqs ADC, 9 Nov 1951.

31. Minutes of ADC Staff Briefing, 17 Mar 1951.

Camera gunnery training was handicapped by the lack of adequate assessing equipment, film, and the inability to properly mount the camera. An interim solution to the camera gunnery problem was sought by mounting the camera on top of the A-1 gunsight head. This make-shift reticle camera photographed pictures as the pilot saw them. A serious disadvantage of this temporary "fix," however, was that the pilot's forward vision was partially blocked by the camera. This, of course, created a hazard to safe flight operations. Outstanding camera gunnery requirements at the end of June 1951 were for a reticle camera and for equipment that would allow complete, accurate processing and assessing of color film at squadron level.[32]

Another training problem, peripheral perhaps to the particular subject of flying training but one which played a major role in the ability of fighter units to convert to new models of aircraft, was the shortage of Mobile Training Detachments (MTDs) for training mechanics.[33] The basis of issue of MTDs in January 1951 was one for each 150 aircraft. For ADC's purposes, this was not

---

32. Hqs ADC, *Command Data Book*, Mar 1951.

33. During equipment conversion, factory familiarization trains key personnel in advance of first equipment delivery for approximately 10 per cent of the Air Defense Command's requirements. As initial equipments are delivered, ATRC establishes temporary specialized courses to train an additional 20 per cent. The balance, or 70 per cent, must be trained by Mobile Training Detachments and on-the-job training. See the following: ADC to ATRC: "J-48 Training Program," 10 May 1951 (DOC 151); and ADC to USAF: "Special Training, F-86E Aircraft," 14 Mar 1951. (DOC 152)

adequate. The deployment of fighter units by squadrons and the equipping of the all-weather units with only twelve aircraft per squadron initially made the assignment of MTDs according to total aircraft inventory an unreal policy. It was ADC's opinion that MTDs should be assigned on the basis of one per wing.[34]

USAF changed the basis of issue of these items to one per two wings. But in May, ADC informed higher headquarters that this was still inadequate. At that time, ADC requested that a minimum of two MTDs be assigned to every three wings.[35] This request, however, was denied; while USAF agreed with ADC that it would be desirable to have a mobile training detachment available for each squadron three months prior to its conversion to new equipment, the assignment of such a large number would mean a great surplus of them after the converting units had completed their transition requirements.[36]

Thus, due to fund limitations, accelerated aircraft production, and the squadron deployment plan, there would not be enough MTDs to meet the demand. ADC's operational proficiency, therefore, was dependent primarily on an aggressive on-the-job

---

34. ADC to USAF: "Mobile Training Detachments, Fighter-Interceptor and Fighter-All Weather," 2 Feb 1951. (DOC 153)

35. ADC to USAF: "Mobile Training Detachments, Fighter-Interceptor and Fighter-All Weather," 8 May 1951. (DOC 154)

36. Ibid., 1st Ind, USAF to ADC, 25 May 1951. (DOC 154)

training program for ground maintenance personnel. Outlines for these programs were published during the first half of 1951.

V

Firm plans were in existence, then, at the end of June 1951, for assuring that by 1953 there would be available the 2,200 jet all-weather pilots and 1,200 radar observers ADC would need to support its 1953 fighter-interceptor program. However, between the middle of 1951 and the latter part of 1952 and early 1953, crew production would lag considerably behind all-weather jet aircraft production. ADC expected to remain about 40 per cent below the required number of all-weather fighter crews required to man its assigned aircraft during this period. This, coupled with the fact that ADC also expected to be called upon to continue to meet overseas fighter pilot replacement requirements for an indefinite period, presented a problem of the first magnitude. At the end of June 1951, ADC was pressing hard for an increase in combat trained pilot strength, both to conduct its air defense mission and to support what in reality was a refresher training program. Until that was done, the operational capability of ADC portended to remain at a dangerously low level.

CHAPTER NINE

THE EVOLVING PATTERN OF AIR DEFENSE ORGANIZATION

I

Although the old Air Defense Command had expended most of its energies for air defense in trying to get the tools with which to accomplish its mission, there had been much activity in planning for the ideal organization of air defense. It will be recalled that the Air Defense Command was originally organized into six territorial air forces - each of which was charged with the execution of all of ADC's responsibilities in its respective area.[1] Early in ADC's history it was realized that this six air force structure was unsuitable for air defense purposes.[2] Not only did each air force reflect ADC's own dilemma in being saddled with so many missions, but the actual territorial areas of the subordinate air forces bore little or no relation to the location of priority defense areas. In both its "Air Defense in Being" and "Long Term" plans ADC sought to rectify this deficiency. In the former plan ADC recommended the defense of five vital target areas by an organizational arrangement of only

---

1. See above, pp. 48-51.
2. *Ibid.*

three air forces. These air forces were to be responsible respectively for: the East Coast; the Mid-west; and the West Coast.[3] ADC's "Long Term" plan, assuming that there would be a greater build-up of air defense capabilities in the distant future, recommended a four air force organization distributed for defense of the following areas: the Northeast and industrial Mid-west; the South and Gulf Coast areas; the entire West Coast; and the North Central Plains area. A feature of this latter plan was the recommendation that each air force be further subdivided into divisions and wings.[4]

ADC frequently sought AAF permission to reorganize its air forces to conform to its air defense plans, but it was not until early 1948 that it found USAF receptive to this suggestion.[5] It had been a feature of War Department policy to have the numbered air force boundaries correspond in area with the six continental armies. After unification, USAF continued to adhere to this policy in theory, though making concessions to ADC's needs.[6]

Early in 1948, USAF agreed to allow a reduction in the

---

3. Ibid.

4. Ibid.

5. USAF to ADC: "Reorganization of the Air Defense Command," 17 Dec 1947.

6. ADC to USAF: "Plan for Reorganization of Air Defense Command," 30 Jun 1948, and 1st Ind. (DOC 155)

number of ADC's air forces from six to four.[7] The reduction took place in mid-1948. In his original request for a reduction, General Stratemeyer had recommended that a "command post" be constructed in each air force area. Exactly what was involved in this suggestion is not clear from the pertinent correspondence. At any rate USAF did not act upon it, and the matter was dropped.[8]

The reduction in the number of ADC air forces and the rectification of their boundaries did much to enable ADC to embark with confidence on preparations for the establishment of an air defense in being in 1948.[9] As soon as the earliest phases of this effort were implemented, however, new organizational problems affecting air defense were born. The Northwest maneuver of March-April 1948 saw the hurried merger of fighter and AC&W resources into a Northwest Air Defense Wing (Provisional), responsible to the Fourth Air Force for the defense of the Seattle-Hanford area.[10] This temporary organization left much to be desired in its composition and procedures, and the end of the maneuver saw its demise.

It had been realized by ADC and all concerned with air defense operations that the very nature of those operations required

---

7. Ibid., 1st Ind. (DOC 155)

8. ADC to USAF: "Plan for Reorganization of the Air Defense Command," 29 Jan 1948. (DOC 156)

9. See above, Chap. III.

10. Ibid.

agencies new in the experience of the Air Defense Command. The necessary synchronization of fighter and ground radar capabilities demanded the formation of local operational headquarters to operate these resources in unison. Any such organization would have to be injected between the numbered air force and its fighter and AC&W components. By mid-1948 provision was consequently made by USAF for the eventual activation and assignment to ADC of a number of air divisions for that purpose.[11]

The gradual build-up of an AC&W network in the Northwest and Northeast during 1948 made certain innovations necessary in the matter of AC&W organization. In the early months of 1948 only one AC&W Group existed within the Air Defense Command - the 505th. The growth of a ground radar network in the Northwest occupied its full attention, however, necessitating the acquisition of an additional AC&W Group for the East Coast area. In May 1948 the 503rd AC&W Group was activated in the First Air Force area.[12] Both AC&W Groups were responsible for the operation of the nascent ground radar system in their respective areas.

The decision of the United States Air Force to embark upon the LASHUP and Permanent Systems in September 1948 necessitated

---

11. USAF, "Department of the Air Force Troop Program," 1 Jun 1948.

12. USAF to ADC: "Constitution and Activation of the Hq. 503d Aircraft Control and Warning Group. . . ." 19 May 1948.

greater activity in the matter of air defense organization. In that month ADC pressed USAF for the immediate activation of two air divisions to operate the defenses of the Northwest and Northeast areas.[13] In consequence, the 25th and 26th Air Divisions were activated and assigned to the Fourth and First Air Forces respectively in the following month.

II

The beginning of large-scale air defense activity in the fall of 1948 was paralleled by a major change in USAF organization. On 1 December 1948 the Continental Air Command was formed, and ADC and the Tactical Air Command were placed under it as operational headquarters. The administrative and logistical functions of the two subordinate headquarters were assigned to the territorial air forces, also under the overall authority of ConAC. The reorganization of December 1948 was of considerable benefit to air defense in that it brought directly under ConAC's authority the total air defense resources of the two commands. This amalgamation was particularly welcome not only because three fighter wings were added to air defense, but also because ConAC acquired a number of sorely-needed personnel experienced in aircraft control operations.

---

13. ADC to USAF: "Preliminary Action for Activating Air Defense Division Headquarters," 25 Aug 1948 (DOC 157); and, ADC to USAF: "Request for the Activation of an Air Division Headquarters," 28 Sep 1948. (DOC 158)

Although the reorganization of December 1948 was generally of much benefit to air defense, it introduced into the air defense picture a situation which was to cause considerable misunderstanding in the immediate future. The concept of a major command which was solely an operational headquarters was a novel one. Although ADC was nominally a major USAF command, with a general officer in charge, its position in the ConAC hierarchy throughout its short existence was an incongruity.14 In theory, ADC was to be the operating agency of the entire continental air defense system under ConAC, and it was to exercise authority through two regional headquarters subordinate to it. As an operational headquarters it was not to possess command authority over any air defense element, but was to operate the system with the resources placed under its operational control from time to time at the discretion of the Commanding General of ConAC.15 Misunderstanding was inherent in such a situation. The anomaly was further emphasized by the fact that the Commanding General of ADC was at the same time Deputy for Air Defense on the staff of the Commanding General, ConAC, so that it was frequently uncertain in what capacity he spoke.16 ADC was to remain in this unfortunate position until

---

14. ConAC, G. O. #2, 1 Dec 1948. The Commanding General of ADC was Maj. Gen. Gordon P. Saville.

15. ConAC Reg. 25-1, "Organization and Mission of the Air Defense Command," 31 Jan 1949. (DOC 159)

16. ADC to ConAC, 2 Dec 1948 and IRS correspondence inclosed as Document 51 in: History of the Continental Air Command, 1 Dec 1948 - 31 Dec 1949.

July 1950, when it was eliminated as a major command.

III

As the new AC&W system, or LASHUP, came into being, the process of creating a hierarchy solely concerned with the operational control of air defense was accelerated. To the air divisions which had been activated in the autumn of 1948 were now added ADC Headquarters itself and two regional headquarters subordinate to it. These latter organizations, called "Air Defense Liaison Groups," were established in close proximity to the headquarters of the First and Fourth Air Forces which were to support them administratively.[17] The implementing agencies of the two Air Defense Liaison Groups (ADLG) were the two air divisions: the 25th and the 26th. The two divisions, however, were assigned directly to the air forces in whose area they operated. The relationship between ADC and the air divisions was nebulous indeed in view of the fact that throughout 1949 major air defense activity lay in construction and deployment of radar, rather than in air defense operations. In theory the divisions had a dual allegiance to the air forces and to the operational hierarchy headed by ADC Headquarters.

Thus, as 1949 progressed, two organizational hierarchies

---

17. ConAC to WADLG: "Mission and Responsibility of the Western Air Defense Liaison Group," 23 Mar 1949 (DOC 160); and, ConAC to EADLG: "Mission and Responsibility of the Eastern Air Defense Liaison Group," 23 Mar 1949. (DOC 161)

were revealed, one concerned with operational matters and the other with administration and logistical support of the air defense elements. Although the number of air forces had been reduced to four in the summer of 1948, the reorganization of December 1948 had raised this number to six again by the addition of two air forces brought into ConAC by the Tactical Air Command.[18] The number of ConAC air forces remained at six until a further reorganization in July 1950 reduced the number once more to four.

The air forces were also placed in an anomalous position as a result of the growth of an operational hierarchy within ConAC. Although in March 1949 ConAC saw fit to transfer air defense responsibilities from the air forces to ADC and to the two liaison groups, for almost a year thereafter the air forces still were the only organizations within ConAC capable of administering and supporting the field units. By their possession of experienced engineering and installations personnel, and by their control of air base facilities for logistical purposes, the air forces were the logical agencies to supervise the construction and deployment effort of both the radar networks in progress.

Lest it be understood that the existence of two command hierarchies so inextricably intermeshed was the result of mismanagement, it must be pointed out that the necessity of integrating

---

18. See: History of ConAC, 1 Dec 1948 - 31 Dec 1949, Vol. I, pp. 30 ff.

so many special military and civilian air defense capabilities posed requirements which the existing air force structure was incapable of meeting. The need for sector and regional control of GCI operations demanded a controlling hierarchy familiar with the requirements and operation of this highly specialized activity. The key points in this air defense operation were the control centers and the GCI stations, and it was at these points that skilled commanders were required to operate, unencumbered with administrative and logistical burdens. The existing air forces were trammeled with responsibilities inherited from the old ADC, which made it difficult for them to grant to the air defense mission the degree of effort called for. Consequently it was quite realistic to leave the air forces responsible for what they could accomplish with their resources, and to create an operational air defense hierarchy side by side with the existing organization.

The necessities which prompted this unique juxtaposition of old and new organizational structures within ConAC, while self-evident to those who planned their development, was not understood too well in the field, and confusion in thought was rife. Fortunately, this confusion affected administrative matters, and did not prejudice the air defense effort during 1949 to any appreciable extent. That it did not do so to a greater extent was perhaps due to the fact that active air defense operations were limited by the greater logistical effort of deployment and construction.

IV

The program for implementing the organizational structure of operational control of the air defense system called for the activation of two operational regional headquarters.[19] As has been seen above, two air defense liaison groups had been organized in March 1949 as a temporary measure pending the activation of the units which were to perform this function permanently. The two liaison groups had been formed by detaching certain key air defense experts from the staffs of the First and Fourth air forces. As has been noted above, the implementing agencies for the decisions of these two liaison groups were the two existing air divisions. The fact that the two liaison groups were made responsible for the operation of the total ConAC air defense effort, meant that this mission was delegated in reality to the two divisions. In the case of the 25th Air Division the assignment of air defense responsibility for the entire western half of the United States caused misgivings to its commander, Colonel Clinton D. Vincent. This officer remonstrated that his responsibility was not commensurate with his ability to meet it, especially since he did not even possess direct telephonic communications with the New Mexico defenses.[20]

---

19. ConAC to 10th AF, "Air Defense Responsibilities," 1 Feb 1949. (DOC 162)

20. TWX, 25th AD to ConAC 18 Feb 1949. (DOC 163)

The dilemma in which Colonel Vincent found himself reflected the transitional nature of air defense organization in 1949. If the situation was so perplexing to Colonel Vincent, it can be no surprise that unindoctrinated USAF Headquarters personnel sent to inspect the West Coast defenses during operation DRUMMERBOY in 1949 were left wondering at the state of organization in the West.[21]

The way in which the dilemma of the 25th Air Division was resolved gives an excellent insight into the problems facing ConAC Headquarters in this thorny question of air defense organization. General Whitehead recognized the predicament in which his subordinates found themselves. He immediately gave the Commanding General of the Fourth Air Force the additional assignment of commanding the western air defenses with the exception of those in the state of New Mexico.[22] The latter area was placed under the operational control of the Commanding General of the 12th Air Force, in whose territory the Albuquerque defenses lay. This arrangement in effect placed the western area under one commander for both logistic and operational purposes, although retaining the fiction of a dual hierarchy. Similarly, the New Mexico area was to be operated and supported by one commander, although it was

---

21. USAF to ConAC: "Special Report of Observation on Exercise DRUMMERBOY," 2 Dec 1949. (DOC 55)

22. TWX, Gen. Whitehead to Gen. Upston, 8 Jul 1949. (DOC 164)

impossible in his case to grant him two titles.

In the eastern part of the United States confusion of the two hierarchies was mitigated by the proximity of ConAC Headquarters to the eastern air defense effort. Furthermore, the critical importance of the Northeast and the relatively advanced state of radar deployment there necessitated a permanently established operational hierarchy. This had been achieved at an earlier date than in the West by transferring a goodly number of ADC Headquarters personnel into an organization known as the Eastern Air Defenses Headquarters, commanded by Major General Robert Webster, hitherto Commanding General of the First Air Force.[23] The 26th Air Division was not presented with the same dilemma which had faced the 25th Air Division because of the fact that the former's area of operation was not so extensive as that of the latter.

It will be recalled that the two air divisions had assumed responsibility for air defense in their areas at the time the air forces were relieved of that responsibility in March 1949. As a result of the "shake-up" of July 1949 described above, the two air divisions were again reassigned to the air forces. In general, the effect of the reorganization of responsibilities in July 1949 was to place all air defense elements in the field directly under the air forces. In the West, the Fourth Air Force commander was

in effect in full control of the entire air defense complex. In
the East, much the same prevailed, with the First Air Force commander in control, except that a group of experts had been created
in EAD Headquarters which worked closely with him. Although the
new arrangement appeared to be even more complicated than that
which existed previously, it had the advantage of crystallizing
responsibility and authority in one man in each area. These arrangements, however, were not intended to be permanent. General
Whitehead made it clear that the operational hierarchy would resume its identity and responsibilities with the activation of the
two regional air defense headquarters late in 1949.[24]

V

In September 1949 the two regional air defense headquarters
came into being under the names of the Eastern and Western Air Defense Forces. Their activation, however, did not mean an immediate end to the problem of command jurisdiction. A question arose
again in the West as to whether integration of the WADF with the
Fourth Air Force was warranted or not. The decision was made,
however, to retain WADF as a separate headquarters, though based
in close proximity to headquarters of the Fourth Air Force at
Hamilton Air Force Base, California.[25] There was little controversy

---

24. TWX, Gen. Whitehead to Gen. Upston, 8 Jul 1949. (DOC 164)

25. IRS, P&O to DAD, "Organization of Hq and Hq Sq, Western Air Defense Force," 6 Sep 1949, and draft of study attached. (DOC 166)

involving the advantages of separation in the East, where the separation had been found to be successful.

While these organizational adjustments were being made, the deployment of LASHUP was progressing rapidly and nearing completion. This latter factor meant that the day of full-scale active operation of the air defense system was drawing near, and that clearly-defined lines of responsibility would have to be drawn soon.

The complicated ConAC structure of six air forces and two operational commands, which included missions concerning the Air National Guard, the Air Reserve, tactical air support of ground forces, air defense and a wide variety of other missions, was far too unwieldy to satisfy General Whitehead and his staff.[26] Early in 1950 ConAC suggested to USAF that a major reorganization of the United States Air Force take place which would see a redistribution of ConAC's many missions among other major commands. ConAC recommended that air defense be reserved as its primary mission. Although USAF failed to consent to ConAC's suggestions, it did agree that a reorganization within the Continental Air Command might be the answer to ConAC's problems. Two additional factors which spurred ConAC to reorganize its household were the decision to redeploy its fighter resources, and the outbreak of war in Korea.

---

26. ConAC to TAC: "Long Range Planning in Hq ConAC," 6 Apr 1950. (DOC 167)

The decision to redeploy ConAC's fighter resources reflected the growing maturity of the LASHUP system and experience in air defense operations.[27] The completion of LASHUP in mid-1950 called for a closer integration with that system of fighter capabilities, and this meant an extensive redistribution of aircraft strength. It was consequently decided to divide ConAC's fighter resources into 23 separate squadrons and deploy them separately upon fourteen bases.[28] This redeployment of fighter squadrons implied a far-reaching readjustment in the conventional relationship of fighter squadron to parent wing headquarters. As this deployment was made, the increased reliance of the fighter squadron upon the air division in operational matters created a corresponding loss in the authority of wing over squadron. In addition it meant a loss in the authority of the numbered air force over fighters and bases, since these units were directly assigned to the numbered air forces.

By mid-1950 a gradual build-up of the operational hierarchy within ConAC's air defense system had witnessed increased manning in the two Air Defense Forces and the establishment of additional air divisions and AC&W Groups. The completion of LASHUP and the completion of engineering preparations and site selection for the Permanent System had deprived the air forces of much

---

27. On the 23-Sq Plan, see Chap VI.
28. See Chap VI.

of their former responsibility to the air defense effort. In consequence of these developments ConAC determined to separate its air defense function from its many other activities.

To this decision the outbreak of war in Korea contributed. Immediately on commencement of hostilities, ConAC's entire establishment was galvanized into extra efforts.[29] The recall of reservists and federalization of ANG units put a strain on all staff activities, particularly within the air forces. The need for tactical support units in the Pacific drained off much of TAC's strength and involved great logistic effort on the part of all to ship fully equipped units overseas. The air defense system based on LASHUP was converted overnight from a token or "model" system to a full-scale air defense system on the alert for an imminent attack. The strain was immediately felt in ConAC Headquarters where all these responsibilities converged.

The separation of the air defense function from ConAC's other chores was made in July 1950.[30] As a result, the Air Defense Forces were metamorphosed into completely self-sufficient organizations and came into full logistical, administrative and operational authority over the air divisions, AC&W Groups and fighter wings. Headquarters ADC was abolished and its functions

---

29. See: *ConAC Historical Study*, "The Continental Air Command and the Korean War, Jun 1950 - Dec 1950."

30. ConAC to USAF: "Proposed Internal Reorganization of the Continental Air Command," 2 May 1950. (DOC 168)

incorporated into ConAC Headquarters itself.[31]

To a great extent this reorganization eliminated the overlapping authority of command functions within the air defense system - but not entirely. The troublesome concept of operational control still existed to plague some divisional commanders in their relationship with the fighter elements.[32] The divisions, it is true, had been given continuous operational control over all fighters in their areas, but these fighter units had been assigned directly to the Air Defense Forces for command. A further complication arose from the fact that the air division, being an operational headquarters primarily, was not designed to render logistic support to the AC&W units under its control. This latter function was performed by the fighter wings which, by controlling air base resources, could render this support.

Another important factor in the continuing controversy over air defense organization arose over the status of fighter and AC&W groups. The dispersal of fighter squadrons away from group headquarters made the tactical fighter group headquarters an anachronism, and there were many within ConAC who advocated

---

31. For a collection of pertinent documents dealing with the reorganization of Jul 1950, see: History of ConAC, 1 Jan 1950 - 30 Jun 1950.

32. See remarks of Col C. R. Vincent, Commander of the 25th Air Division in Report of Operation WHIPSTOCK. See WADF monograph on Operation WHIPSTOCK, Jun 18-24, 1950; also Gen. Smith to Gen. Myers, 6 Jun 1951. (DOC 169)

the complete elimination of the fighter group.[35]

A similar problem arose concerning the AC&W group. Originally the AC&W groups had been independent organizations, responsible for the operation of the ground radar under their control. With the formation of the air divisions, however, the group and division headquarters had been integrated into one organization, though retaining the fiction of separate identities.[34] So long as one AC&W group performed its function alone in a division area, the necessity of retaining a separate AC&W group headquarters was seriously questioned.[35] However, the influx of manpower into the AC&W system after Korea, and the expansion of the system itself to include more radar stations, resulted in the activation of a number of new AC&W groups, with the result that in several instances in 1951 two groups handled the AC&W function within one divisional area. This complicated the suggestion to eliminate the AC&W group headquarters as unnecessary.[36]

As a direct product of the Korean conflict, the process of air defense organization was given a great forward impetus. At

---

33. EADF, Memo, "Recommended Organization for Fighter-Interceptor Wing in Air Defense," 16 May 1951. (DOC 170)

34. See: *History of the 25th Air Division, Oct – Dec 1949*; and, *History of the 26th Air Division, Oct – Dec 1950*.

35. EADF to ADC: "Plan for Reorganization of the Air Division (Defense)" 12 Jan 1951. (DOC 171)

36. EADF to ADC: "Organization for Air Defense," 31 May 1951.

ORGANIZATIONAL CHART
AIR DEFENSE COMMAND
1 JULY 1951

HEADQUARTERS AIR DEFENSE COMMAND

SPECIALIZED UNITS
- 4600th AIR BASE GP
- 47th COMM SQ
- 504th AF BAND

HEADQUARTERS EASTERN AIR DEFENSE FORCE

26th AIR DIVISION
- 561st AC & W GP

52nd F/I WING
- 2nd F/I SQ
- 5th F/I SQ
- *105th F/I SQ

101st F/I WING
- 152nd F/I SQ
- 134th F/I SQ
- 136th F/I SQ

103rd F/I WING
- *21th F/I SQ
- *71st F/I SQ
- 118th F/I SQ

113th F/I WING
- 121st F/I SQ
- 142nd F/I SQ
- 148th F/I SQ

30th AIR DIVISION
- 541st AC & W GP

56th F/I WING
- 61st F/I SQ
- 63rd F/I SQ
- 122nd F/I SQ

122nd F/I WING
- 183rd F/I SQ
- 163rd F/I SQ
- 166th F/I SQ

142nd F/I WING
- *62nd F/I SQ
- *97th F/I SQ

32nd AIR DIVISION
- 540th AC & W GP

23rd F/I WING
- 74th F/I SQ
- 75th F/I SQ
- 134th F/I SQ

33rd F/I WING
- 58th F/I SQ
- 59th F/I SQ
- 60th F/I SQ

SPECIALIZED UNITS
- 47th COMM SQ
- 579th AF BAND
- 4700th AIR BASE GP
  - 4613th AIR BASE SQS
  - 4651st
  - 4652nd WAF SQS
- 7th 109th RADAR CALB SQS
- 4670th 4671st 4612nd GROUND OBS SQS
- 11th 12th 32nd CRASH RESCUE BOAT FLTS

HEADQUARTERS CENTRAL AIR DEFENSE FORCE

31st AIR DIVISION
- 543rd AC & W GP

128th F/I WING
- 126th F/I SQ
- 176th F/I SQ

133rd F/I WING
- 109th F/I SQ
- 175th F/I SQ
- 179th F/I SQ

33rd AIR DIVISION
- 159th AC & W GP

SPECIALIZED UNITS
- 50th COMM SQ
- 680th AIR BASE GP 4674th
- 4672nd GROUND OBS SQ

HEADQUARTERS WESTERN AIR DEFENSE FORCE

25th AIR DIVISION
- 636th AC & W GP
- 635th AC & W GP

81st F/I WING
- 91st F/I SQ
- 92nd F/I SQ
- 166th F/I SQ

325th F/I WING
- *123rd F/I SQ
- 318th F/I SQ
- 319th F/I SQ

29th AIR DIVISION
- 545th AC & W GP

27th AIR DIVISION
- 544th AC & W GP

1st F/I WING
- 94th F/I SQ
- *198th F/I SQ

34th AIR DIVISION
- *93rd F/I SQ

28th AIR DIVISION
- 542nd AC & W GP

78th F/I WING
- 82nd F/I SQ
- 83rd F/I SQ
- 84th F/I SQ

SPECIALIZED UNITS
- 43rd COMM SQ
- 513th AF BAND
- 4750th AIR BASE SQ
  - 4725th 4726th
  - 4727th 4728th
  - 4729th 4730th WAF SQS
- 11th 112th RADAR CALB SQS
- 4770th 4771st 4772nd 4773rd GROUND OBS SQS
- 13th CRASH RESCUE BOAT SQ
- 472nd SIG AVN HVY CONST CO

---

*ATTACHED SQUADRONS

RESTRICTED

the end of 1950 the Continental Air Command was split into three components, each of which became an independent major command. On 1 January 1951 the air defense hierarchy of ConAC was incorporated into a new command bearing the familiar title of the Air Defense Command.[37] Its sole mission was that of providing for the air defense of the United States. The Tactical Air Command was also reestablished as a separate command. ConAC was left with its air force structure and the Air Reserve and Air National Guard missions.

Early in 1951 a commanders' conference was convened at Headquarters, ADC, to consider the many problems of air defense organization which remained after the reorganization of ConAC. In view of the many imponderables in the situation and the conflicting views aired, it was determined that a period of experimentation by each air defense force commander would do much to help determine the best form of organization. By June 1951 the experiment was still continuing.

A feature of the organizational growth of the new Air Defense Command early in 1951 was the establishment of a third Air Defense Force to operate the air defense of the central and southeast

---

37. AF Reg 23-9, 15 Nov 1950, and, ADC G. O. #2, 1 Jan 1951.

portions of the United States.[38] This organization became known as the Central Air Defense Force, with headquarters located at Kansas City, Missouri.

---

38. ConAC to USAF: "Establishment of a Central Air Defense Force," 27 Jul 1950 (DOC 172); ConAC to USAF: "Location of Headquarters of Proposed Central Air Defense Force," 6 Sep 1950; USAF to ConAC: "Establishment of a Central Air Defense Force," 5 Oct 1950 and 1st Ind (DOC 173); USAF to ConAC: "Establishment of a Central Air Defense Force," 13 Dec 1950 (DOC 174); USAF to ADC: "Assignment of Central Air Defense Force," 5 Feb 1951.

CHAPTER TEN

THE ARMY AND AIR DEFENSE

At no time did either USAF or its air defense agencies propose that the air defense of the United States be a unilateral occupation of any one service. Both of the other services possessed tactical resources which could be effectively employed in air defense, and from the beginning USAF strove to lay the basis for inclusion of those resources into any future air defense system. The Army's antiaircraft artillery was a major air defense weapon, expressly designed as such, while the Navy possessed quantities of fighters, antiaircraft, and radar. In the lean years of reduced military appropriations which followed the end of World War II, inclusion of both Army and Navy air defense capabilities to the maximum extent was a major preoccupation of USAF planning.

Though the road of inter-service cooperation in air defense was clearly defined to both ConAC and ADC, the years from 1946 to 1948 were characterized by a serious absence of doctrine and procedural precedents for common service participation in a national air defense effort.[1] Indeed, until mid-1947 the Air Forces were

---

1. See Chapter Two, pp. 30-52.

still an integral part of the War Department, and theoretically under the command of the Army Chief of Staff. In such a situation, an integrated War Department effort including Army and AAF resources was possible, but in view of the impending reorganization of the military establishment which pointed to the erection of the Air Forces as a third and independent service, little or nothing was done towards common War Department integration of air defense plans and capabilities. The issue was further confused by the fact that much of the tactical doctrine evolved during the war, and given official sanction in the form of field manuals, was still on the books. This body of doctrine had in effect placed all active air defense measures, including antiaircraft artillery, under Air Force operational control.[2] With the impending separation of the Air Force from the War Department, a continuation of such a state of affairs was deemed anomalous by the Army Ground Forces, commanding Army antiaircraft. In June 1946, as recounted in Chapter Two of this history, the Army Ground Forces proposed a redefinition of air defense doctrine to award the Air Forces command of all air-to-air capabilities, while reserving to the Ground Forces command of all ground-to-air resources, including antiaircraft artillery.[3] When this matter was referred to the War Department for decision, that agency determined that operational control

---

2. See Chapter One, pp. 24-29.

3. See Chapter Two, pp. 45-6.

of AAA in air defense should remain vested in the AAF, thus advocating a policy of the *status quo* in the matter. In theory, therefore, the AAF retained control of antiaircraft operations for air defense. In reality, the entire matter within the Zone of the Interior was an academic one in view of the fact that no antiaircraft resources were allocated to air defense, and indeed, no air defense in being was established at all until late in 1948.

Unification, occurring in mid-1947, created a doctrinal vacuum where antiaircraft was concerned. AAA was now out of the reach of USAF, and in the absence of joint doctrines laid down by the new Department of Defense, this important capability was to all intents and purposes removed from USAF air defense planning considerations, except through the tortuous channels of joint agreements.[4] USAF's attitude to this predicament was well-expressed in an Air Defense Policy Panel report in February 1948 which stated that the "present assignment of AAA and ground-to-air missiles to the Army is contrary to good organization and to the most efficient utilization of the weapons in air defense."[5] It was the opinion of this panel that the responsibility for organizing,

---

4. The process of negotiation during this period may be followed in the following documents which are included in the supporting documents to this history: 1st AF to ADC: "Joint Agreements" 7 Mar 1947 (DOC 175); AAF to ADC: "Use of Ground Assigned Antiaircraft Artillery in Air Defense," 18 Aug 1947 (DOC 176); USAF to ADC: "Air Defense Standardization" 17 Sep 1948 (DOC 177).

5. "Report to the C/S USAF by the Air Defense Policy Panel" 3 Feb 1948.

manning, training, equipping and employing AAA and ground-to-air missile units should be given to USAF, and it was strongly urged that USAF keep as a long range goal the adoption of this policy.

At the Key West Conference in the spring of 1948, a basis of inter-service cooperation was established. The Army's primary responsibilities for air defense, as laid down at that meeting, were:[6]

> To organize, train and equip Army antiaircraft artillery units. To provide Army Forces as required for the defense of the United States against air attack, in accordance with joint doctrines and procedures approved by the Joint Chiefs of Staff.

In June 1949, a JCS-sponsored "Policy on Doctrines and Procedures for the Air Defense of the United States" enlarged on the Key West statement as follows:[7]

> To provide U. S. Army Antiaircraft forces for the air defense of the United States in accordance with /the Key West statement/ and allocations of the Joint Chiefs of Staff and to place all such units under the operational control of the Air Defense Command.
>
> To make available to the Air Defense Commander the maximum effort of all U. S. antiaircraft units physically present in the United States and assigned a mission other than the air defense of the United States, consistent with the accomplishment of their assigned missions, the Air Defense Command to exercise operational control over the air defense effort of the units concerned to include authority to redeploy only at the discretion of the Army Commander concerned.

---

6. Functional Agreement of the Key West Conference, Mar 1948, pp. 5-6. (See DOC 16)

7. Hqs USAF, "United States Air Force Policy on Doctrine and Procedures for the Air Defense of the United States," 10 Jun 1949, p. 54.

To a great extent, the decisions reached at Key West were beneficial to Army-USAF cooperation in air defense in that a single fountainhead of doctrine and policy was created in the Joint Chiefs of Staff, and in that the vast accumulation of pre-Key West traditions and precedents was theoretically wiped away. In reality, as will be seen, the Key West arrangements were insufficient to provide a concrete guide for joint USAF-Army procedure in the matter of AAA utilization, since the Joint Chiefs themselves were tardy in development of a program of action in this matter. Of much importance in contributing to the slowness of development of tactics and procedures for the use of AAA was the total lack of in-being capabilities in air defense, either in the form of an AC&W system or of AAA units.[8]

In view of the nascent stage of AC&W deployment in 1949, characterized by the hasty putting together of the LASHUP system, and the painfully slow rebirth of AAA capabilities, standardization of AAA air defense tactics, techniques and policies remained on a fictional level, while a top-level planning and doctrinal vacuum contributed in maintaining the status quo. The influence of this latter factor can be judged from two interchanges between Army and Air Force representatives during 1949.

---

8. 1st Army to ADC: "Use of First Army Antiaircraft Units in an Air Defense Mission" 18 Jun 1949. (DOC 178)

At a Fifth Army briefing by the Eastern Air Defense Liaison Group, the Fifth Army wanted to know when ADC was going to publish Standard Operating Instructions for AAA.[9] EADLG's comment was that ADC was holding off on any such publications until certain differences at Joint Chief of Staff level were resolved and a decision made. Later in the year, the First Army requested ADC's recommendations on a "rules of fire" SOP for AAA units employed in the air defense of the First Army area.[10] ADC replied that such recommendations were not feasible until the Joint Chiefs made some dispensation on overall deployment policies and plans. The First Army replied that it seemed necessary that interim agreements be effected until such time as the appropriate joint doctrines and procedures were published by the JCS. It conceived that the agreement might be limited to simple "rules of fire" to serve as a guide to whatever units might be deployed under the proposed plans. To this end the First Army requested that "rules of fire" proposed by ADC be furnished to permit the Fifth Army to formulate a basis of an interim agreement.

II

The flaws and gaps in working AAA-air defense arrangements

---

9. Eastern Air Defense Liaison Group to CG 5th Army: "Answers to Questions Pertaining to Air Defense," 27 Apr 1949. (DOC 179)

10. 1st Army to ADC: "Use of First Army Antiaircraft Units in an Air Defense Mission," 16 Sep 1949. (DOC 180)

became all too apparent in the latter part of 1949. The newly established air defense forces now began in earnest to resolve the problem of effectively integrating AAA into their respective air defense systems.

Late in 1949, the 25th Air Division and the 31st AAA Brigade had come to an agreement with the Manager of the Hanford Engineering Works whereby the immediate area would be protected by an inner artillery zone (IAZ). Aircraft would be fired on according to the established rules of engagement, with certain authorized exceptions. This agreement was approved as an interim arrangement. When 24-hour operations were ordered in January 1950 for certain areas in the 25th Air Division, Hanford was included. The 25th Air Division felt that the prohibited area should be enlarged and both the AAA Commander and the Hanford manager agreed. The request for enlargement was approved by WADF and ConAC.[11]

But then things began to happen. Modification of an IAZ to permit passage in certain cases had long been galling to the AAA commander. The WADF rules of engagement governing aircraft and AAA were also considered by him to be entirely too compromisingly in favor of unidentified aircraft, particularly in view of modern day aircraft capabilities. All in all, he felt that Hanford defenses were in effect being emasculated and he requested, through

---

11. The following discussion is based on textual and documentary data contained in the History of the Western Air Defense Force, 1 Jan - 30 Jun 1950, pp. 94-104.

Sixth Army, that something be done to work out more realistic rules of engagement and to reconsider the present procedures for establishment of AAA defended areas. This position was fully endorsed and passed to WADF by Sixth Army. WADF, in turn, asked ConAC for specific advice on IAZs and GDAs (gun defended areas) and wanted to know if any authorization existed for their establishment as defined by the Army.

ConAC's unequivocal "no" started a violent chain reaction. WADF notified the 25th Air Division that no GDA and IAZ areas would be established in peacetime and wrote to the Sixth Army abrogating the 25th Air Division - 31st AAA Brigade - Hanford Engineering Works agreement because it was based on an unauthorized IAZ. WADF also emphasized to the Sixth Army that all AAA under WADF operational control would submit to its SOP #4, which meant that the AAA could fire only when released by ADCC or when actually attacked by hostile aircraft.

The Sixth Army reacted explosively to the prescription of AAA embodied in ConAC letter 300-1 and WADF SOP #4, stating that its hands were being tied, leaving Hanford defenseless for all practical purposes. The commander of the Sixth Army further stated that he thought the matter of such vital interest to the nation's security that he was sending on his recommendations to the Department of the Army with the request that the Joint Chiefs of Staff consider the case.

The crux of the problem which WADF felt that the Army had

not fully appreciated was that if AAA were given the release fire and IAZ provisions it desired, nasty accidents involving friendly civil and military air traffic would be bound to happen. As yet the means simply did not exist whereby vital friendly air traffic could be identified and controlled adequately for AAA to enjoy wide latitudes on engagement. A calculated risk had to be taken in order to give friendly aircraft the benefit of the doubt.

The Eastern Air Defense Force like its western counterpart felt strongly its duty to consummate agreements with the armies within its area whereby AAA capabilities might be used in its air defense system.[12] For example, during the eleven month period December 1949 - November 1950, four separate agreements were discussed with the First Army alone.

The first proposed agreement (28 December 1949) and the resultant SOP which outlined rules for engagement and alert status for AAA, were in general accord with the policies established at a conference of the Joint Defense Planning Committee called by the First Army in late 1949. It was not long, however, before EADF discovered that its agreements with the First Army were not in line with ConAC's thinking on the subject. ConAC Letter 300-1 was published on 16 January 1950 for the avowed purpose of provid-

---

12. The following discussion is based on textual and documentary data contained in the History of the Eastern Air Defense Force, 1 Jan - 31 Dec 1950, pp. 45-63.

ing guidance for ConAC commanders. This guidance was, however, qualified by the realization that, "latitude must be allowed the Air Defense Force Commanders to arrive at mutual agreements."

The nub of the difference between EADF and the Army on one hand and ConAC on the other lay in the two questions raised in the Western Air Defense Force area. ConAC letter 300-1 held that "hold fire" should be the normal AAA status and also postulated that while in some exceptionally vital area outside the aircraft control and warning system an IAZ might be warranted, the presence of AAA within the AC&W system did not necessitate flight restrictions or special approach procedures. The December agreement and SOP had set up both IAZs and GDAs and established "release fire" as normal. EADF's excuse was that to get any kind of agreement in which EADF would have the vitally necessary operational control of AAA, EADF had to accede to the Army concepts of release fire and accompanying restricted areas. In fact, the EADF Commander could find little to quarrel with in the idea of release fire so long as he retained ultimate operating control.

As previously indicated, however, ConAC was worried over the identification requirements of the aircraft control and warning system for a release fire status and concomitant use of restricted AAA areas. To ConAC no compromise was possible over the "hold fire" and "no restricted area" concepts, whereas compromise was possible over operational control. EADF found these provisions difficult to countenance in the face of First Army demands and asked that letter 300-1 be rescinded. ConAC replied that its policy would remain unchanged, pointing out that enough latitude was extended to permit the Air Defense Forces to make certain concessions while still remaining within suitable agreement.

EADF's attempt to compromise with both the Army and ConAC was embodied in another proposed agreement, dated 23 February 1950. Apparently, this proposal was not accepted, for negotiations with the Army were not resumed until July when a Department of the Army message to the numbered armies "directed adherence" to the principles established in ConAC regulation 55-6 and the controversial ConAC letter 300-1 in the absence of prescription by the appropriate air defense commander. The guiding principle for any and all rules for engagement, SOPs, and agreements was that no engagement was to be permitted unless the aircraft was positively and without doubt identified as hostile.

Thus, both ConAC and EADF were upheld in some respects: ConAC's fear of uncontrolled, released AAA fire was allayed, while the air defense commanders were permitted considerable latitude of action for local variations so long as the basic rule was adhered to.

This clarification resulted in the signing of an agreement on 17 July 1950 and the publication, on the same date, of EADF SOP 355-2. But adherence to Air Force concepts on rules of engagement and restricted areas had been bought at a price. Points which had been originally considered the particular province of the Commanding General EADF were now subject to joint determination. For instance, the responsibilities of the EADF commander for promulgation of procedures, prescription of objectives and priorities in providing defense, and prescription of the type of AAA defense, as laid down in the July 1950 Joint Agreement, were no longer matters for his unilateral decision. The phrases "as coordinated with the Army Commanders concerned," "as coordinated with and agreed to by the Army commander," and "as coordinated with the Army commander," had been added.

Air defense of the Eastern United States was in truth now a _joint_ operation. EADF and ConAC's earlier fears of a joint air defense had been realized. However, this breach in a previously impregnable doctrinal bastion was academic in the face of the establishment of the Army Antiaircraft Command on 1 July 1950.[13]

III

The whole AAA question was revolutionized with the signing of the Air Force – Army Memorandum of Agreement (known as the Vandenberg – Collins Agreement) on 1 August 1950.[14] The organiza-

---

13. Department of the Army to CGs, Continental Armies: "Command and Staff Structure for an Army Force in Air Defense of the United States," 11 July 1950. (DOC 181)

14. Memorandum of Agreement, signed by Gen. Hoyt S. Vandenberg and Gen. J. Lawton Collins, 1 Aug 1950. (DOC 182)

tional-operational implications of this agreement cannot be over-emphasized. Operationally, the agreement was eminently successful in untangling the AAA operational controversy. It made possible a hard core of workably defined practices and procedures for the employment of AAA in air defense. Further, it authorized considerable latitude for local experimentation and arrangements around this hard core.

Organizationally, a completely new concept of Army AAA organization and of its relationship to the Air Force air defense agency was recognized. Each Air Defense Command echelon was henceforth to be furnished an AAA officer as a component of its staff and for liaison purposes. This constituted official notice of the wedding of the newly established Anti-Aircraft Command and of the Air Defense Command. This represented a deviation from earlier Air Force statements regarding the essentiality of a complete and organic integration of all primarily military air defense capabilities.

One immediate result of the Vandenberg - Collins Agreement was that joint agreement negotiations were put on a firmer and broader basis.

The 17 July Agreement between EADF and the First Army was renegotiated and signed on 7 November 1950.[15] The latter part of

---

15. *The History of the Eastern Air Defense Force, 1 Jan-31 Dec 1950.* pp. 62-63.

1950 also saw EADF attempting to secure some sort of uniformity of agreement with AAA in its area.[16] This was to have been achieved either by (1) standardization of all agreements with numbered armies in the EADF area into one prototype, or (2) accomplishment of a single agreement with EADF's new sister Eastern Antiaircraft Command covering all AAA resources in the EADF-EAC area.

As the mission of the Antiaircraft Command was gradually expanded and that command given more operational resources by the Army (culminating in the assignment of command of AAA units on 10 April 1951), the second of the alternatives mentioned above became the more feasible and preferable.[17] The "Joint Agreement for the Air Defense of the Eastern United States" of 1 May 1951 was the logical and much to be desired outcome.[18] Publication of implementative ADC regulation 55-1[19] and EADF SOP 355-2[20] with respect to the rules of engagement for AAA in air defense completed the rounding out of the operational cycle (using EADF as an example) begun by the Memorandum of Agreement of August 1950.

---

16. Ibid., pp. 47-48.

17. Briefing for CG ADC by Lt. Col. Z. L. Strickland, Jr., Hqs AAC, "Missions and Organizations of the Army Anti-Aircraft Command," 10 Sep 1951. (DOC 183)

18. "Joint Agreement for the Air Defense of the Eastern United States," 1 May 1951. (DOC 184)

19. ADCR 55-1, "Operations, Rules of Engagement for AAA in Air Defense," 14 Feb 1951. (DOC 185)

20. EADF SOP 355-2, "Defense, Rules of Engagement for AAA in Air Defense," 25 May 1951. (DOC 186)

Coincident with the doctrinal developments in Air Force-Army relations with regard to cooperation for air defense, as represented by the above, actual integration of AAA into air defense systems was commenced.[21]

The air defense exercises held during the first six months of 1951 revealed how far the integration of AA into the air defense system had progressed. They also revealed ADC's responsibilities for insuring the effective employment of this weapon. The ADC aircraft control and warning system was made responsible for the passage of reliable early warning information, including such raid data as altitudes, to assist AA gunlaying and target acquiring radar. ADC was solely responsible for identification of AA targets. ADC also exercised operational control of AA, to include the announcement of the basic rules of AA engagement, the authority to specify the condition of alert, and to direct the engagement and disengagement of antiaircraft fire. Air defense agencies were further responsible for establishing proper communications facilities to their associated AA, whereby EW, identification, alert, and rules of engagement information could be passed and operational exercise of control assumed. In short, ADC had become responsible for almost

---

21. Hereinafter, Army antiaircraft will be referred to simply as AA, in conformity with 1951 usage adopted by the newly activated Anti-Aircraft Command.

everything operational but the firing of the AA gun itself.

A deficiency in any one of the ADC warning and control functions would reflect immediately on its ability to effectively employ the dependent combat elements, fighter-interceptors and AA. Such was the case in the full-scale 1951 exercises, especially with respect to AA. Antiaircraft suffered ineffective utilization even more than its counterparts, the fighter-interceptors, because its weapon capabilities were still a relatively unknown quantity to Air Force personnel, and because of its late and as yet loose alliance with its controlling air defense organization.

The results of the several exercises held during the first six months of 1951 shed considerable light on the air defense AA problem.[22] Generally speaking, the early warning information passed on from the GCIs to the antiaircraft operations centers (AAOCs) in these maneuvers lacked sufficient height readings. The absence of adequate cross-telling was also a constant source of operational disturbance. In many instances, gun batteries found it difficult to pick up and correlate with absolute certainty a given GCI target, and in some cases where pickup was obtained, the time of pickup was so late than an effective engagement proved impossible. Even when early

---

22. WADF Summary of Operations Plan 2-51, 1-4 Feb 1951; WADF Summary of Operations Plan 3-51, 7-9 Apr 1951; WADF Summary of Operations Plan 7-51, 22-24 Jun 1951; ORT Report, 26th Air Division, 22-27 Jun 1951; EADF Report of Air Defense Exercise, 8-11 Feb 1951.

warning was judged good, the problem of obtaining EW on low level flights was admittedly unsolved.

Height-finding, cross-telling, and low level early warning would undoubtedly wait upon equipment and other improvements for complete solution. Some improvement, however, was bound to result as the GCI and AAOC personnel became more proficient individually and learned better how to work together in future exercises. Later maneuvers in this period showed some individual improvements.

The identification problem continued to remain a major irritant. Too much effort was required to positively identify friendly aircraft, with the result that many undetected penetrations and more late interceptions were permitted. AA was particularly helpless and dependent in this matter of identification. In at least one instance, GCI stations withheld information on certain tracks until identified as "aggressor" and then stopped telling them before the aircraft got in range of AA radar. As a result, the AA could not obtain identification on targets detected by AA radar in the defended area. It was expected that equipment and training measures would bring an improvement in GCI identification ability. It was also believed that under actual combat conditions much of the problem of identifying friendly air traffic would disappear because of grounding and other very rigid regulations.

These expectations, however, did not entirely dispel trepidations aroused by the fact that identification consistently was cited as a major weakness. "Limited identification capabilities," revealed one of the analysts of the February 1951 Western Air Defence Force exercise, were disturbingly typical. To say the very least, "the responsibility on GCIs for identification [would become] of increasing importance as more AA units [were] deployed."

Operational control, chiefly with regard to rules of engagement, understandably showed itself to be a little shaky and uncertain in some respects. Some improvement over earlier exercises was generally shown because of the publication of ADC regulation 55-1 in February 1951. For instance, the tendency was towards "release fire" in the later operations in contrast to the "hold fire" of previous exercises. But no amount of prescription could tell the air defense controller when to have his AA hold fire to protect friendly fighters, or when to pull off his fighters and give the show over to AA, or when to employ both AA and fighters at the same time. One of the facts underlined in the maneuvers was the importance of indoctrinating aircraft control and warning controllers in the employment of both AA and fighter-interceptors in meeting a hostile attack.

During the June 1951 exercise in the Western Air Defense Force area an incident occurred which exemplified the need for greater awareness on the part of controllers of the AA potential. A bomber flying East over the Cascade Mountains toward Hanford was tracked by ground radar up to the mountains. When the bomber reappeared, Larson ground radar picked it up late and scrambled its fighters tardily with interception taking place only after the bomber had penetrated well into the gun defended area. AA was forgotten, for all tactical purposes. At the critique of the exercise, General Vincent of the 25th Air Division pointed out that the controller should have held his fighters short of the Hanford boundary and turned the "enemy" plane over to the AA. Such a decision would not only have provided an excellent opportunity for AA training, but it would have been the correct tactical decision had the raid been in earnest. "Don't ever sell these AAA boys short, they can knock down lots of planes given half a chance," was General Vincent's pithy advice.[23]

V

The maximum utilization of AA as an air defense weapon had not been realized at the end of June 1951; however, the joint exercises of the first half of the year had served to clarify the major problems which were thwarting its full-scale employment. Permanent and continuous joint operations between AAOCs and GCIs were underway to provide requisite coordination and understanding and for developing effective operating procedures. Additionally, courses were scheduled for acquainting controllers and AA personnel with one another's capabilities and problems. Certainly,

---

23. *The History of the 25th Air Division (Defense), 1 Apr-30 Jun 1951*, pp. 45-46.

the outlook was bright at the end of June 1951 for a rapid and harmonious integration of AA into the ADC's air defense system in the near future.

CHAPTER ELEVEN

THE ROLE OF THE NAVY IN AIR DEFENSE

I

The Navy possesses fighter-interceptor aircraft, ground radar, airborne early warning radar (AEW), radar picket ships, and antiaircraft artillery. In the post-war years, the Air Force has directed considerable attention to coordinating with the Navy for the use of the latter's tactical resources in the nation's air defense system.

Primary advancement in joint Air Force-Navy relations in this regard has been made in readying Navy fighters for an air defense role in time of emergency. Corollary effort to integrate Navy AEW and radar picket ships has met with less success. Air Force requirements for use of these Naval resources in extending permanent early warning capabilities seaward have run into reluctance on the part of the Navy to allocate equipment on anything but an emergency basis. With regard to utilization of Navy ground radar and antiaircraft for air defense, relatively little had been accomplished through June 1951.

II

As told previously in the history, the first post-war Air Defense Command was given the responsibility for establishing the air defenses of the nation. In its determination to provide some measure of air defense, ADC repeatedly requested higher headquarters to take action whereby Army and Navy tactical resources could realistically be used for air defense. So far as the Navy was concerned, General Stratemeyer wanted to "integrate Naval aircraft control and warning units and fighter units into the air defense system." This, General Stratemeyer felt, could not be done at ADC level, but had to be "initiated on the Joint Chiefs of Staff level." It seemed to him "impractical of accomplishment on a 'cooperation' basis on Air Defense Command-Sea Frontier level and even more difficult of accomplishment on the Numbered Air Force-Naval District level."[1]

The Northwest Naval maneuver NOVFLEXPAC in late 1948 emphasized the inadequacies of extant arrangements for Air Force-Navy cooperation, as exemplified by the 1947 Northwest Joint Agreement (Joint Interim Defense Plan for Pacific Coastal Frontier).[2] For the first phase of NOVFLEXPAC a complicated Joint Command Post-Joint Operations Center (JOC) was established. This organization did not function satisfactorily from the air defense point of

---

1. ADC to USAF: "Air Defense of the United States," 24 Apr 1948. (See DOC 30)

2. The Fourth Air Force was authorized by AAF to sign the "Joint Interim Defense Plan for Pacific Coastal Frontier, 1947," on 18 Jun 1947.

view in that several times Navy fighters were proffered to and withdrawn from the air division with no notice given the JOC. As a result, the Air Defense commander did not know the exact status at all times of the forces available to him. Another major discrepancy noted was the absence of standardized doctrine, nomenclature, operating procedures and aircraft radio. The maneuver had not been planned too well at the top and the governing joint agreement itself was full of loop-holes. Even so, the Air Force commander was confident that "the friendships which were formed /would/ bear fruit in better plans, closer relations, and more efficient joint operations in the future."[3]

III

Post-unification top level attention to the subject of joint Air Force-Naval cooperation for air defense began at Key West. As did the Army, the Navy at that meeting agreed to accept responsibility for providing its tactical forces for an air defense mission. Specifically, the Navy agreed:[4]

> To provide sea-based air defense and the sea-based means for coordinating control for defense against air attack, coordinating with the other services in matters of joint concern.

---

3. *The History of the Fourth Air Force, 1 Jan 1948 to 30 Nov 1948*, Volume II, pp. 18-22.

4. Functional Agreement of the Key West Conference, Mar 1948, pp. 5-6. (See DOC 16)

> To provide Naval (including Naval air) forces as required for the defense of the United States against air attack, in accordance with joint doctrines and procedures approved by the Joint Chiefs of Staff.

In June 1949, the "USAF Policy on Doctrine and Procedures for the Air Defense of the United States" was published. This document was to serve as a planning blueprint until more adequate agreements could be reached. The Navy's responsibilities for cooperating in air defense were set forth as follows in this document:[5]

> To provide and operate off-shore ship-borne early warning radar stations in Naval picket ships, where and when requested by the USAF as allocated by JCS to the air defense forces, to operate as integral elements of the AWS of the U.S.
>
> To coordinate the air defense operations of forces operating in the air defense of Naval forces at sea within the geographic area covered by the aircraft warning system for the air defense of the United States, with those forces operating in air defense of the United States in such a manner as to ensure maximum over-all effectiveness of both forces against the enemy.
>
> To provide for the mission of air defense of the U.S. such Navy (including Marine Corps) fighter forces as are available and not more urgently required for the establishment of missions of primary interest to the Navy; and to allocate such forces to the operational control of the Air Defense Command.

---

5. Hqs USAF, "United States Air Force Policy on Doctrine and Procedures for the Air Defense of the United States," 10 Jun 1949, pp. 45-46, 51.

Some months later, the Chief of Naval Operations set forth the Navy's intentions for supporting the air defense system. The "Interim Statement of the Chief of Naval Operations Concerning Emergency Employment of Naval Forces and Facilities in Air Defense of the United States," stated: "It is the desire of the Chief of Naval Operations to support fully the activities of the Chief of Staff, United States Air Force, in the execution of the latter's primary responsibility for the air defense of the continental United States."[6] In this document, the Sea Frontiers were designated as the responsible Naval coordinating agencies for consignment of Naval forces for air defense. The guiding principle to be observed was that "those Naval forces having important air defense capabilities /would/ be trained and prepared for emergency allocation to reinforce and augment forces regularly assigned" the air defense function. It was not contemplated by the Navy that any of its forces, except those which might be so allocated by the Joint Chiefs of Staff, would be required to participate in air defense operations on a routine and continuing peacetime basis.

With the laying of the requisite doctrinal foundation, the Air Defense Forces and the Sea Frontiers were able to complete

---

6. "Interim Statement of the Policy of the Chief of Naval Operations Concerning Emergency Employment of Naval Forces and Facilities in Air Defense of the United States." (DOC 187)

interim bilateral agreements by late 1949 and early 1950.[7] These agreements, in turn, enabled EADF and WADF[8] to proceed with their corresponding Sea Frontiers in drawing up implementative SOPs and joint training agreements. For example, in the eastern area an EADF SOP 355-3, titled: "Employment of Naval Interceptors in the Air Defense System," was published in August 1950.[9] This document provided that the EADF commander would, in case of active air defense operations, either during peacetime or emergency alert, request allocation of Naval interceptors from the ESF commander normally on a one and/or three hour state of preparedness basis. Upon allocation, the Air Division commanders would receive availability notification. GCI controllers, in turn, would send requirement notification to the Fleet Air Detachment commanders concerned and then employ all one hour availables as First Category Aircraft.

In September 1950, a "Joint Agreement for the Training of Navy and Marine Corps Units in the Air Defense of the Eastern United States," was published.[10] The purpose of this document was

---

7. "Joint Agreement for the Air Defense of the Eastern United States," 5 Dec 1949; "Bilateral Agreement for the Air Defense of the Western United States," circa May 1950. (DOC 188)

8. *The History of the Western Air Defense Force, 1 Jan - 30 Jun 1950*, pp. 104-114.

9. EADF SOP 355-3, "Employment of Naval Interceptors in the Air Defense System," 7 Aug 1950. (DOC 189)

10. "Joint Agreement for the Training of Navy and Marine Corps Units in the Air Defense of the Eastern United States," 25 Sept 1950. (DOC 190)

243

to ensure that those Naval interceptors allocated, made available, and employed would be familiar with EADF operational procedures and be able to work with the aircraft control and warning system. The agreement was limited to the training of fighters and airborne early warning units. It was stated in the agreement that participation in air defense training by Naval and Marine Corps forces was to be entirely voluntary, although requests could be initiated through unit and division level channels by either party. The Air Division commanders were made responsible for all coordination with GCI controllers.

Once the documentary groundwork had been laid, attempts were made to refine operational procedures by means of widespread use of Naval and Marine fighters in "Big Photo" and other more or less standard training exercises. As expressed by one observer, advantages of this training were:[11]

> It offers the pilots training and experience in flying intercepts and identification missions; it offers the controllers much needed experience and training which often would not be available if we had only USAF facilities to depend upon; and most important, it affords a more effective air defense for the area since the degree of protection we are able to afford will vary directly with the availability of well trained defense units.

Of the need for preparing Navy and Marine fighters for their air defense role:[12]

---

11. *The History of the 26th Air Division (Defense), 1 Apr – 30 Jun 1951*, p. 50.

12. *Ibid.*, p. 51.

The desirability of utilizing Navy and Marine Corps airpower to the fullest possible extent in active air defense becomes obvious when the capabilities of USAF Fighter-Interceptor Units are examined. Though we are more effective now than we have been in the past, there is no doubt but that we are in dire need for more fighter coverage. The basic difficulty is not concerned with the actual deployment of fighter units and bases (though coverage is hardly considered satisfactory especially in the south), but is primarily due to insufficient quantities of fighter aircraft and combat-ready pilots.

V

The USAF Air Defense Policy Board Report of 3 February 1948 had conceded that the Navy was the only service that could continuously search an air space hundreds of miles to sea.[13] But post-war Air Force attempts to extend its permanent early warning system seaward by use of Navy AEW and radar picket vessels ran into the difficulty that the Navy, as posited in the CNO's Interim Statement, did not contemplate the use of its forces on any but an emergency basis. Nor, as events proved, did the Navy have at its disposal sufficient AEW and picket vessel resources to meet Air Force requirements.

In Operations BLACKJACK (June 1949) and WHIPSTOCK (June 1950), radar picket ships were employed. In BLACKJACK, four picket vessels were used, three of which were deployed offshore

---

13. "Report to the C/S USAF by the Air Defense Policy Panel," 3 Feb 1948.

at designated locations for a period of a week while the fourth performed a roving gap-filler function.[14] For several reasons, chiefly communication difficulties and obsolescent equipment problems, participation by the picket ships in this maneuver was adjudged to be unsatisfactory. This judgment, however, it was carefully pointed out, did not infer that picket ships did not have a definite place and function in the air defense system. It did mean that more training and testing prior to future exercises would be necessary, particularly in the field of communications.

During WHIPSTOCK the Coast Guard provided a radar picket vessel spotted 150 miles west of Pacific Beach, Washington.[15] This ship relayed plots to the Paine GCI station via Pacific Beach, using high frequency radio. As reported by the 25th Air Division, this ship "proved a valuable asset in the extension of early warning, and serious consideration should be given to the provision of radar picket vessels as an integral part of the permanent Air Defense system."[16]

In October 1950, ConAC requested its air defense forces to discuss with their respective Sea Frontiers the feasibility and capabilities of picket ship utilization.[17] Besides a relatively

---

14. Report of Air Defense Exercise BLACKJACK, pp. 4-5.

15. Report of Air Defense Exercise WHIPSTOCK, June 1950.

16. Ibid., p. 25.

17. ConAC to WADF: "Requirement for Radar Picket Stations to Supplement the Permanent Radar System," 10 October 1950. (DOC 191)

complete survey of the mechanical and technical capabilities of equipment, ConAC wished its defense forces to obtain from the Sea Frontiers: (1) Information on Navy peacetime and emergency capabilities to provide and sustain "on station" radar picket ships; and (2) a statement of Navy use of picket ships. If additional missions were assigned by the Navy, ConAC wished to know if they would interfere with their radar capability.

After these surveys had been made and the results interpreted, ConAC concluded that neither the Eastern nor Western Sea Frontier possessed the necessary resources for extending the permanent land-based radar net. At this time, ConAC asked USAF to undertake at that level the securing of additional picket ships.[18]

While the Navy seemed to be in general agreement with the requirement for and the advantages of a radar picket vessel line, it was physically unable to meet air defense requirements. Further, the problem was complicated by the fact that the Navy really had not seriously considered such a request, except as might be prescribed by the Joint Chiefs of Staff. As was stated in the CNO's Interim Statement, "the Navy did not contemplate allocating any of its forces for air defense except on an emergency basis."

Until such time, however, as higher authorities dealt with the matter, the Navy was willing to lend picket ships for the purpose of developing standard procedures and practices so that this

---

18. ConAC to VC/S USAF, "Radar Picket Vessel Utilization in Air Defense," 13 Dec 1950.

type of radar capability might be effectively integrated at a time of emergency.

Operation TUNA, held from 20 February through 19 March 1951, off the East Coast from Santini, Montauk, and Palermo, was conducted by EADF and ESF to determine picket ship capabilities.[19] The following functions were tested during the course of this maneuver: Radar early warning and reporting by picket ships; identification point reporting; intercept control; navigational aid; detection of airborne radar emissions; and weather reporting. The 26th Air Division drew up the final operations order for the maneuver.

The final report on the maneuver revealed that everyone concerned thought the operation a huge success. Air Force and Navy personnel were impressed with each other's cooperative spirit and capability. The Santini Direction Center was particularly enthusiastic, reporting that the picket ships had proved invaluable in every respect — in early warning, in control and interception, and in identification. On the debit side, the one weak link in TUNA had proved to be in the matter of communications. It was generally agreed that this problem would have to be corrected as soon as possible. The Navy did feel, too, that much of the combat capabilities of the destroyer picket vessel would be wasted

---

19. Report on Operations TUNA, by 26th Air Division, 27 Apr 1951.

in being for such a purpose on a continuing basis. Their observation was that any vessel equipped with proper radar and communications equipment and with adequate sea-keeping qualities, such as the Coast Guard operated, would be sufficient.

At the close of June 1951, then, the primary obstacles to the use of picket ships in the air defense system were (1) a shortage of these vessels, and (2) the Navy's reluctance to make its picket resources available for permanent continuing operations unless so directed by the Joint Chiefs of Staff. Colonel Minty, commander of the 26th Air Division, was quick to point out the air defense fallacy of the Navy's affirmed policy of making picket vessels available only on 24-hour notice in event of an emergency. Twenty-four hours after an attack might very well be too late. Epitomizing ADC's position, Colonel Minty stated his recommendation "that strenuous efforts be made to strengthen our defense against the initial attack by obtaining radar picket vessels prior to and during the initial attack."[20]

VI

The 1948 Policy Panel Report regarded airborne early warning as the most promising form of seaward surveillance.[21] The later evidence of BLACKJACK and succeeding exercises and tests

---

20. *The History of the 26th Air Division (Defense), 1 Jan - 31 Mar 1951*, p. 76.

21. "Report to the C/S USAF by the Air Defense Policy Panel," 3 Feb 1948, Tab "A", p. 6.

was favorable to the utility of this type of equipment as a gap-filler for land-based radar and for surveillance of low approaches. As the air defense requirements for AEW to extend its permanent radar system grew, it became more apparent that the Navy was unwilling and, in fact, unable to meet these requirements.

In attempting to fulfill its responsibilities on this count, the Navy queried USAF in October 1949 as to the possibilities of fully exploring the use of AEW as an adjunct to land-based radar, and as to the adaptability of this equipment to performing both air defense and anti-submarine warfare missions concurrently.[22] USAF was considerably interested in investigating these questions, of course. Consequently, that headquarters directed ConAC to have WADF arrange with the WSF commander and the Commander in Chief of the Pacific to work out the details of making such tests. ConAC, in relaying this directive to WADF, suggested that "Big Photo" missions, as well as any local arrangements that could be made, be used for testing purposes.[23]

The results of these tests, which were completed in the fall of 1950,[24] led ConAC to commence studies in order to substantiate

---

22. USAF to ConAC: "Use of Navy Airborne Early Warning in Air Defense Exercises," 30 Dec 1949; USAF to CNO: "Use of Navy Airborne Early Warning in Air Defense Exercises," 30 Dec 1949. (DOC 193)

23. Ibid., 1st Ind, ConAC to WADF, 18 Jan 1950.

24. WADF to USAF: "Use of Navy Airborne Early Warning in Air Defense Exercises," 10 Jul 1950. (DOC 194)

a firm requirement to USAF for the express "integration of AEW aircraft into the Air Defense system." To this end, EADF and WADF were requested to submit by 15 March 1951 their detailed recommendations and comments regarding the type, number and deployment of AEW equipment within their respective commands.[25]

The result of these investigations was a request by ADC in April that USAF establish a project as soon as possible to provide ADC an assigned AEW capability. First, there was an immediate requirement for three AEW aircraft to work out operational procedures and means of integrating AEW capabilities into the air defense system. There was also a further initial requirement for five squadrons (equipped with eight aircraft each) of airborne early warning and control aircraft. Two of these squadrons would be deployed along the Northeastern coastal area, one along the Northern boundary, and two along the Northwestern coastal area.[26]

---

25. *Ibid.*, 3d Ind, ADC to WADF, 16 Feb 1951.

26. ADC to USAF: "Requirement for Airborne Early Warning and Control Equipment," 9 Apr 1951. (DOC 195)

CHAPTER TWELVE

THE GROUND OBSERVER CORPS

I

The participation of civilians in the defense of the United States against air attack during World War II was the first serious attempt in the nation's history to enlist the home-front actively in preparation for its own defense. The actions taken to effect a wedding of military and civilian resources in defense during this period provided many of the basic premises upon which a post-war system of civil air defense was based.

Six months before Japan's attack on Pearl Harbor, the War Department set out to create an air defense system. Since America had no precedent for such action, military leaders decided to model the United States air defenses on the English system which had worked so successfully in the Battle of Britain. Accordingly, an Aircraft Warning Service (AWS) was established with two basic components: a coastal radar network and a supporting ground observer system. The purpose of the AWS was to locate enemy aircraft approaching the shores of the nation and to disseminate warnings to military and civilian agencies in the path of the attackers.

Limitations of radar equipment in 1941 made it possible for enemy aircraft to penetrate our defense areas at certain low altitudes without detection. To plug this gap, the War Department sent out a call for civilians to serve on a voluntary basis as ground observers to report on the identity and movement of low-flying aircraft. By 7 December 1941 the existing radar coverage in the United States had been supplemented by 4000 civilian-manned observation stations on the East Coast, and by approximately 2400 stations along the Pacific. Additionally, civilian volunteers were actively employed as plotters and tellers in filter and information centers which relayed reports from ground observers and radar stations to appropriate military facilities.

At the outset, the decision to rely upon civilian volunteers as ground observers, plotters, and tellers, was seriously questioned by civilian and military experts.[1] Doubts were raised as to whether this system, which depended so heavily on volunteer workers who were "unpaid, un-uniformed and uncontrolled,"[2] could function efficiently. In some military quarters the protest was made that around-the-clock operation of observation posts seven days a week was extremely difficult to accomplish even with well-trained military personnel. If this were the case, how could unpaid volunteer personnel hope to succeed?

---

1. For a discussion of the pros and cons regarding the use of civilian volunteers in World War II, see: <u>Fourth Air Force Historical Study III-2</u> (Defense Plans and Operations in the Fourth Air Force, 1942-1945).

2. This was the considered opinion of Mr. R. A. Watson-Watt, the distinguished British air defense specialist. See: <u>4AF Study III-2</u>, I, 78.

When the civilian volunteers actually commenced to demonstrate their ability to handle many vital jobs, however, adverse criticism slowly receded. Recognition of the role they were performing was soon forthcoming. In the summer of 1942 a system of measuring the efficiency of operation of ground observer posts was set up by the military along the Pacific Coast. The "efficiency as measured /was/ exceptionally high."[3] A year later, both military and civilian officials were emphasizing the contributions made by civilian volunteers to the air defense system. Brigadier General Edward M. Morris of the IV Fighter Command stressed the importance of the work done by plotters and tellers at various warning centers on the West Coast in the following words: "You are soldiers with a mission as important as that assigned to the military personnel of this command."[4] Tribute was also paid to the civilian volunteers in a proclamation issued by Governor Earl Warren of California in 1943 which set aside an Aircraft Warning Service week. The proclamation read:[5]

> Volunteers in the Aircraft Warning Service have served with unceasing vigilance on our observation and in our filter and information centers. They have guarded this vital American frontier 24 hours a day.
>
> Families have slept in safety; men and women have worked in our vital war industry without fear of sudden and unexpected death; trained military personnel have been released to carry the war to the enemy's shores . . .

---

3. See: Document #80 in <u>4AF Historical Study III-2</u>, III.

4. <u>Ibid.</u>, I, 87.

5. <u>Ibid.</u>, I, 100.

In spite of these glowing reports, it is difficult to make an evaluation of the civilian performance in the AWS during World War II since the system was never battle-tested. However, the fact that more than 6000 observer posts in the United States along with numerous filter and information centers were manned by civilians during the war, provided evidence to post-war analysts that civilians could be effectively integrated into an air defense network.

II

Thus, it was only natural that plans for the postwar air defense of the United States would include provisions for the continued use of civilian volunteers. The Bull Board Report rendered by the War Department Civil Defense Board and the Hopely Report issued by the Office of Civil Defense Planning, both documentary landmarks in the civil defense planning of the postwar period, proceeded on the assumption that civilians were to figure in future plans for air defense.[6] This was also the assumption made by the staff of the first post-war Air Defense Command (ADC). During its entire two and one-half years existence, ADC included in its preparations for an air defense system provisions for the integration of civilians into the air defensive network.

However, there were still some who did not go along with the idea of civilian participation in air defense activities. Immediately

---

6. *Civil Defense for National Security*, Report to the Secretary of Defense by the Office of Civil Defense Planning (Washington, 1948).

upon its activation in March 1946, the ADC requested Army Air Force (AAF) Headquarters to give it <u>carte</u> <u>blanche</u> authority to solicit the assistance of civil defense agencies for air defense.[7] Such a directive was not forthcoming, however, for higher headquarters at this time was engaged in a controversy with the Army Ground Forces over postwar responsibilities in the air defense mission and was not in a position to delegate this authority to ADC.[8] Furthermore, at this time, certain members of the staff at AAF itself were not convinced of the efficacy of permitting civilian defense agencies to participate actively in the air defense system during peacetime.[9]

Undeterred by these actions, ADC went ahead with its preparations for civilian participation in air defense activities. ADC's view was that limitations on regular military forces engaged in the air defense mission at this time made it necessary to engage the assistance of all civilian and semi-military organizations which could contribute to a combined national air defense. As General Stratemeyer, Commanding General of the Air Defense Command, so forcibly put it:[10]

---

7. ADC to AAF: "Air Defense of the United States," 3 May 1946. (DOC 196)

8. For the story of this controversy see above pp. 40-46.

9. AAF to ADC: "Air Defense of the United States," 13 Jun 1946. (DOC 197)

10. ADC to AAF: "Responsibilities for Air Defense, Project No. 14," 20 Jul 1946. (DOC 198)

It will be necessary for the American public to realize that air defense of the United States cannot be secured by the action of the Armed Forces alone. Continental Air Defense will require preparations to mobilize the potentials of civilians and industry to assist such defenses. They also must realize that neither time nor distance will shield them from the necessity of being prepared in peacetime to cope with the threat of air attack. It will be the responsibility of the Air Defense Command to determine the necessity of civilian participation in air defense and when so determined to take such steps as are necessary to secure civilian cooperation.

With a firm determination to secure authority for using civilians in the air defense system, General Stratemeyer seized upon that part of his assigned mission which read, "The Air Defense Command will . . . . coordinate all passive means of defense," and gave it new meaning.[11] He interpreted this phrase to mean that he had authority to coordinate the work of civilian agencies for participation in the air defense system.[12] In the end, this analysis of the ADC mission was approved by AAF Headquarters and the post-war battle to include civilians in the air defense picture was won.[13]

From this point on, ADC forged ahead with its ideas for incorporating civilians into the air defense system. Plans were laid for the use of civilian volunteers in a ground observer system.[14]

---

11. "Mission of the Air Defense Command as Assigned by the Commanding General, Army Air Forces," 5 Aug 1946. (DOC 199)

12. Ibid.

13. Memo, ADC to C/S, 13 Aug 1947. (DOC 200)

14. Ibid.

The recommendation was also made to create a civil defense agency to expedite the marshalling of civilians for air defense purposes.[15] At the time of ADC's absorption into Continental Air Command, in the fall of 1948, civilians as yet were not actively employed in the air defense system. But the authority had been established and the plans laid for their utilization. In other words, the stage was set for the actual implementation of the civil air defense program.

III

At the time of ConAC's activation, steps were underway to establish a radar network. From the beginning, it was apparent that radar alone would not suffice as an early warning system. Radar beams operate on a line-of-sight principle, and "gaps" appeared in mountainous regions. Also, because of earth curvature it was possible for low flying enemy planes to get within fifty miles of a target before registering on a scope. Although it was theoretically possible to build radar warning units so closely together that their surveillance would overlap and form an unbroken ring, the cost of such an electronic fence was prohibitive. The only apparent solution to the problem was the establishment of a corps of civilian volunteer ground observers.

Ground observers could perform other duties besides complementing the radar system. They could report the dropping of paratroopers or specify the presence of gliders, thus indicating that

---

15. ADC to AAF: "Suggested Priority on ADC Matters Requiring Action by ACAS-5 Headquarters, Army Air Forces," 16 May 1947. (DOC 201)

airborne landings were in the offing. They could also report when enemy fighters were committing hostile acts, and the results of enemy air action.[16]

There was yet another attractive feature of the ground observer system, its relatively low cost. Since civilians volunteered their services to fill most of the positions in a ground observer network, personnel expenses could be kept to a minimum. In the initial phase of planning, it was estimated that the system for the entire United States would cost less than $2,000,000 for the first year, including the construction, installation, and operation of facilities.[17]

Concurrent with the construction of radar sites, therefore, ConAC commenced the organization of a civilian ground observer corps. Before establishing a permanent GOC, however, it was necessary first to experiment with such a system to see if it could meet the requirements of present day aircraft speeds and capabilities. Implementation and testing went hand in hand as the twin purposes of LOOKOUT, the air defense maneuver conducted in the northeastern United States in the fall of 1949 by ConAC in conjunction with the Office of Civil Defense. The exercise was intended to test the efficiency of a

---

16. Office of the Secretary of Defense, Assistant for Civil Defense Liaison, Conference of Governors on Expansion of Aircraft Warning System, 19-20 Jan 1950, pp. 51-52.

17. Summary Report to DO, ConAC: "Operations Analysis, Air Defense," (ca. Oct 1949) (DOC 202)

combination of ground observers and radar stations in operating an aircraft warning system. At the same time its purpose was to create the nucleus for the proposed Ground Observer Corps in the northeastern states. The maneuver succeeded, both in creating a standby organization which would serve as a ground observer network in parts of ten northeastern states, and in testing in its embryonic form the techniques and tactics of a national ground observer system.[18]

The pragmatic results of operation LOOKOUT encouraged ConAC to request authority from higher headquarters to officially activate the GOC. In mid-December 1949 ConAC asked that the necessary orders be issued to form the GOC, that action be initiated to enact Federal legislation required to give the GOC official status as an auxiliary of the United States Air Force, and that funds be furnished to implement the program.[19]

By February 1950 the necessary directives were forthcoming from Washington, and ConAC was given the go-ahead signal to provide facilities and supervision for a GOC. It was agreed that the GOC would be composed of civilian volunteers and that recruiting of such volunteers would be on a mutually cooperative basis between the civil authorities of the state concerned and ConAC. The GOC was to be

---

18. Conference of Representatives on Expansion of Aircraft Warning System, Office of the Secretary of Defense, Assistant for Civil Defense Liaison, 10 Jan 1950, p.8.

19. ConAC to C/S, USAF: "Implementation of Ground Observer Corps - Aircraft Warning Service," 15 Dec 1949. (DOC 203)

operated on a permanent basis as an adjunct to the Aircraft Control and Warning System.[20]

While action was being taken by the United States Air Force to utilize civilians in an air defense program, planning was going on in higher levels to establish a national civil defense program in which all the services would participate. In the spring of 1950 the Defense Department clarified the role which the Air Force would play in this national civil defense program.[21] The Air Force in turn delegated to ConAC many of those responsibilities for which it had been charged within the program.[22] ConAC's mission with regard to civil air defense consisted of: an Aircraft Observer System which ConAC had chosen to designate as the Ground Observer Corps; a limited interim Civil Air Raid Warning System; and a Military Air Raid Warning System.[23]

---

20. Ibid.

21. Memo for the Secretaries of the Military Departments: "Responsibility for Planning and Preparation of Certain Civil Defense and Allied Programs Within the Department of Defense," 24 Apr 1950. Incl to (DOC 204)

22. DAF to ConAC: "Responsibility for Planning and Preparation of Certain Civil Defense and Allied Programs Within the Department of Defense," 1 Jun 1950. (DOC 204)

23. ConAC to CGs EADF-WADF: "Civil Air Defense Responsibilities and Organization," 14 Jul 1950. (DOC 205)

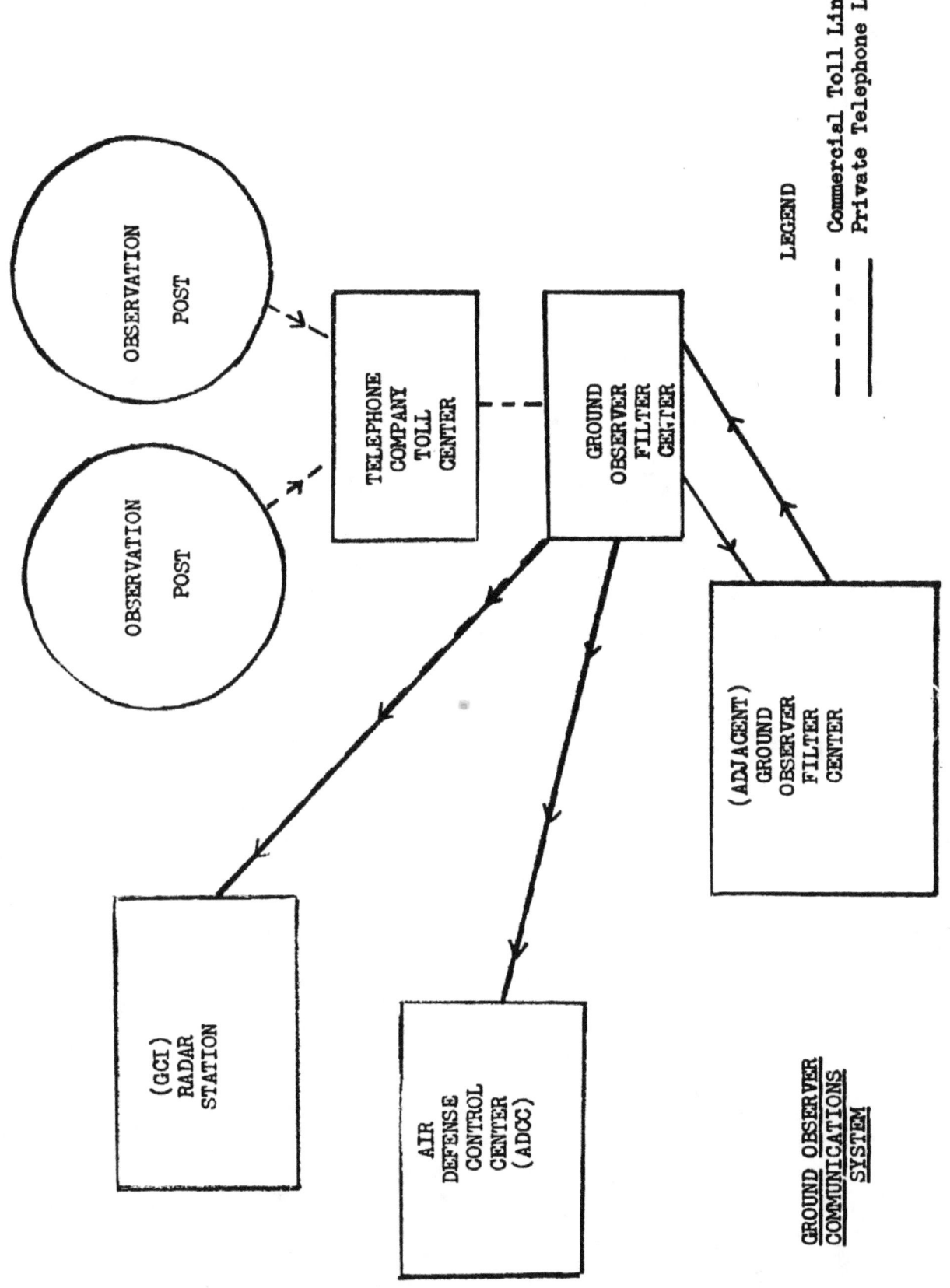

IV

Once the original authorization had been approved to higher headquarters in February 1950, ConAC undertook the task of preparing a master plan for the establishment and functioning of a Ground Observer Corps. Civilian volunteers at observation posts were to make "aircraft flash" calls to their assigned filter centers whenever an airplane was seen or heard in the vicinity. These messages would include information on the altitude, direction of flight and number of aircraft seen or heard by the observer. This information together with reports from other observation posts was to be plotted on a grid map of the area at the filter center. After this information had been evaluated, a report was to be made from the filter center to a ground control intercept unit or air defense control center where action could be taken to scramble fighters.

The observation post was to be the first link in this chain of information. The observation post was to be in a properly located position and equipped with a telephone. Two or more observers were to be assigned each post. It was estimated that approximately twenty part-time volunteers would be required for sustained operations 24 hours per day. Observation posts were to be spaced approximately eight miles apart throughout those areas where the Ground Observer Corps was organized, since tests and experiments had indicated that four miles is the limit at which an ordinary person can see and identify an aircraft in flight.

The Air Defense Forces under the Continental Air Command were to be responsible for selecting the specific towns, villages or parts of larger cities in which observation posts would be required to give the desired spacing of approximately eight miles apart. However, each observation post was to be commanded by a civilian observation post supervisor who would be responsible for the exact physical location of the post within the designated town, village and city.

Each observation post was to be near an established telephone whose subscriber would volunteer its use for the reporting of aircraft movement. A standard was created whereby each post had to be within fifteen seconds walking time to an existing commercial phone. Although the use of each phone was to be volunteered, all calls made by ground observers on the movement of aircraft were to be at government expense.

The filter centers were the key points from which information obtained from the ground observers was to be fed to the radar network. These centers were to be manned both by volunteer civilian personnel and supervisory military personnel. The civilian volunteers were to serve as plotters, tellers and filterers in the center. It was estimated that each filter center would require approximately 500 part-time volunteers for sustained operations 24 hours per day.

---

24. Historical Report, Directorate of Civil Air Defense, ConAC, Jan-May 1950.

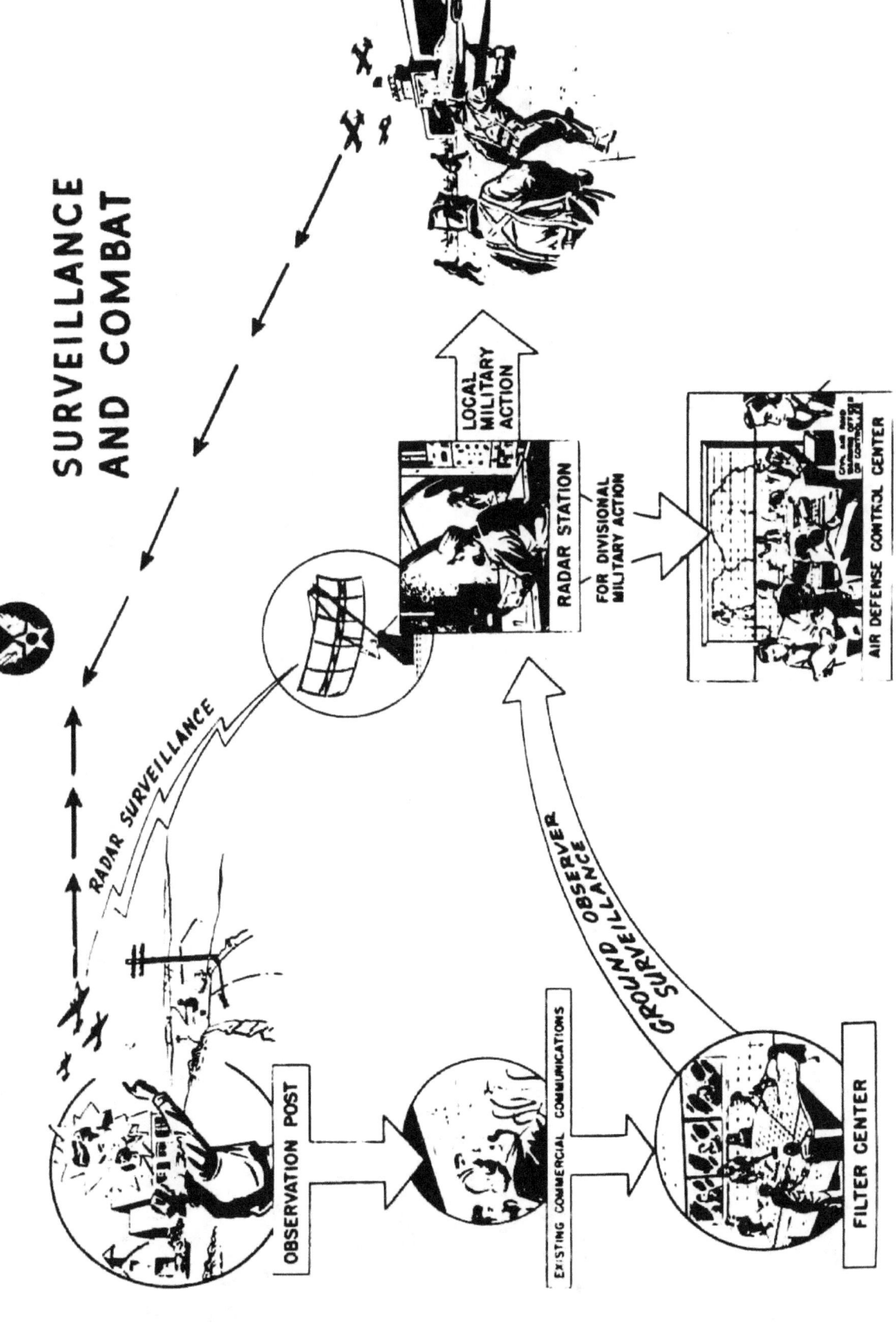

The selection of filter centers was to be based primarily upon the long-line telephone facilities and telephone routing as determined by the officials of the telephone companies. In addition, filter centers had to be located in cities with reasonably good transportation systems so that the 500 volunteer workers required could be recruited. Still another consideration to be taken in the locations of filter centers was a selection of cities which would not be priority targets for enemy attacks.

In the administration of the above system, both the military and civilian organizations concerned found it necessary to create agencies to handle GOC matters. Within ConAC itself, a Civil Air Defense section was added in December 1949 to prepare plans and procedures for GOC and other civil air defense measures.[25] The Department of Defense, which was responsible for national civil defense matters, established the Office of Civil Defense Liaison. It was the function of this office to establish contact with various state governments, and in conjunction with ConAC to institute procedures whereby each state could organize its GOC and other aspects of civil air defense.[26] The civilian – military spheres of authority were roughly outlined as follows: civil authorities were responsible for manning the observation posts and filter centers with civilian volunteers; ConAC was to be responsible for the training and operation of the Corps.

---

25. ConACR 21-1A, "Organization – Continental Air Command," 29 Dec 1949. (DOC 206)

26. ConAC to CG, 1AF: "Public Information Policy for the Air Defense Program," 17 Feb 1950. (DOC 207)

V

Thus, in February 1950, ConAC was able to commence expansion of its GOC program. The expansion program was phased in two parts. Phase I provided for the establishing of approximately 6000 observation posts and nineteen filter centers in EADF's area; WADF was to have about 2000 observation posts and seven filter centers. The location of GOC posts during Phase I was to be confined to the East and West coasts and the Great Lakes region, the areas in which radar installation was taking place.[27] ConAC estimated that it could completely organize, install and test this first phase of the GOC program within five months. Consequently, a target date was set for July 1950.

This date for completion of Phase I of the GOC was not met by ConAC. Indeed, so many obstacles arose that the date had to be pushed back to November 1950. Four major causes for ConAC's inability to implement Phase I of the GOC within the five month period originally estimated were: difficulty in "recruiting" observers, inadequacies of USAF directives, filter center problems, and obstacles encountered in properly spacing ground observer posts. Additionally, there were certain general problems which contributed to ConAC's failure to meet its goal as originally planned.

Perhaps the most persistent problem which ConAC encountered in its struggle to complete Phase I of the GOC was the apathetic

---

27. ADC, "Ground Observer Corps Plan," 18 Jan 1951. (DOC 208)

reaction of civilians to the AF proposal that they man the GOC.[28] The volunteer status of the ground observers and of the plotters and tellers in filter centers made the success of the entire program contingent upon the number of civilians who would offer their services. Public support of the program, however, was extremely feeble. In spite of a great publicity program waged by ConAC, USAF and the Civil Defense Board, only 402 of the total 8,224 observation posts planned (slightly less than five per cent) were manned by July 1950, the original target date for completion of Phase I.[29]

The outbreak of hostilities in Korea did much to bring about a change in public interest towards the GOC: there was a substantial increase in the number of civilian volunteers during the second half of 1950. On the other hand there were times when our military progress in Korea did not aid the program. "Whenever the situation in Korea improved, the interest of the public at home in serving with the Ground Observer - Aircraft Warning Service declined proportionately."[30] In the final analysis, the Korean war did inject a note of realism for the necessity of an air defense system, and the public responded by providing more volunteers in the last six months of 1950.

---

28. History of EADF, Jan-Dec 1950, pp. 36-37; History of WADF, Jan-Jun 1950, pp. 30-32; and History of WADF, Jun-Dec 1950, pp. 143-145.

29. ConAC to CG, 4AF: "Increased Emphasis, Organization of Ground Observer Corps," 21 Jul 1950. (DOC 209)

30. History of WADF, 1 Jul-31 Dec 1950, p. 145.

However, ConAC was not content to allow current events alone to determine the success or failure of its recruiting campaign for GOC. In an attempt to overcome civilian apathy, an aggressive public information campaign was initiated. An appeal for more publicity was made by ConAC to both the higher and lower echelons of command. From USAF, ConAC received assurances that greater publicity would be given the program to create public interest.[31] EADF, for its part, conducted an exercise whose primary purpose was to stimulate interest in the GOC.[32] At the same time ConAC impressed upon its numbered air forces their responsibility for disseminating publicity to all agencies which were organizing civil air defense activities.[33]

As a result of both the Korean war and these publicity efforts, manning of the GOC posts was considerably improved. By the end of 1950, 61 per cent of the observation posts in the EADF were completely manned and 52 per cent in the WADF.[34]

John Doe was not the only one guilty of apathy toward the GOC program; the virus of disinterest infected responsible state officials as well. There appeared a marked reluctance on the part of

---

31. 1st Ind, USAF to ConAC, 13 Aug 1950 to ConAC to USAF: "Status of Ground Observer Corps," 10 Jul 1950. (DOC 210)

32. EADF to ConAC: "Ground Observer Corps Exercise 4 and 5 November 1950 – Preliminary Report," 21 Nov 1950. (DOC 211)

33. ConAC to CGs, numbered AFs: "Civil Defense Responsibilities," 30 Sep 1950. (DOC 212)

34. Information supplied by the Directorate, Civil Air Defense, ADC.

some state authorities to cooperate in the implementation of the GOC. A major weakness in the program lay in the fact that in order to bring pressure to bear on states lagging behind in the program, ConAC had to fall back on civilian channels. However, because of the constitutional predicament involved in states rights, the civilian chain of command carried relatively little authority, and the Office of Civil Defense Liaison had no authority to direct state agencies. As a result, ConAC frequently found itself hamstrung in getting those states which were slow in organizing the GOC "on the ball."[35]

A second major reason for ConAC's inability to meet the initial target date it set for completing Phase I was the inadequacy of the directives received from higher headquarters. Lacking detailed directives from USAF, ConAC was unable to publish directives to its subordinate air defense forces and numbered air forces clearly outlining their respective responsibilities. From the time that ConAC was authorized to organize the GOC in February 1950 until the middle of the year, this problem of blurred responsibilities seriously hindered the program.

A major aid in resolving this difficulty was a directive from Headquarters, USAF, which delegated to ConAC in verbatim form most of the responsibilities of civil air defense for which the Air Force itself had been charged.[36] The receipt of this directive evoked

---

35. ConAC to WADF: "Increased Emphasis, Organization of Ground Observer Corps," 19 Aug 1950. (DOC 213)

36. DAF to ConAC: "Responsibility for Planning and Preparation of Certain Civil Defense and Allied Programs Within the Department of Defense," 1 Jun 1950. (DOC 204)

considerable discussion among the staff relative to the responsibilities of the various directorates for each item with which ConAC was charged. The final decision on this matter, made in early July 1950, placed responsibility for the administration of not only the Ground Observer Corps but of the Civil and Military Air Raid Warning Systems as well in the Directorate of Civil Air Defense.[37]

The receipt of this directive also permitted ConAC to delegate responsibilities for the GOC to its lower echelons. In the middle of July 1950, the responsibilities of the Eastern and Western Air Defense Forces were outlined in detail, and they were directed to conduct planning, organization and control of the GOC with the objective of developing maximum operation capability as soon as possible.[38] At the same time, ConAC ordered its numbered air forces to work with the air defense forces to expedite the organization of the GOC.[39] By delineating the responsibilities of its major subordinate units, ConAC removed a handicap which had crippled the GOC program in the first five months of its existence.

The innumerable problems encountered in putting the filter centers in working order constituted a third major reason why ConAC was unable to meet its initial target date for Phase I of the GOC.

---

37. IRS, P&R to DO: "Civil Air Defense Planning," 3 Jul 1950. (DOC 214)

38. ConAC to CGs, EADF and WADF: "Organization and Operation of the Ground Observer Corps," 21 Jul 1950. (DOC 215)

39. ConAC to CG, 4thAF: "Increased Emphasis, Organization of Ground Observer Corps," 21 Jul 1950. (DOC 209)

In some areas difficulties were met in securing appropriate filter center sites. Equipment shortages arose, and bottlenecks developed in the attempts to obtain the military and civilian personnel needed to man the filter centers.

Perhaps the most serious problem faced by the filter centers was the shortage of personnel. Both civilians and military personnel were needed for manning the centers. The civilians were to be recruited by the civil defense authorities of the various states, while the military personnel were to be drawn from Air Reserve Corollary Units. The results in both cases were somewhat disappointing.

For the most part it was easier to secure civilian volunteers to man filter centers than it was to recruit civilians as ground observers. But even securing the 500 volunteers needed to man each center on a 24-hour basis was bound to be difficult. It was impossible to keep such a large number of volunteers constant over a long period of time. In some instances too, the recruiting of filter center personnel was delayed because state authorities required security clearances for its volunteers.[40] The result of these problems was a lack of qualified volunteers to man the filter centers.

A much more serious personnel problem occurred with regard to the military. The need of military personnel, both officers and men, to be assigned to permanent duty with filter centers had been realized for some time, since even the most loyal and willing civilian personnel

---

40. <u>WADF History, 1 Jun-31 Dec 1950</u>, p. 142.

could not carry on duties of the center efficiently unless they were given the needed supervision and direction by qualified military personnel. The first attempt to secure military personnel for assignment to filter center duties was aimed at getting volunteer Air Reserve officers. Those officers who volunteered were to be given Reserve Corollary Unit assignments. However, it was necessary that such corollary units be activated by USAF, and ConAC requested this authorization. It was not until the summer of 1950 that approval was obtained for activating these reserve corollary units as Ground Observer Squadrons for manning the filter centers with reserve officer personnel.[41] This delay in providing military personnel created a problem that played no small part in equipping filter centers. Until a responsible officer was assigned, there was no one to sign for the approximately $2,000 worth of Air Force property installed in each filter center. The problem was resolved when the use of reserve officer personnel in the filter centers was authorized; officers were issued the property on a hand receipt as soon as they were assigned to duty.[42]

However, the assignment of Air Reserve officers did not fully meet the requirements for military personnel in the filter centers. Under the regulations governing the Reserve Forces, these officers

---

41. ConAC Training Standard 10-15: "Ground Observer Squadron," 26 Aug 1950. (DOC 216)

42. TWX, ConAC to WADF: "Responsibility for Property Issued for Use in Filter Centers of the Ground Observer Corps," 28 Jun 1950. (DOC 217)

were available for training infrequently and only for relatively short periods of time. This arrangement was hardly satisfactory in view of the need for continued supervision of filter center personnel and coordination with civil authorities. Consequently, in July 1950, ConAC granted its approval of the assignment of one full time regular officer and two full time airmen for each filter center.[43]

The fourth major difficulty which confronted ConAC in setting up the GOC was the problem of properly spacing the ground observer posts. Even when observation posts were completely manned they frequently did not meet the spacing principle of eight mile intervals laid down by ConAC. Despite the many weeks of work which had gone into the plans for properly locating observation posts in order to get the desired tactical coverage, local factors frequently made changes necessary. In many areas which were sparsely populated or entirely uninhabited the problem of finding people to man the posts was, at best, difficult, oftentimes impossible. In a surprisingly large number of communities the necessary telephone facilities did not exist. When either personnel or communications were totally lacking there was no recourse but to abandon the site. Situations of this nature forced WADF to reduce the planned number of observation posts in its area from 2000 to a little more than 1600.[44]

---

43. Historical Report, Directorate of Civil Air Defense, ConAC, Jun-Jul 1950.

44. History of the WADF, 1 Jan-30 Jun 1950, p. 27.

Fortunately, in some areas the facilities of the State and Federal Forest Service provided an opportunity for establishing ground observer posts. This system of using forest service personnel and equipment had been satisfactorily employed in World War II. By the end of July 1950, ConAC had succeeded in securing authority from the Department of Agriculture for the utilization of U. S. Forest Service installations, and the air defense forces had been authorized to contact the appropriate state officials for the use of state forestry locations.[45] Some indication of the aid received as a result of this move was the plans made at Headquarters WADF to incorporate some 400 forestry installations into the ground observer system in its area.[46]

Another windfall in the search for sites for observation posts was the utilization of Coast Guard stations. Since they were manned continuously, integration of such stations was considered very desirable in areas where no civilian posts were available. Arrangements were made with Coast Guard officials to incorporate their installations into the ground observer network.[47] It should be noted that the use of Coast Guard and Forestry Service personnel represented a deviation from the normal practice of using civilian

---

45. ConAC to CGs, EADF and WADF: "Utilization of U. S. Forest Service Installations in Air Defense," 31 Jul 1950. (DOC 218)

46. History of the WADF, 1 Jan-30 Jun 1950. p. 28.

47. WADF to Dir. CAD, ConAC: "Periodic Progress Report," 6 Jun 1950. (DOC 219)

volunteer personnel in the capacity of ground observers.

After the problems in the filter centers and observation posts of the GOC had been overcome, there still remained the general problem of putting the entire organization into motion in the event of hostilities. Except for periods of maneuvers or emergencies the GOC was to be maintained only on a standby basis.[48] The beginning of the Korean War introduced into this matter an element of urgency. Consequently, in the last six months of 1950, a procedure was evolved for alerting the GOC in the event of imminent hostilities or actual attack. Briefly, ConAC was to authorize the air defense forces to alert the GOC when the situation so required. The air defense forces then were to alert the subordinate elements of the ground observer system in accordance with prescribed SOPs.[49]

Another overall problem of major proportions facing ConAC was that of joining Canadian and United States GOC capabilities. The vulnerability of certain key areas bordering Canada to surprise air attacks made it imperative that the Canadian ground observer network be linked to that of the United States. Complete low altitude coverage of the U. S. radar system required that the U. S. ground observer system should be augmented by coverage in Canada north of Lake Ontario, Lake Erie and Lake Huron by a Canadian ground observer

---

48. ConAC to CGs, EADF and WADF: "Implementation of Civil Air Defense System," 10 Oct 1950. (DOC 220)

49. ConAC to CGs, EADF and WADF: "Standing Operating Procedure for Alerting the Ground Observer Corps," 6 Dec 1950. (DOC 221)

system. Without this coverage such key cities as Detroit, Toledo, Cleveland, Erie, Buffalo and Rochester would be exposed to attack by low altitude bombing.[50] The northwestern portion of the United States also required augmentation of the American GOC by a Canadian ground observer system. Radar detection of aircraft in that area is difficult except at high altitudes because of the terrain. A positive coordination of Canadian and United States ground observer systems in that area was absolutely mandatory.[51]

Cognizant of the benefits to be derived from such a union, ConAC commenced very early its efforts to enlist Canada's aid in establishing a joint Canadian-United States ground observer system. In the middle of 1949, a representative of the RCAF's Air Defense Group visited ConAC and participated in discussions of the general system. At this time arrangements were also made to have responsible officials of the Bell Telephone Company of Canada visit ConAC to study the technicalities involved in forming a Ground Observer Corps. In the fall of 1949, three officials of the company visited this country and were fully briefed on the United States ground observer and civil air raid warning systems, and on the construction and operation of air defense control centers and filter centers. During Exercise "LOOKOUT" another RCAF representative was assigned

---

50. ConAC to C/S, USAF: "Coordination with Canada on Ground Observer System," 15 Dec 1949. (DOC 222)

51. WADF to ConAC: "Canadian Participation in the Ground Observer System," 30 Jun 1949. (DOC 223)

to Headquarters Eastern Air Defense Force to observe operations.[52]

In mid-December 1949 the Continental Air Command requested that authority be granted for communication directly with the proper Canadian authorities on this matter of ground observer systems. A month later ConAC was informed that the Joint Chiefs of Staff had designated the RCAF Headquarters and the United States Air Defense Command under ConAC as planning agents for the joint air defenses for Canada and the United States.[53] This authorization permitted direct communications between these agencies and such coordinated planning as was necessary for air defense.

Until the outbreak of hostilities in Korea, little was done either by the Continental Air Command or the Canadian government to implement the plans for linking the ground observer systems of the two countries. After an investigation, the Continental Air Command, in August 1950, came to the conclusion that there were latent Canadian ground observer capabilities in the various wireless communications stations throughout Canada (about 500 in number). Consequently, ConAC requested that higher headquarters furnish the Canadian wireless stations with an SOP for reporting all aircraft sightings and movements or other unusual activities that might prove of

---

52. See: ConAC to C/S, USAF: "Coordination with Canada on Ground Observer System," 15 Dec 1949. (DOC 222)

53. 1st Ind, USAF to ConAC, 16 Jan 1950 to ConAC to C/S USAF: "Coordination with Canada on Ground Observer System," 15 Dec 1949. (DOC 222)

interest to the air defense forces.⁵⁴

As a result of an earlier request, action had already been taken to establish a warning system of sorts in northern Canada. Arrangements had been made with the personnel of the Hudson Bay Company, weather stations, the Royal Canadian Mounted Police, the Canadian Armed Forces and the Canadian Department of Transport to report the movement of aircraft. Since the majority, if not all, of these reports would be reports of movements of friendly aircraft, and since it was assumed that only four-engined aircraft could reach the continent from Soviet bases, no aircraft movements other than those of four-engine aircraft were to be reported in this area. The movement of unidentified aircraft of this type was to be relayed through channels to the appropriate American authorities.⁵⁵

Expansion of the Canadian ground observer system beyond this somewhat sparse coverage was slow. The growth of the Canadian system was phased with and limited by the establishment of Canadian ADCCs to which the reports of observers were to be channeled. Since progress on the control centers proceeded very slowly, the Canadian ground observer system remained in the organization stage. First priority in implementing the Canadian GOC was to be given to the

---

54. ConAC to DP&O, USAF: "Canadian Capability for Ground Observer Augmentation of USAF Early Warning System," 2 Aug 1950. (DOC 224)

55. Journal of Meetings of the Permanent Joint Board on Defense, Canada-United States, 2-5 Oct 1950. (DOC 225)

Montreal-Ottawa-Toronto area.

In summary, it should be noted that despite the delays and frustrating problems which ConAC encountered in the GOC program, considerable progress was made. By the end of 1950, when ConAC relinquished its GOC responsibilities to the Air Defense Command, 26 filter centers had been installed and were operating. In addition, 61 per cent of the ground observer posts were completely manned in EADF, and 52 per cent in WADF. And the groundwork had been laid to coordinate the United States and Canadian ground observer systems.

VI

The Air Defense Command activated on 1 January 1951 inherited the responsibility for the GOC from ConAC. The legacy of ConAC to the new command included a blueprint for enlarging the GOC. This expansion program was designated as Phase II, and the major GOC activities of ADC in the ensuing six months were centered on its implementation.[57]

---

56. *Ibid.*

57. This plan had a curious history. It was drawn up by ConAC in November 1950 and submitted to USAF Headquarters for approval. This plan called for the GOC program to be phased in two parts. Phase I provided ground observer coverage in 25 states along the East and West coasts and Great Lakes regions where permanent radar installations had been built. GOC implementation for Phase I had already been started in February 1950 with the authorization of USAF. Phase II was intended to expand GOC coverage in the original 25 states as well as to extend the GOC to 11 new states. By the time this plan was returned, ADC had assumed responsibility for the GOC. After making certain changes, the new command re-submitted the plan to higher headquarters. By the end of March 1951, the Secretary of Defense had approved it, and thus the plan cleared its last barrier. See: USAF to ADC: "Implementation of the Ground Observer Corps Plan," 12 Jan 1951. (DOC 226); also, USAF to ADC: "USAF Ground Observer Corps Plan," 30 Apr 1951. (DOC 227)

Phase II was designed to close the gaps which existed in areas where the GOC was already organized as well as to implement the GOC in those regions where new permanent radar installations were being built. This meant enlarging the area covered by Phase I in 25 states along the East and West coasts and the Great Lakes region, and at the same time extending ground observer coverage to eleven new states in the Southeastern and North Central areas of the United States.[58] Phase II called for the establishment of 11,400 observation posts and 24 filter centers. The target date set for the completion of Phase II was 1 July 1951.[59] When Phase I and Phase II of the GOC program had been completed the ADC was to control 500,000 civilian volunteers, a force outnumbering by far the total cadre of military personnel engaged in air defense. There were to be 19,400 ground observer posts and 50 filter centers along the northern part of the United States and on the two coasts to augment the radar screen in those areas. Thirty-six states were to be linked with the ground observer network and ADC would maintain liaison with each. Approximately five million dollars a year was to be expended to maintain this "full-grown" GOC.

There were many important changes incorporated in the GOC plan which were designed to facilitate the expansion of Phase II. It has been noted that one of the difficulties encountered earlier was

---

58. See: ADC, "Ground Observer Corps Plan," 18 Jan 1951. (DOC 208)

59. Ibid.

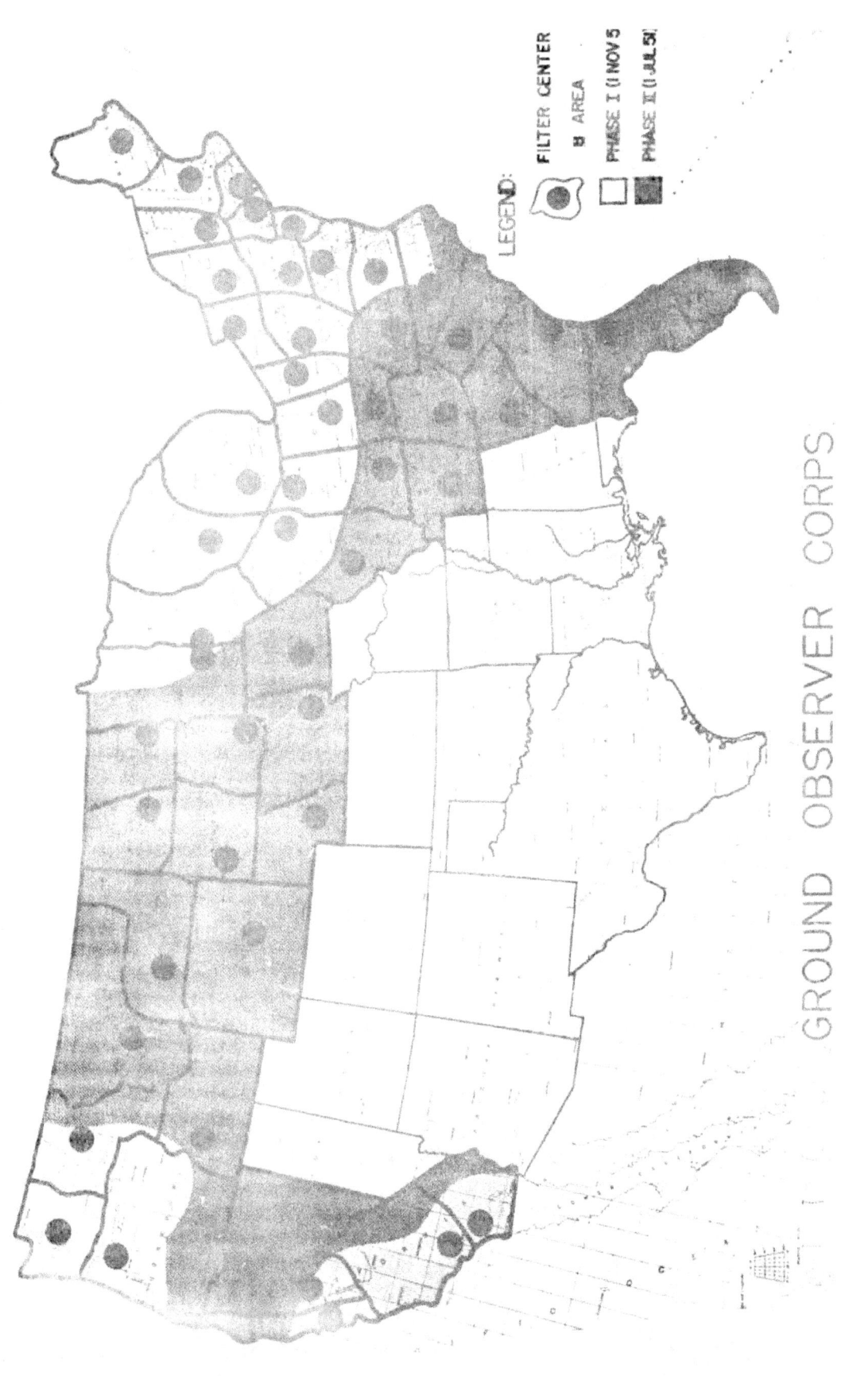

the lack of military personnel on duty in the filter centers. The assignment of one full time officer and two full time airmen to each filter center had not completely remedied the situation. These men soon found themselves bearing a very heavy burden. For example, WADF reported that ". . . the average duty day in filter centers in the past and at present has been and is over 12 hours. All centers have been operating on a seven day week, although efforts are being made to reduce the number of work days."[60] The new plan took cognizance of this situation and authorized five officers and ten airmen to form a regular Air Force cadre for each filter center. In addition, three officers and four airmen were to establish a squadron for the purpose of training and administering the regular Air Force personnel assigned to the filter center detachments in the area of each Air Division.[61] It was anticipated that this manning would obviate many of the filter center difficulties which had been encountered during Phase I.

Another change in the new plan called for the appointment of liaison officers to each state to insure full cooperation with state officials. The experiences of Phase I had revealed certain shortcomings in those states where responsible civilian authorities were lax or reluctant in implementing the GOC. Consequently, the new plan authorized one officer to be assigned for purposes of liaison in each

---

60. History of WADF, 1 Jul-31 Dec 1950, III, 140.

61. IRS, ADC, CAD to P&O: "Ground Observer Corps Squadron Organization," 28 Feb 1951. (DOC 228)

state where the GOC was organized.

It is also important to note that the plan indicated a new federal agency in the civilian chain of command. The newly-created Federal Civil Defense Administration was designed to co-ordinate all matters of civil defense on the national or interstate level. Coordination of civil air defense measures such as the GOC was to be accomplished with this agency through the Assistant for Civil Defense Liaison, Office of the Secretary of Defense.[62]

These highlights of the new plan seemed to indicate that Phase II of the GOC program would progress more quickly than had Phase I. However, a critical defect soon became evident. Despite the fact that the plan had been approved in substance, it was discovered that separate action was necessary to obtain personnel and budgetary authorization to implement the new phase.

This meant that action had to be initiated by the Directorate of Civil Air Defense of ADC to secure the personnel changes authorized by the new plan. Accordingly, a request was made that T/D squadron organizations be established for each Air Division to which there would be assigned the filter center and squadron personnel which had been authorized under the new plan. The result was the activation of nine ground observer squadrons.[63]

---

62. See: ADC, "Ground Observer Corps Plan," 18 Jan 1951. (DOC 208)

63. ADOMO 322, 27 Mar 1951, to EADF authorized activation of four Ground Observer Squadrons in the eastern area; ADOMO 322, 27 Mar 1951, to WADF authorized activation of four Ground Observer Squadrons in the western area; ADOMO 322, 31 May 1951 to CADF authorized activation of one Ground Observer Squadron for the central area.

What effect was this to have on the ground observer squadrons which had previously been organized as corollary units and to which Air Reserve officers had been assigned for filter center duty? Upon activation of the new Ground Observer Squadrons, it was anticipated that the Reserve officer in the corollary units would be called to extended active duty and transferred from the corollary units to the newly activated squadrons. When this had been accomplished, the corollary units would in all probability be inactivated or merely set aside.[64]

Numerous difficulties were encountered in the recall of corollary personnel. In some instances the corollary recallees were alerted for overseas assignment almost as soon as they were recalled to active duty. In view of the fact that these corollary recallees represented the bulk of the trained military personnel in the ground observer system, a request was made to freeze such personnel for filter center duty for a period of one year.[65] Moreover, these corollary recallees had to be equitably distributed between the air defense forces. Since CADF had been activated in the spring of 1951, it was vital that some Reserve officers be assigned to the ground observer squadrons of this newly activated command to afford CADF a source of supply of at least partially trained personnel.[66]

---

64. See: IRS, ADC, CAD to P&O: "Ground Observer Corps Squadron Organization," 28 Feb 1951. (DOC 228)

65. IRS, ADC, OCD to Mil Personnel: "Recap of Officer Personnel Assignments," 3 Jul 1951. (DOC 229)

66. IRS, ADC, OCD to PPM: "Ground Observer Corps Personnel," 15 May 1951. (DOC 230)

By the end of June, this problem of placing the right men in the right place still was not solved satisfactorily. In WADF there were eleven filter centers with only 31 officers on duty. Of the 31, on four were completely qualified, and six were partially trained, while the balance with little or no training had to be assigned to filter centers.[67] EADF was more fortunate because the bulk of those officers on filter center duty were corollary recallees with an average of eight to ten months reserve training in filter centers. Action was initiated to assign some of this trained personnel from EADF to CADF in order to expedite the training of the new command.[68]

It was also necessary under the new plan to requisition by separate action the officers who were to be assigned to each state for liaison purposes. These liaison officers were redesignated as Ground Observer Corps Coordinators, and one was assigned to each state to actively encourage the organization of the GOC within the state, as well as to maintain continuous contact with the appropriate air defense force. In an advisory capacity only, this officer would aid the state organization responsible for Civil Defense in selecting and organizing observation posts and in clarifying Air Force policies in all matters related to Civil Defense.[69] The air defense forces were

---

67. See: IRS, ADC, OCD to Mil Personnel: "Recap of Officer Personnel Assignments," 3 Jul 1951. (DOC 229)

68. Ibid.

69. ADC to EADF: "Ground Observer Corps Co ordinators," 10 Mar 1951. (DOC 231)

requested to fill these new position vacancies with able and mature officers, since this assignment would necessitate tactful and diplomatic relations with responsible state officials.

Despite the incorporation of these features in the new plan to expedite matters, and in spite of the schedules prepared to implement Phase II, the target date of 1 July 1951 was not met.[70] Inability to adhere to this schedule necessitated a revision of earlier plans.[71]

Another major reason for this failure of ADC to meet the target date assigned for the completion of Phase II was the difficulty encountered by the air defense forces in locating additional filter center sites. In the EADF area, eight sites were inspected, but only one was considered satisfactory.[72] The remaining seven did not meet with required specifications. As a result of this problem EADF was forced to report that it would not have its filter centers operational until 1 August 1951.[73]

---

70. ADC to EADF: "Schedule for Implementation of the Ground Observer Corps," 7 Feb 1951. (DOC 232)

71. ADC to EADF: "Schedule for Implementation of Phase II Filter Centers," 27 Apr 1951. (DOC 233)

72. TWX, EADF to ADC: "Filter Center Sites," 28 Mar 1951. (DOC 234)

73. 1st Ind, EADF to ADC, to ADC to EADF: "Schedule for Implementation of Phase II Filter Centers," 27 Apr 1951. (DOC 233)

During the first half of 1951, the ADC engaged in an interesting battle of semantics concerning the status of GOC as an auxiliary of the Air Force. Many state Civil Defense officials were inclined to believe that civilian volunteers of the GOC should not be considered as Civil Defense personnel since the GOC was viewed as an auxiliary to the military activities of the Air Force.[74] ADC maintained, however, that the GOC was not a federally constituted auxiliary of the Air Force and that the military was only the "using service" of this volunteer organization and responsible only for the training and operation of the GOC. This interpretation would leave the selection and administration of civilians to man the organization a responsibility of the federal and state Civil Defense agencies, thereby permitting ADC to avoid conflicts with those political, governmental and personnel factions usually incident to the administration of a civil organization.

Pragmatically, the ADC interpretation of the GOC worked successfully. ADC submitted its requirements for GOC to selected state officials, and then assumed responsibility only for the training and operation in ground observation posts and filter centers. The administration of personnel, however, remained in the hands of civil authorities. In this manner the affairs of the Ground Observer Corps

---

74. WADF to ADC: "Ground Observer Corps as Civilian Auxiliary to Military Activities," 6 Apr 1951. (DOC 235)

progressed satisfactorily. Accordingly, ADC recommended that this dichotomy of responsibilities be concurred in by federal civil defense authorities and USAF headquarters.[75]

The reply from higher headquarters was disappointing and unsatisfactory: "The Ground Observer Corps must be considered as a voluntary Air Force auxiliary which is neither a constituted Air Force auxiliary or an integral part of the Civil Defense Organization . . . ."[76] This left the status of the GOC in a state of limbo until such time as a policy could be determined or clarified.

VIII

To provide realistic training for the ground observers during the first six months of 1951, ADC planned and executed a number of training exercises. Exercises of this type, simulating wartime conditions, were deemed the best means the Air Force has of evaluating the combat potential of units and individuals engaged in air defense. In the case of the GOC there was an added advantage in holding exercises. Decided spurts in volunteer enlistments were noted as a result of each air defense force exercise involving ground observers.

The most interesting of these exercises was held in the area of EADF in the middle of April. The results of this exercise

---

75. 1st Ind, ADC to DC, USAF, 17 Apr 1951 to WADF to ADC: "Ground Observer Corps as Civilian Auxiliary to Military Activities," 6 Apr 1951. (DOC 235)

76. 2d Ind, USAF to ADC, to WADF to ADC: "Ground Observer Corps as Civilian Auxiliary to Military Activities," 6 Apr 1951 (DOC 235)

indicated considerable improvement in performance as compared with previous exercises. Although there was still evidence of need for additional training at both the observation posts and at the filter centers, the progress made in most areas was "encouraging."[77]

In many instances the reporting procedure of the ground observers reflected their inexperience. They frequently failed to identify their posts, to write down their report before calling, to deliver the entire message before stopping for acknowledgment, and to follow other operating directions. At the filter centers, faulty technique and transposition of details in passing reports revealed the uncertainty and inexperience of the personnel assigned this duty. The Telephone Company representatives who observed filter centers during this exercise furnished constructive criticisms to help improve the efficiency of operation.

An ambitious training exercise was scheduled for 23 - 24 June 1951.[78] This exercise called to duty approximately 210,000 members of the GOC to man some 8000 observation posts and 26 filter centers in the Northeast, Great Lakes and West Coast regions. The exercise was the largest of its kind since World War II and the first joint maneuver in the Eastern, Western and Central Defense Commands in more than two years. It was also the first exercise to include night

---

77. H. J. Schroll to C/CDD, EADF: "Results of Ground Observer Exercises - EADF - Apr 14-15 1951," 17 May 1951. (DOC 236)

78. TWX, ADC to CGs, EADF, WADF and CADF: "Training Exercise," 25 May 1951. (DOC 237)

training for ground observers since 1949.[79] In this manner, ADC hoped to test the GOC under simulated battle conditions.

---

[79]. Since the results of this exercise were still forthcoming at the time this chapter was written, they will be dealt with in the history of this command for the last six months of 1951.

CHAPTER THIRTEEN

AIR RAID WARNING SYSTEMS

I

Modern military strategy indicates that in all probability the United States will be subjected to initial surprise air raids in an effort to cripple vital installations and to destroy the will of the American people to resist. To guard against such an eventuality, the Air Force has literally "wired the continent" to provide a Civil Air Raid Warning System (CARW) to warn civilians, and a Military Air Raid Warning System (MARW) to alert military installations.

The genealogy of CARW, like that of the Ground Observer Corps, may be traced back to World War II origins. In the second World War, the issuance of warnings of impending air raids to towns and cities was a major responsibility of the Air Force.[1] In contrast to the postwar efforts of the Air Force to establish an air raid warning system, there were only feeble preparations for a CARW system when war was declared in 1941. On the day following the sneak attack on Pearl Harbor, an alert was sounded on the West Coast, and it was noted that "In the absence of adequate preparations, sirens on police cars were used to warn the people, and self-appointed neighborhood wardens

---

1. *4th Air Force Historical Study III-2*, I, 119.

rushed from door to door to enforce the blackout."[2] On the ninth of December 1941, an air raid warning swept New York City and the Northeast states. Since there was no system for warning the public—New York's air raid sirens were not installed until February 1942—the police took the initiative in spreading news of the alert.[3] Thus, we entered the war with both of our coasts bare of any means to alert the civilian populace in their areas.

Within a very short time, however, civil air raid warning procedures were worked out, and telephone communications were installed. Warnings were transmitted from specified Air Force units on the East and West coasts, to civilian defense agencies which disseminated air raid warnings to the public. Military responsibility ended once the warning had been acknowledged by the civil defense organization.[4] From this point on, the dissemination of warnings and enforcement of precautionary measures against air raids, such as blackouts, became a civilian responsibility.[5]

Needless to say, the CARW system during World War II never received its baptism under fire. Nevertheless, mistakes were made resulting in false alerts, as hundreds of planes were in the air each day, and the task of identifying each flight assumed major proportions.

---

2. USAF, I, 278.

3. Ibid., pp. 279-280.

4. 4th AF Historical Study HI-2, I, 121.

5. Ibid., p. 129.

On the West Coast alone from the outbreak of hostilities to 31 December 1942 there were 25 alerts and eighteen blackouts, and during 1943 there were six alerts and five blackouts in that same area.[6] The CARW system continued to function down to the very end of the war.

Without doubt, the CARW had a significant psychological effect, since it provided assurance to the civilian population that the means existed to warn the public in the event of an enemy air attack.

II

In the period after the cessation of hostilities, the first postwar Air Defense Command continued to plan for CARW. ADC maintained that military responsibility should be confined to furnishing appropriate information to authorized civil defense representatives and that the responsibility of disseminating air raid warning to the general public should be in civilian hands.[7] This was in keeping with the concepts of World War II, and this delineation of military and civilian responsibilities was applied to future plans for CARW.

By the fall of 1948, the Office of Civil Defense Planning had given USAF the responsibility for providing an air raid warning

---

6. Ibid., p. 123.

7. ADC to C/S, USAF: "Relationship of Civil and Military Air Defense Activities," 25 May 1948. (DOC 238)

system.[8] To discharge the USAF function, the ADC was directed by higher headquarters to provide an interim plan for the emergency dissemination of air raid warning information to responsible civilian authorities.[9]

This plan was drawn up by ADC in October 1948. It was a loose interim arrangement which merely called for the dissemination of air raid warnings to the top levels of civil government, and made no provisions for local dissemination of information. Arrangements were made with the air forces under ADC to alert governing authorities.[10] Selective as this system was in the dissemination of air raid alerts, it represented a step towards the establishment of a national air raid warning system.

III

In December 1948, ConAC had assumed the responsibility for the warning system inaugurated by ADC. But at the same time, the decision was made to establish a CARW system which would provide for local dissemination of air raid warnings.

During exercise LOOKOUT in the fall of 1949, ConAC examined the concepts of this more extensive CARW system. Two means of

---

8. USAF to ADC: "Emergency Dissemination of Air Raid Warning Information," 7 Oct 1948. (DOC 239)

9. Ibid.

10. ADC to 1st AF and all ADC Air Forces: "Interim Plan for the Issuance of Air Raid Warnings to Civil Authorities," 18 Oct 1948. (DOC 240)

relaying information were tested, a telephone method and the use of sub-audible radio frequencies. The telephone method took longer to transmit warnings, but the acknowledgment process from civilian sources was reliable. The sub-audible method would pass alerts almost instantaneously, but technical difficulties prevented the receipt of acknowledgments. Consequently, it was decided to rely upon the telephone method.[11]

Exercise LOOKOUT proved the feasibility of a CARW system which could disseminate warnings to the local level. Accordingly, ConAC completed plans for inaugurating this system on a nation-wide basis, and submitted them to USAF for approval in December 1949. ConAC estimated that this system could be operational within five months from the date USAF authorized implementation.[12] By February 1950, the desired authorization had been received from higher headquarters.[13]

As designed by ConAC, the CARW system was to consist of facilities and services provided by the Air Force to alert key civilian agencies. At each of the air defense control centers located throughout the country, there was to be a Civil Air Raid Warning Officer whose duty it was to transmit warnings of an impending

---

11. *History of the EADF, 1 Sep-31 Dec 1949*, Doc 49, p. 12.

12. ConAC to C/S, USAF: "Implementation of Civil Air Raid Warning System," 15 Dec 1949. (DOC 241)

13. *Ibid.*

air attack to designated key point air raid warning centers. To receive these warnings, civil air raid warning telephones were to be installed at selected key point air raid warning centers throughout the United States. From here, calls were to be disseminated to sub air raid warning centers in surrounding local areas.[14]

In those states which were to be provided with only one key point air raid warning center, the installation was to be designated as a State Wide Key Point (SWKP). The SWKP generally consisted of a special telephone in the governor's mansion or in the state police headquarters. Where two or more key point air raid warning centers were to be located in one state, they were to be designated as Key Points (KP). The monitoring of the CARW telephones in the SWKPs and KPs was to be carried on by civil authorities 24 hours a day. Once the SWKPs or KPs were notified and acknowledgment had been received at the air defense control center, military responsibility for the CARW would be ended. It was to be a civilian responsibility to further disseminate the warning information.

ConAC was to assume the responsibility for choosing the KP and SWKP locations. Such factors as population, industrial importance, communicators, vulnerability to enemy attack, and the ability of a Key Point to further disseminate warnings, were to enter into the selections which were made. The Directors of Civil Defense in

---

14. See Chart.

each state were asked to approve the location of KPs and SWKPs. Where differences arose they were to be worked out on a mutually cooperative basis between the Director of Civil Defense and the air defense force concerned.

These ConAC plans for a CARW system were designed to relay timely warning to designated local civil defense agencies, so that action could be initiated to safeguard lives and property and to minimize the effects of enemy action. Such civilian organizations were to include fire and disaster control, chemical detection, biological and nuclear detection, decontamination, bomb disposal, rescue and medical aid, and other post-attack facilities. With the advantage of an early warning, civilian agencies could consider the advisability of a partial evacuation of critical target areas, and alert the civilian population to take cover in preconstructed personnel shelters.[15]

With the authority granted by higher headquarters in February 1950, ConAC was ready to implement the CARW system as described above. In all six of the ADCCs in existence at that time, the necessary equipment to disseminate air raid warning information was quickly installed.[16] As for the installation in civilian locations, a blanket order was placed through the New York Telephone Company for

---

15. See Chart.

16. These Air Defense Control Centers were located at: Roslyn AFB, N.Y.; Silver Lake, Everett, Wash.; Stewart AFB, N.Y.; Hamilton AFB, Calif.; Selfridge AFB, Mich.; Ft. McArthur, Calif.

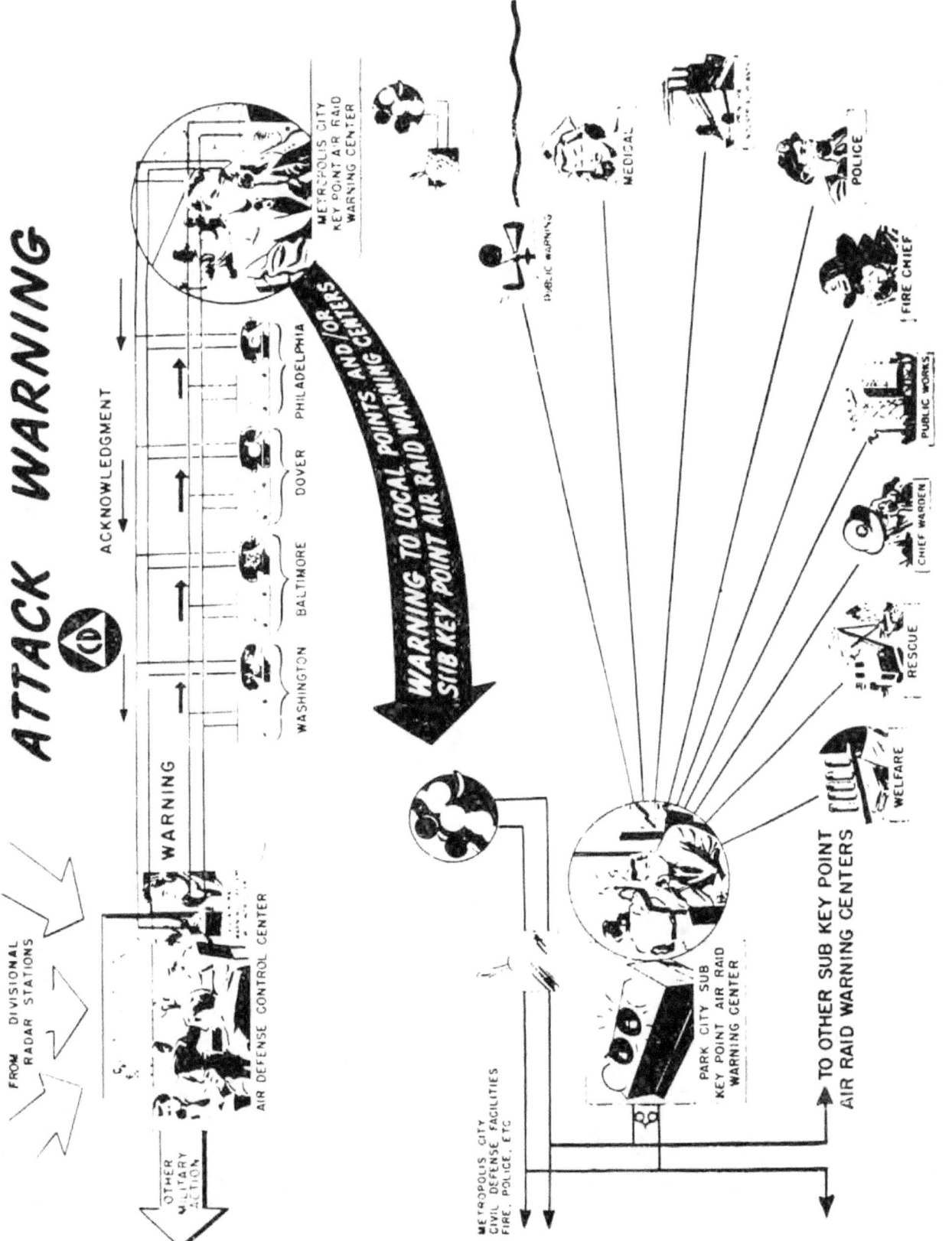

special air raid warning telephones in 147 KPs and 24 SWKPs which had been designated. A target date of 1 July 1950 was set for the completion of installations in KPs and SWKPs.[17]

This target date was not met. It was not until early October that the designated KPs and SWKPs were completely installed.[18] Consequently, the fall of 1950, instead of 1 July 1950, marked the completion of a national CARW system physically capable of disseminating air raid warnings to KPs throughout the nation.

The installation of facilities was only the beginning of the problems which were to be encountered in the CARW system. Frequent tests of this national system soon revealed flaws which had not been anticipated by exercise LOOKOUT. The major drawback was that the time required to alert various KPs was excessive. Consequently the CARW failed to reach a point of acceptable efficiency.

One major reason for ineffective operation of the CARW lay in the failure of the monitors at KPs to answer calls rapidly and accurately. As ConAC stated to its air defense forces:[19]

---

17. One difficulty in establishing the CARW system was the slow receipt of installation information on air raid warning telephones from civil defense authorities. When installation of telephones at KPs and SWKPs had been completed, the State Directors of Civil Defense were to notify ConAC but they frequently failed to do so promptly.

18. ConAC to C/S, USAF; "Status of Civil Air Raid Warning," 4 Oct 1950. (DOC 242)

19. ConAC to EADF: "Increased Efficiency of the Civil Air Raid Warning System," 5 Sep 1950. (DOC 243)

It appears obvious that regardless of how efficiently the military of the Civil Air Raid Warning becomes, unless the personnel on duty at the Key Point perform their function quickly and correctly, the time required to alert various Key Points will remain excessive and inacceptable.

Consequently, ConAC suggested that field visits be made and written instructions be prepared by the air defense forces to properly indoctrinate civilian personnel at the KPs.[20]

A second major reason for the inability of the CARW to reach a point of acceptable efficiency was the delay encountered in initiating single calls to each KP from the CARW switchboard. Experimental tests conducted in the 26th Air Division indicated that the use of a predetermined sequence list filed with the central office of the local telephone company reduced the transmission time about 50 per cent under the individual calling method.[21] The use of a sequence list permitted the operator at the telephone company to initiate the call to KPs, while the military personnel at the CARW switchboard were responsible only for monitoring the conversation. This time-saving device was recommended by ConAC to its air defense forces. Nevertheless, the best results obtained by this method to alert the 26th Division area was eighteen minutes. ConAC planners, on the other hand, had set for themselves a goal of ten minutes as the

---

20. Ibid.

21. ConAC to WADF: "Use of Sequence Lists for Civil Air Raid Warning," 16 Sep 1950. (DOC 244)

maximum time allowable for alerting a division area.[22]

Another step which was taken to speed up the CARW system was the reduction in the number of types of alerts. As originally planned, the CARW was so designed that four different degrees of color code alert were to be given to civilian agencies, depending upon the information available in the control center. However, in August 1950 it was deemed impractical to continue with these four degrees of alert, and three degrees of alert were determined upon:[23]

> 1. Yellow alert: Attack likely – This warning to be given as a result of intelligence indicating that hostile aircraft are enroute to attack the United States. This is considered to be informatory only for purpose of alerting key people and installations. This was not to be transmitted to the general public.
>
> 2. Red alert: Attack imminent – This warning to be given as a result of an Air Division Commander identifying hostile aircraft within his area of responsibility. This is the final warning received at the key point air raid warning center prior to actual attack.
>
> 3. White alert: All clear – This notification to be given when the danger of either Yellow or Red type air raid warning is over. To be transmitted to the general public.

Although these three efforts to cut down on the time for transmitting warning information had limited success, ConAC planners remained unsatisfied and it was decided that the system then in use should be changed. During World War II and from the latter part of

---

22. Historical Report, Directorate of Civil Air Defense, ConAC, Aug 1950.

23. ConAC to DP&O, USAF: "Implementation of Civil Air Raid Warning System," 8 Aug 1950. (DOC 245)

1949 through 1950, civil air raid warnings had been transmitted from ADCCs to CARW KPs by means of individual telephone calls over the common intertoll facilities. These calls originating in each ADCC were transmitted over toll subscriber lines to the nearest toll office. From there they were extended over common intertoll trunk lines to the remote toll offices nearest to the CARW KPs. At these offices they were connected to toll subscriber lines that terminated in special telephone sets at the KP stations. Because trunk lines were frequently busy when calls were placed to CARW KPs, and because there were a number of intermediate points used to process these calls, the intertoll facilities system failed to meet the speed desired to cope with current attack concepts.

ADCC	Toll Subscriber Line	Toll Office Nearest ADCC	Toll Trunk Line	Toll Office Nearest CARW KP	Toll Subscriber Line	CARW KP

During World War II, the speed of aircraft had been slow enough to permit adequate protection of civilians by transmitting CARW warnings in individual telephone calls over intertoll facilities. In 1950, the aircraft speeds were so much greater that it was necessary to transmit CARW alerts to groups of KPs almost simultaneously.[24] Consequently, a multi-point private line telephone network was devised which was capable of rapidly alerting a number of KPs.

---

24. Using this group warning concept the Air Force established the objective of consuming not more than 2 minutes for alerting all keypoints in each area served by an ADCC.

This new system overcame some of the disadvantages inherent in the intertoll system. By leasing telephone lines full time from the ADCC to each CARW KP, the possibility of encountering a busy trunk line was cancelled out. At the same time the use of leased lines eliminated the physical handling of calls at intermediate points which had been employed between the ADCC and the CARW KP in the intertoll system.[25]

In December 1950, the ConAC planners decided to initiate experimentation on a new push button system for a telegraphic multi-point private line network connected to all CARW KPs. This telegraphic procedure was expected to transmit a warning tone to each KP and at the same time light a lamp corresponding to the color of the alert. In this manner the KP operator would be provided with a visual and audible aid. The recipient would merely depress a button corresponding to the color lamp in order to acknowledge the alert.[26]

The ADC became heir to these two programs when it was assigned the mission of air defense on the first of January 1951. Experimentation was continued for a time on the telegraph signalling system, but because of technical disadvantages which soon became evident, work on this project was discontinued.[27] However, the multi-point

---

25. Switching Engineering Report #1, "Civil Air Raid Warning Systems for Dissemination of Alerts from Air Defense Control Centers to CARW Key Points." Bell Telephone Laboratories, 23 Jul 1951.

26. Ibid.

27. Ibid.

voice private wire network was installed almost immediately. It was immediately tested and proved very satisfactory to all users. After testing, it was determined that the new private line telephone system had the capability of disseminating warnings from each control center to all KPs and SWKPs within a division area inside of two minutes, and that acknowledgment from each of the CARW KPs could be received back at the control center within five minutes.[29] Thus, the hope of the ConAC planners to achieve a system which would alert an air division area in ten minutes or less was realized.

Under this new system, each KP was provided with new equipment consisting of a loudspeaker and a push-to-talk telephone hand set which was wired for control to the loudspeaker. In order to disseminate a warning, the control center operator operated a key that placed a distinctively audible tone on the circuit which was received simultaneously at all KPs over the loudspeaker. This alerted the KP personnel that a warning was to follow. After an appropriate signalling interval, the control center operator proceeded to announce the warning, and this was also received simultaneously at all KPs through the loudspeaker. After the conclusion of the warning, the control center operator called the roll of all KPs on the network, and the proper acknowledgment was given by the KP personnel

---

28. ADC to WADF: "Civil Air Raid Warning," 23 Jan 1951. (DOC 246)

29. EADF to All State Directors of Civil Defense, 9 Jan 1951. (DOC 247)

over the push-to-talk telephone hand set.[30]

The old warning system which had employed toll facilities for transmitting alert information to KPs was not wholly abandoned however. It remained in service as a standby for alerting KPs in the event the multi-point voice system failed to function because of sabotage or line failure.[31] The old system was also continued in service in the SWKPs which were not included in the multi-point private line net until 1 April 1951.[32] However, by the end of the first six months in the life of the new ADC the new system was servicing all the air division control centers, with the exception of the 34th Air Division where two KPs with toll facilities were maintained.[33]

During the first six months of 1951, questions were raised by civil defense officials concerning the transmission of alerts by ADC. It was undecided whether the ADC would disseminate warnings with reference to surface or subsurface vessels, or whether such warnings lay within the province of naval responsibilities. Since it was understood that such vessels were capable of launching guided

---

30. Air Defense Warning System ADCC Instructions for Operations of Private Line Voice Network, 11 Jan 1951. (DOC 248)

31. American Telephone and Telegraph Company to All Chief Engineers, 9 Jan 1951. (DOC 249)

32. ADC to USAF: "Status of Civil Air Raid Warning," 13 Mar 1951. (DOC 250)

33. See Chart.

missiles or rockets, a problem of inter-service responsibility arose. To dispel the confusion ADC requested higher headquarters to define the Air Force policy in this respect.[34]

Still another question raised by civil defense officials concerned the definition and degree of dissemination of the white alert in the CARW system. It will be recalled that the white alert indicated an all clear condition, and notification was to be given when either the red or yellow type of air raid warning was over. ADC had specified that the white alert should be given to the general public. However, the yellow signal alert was of a confidential nature, and was issued only to key civil defense personnel and agencies. This immediately brought up the problem as to whether a white signal following a yellow alert should be disseminated publicly. Considerable confusion would result from public issuance of a white all clear signal where no previous public announcement had been made of the confidential yellow alert.[35]

In order to prevent misunderstandings, ADC took steps to qualify its definition of the CARW white alert. The change now read: "Dissemination of the White alert will be consistent with the dissemination of the Air Raid Warning conditions currently in force."[36]

---

34. WADF to ADC: "Air Raid Warning," 28 Apr 1951. (DOC 251)

35. WADF to ADC: "Civil Air Raid Warning," 3 Mar 1951. (DOC 252)

36. TWX, ADC to Major Subordinate Commands, 19 Mar 1951. (DOC 253)

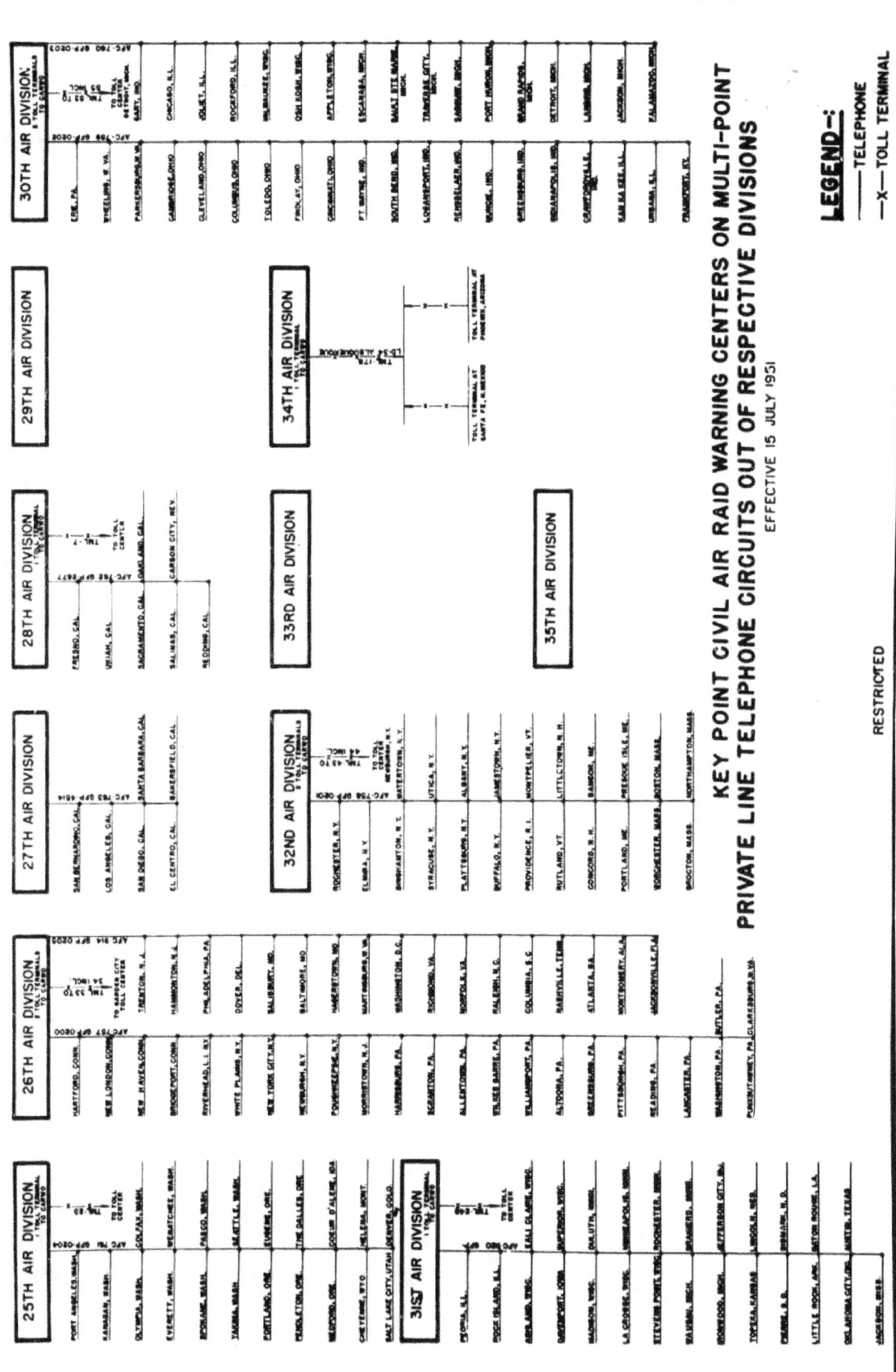

In other words, in those cases where a confidential yellow alert was given only to key civil defense people and installations, the all clear white alert would be confined to these same elements if the anticipated attack did not develop.

During the period under consideration, steps were taken to insure the alerting of the entire CARW system in the event of a surprise attack. Since the existing concepts envisaged a simultaneous mass attack against a maximum number of strategic targets, it was considered essential that the CARW system be so operated that the issuance of an air raid warning by one air division will serve to alert the entire air defense system. Consequently, the following policy was announced as an SOP for the initial attack:

> a. When one Division determines a requirement for issuing a "Yellow Alert" warning, all other Divisions will similarly issue Yellow Alert.
>
> b. When one Division determines a requirement for issuing a "Red Alert" warning, all other Divisions will issue or remain on, a Yellow Alert. Unless further enemy action is discovered in other Division Areas, or unless hostile aircraft move toward and threaten other Division Areas, all Divisions will remain on Yellow Alert for the Initial Attack---the end of which will be determined by Commanding General, Air Defense Command.[37]

A major development in the history of CARW came about when civilian and military authorities engaged in controversy over control of certain aspects of the system. In January 1951, under the terms of Public Law 920 of the 81st Congress, the Federal Civil

---

37. ADC to WADF: "Air Raid Warning," 21 Mar 1951. (DOC 254)

Defense Administration was brought into existence. This organization was destined to fill the vacuum which existed for a federal agency to have a primary responsibility for the defense of the civilian population. It was intended to top the pyramid of authority in the civilian chain of command in the civil defense program by making decisions upon which the nation-wide civil defense system would operate during times of emergency. In certain civil defense matters having to do with air defense, such as CARW, both the FCDA and ADC held responsibilities.

In February 1951, a meeting was held between FCDA representatives and members of Air Force Headquarters to delineate responsibilities for the CARW system. Two basic points were unresolved at the close of that meeting. The first was the question of which agency should determine the degree of air raid alert. The second moot point was which of these two agencies should operate, maintain and budget for the communications between control centers and the KPs.[38]

On the first point the Air Force view prevailed. It was recognized that the Air Division Commanders at the control centers should have the authority to interpret the type of warning and the time of issuance of such a warning to the civilian population, and FCDA stated that it would abide by those decisions.[39]

---

38. USAF to ADC: "Liaison Personnel at Air Defense Control Centers," 23 May 1951. (DOC 255)

39. Ibid.

However, on the second issue the FCDA stood firm. Citing Public Law 920, the FCDA claimed that the Federal Civil Defense Administrator had been given the responsibility for providing the necessary civil defense communications and for disseminating warnings of enemy attacks on the civilian population. It was argued that the Air Force, in fulfilling its responsibility for the air defense of the nation, had organized the present CARW system on an interim basis only, since there had not previously existed a federal agency which had a primary responsibility for the defense of the civilian population. Now that the FCDA had been created, it was prepared to assume the responsibility for operating the CARW system. Accordingly, the FCDA asked for authority to station liaison personnel at the control centers for the purpose of operating the CARW system "which the Air Force has so ably installed and operated during this interim period."[40]

ADC was not prepared to accept a proposal which might adversely affect the efficiency of the CARW system. ADC felt that it should control all communication facilities emanating from its control centers. Since these facilities were becoming more critical every day, it did not wish to have any other agencies, military or civilian controlling any operation within this "most critical installation in the air defense system."[41]

---

40. Ibid.
41. Ibid.

ADC also pointed out that its primary responsibility for a CARW system had been to the state governments, and not the Federal Government. The defense force commanders, in conjunction with the state officials, had selected the KPs to which the ADC would pass alerts. In rebuttal to the citation of Public Law 920 by FCDA as the basis for its powers, ADC quoted parts of the law which upheld its contention on this matter: "/It is/ the policy and intent of Congress that this responsibility for Civil Defense shall be vested primarily in the several states and their political subdivision."[42] In outlining the role of the Federal Government as one of coordination, guidance, and assistance, the law appeared to support the appropriateness of the ADC concept as to how the system should be operated. The issues discussed above were still unresolved by the end of June 1950.

But perhaps of greater importance to the people of the United States than the question whether military or civil agencies will control certain parts of the CARW system, was the positive existence of the system itself. Emanating from the Air Defense Control Centers and connected to 160 KPs throughout the country, the CARW now appeared capable of warning civilians with the speed desired to meet existing attack concepts. The sentinel CARW system provided strong assurance that in the event of surprise enemy air raids the American people would be forewarned.

---

42. Ibid.

IV

The sister system of CARW is the MARW, which was designed primarily to provide warnings of an impending air attack to major military commands and installations throughout the country. In addition, the MARW was also responsible for alerting such critical civilian agencies as Atomic Energy Commission (AEC) installations.

The initial steps to institute such a system came in June 1950, when USAF delegated the responsibility for planning and operating an MARW to ConAC.[43] Within six weeks, ConAC had issued a directive to its air defense forces calling for the establishment of an MARW system which would alert the military and critical civilian agencies concerned.[44]

The principles of operation of MARW were modeled after those of CARW. Alerts were to be initiated at the air defense control center and relayed by means of priority toll terminal circuits to all major military and AEC agencies within the air division area. At each of these installations one telephone was to be designated as a military KP to receive air raid warning information. As soon as the military KPs had acknowledged the alert, the responsibility of the air defense control center was to be ended. Any further dissemination of the warning past this point was to be the function of

---

43. ConAC to CGs, EADF and WADF: "Civil Air Defense Responsibilities and Organization," 14 Jul 1950. (See DOC 205)

44. ConAC to WADF: "Establishment of a Military Air Raid Warning System," 14 Jul 1950. (DOC 256)

the major military command or AEC agency involved.[45]

In addition to providing the design for MARW, ConAC was also responsible for organizing and operating the system. From the time of its inception, the MARW like the CARW was to be considered in full wartime operation at all times. By this means, greater precaution was taken to achieve a more effective defense against surprise enemy attacks.[46]

When the time came to set up the MARW system in the summer and fall of 1950, implementation of this system began smoothly. The solution of many problems of installation which had been overcome in setting up CARW earlier in the year had "greased the skids" for MARW. A few problems were encountered in standardizing the system, defining degrees of alerts, and providing for the installation of some facilities, but by the fall of 1950 the MARW was ready for operation.

A major difficulty confronting the establishment of MARW came in the degree of alerts to be used. It was finally decided by ConAC to design the degrees of alert for MARW to parallel those used in the CARW system.[47]

>   (1) Yellow: Attack likely – This warning to be
>   given as a result of intelligence indicating that
>   hostile aircraft are enroute to attack the United
>   States. Yellow warning will include information

---

45. The Air Force in many cases makes use of the Military Flight Service net to alert its bases.

46. ConAC to CGs, EADF and WADF: "Implementation of Civil Air Defense Systems," 10 Oct 1950. (See DOC 220)

47. ConAC to EADF and WADF: "Organization and Operation of a Military Air Raid Warning System," 11 Aug 1950. (DOC 257)

as to approximate number of hostile aircraft, position and direction, if available. It is considered informatory only.

(2) Red: Attack imminent - This warning to be given as a result of an Air Division Commander identifying hostile aircraft within his or adjacent area of responsibility. A Red Warning will include information as to approximate number of hostile aircraft, position and direction. Further information will be distributed when the Air Division Commander deems necessary, and when raiding aircraft has passed beyond his area of responsibility.

(3) White: All clear - This notification to be given when the danger of either Yellow or Red type air raid is over.

When ADC took over the responsibility for the MARW at the beginning of 1951, steps were taken to further standardize the procedure in the alerting process. Definitions of air raid warning alerts in certain basic military documents used by all three services were changed to coincide with definitions used by ADC.[48] In this manner ADC hoped to eliminate any confusion in its transmission of alerts to Army and Navy commands and installations.[49]

An extensive review of the MARW system by ADC soon revealed that excessive delays were encountered in transmitting alerts over toll terminal facilities. Consequently, in February 1951 ADC initiated the installation of a private line multi-point voice network

---

48. ADC to USAF: "Military Air Raid Warning Definitions," 12 Feb 1951. (DOC 258)

49. The phraseology in the Dictionary of Military Terms for Joint Usage, and the Joint-Army-Navy-Air Force Publications was changed for this purpose.

for the MARW system similar to the system which had been employed so successfully for CARW.[50] As in the case of CARW, toll terminal facilities were to be maintained as a back-up system.

The new system was in operation by the end of the period under consideration and linked ADCCs to 56 military KPs throughout the country. It had been subjected to a series of test alerts and had reduced the time for transmitting alerts over the MARW net. This was a highly desirable improvement, for nowhere does the old adage "forewarned is forearmed" apply more truthfully than in the case of the MARW system.

---

50. ADC to EADF: "Military Air Raid Warning," 21 Feb 1951. (DOC 259) These systems were similar in all but one respect. In the CARW system, the acknowledgment by one Key Point is not heard by the rest of the net because of a lock-out feature. However, in the MARW system, the acknowledgment of one Key Point is heard by all other Key Points on the network. For a detailed description of the operation of the MARW multi-point network see: Ltr, ADC to EADF: "Military Air Raid Warning," 20 Apr 1951. (DOC 260)

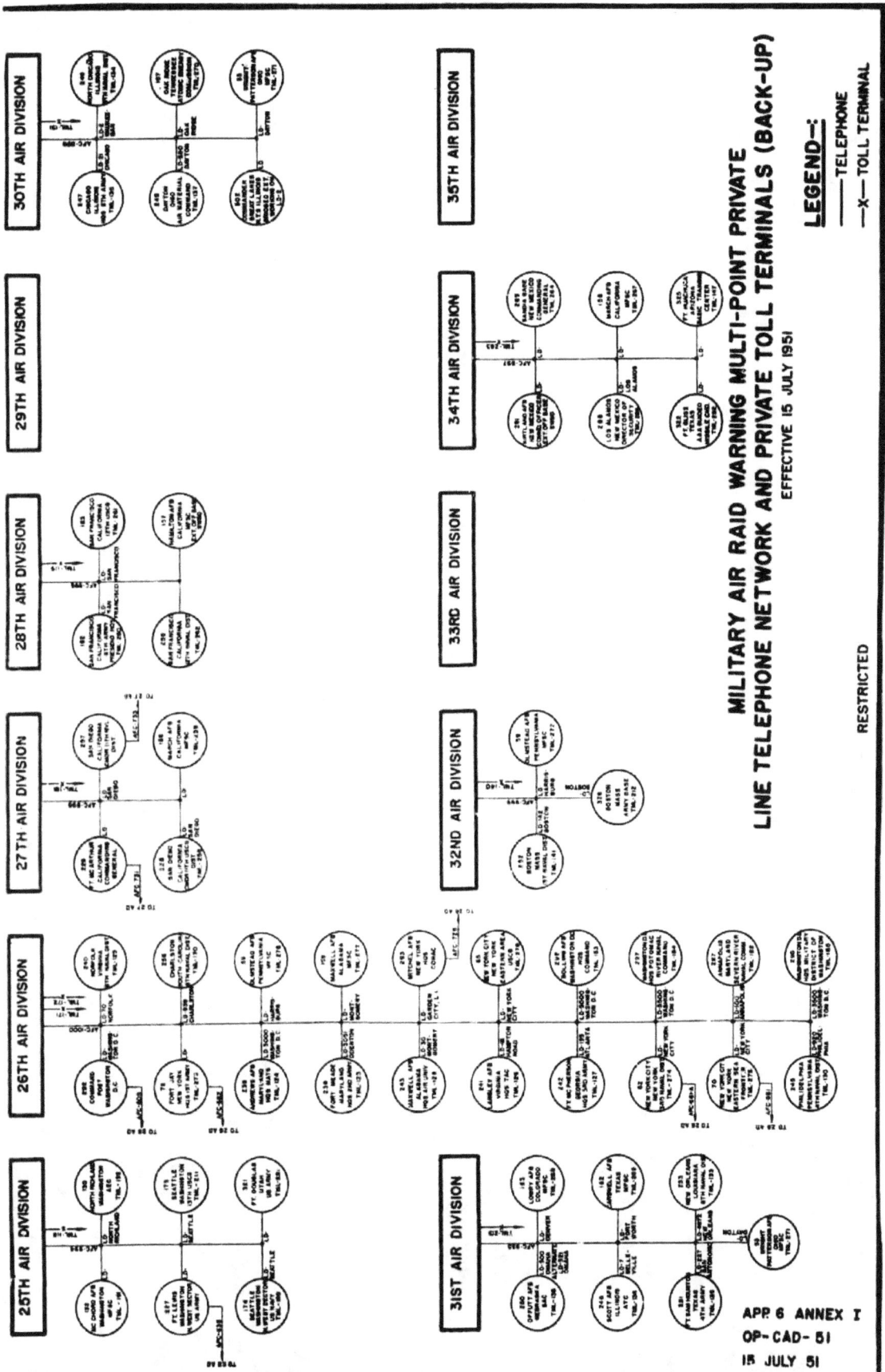

CHAPTER FOURTEEN

AIR TRAFFIC CONTROL[1]

I

World War II witnessed the first attempts by this country to control air traffic. Two months after the outbreak of hostilities, active air defense zones were established along the coastal frontiers of the United States.[2] Within these zones the Air Force created an aircraft warning service. One of the duties of the aircraft warning service was to identify aircraft.

To enable units of the aircraft warning service to distinguish between friendly and enemy aircraft, a system of pre-plotting was employed. All friendly planes operating within active defense zones were required to submit flight plans in advance. On the basis of this pre-flight information the course and position of friendly aircraft were plotted in advance. In

---

1. The term "air traffic control" has many connotations in aeronautical terminology. In this chapter it is used in a restricted sense, and refers only to those efforts made to control air traffic for purposes of identification within the air defense system.

2. The Eastern active air defense zone covered the coastal strip from the Canadian border to the tip of Florida, and extended 150 miles inland and 200 miles out to sea. On the West Coast the active air defense zone comprised the air space extending along the Pacific from Canada to Mexico, and stretched 150 miles inland and 200 miles to sea.

this manner the aircraft warning service was able to identify the track of these aircraft as they appeared within the active defense zones, and all other tracks which appeared were labelled as unidentified.

While the pre-plotting method remained the chief means of identifying air traffic throughout the war, other systems of identification were employed. The pre-plotting method proved to be very cumbersome for the identification of *military* aircraft in view of the intensive flying activity of all the services. The installation of electronic equipment, called IFF, on planes and at radar stations for identification helped to solve the problem. However, this equipment was not available in quantity in the United States until late in 1943.[3]

In addition to the pre-plotting method for controlling civil air traffic, rules were laid down which curbed or prohibited civilian flying in the air defense areas. In the Western air defense zone, during the early part of the war, "private flying was prohibited so as to prevent confusion on the filter and information board which /might have caused/ unnecessary blackouts."[4] In the Eastern air defense zone, regulations curbing civilian

---

3. Even during 1944, after IFF equipment had been installed, it did not operate successfully. A test of IFF along the West Coast during 1944 revealed that nearly 80% of the aircraft plotted along the entire coastline did not display any IFF. See: 4th Air Force Historical Study III-2, I, 138-143.

4. *4AF Historical Study, III-2*, I, 8.

flying were stringent, and extra precautions were taken to protect this zone from aerial observation because of its highly concentrated industrial areas.[5] These controls were not very effective. They generally lacked means of enforcement and no punitive measures for violators were prescribed.[6]

II

After World War II the aircraft warning system was dismantled, and our air defenses were neglected. Consequently, during the postwar years, 1946-1947, little attention was paid to the problem of air traffic control.

In March 1948, ADC ordered a maneuver for the Northwestern part of the United States, and for the first time in the post-war period an air defense in being was operated on a continuous 24-hour basis. As a result of this exercise, the Fourth Air Force, which was in charge of the air defense operations, made the observation that as important as any other element in an air defense system was "a means of controlling absolutely all friendly flying in the defense area."

About the same time that the maneuver in the Northwest had underscored the need for controlling friendly aircraft within the air defense system for means of identification, ADC was engaged

---

5. History 1st AF, Vol I, Project I, 43.

6. ADC to USAF: "Air Defense of the United States," 24 Apr 1948. (DOC 30)

in a study of the same problem. Members of the ADC staff became
convinced that no matter how effective other elements of the air
defense system might be, without immediate and accurate identification of all targets detected by the radar systems no defense
could be provided. Since the IFF equipment used during World War
II had been compromised, no other electronic means of identification were available at that time.[7] The ADC staff concluded that
the only known alternative solution lay in the cumbersome but workable method, which had been employed in World War II, of pre-plotting flights.[8]

The aims of ADC with regard to air traffic control were
set down by the same staff members as follows:

> Control and regulation of all friendly air traffic
> in the air defense areas are mandatory to the
> effectiveness of the pre-plot identification system.
> Such controls and regulations must be exercised by
> the air defense commander and must be binding upon
> all air operations agencies, civil, private and military.

For ADC to successfully identify friendly air traffic
during peacetime by means of the pre-plot method, it was necessary that all aircraft flying within active defense zones file
flight plans. The two main sources for such flight plan information were the Civil Aeronautics Authority (CAA) and the Military

---

7. See chapter on Identification.

8. ADC to USAF: "Air Defense of the United States," 24 Apr 1948. (DOC 30)

Flight Service (MFS) which acted as the coordinating agencies for civil and military traffic respectively. The ideal solution would have been to make mandatory the filing of flight plans with these agencies. However, the first post-war ADC did not possess the authority to make the filing of flight plans compulsory for either civil or military aircraft.

Since no legislative authority existed to compel civilian fliers to file flight plans with the CAA, ADC attempted to secure the voluntary cooperation of civilian pilots in this matter. In the case of military aircraft, ADC had no authority to regulate or otherwise control air traffic in peacetime except for aircraft under its command.[9] This meant that the filing of flight plans by military aircraft of other services would also be on a voluntary basis only.

Based on a system of voluntary controls, ADC inaugurated air traffic control in certain sections of the United States in the fall of 1948. The Seattle-Hanford area and the New York area were designated as active defense areas, and within these areas a limited form of air traffic control was put into effect.[10] All aircraft entering these active defense areas from the sea were to file flight plans.

---

9. ConAC copy of ADC ltr to 1st, 10th and 14th Air Forces: "Identification of Aircraft for Air Defense," 2 Sep 1948. (DOC 261)

10. Ibid. See also ADC Reg 100-5, 30 Jun 1948.

It was soon evident that this system of voluntary controls was not strict enough. In the over-water sector of the Seattle-Hanford area during a given period the system of identification by correlating tracks with flight plans proved to be relatively effective. However, failure of military and civilian aircraft to file pre-flight plans was reported as the main cause for the large number of aircraft which were not identified in this manner.[11]

III

At the same time that it was attempting to establish voluntary controls over air traffic during peacetime, ADC was planning for strict control of all air traffic during a period of emergency. General Stratemeyer felt that the system of voluntary controls over air traffic could not be tolerated in times of emergency. Consequently, at his request, ADC was designated as the agent to represent the Chief of Staff, USAF, in the formulation of basic policies for emergency control of all air traffic.[12]

By the fall of 1948, ADC, in conjunction with the CAA, submitted a proposed detailed plan for the control of civil air traffic in an emergency.[13] A companion plan for the control of military

---

11. 4AF to ConAC: "Progress Report on Identification of Aircraft for Air Defense," 20 Jan 1949. (DOC 262)

12. ADC to C/S USAF: "Air Traffic and Air Communications Control," 3 May 1948. (DOC 263)

13. ADC to C/S USAF: "Security Control of Air Traffic," 21 Oct 1948. (DOC 264)

air traffic during an emergency period was also proposed by ADC at the same time.[14] By making provisions in advance for both civil and military air traffic, ADC hoped to eliminate confusion in applying controls with the sudden advent of an emergency.

In December 1948, the plan for security control of civil air traffic in an emergency was jointly approved by the CAA and USAF.[15] It was felt that it would be essential to the prosecution of the war effort to permit flying by civil aircraft in active air defense areas in time of war. At the same time it would be necessary to rigidly control the flying of civil air traffic within active defense areas during wartime in order to expedite the identification of friendly and enemy aircraft. Therefore, this plan was aimed at conducting a safe, orderly and expeditious flow of vital, civil air traffic during wartime in consonance with the military requirements for the air defense of the United States.

The plan stated that the Commanding General, ADC, in the performance of his air defense mission, was to define the areas which would require air traffic control.[16] The CAA was named as the responsible agency to administer strict security control over

---

14. ADC to C/S USAF: "Control of Military Air Traffic in Emergencies," 20 Oct 1948.

15. ADC, A Plan for the Security Control of Civil Air Traffic, 1 Apr 1949.

16. At this time ADC was under the command of the Commanding General, ConAC. See Chapter Nine.

civil air traffic in those areas designated by the Commanding General, ADC.

Following the approval of this plan, it was decided to test the procedures incorporated in the plan during the coming air defense maneuvers. Accordingly, in the air defense exercise BLACKJACK, held in June 1949, CAA participation was based on the concepts embodied in the plan and consisted generally of providing flight plan data on Instrument Flight Rules (IFR) and overwater flights in or near the defended area.[17] During exercise LOOKOUT, held in the fall of 1949, these basic procedures were again put to the test and proved their practicability.[18]

The plan for the control of military air traffic in an emergency which had been submitted by ADC did not fare as well. This plan required coordination and concurrence from all major military commands which possessed aircraft, and these agencies were not as cooperative as the CAA had been.[19] Consequently, the plan was not approved, and no formal procedures comparable to those on civil air traffic in an emergency were established.[20]

---

17. ConAC, "Report of Air Defense Exercise BLACKJACK, 1-30 Jun 1949," (DOC 52)

18. ConAC to DO USAF: "Control of Air Traffic," 15 Dec 1949. (DOC 265)

19. The plan needed the approval of the Chief of Naval Operations; Chief of Staff, U. S. Army; Commandant, U. S. Coast Guard; Commander, Military Air Transport Service; and Commanding General, Strategic Air Command.

20. ConAC to USAF: ADC Plan, "Control of Military Air Traffic in Emergencies," 15 Apr 1949. The plan was approved for planning purposes only

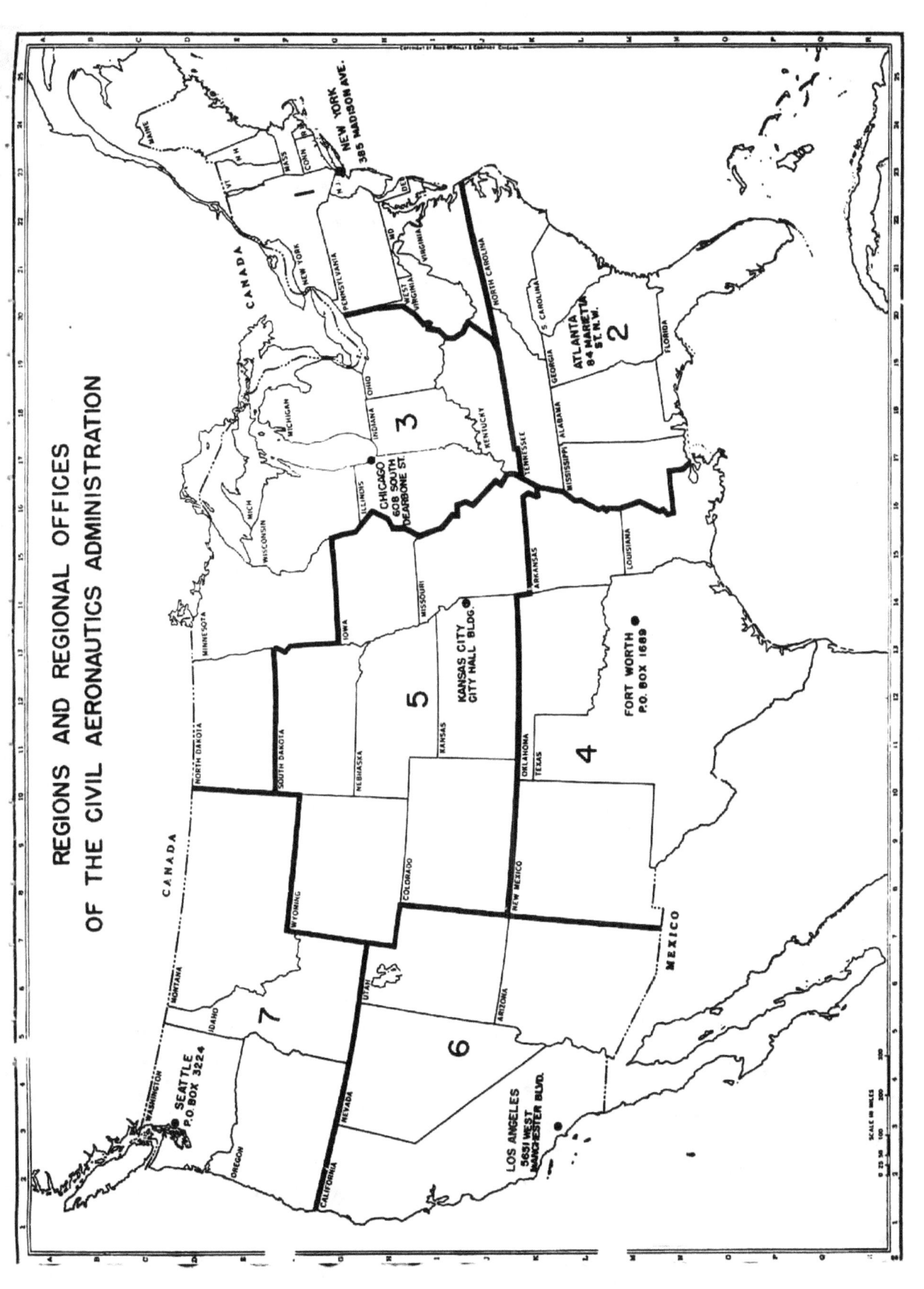

It has already been mentioned that neither the CAA nor USAF had the legal authority to restrict civil aviation or to enforce the filing of flight plans in time of peace. The CAA and USAF jointly sponsored legislation which would give both the command charged with air defense and the CAA this authority.[21] Until such authority was granted, it was agreed that the only solution for the interim period was to secure full voluntary cooperation from civilian pilots with regard to the restrictions imposed by active defense areas and the filing of flight plan data.

It was further agreed that CAA, not USAF, should initiate the publicity to secure the voluntary cooperation of civilian pilots. There were two reasons for this decision. A letter from General Vandenberg had indicated that it would be less disconcerting to the general public if the initial publicity for restrictions on civil air traffic came from a civil agency.[22] The other reason was that CAA had direct contact with civilian pilots through various publications, and information concerning the voluntary control of civil air traffic could be disseminated through these channels.

In February 1950, the voluntary controls over civil air traffic which were desired by USAF achieved the status of a gentlemen's agreement. At the request of the Secretary of the Department

---

21. Report of WADF Conference, Kirtland AFB, 11 Jan 1950. (DOC 266)

22. Ibid.

of the United States Air Force, various civil agencies agreed that all flying in certain critical areas would be conducted above 2000 feet and under IFR.[23] Flight plans were to be filed with the appropriate CAA facility.[24]

Two major difficulties were encountered by ConAC as it attempted to put this agreement in force.[25] The screening by the CAA of all plans for flights in critical areas was a greater task than the CAA could perform with its limited resources; and civilian pilots oftentimes neglected to file flight plans.

Because of budgetary and personnel limitations, the CAA was not able to increase its handling of flight plan information in certain critical areas to provide the coverage desired. At this time there were four active defense areas in the WADF area: Seattle-Hanford, San Francisco, Los Angeles and Albuquerque.[26] Because of the limited CAA facilities, no provisions were made for information on flights penetrating the San Francisco or Los Angeles areas other than from the seaward side. As pointed out by General

---

23. ConAC to USAF: "Identification of Federally Owned Aircraft by Air Defense System," 24 Feb 1950. (DOC 267)

24. Later in AFR 60-22, 19 Jul 1950, Air Defense Identification Zones were established and filing of voluntary flight plans with CAA was requested for all civil flights through these zones.

25. Another problem arose because the agreement did not extend to Canadian pilots flying over critical areas, and an agreement had to be made with Canadians for the filing of flight plans. See chapter on Canada.

26. Col. Israel to Maj. Gen. Rush, CG, WADF, 18 Apr 1950. (DOC 268)

Whitehead, information was required on air traffic entering these active defense areas from all directions.[27]

About this time the entire question of air traffic control became so vital to air defense, and so delicate in view of the non-existent authority of the Federal government over civil air traffic, that General Whitehead had taken the precaution to appoint a member of his staff, in the person of Colonel Robert S. Israel Jr., as liaison agent with the CAA for purposes of joint planning and information. In March-April 1950, it was decided to create a Board for the consideration of matters of joint concern to the CAA and USAF.[28] Colonel Israel was designated as an Air Force member. It was before this Board that the question of complete flight plan information in the Los Angeles and San Francisco areas was deliberated.

General Whitehead also brought this matter of flight plan information in these same areas to the attention of USAF in a letter to the Director of Plans and Operations, Major General S. E. Anderson.[29] General Anderson's reply indicated that the Joint CAA-USAF Air Defense Planning Board had taken action in this matter. He wrote that the CAA had agreed to obtain flight plans from all civil air carrier and executive type aircraft penetrating the

---

27. Gen. Whitehead to Col. Israel, 19 Apr 1950. (DOC 269)

28. "Joint CAA-USAF Air Defense Planning Board," Draft Charter, Apr 1950.

29. Gen. Whitehead to Gen. Anderson, 19 Apr 1950. (DOC 270)

"back doors" of the San Francisco and Los Angeles areas. This would leave little more than the smaller privately-owned types of aircraft without the desired flight plans. General Anderson concluded his letter as follows:[30]

> Since participation in this program by civil aircraft is voluntary, I believe the present agreements are the best we can hope for until appropriate legislation can be enacted. However, we will continue to press the Civil Aeronautics Administration for complete coverage.

Despite General Anderson's optimistic view of the agreements reached with the CAA for the submission of flight plans in the "back door" areas of Los Angeles and San Francisco, staff members at ConAC continued to be disturbed over this problem. Under their joint signatures, Colonels James H. Price and Joseph D. Lee of the Directorate of Plans, Organization and Requirements, prepared a memorandum on the subject of the status of identification negotiations with the CAA.[31] It was the opinion of these staff members that USAF was not following up on the necessary action to get flight plans on civil air carriers penetrating the San Francisco and Los Angeles areas from the north and east. It was pointed out that the CAA would require considerable time to train personnel and acquire communications facilities to undertake the important work of feeding all civil flight plans into the aircraft control network,

---

30. Gen. Anderson to Gen. Whitehead, 11 May 1950. (DOC 271)

31. Memo: "Status of Identification Negotiations with CAA," by Colonels Price and Lee, 24 May 1950. (DOC 272)

and that a delay of six to eight months could be expected before complete coverage materialized.

The problems raised in these negotiations with the CAA in planning for air traffic control have been dealt with at some length because they illustrate so well one of the major difficulties encountered by ConAC in its efforts to institute voluntary controls over civil air traffic.

The second difficulty in this system of voluntary controls was the failure of civilian pilots in some instances to abide by the gentlemen's agreement which required them to file flight plans. Donald W. Nyrop, Administrator of Civil Aeronautics, stated: "We have been gratified by the response to our request for voluntary flight plans. Unfortunately, there have been a small number of pilots who have failed to cooperate in this matter."[32] Fighter interceptor aircraft were frequently forced to intercept unidentified aircraft which had either failed to file flight plans with CAA or which had deviated to a considerable extent from their course. In some cases air defense interceptors were forced to fly perilously close to the civilian aircraft in an effort to ascertain identification numerals and markings, thus endangering the civilian passengers.[33]

---

32. Announcement, CAA-476: "Flight Plans to be Mandatory in Defense Identification Zones," 21 Dec 1950. (DOC 273)

33. WADF to ConAC: "Violation of Prohibited Areas by Private Pilots," 21 Sep 1950. (DOC 274) In the absence of legally permissible controls over civilian air traffic, ConAC resorted to a policy of intensive education of civilian pilots in order to minimize violations in identification zones. EADF to ConAC: "Briefing of Civilian Pilots," 21 Sep 1950. (DOC 275)

In view of the difficulties encountered in this system of voluntary controls, it was obvious that a more rigid control of civil air traffic was necessary. In September 1950, Public Law 778 was passed, giving the CAA power to develop plans, regulations and procedures to govern civil air traffic during peacetime. As a result of Public Law 778, Part 620 of the regulations of the CAA, published in December 1950, required that filing of flight plans would be mandatory for all civil aircraft entering or flying within designated air defense identification zones (ADIZ) over and adjoining the continental United States.

In those identification zones within the United States, flight plans and position reporting were not required for aircraft operating below 4000 feet.[34] This below – 4000 feet exemption permitted aircraft without radio to fly within identification zones, providing they remained below that altitude. In the Atlantic, Pacific and International Boundary Zones, flight plans were required regardless of altitude.[35]

In addition, Public Law 778 authorized the Secretary of Commerce to prohibit civilian flying in certain areas. Three of the ADIZs were several hundred miles in diameter, and surrounded atomic energy plants. These were the Northwest, Albuquerque and

---

34. See: AFR 60-22, 19 Jul 1950, for Air Defense Identification Zones in effect at this time.

35. Announcement, CAA-476, 21 Dec 1950. (DOC 273)

Knoxville Zones. Close to the plants themselves small prohibited areas were established, and within these sectors all flying was excluded regardless of flight plans.[36]

Public Law 778 also contained provisions for anyone who knowingly or willfully violated Part 620 of the CAA regulation. Maximum penalties of a year in prison, a $10,000 fine, and possible pilot license revocation faced the violator.[37] By putting teeth into the law, Congress hoped to eliminate those violations of air traffic control which had persisted under the system of voluntary controls.

During the first six months of 1951, the provisions of Public Law 778 provided ADC with the authority to make mandatory the filing of flight plans by civil aircraft in ADIZs. This procedure has materially enhanced the identification capabilities of the air defenses of the United States.

V

The control of military air traffic during peacetime presented almost as serious a problem of jurisdiction as had the control of civil air traffic. Reference has been made to the fact

---

36. *Ibid.* Two prohibited areas had been established earlier in the WADF area by Executive Order of the President. These were in the Los Alamos, New Mexico and the Richland, Washington areas where atomic energy and other engineering projects of vital importance were located. See: History of WADF, 1 Jan - 30 Jun 1950.

37. Public Law 778, 9 Sep 1950. (DOC 276)

that during 1948 ADC had no authority to regulate any military aircraft for purposes of air traffic control in peace-time, except for aircraft under its command. In the absence of such authority ADC could only request that military aircraft of other services file flight plans on a voluntary basis.

As soon as air traffic control procedures were initiated for military aircraft, it was clear that voluntary controls were not strict enough. In October 1948, all civil and military pilots were requested to file flight plans for all over-water flights in the Seattle-Hanford area and in the vicinity of New York.[38] One of the progress reports that were submitted periodically to determine the success of the identification system in the Seattle-Hanford area stated:[39]

> The fact that all flight plans on Naval Aircraft . . . . . are not forwarded . . . . is the major item at present which makes the identification and preplotting on all aircraft difficult.

It was necessary that the filing of flight plans be mandatory if the pre-plot method was to be used successfully to identify friendly military aircraft. The fact that a number of military agencies, such as the Army, Navy, Marines and Coast Guard, operated aircraft, made it difficult for ADC to obtain the authority to enforce the filing of flight plans. In fact, ADC did not even have

---

38. ADC to 1st, 10th and 14th AFs: "Identification of Aircraft in Air Defense," 2 Sep 1948. (DOC 261)

39. 4AF to ConAC: "Progress Report on Identification of Aircraft for Air Defense," 20 Jan 1949. (DOC 262)

the authority to make mandatory the filing of flight plans by other commands within the Air Force.

After the activation of ConAC, a regulation was proposed by ConAC staff members which would have required all USAF aircraft to conduct all flights within and through certain identification zones under instrument flight rules regardless of weather conditions.[40] It was felt that the stringent requirements contained in instrument flight rules would expedite the identification of aircraft. At the same time it was recommended that USAF extend this same policy to the Army, Navy, Coast Guard and other federally-owned aircraft.[41]

USAF rejected this regulation and the recommendation proposed by ConAC. Instead, USAF favored a proposed Joint Army-Navy-Air Force regulation which outlined procedures to facilitate the identification of all military aircraft. All military pilots would be required by the terms of this regulation to file a flight plan, either operating under Visual Flight Rules (VFR) or Instrument Flight Rules (IFR), whenever over the continental United States or its approaches.[42]

---

40. Proposed AFR No. 60- "Flying: Flight Procedures for Identification in Air Defense Areas," [n. d.] 1950.

41. ConAC to USAF: "Identification of Federally Owned Aircraft by Air Defense System," 24 Feb 1950. (DOC 267)

42. 1st Ind, USAF to ConAC, 4 Apr 1950, to ConAC to USAF: "Identification of Federally Owned Aircraft by Air Defense System," 24 Feb 1950. (DOC 267)

The progress made in formulating a Joint Army-Navy-Air Force regulation was very slow. It was not until mid-July 1950 that the joint regulation was published as AFR 60-22.[43] The regulation listed certain air defense identification zones (ADIZ) in the ZI and bordering ocean bodies.[44] It was made mandatory for all military pilots flying within and through these zones to file flight plans, either VFR or IFR. Furthermore, position reports were required by all military aircraft in ADIZs at given intervals.[45] However, flight plans were not required for local military operations provided that suitable provisions were made for the identification of this traffic between local commanders and local air defense commanders. Thus, the regulation gave ConAC authority to regulate and control all military flights in ADIZs.

The publication of AFR 60-22 did not completely solve the problem of identifying military flights in ADIZs. Two major obstacles arose. The first obstacle was the deficiency in AFR 60-22. It has been previously noted that AFR 60-22, 19 July 1950,

---

43. Joint Regulation, AR 95-210, CNO letter 767P53, and AFR 60-22, "Recognition of Military Aircraft in Certain Areas," 19 Jul 1950.

44. This was a change in the Joint Army-Navy-Air Force regulation originally proposed by USAF which would have required identification for all military aircraft within the United States and its approaches, instead of within our specified identification zones.

45. Position reports required by VFR and IFR flights in ADIZs may be found in USAF and USN publication AN 08-15-1, 19 Jun 1951.

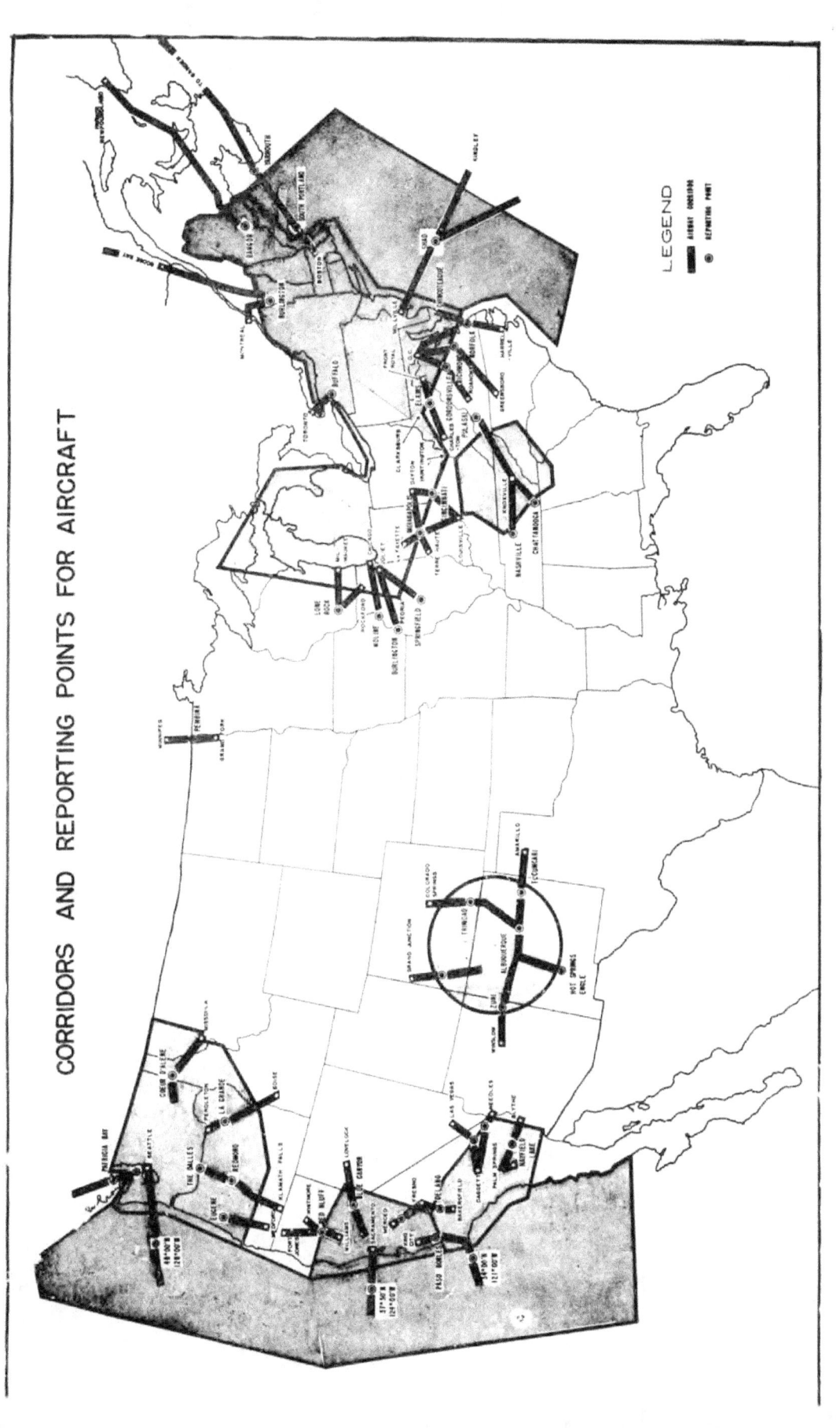

did not require local military flights to file flight plans when operating in ADIZs, as long as arrangements were made with the local air defense commander. The matter of local flying within ADIZs caused considerable difficulty to the air defense system. Consequently, it was recommended that the air division defense commander be given the right to approve or disapprove local flying procedures and boundaries which were established by local commanders.[46] Another change in AFR 60-22, 19 July 1950, recommended by ConAC, concerned the coastal identification zones. In the Joint Regulation, the boundaries of the coastal identification zones were made coincidental with the shoreline. This did not allow the air defense system sufficient time to identify aircraft approach-ADIZ areas from the sea. It was proposed by ConAC that the coastal ADIZ boundaries be established 25 miles offshore.[47]

The two changes requested by ConAC in the Joint Regulation of 19 July 1950 were incorporated in the AFR 60-22, dated 15 January 1951. The revised regulation required the approval of the air division commander on all recognition procedures for military air traffic within ADIZs.[48] It also made provision for moving the

---

46. IRS, ConAC O&T to AAG: "Recognition of Military Aircraft in Certain Areas," 17 Nov 1950. (DOC 277)

47. ConAC to USAF: "Recognition of Military Aircraft in Certain Areas," 22 Nov 1950. (DOC 278)

48. ADC to USAF: "Unidentified Tracks at George AFB," 21 Mar 1951. (DOC 279)

coastal ADIZs some distance out to sea.

The second major obstacle in identifying military aircraft, even after the publication of AFR 60-22, 19 July 1950, arose from the failure of military planes to adhere to the flight plans which had been filed. This problem caused great concern because fighter interception was made on all unidentified planes. In a letter to the commanding generals of Strategic Air Command, Air Training Command, and Military Air Transport Service, the WADF commander stated:[50]

> The navigational facilities available to your aircraft operating between the Pacific Ocean area and the West coast area of the United States admittedly have their limitations, particularly when unfavorable weather and atmospheric conditions prevail. Bearing this deficiency in mind it is requested you inaugurate a program which would substantially improve the accuracy with which your aircraft are being navigated within 400 miles of the Continental United States. It is further requested that this requirement for precise navigation be given wide dissemination to include all operating crews. This will assuredly result in the elimination of costly, and under certain conditions, hazardous fighter interception for identification which inevitably results from inaccurate navigation and non-adherence to proper flight planning.

---

49. Army Regulation 95-210, CNO Serial Ltr 1775P53, AFR 60-22, 15 Jan 1951.

50. WADF to SAC, ATC and MATS: "Identification of Aircraft Approaching the Continental United States," 27 Nov 1950. (DOC 280) With respect to this problem of identifying aircraft approaching ADIZs from the sea, ADC has requested USAF to ask the chief of Naval Operations to make available ocean-going vessels to serve as beacon and picket ships. See ADC to USAF: "Unidentified Tracks at George AFB," 21 Mar 1951. (DOC 279)

In view of the continued violations of military aircraft with respect to adherence to flight plans, ADC had realized the need for a revision of AFR 60-22. The regulation was criticized because it provided no measures for dealing with military pilots who violate its provisions. It was expected that a revision of the regulation would set up certain procedures for handling violators. By this means, ADC hoped to reduce the number of violations and to increase its control over military air traffic for purposes of identification.[51]

VI

Despite the peacetime authority that had been given ADC to make mandatory the filing of flight plans by all air traffic within ADIZs, the air defense system was still unable to identify all aircraft within these zones. It was discovered that in certain areas within the ADIZs, where there was a large volume of air traffic, the task of correlating and plotting all flight plans for the pre-plot method of identification was too great. To alleviate this situation, ADC established "free areas" within ADIZs where there was a high traffic density. All uncorrelated tracks of aircraft which originated in a "free area" were to be identified as friendly. However, tracks appearing outside the "free area"

---

51. It should be noted that IFF as well as the pre-plot method of identification is being employed on a large scale to identify military aircraft. See chapter on Identification, Section IV.

which were inbound to the "free area" were to be identified as questionable unless correlation with flight plans could be effected.[52]

Thus, ADC conceded that identification of aircraft by correlation of flight plans was not possible in areas of heavy air traffic density, even if the flight plan information were available. Therefore, a calculated risk in the identification of aircraft was taken by establishing "free areas."

"Free areas" were set up in the Los Angeles, San Francisco and Northwest ADIZs on an experimental basis.[53] The noticeable decline in the number of unidentified tracks in these areas was partially attributed to the use of this "free area" concept.[54] It was expected that "free areas" would be established in other congested areas. However, it has been decided by ADC that "the numbers and size of these areas must be kept to a minimum and their establishment must, in each case, be justified."[55]

The establishment of "free areas" was to apply only to peacetime operations. In the event of imminent hostile air attacks,

---

52. ADC to WADF, CADF and EADF: "(Restricted) Policy on Establishment of Free Areas," 13 Apr 1951. (DOC 281)

53. ADC Headquarters Staff Briefing, "Current Operational Problems," 17 Mar 1951. (DOC 282)

54. ADC, *Command Data Book*, Mar 1951.

55. ADC to WADF: "(Restricted) Policy on Establishment of Free Areas," 13 Apr 1951. (DOC 281)

the "free area" concept was to be abandoned, and more stringent controls of local air traffic were to be inaugurated.

VII

It will be recalled that the first post-war ADC had submitted two plans for strict control of all air traffic during a period of emergency. The plan for the security control of civil air traffic in an emergency had been approved by USAF and the CAA by 1 April 1949. The companion plan for the control of military air traffic under emergency or war conditions had failed to gain the approval of the other major military commands. Here matters stood until April 1950, when it was reported to ConAC that the plan for the security control of civil traffic under emergency conditions was being revised and expanded to apply to all air traffic, civil and military.[56]

It was eleven months before a plan was adopted which gave the air defense system authority over civil and military air traffic in the event of an emergency.[57] While this matter was under consideration, three steps were taken by ConAC to ensure some measure of control over civil and military air traffic in case of war or a sudden emergency.

---

56. Col. Israel to Gen. Whitehead: "Report on CAA-USAF Air Defense Planning Board," 28 Apr 1950. (DOC 283)

57. ADC, "Interim Joint Plan for Movement Control of Military and Civil Aircraft Entering, Departing, or Moving within the Continental United States under Military Emergency," 1 Mar 1951.

The first step taken by ConAC was to authorize the air defense forces to make detailed arrangements with CAA regional administrators for governing the control of civil air traffic during a period of alert. The air defense forces in turn directed that plans and SOPs be made on a local level by air division commanders and local CAA officials, since requirements and conditions varied in each air division area.[58] The procedures agreed upon were to be considered as interim arrangements and were to remain in effect until a final plan for the control of all air traffic was developed.

The second step taken by ConAC was to impress USAF with the necessity for controlling military air traffic under alert conditions. The problem of controlling military aircraft in an emergency was presented as follows:[59]

> Control of Military Air Traffic, however, is not as yet provided. SAC has agreed to certain routes and procedures through the defended areas of the Continental U.S. during critical periods of their operations, but other USAF aircraft and/or US Navy aircraft cannot be controlled until instructions are issued by their respective Command Headquarters indicating action to be taken under alert conditions.

The third step taken by ConAC was to submit a plan to USAF for the control of both civil and military air traffic in

---

58. ConAC to USAF: "Control of Military Air Traffic During Alert," 27 Oct 1950. (DOC 284)

59. ConAC to EADF: "Movements of Military and Civil Aircraft," 10 Aug 1950. (DOC 285)

the event of an emergency.[60] It was this plan which was adopted by USAF, after a few minor changes, as the plan to govern all air traffic under emergency conditions.

In submitting this plan, ConAC again called to the attention of USAF the absence of any control over military air traffic under emergency conditions:[61]

> In order, however, to provide for control of all aircraft in the event of sudden emergency all military agencies operating aircraft must be aligned to conform to the provisions of this plan to insure identification of friendly aircraft and offer minimum interference to the protection of vital areas of the United States against hostile aircraft.

After the activation of ADC, the plan submitted by ConAC was approved by USAF and returned to the ADC Headquarters.[62] It is of great importance to note that USAF had coordinated this plan with all other services and that the provisions of the plan were made binding on all military units with aircraft.[63]

This Interim Joint Plan, as it came to be known, outlined

---

60. ConAC, "Interim Joint Proposal for Movement Control of Military and Civil Aircraft Entering, Departing or Moving within the Continental United States under Emergency Conditions," 7 Dec 1950.

61. ConAC to D/O USAF: "Control of Air Traffic," 11 Dec 1950. (DOC 286)

62. ADC, "Interim Joint Plan for Movement Control of Military and Civil Aircraft Entering, Departing or Moving within the Continental United States," 1 Mar 1951.

63. IRS, O&T to DO: "Control of Air Traffic," 9 Mar 1951. (DOC 287)

procedures for the security control of all air traffic during an emergency, and included corridors and reporting procedures for all aircraft moving in ADIZs.⁶⁴ This plan was to become effective automatically upon the declaration of an emergency or in the event of hostile action by an enemy. As defined, the following situations would constitute grounds for putting the Interim Joint Plan into effect: A Presidential proclamation declaring a national emergency; a tense military situation whereby the Commanding General, ADC, declares a state of emergency; an enemy attack on targets in the continental United States, a known impending enemy attack,⁶⁵ or when an aircraft bearing USSR markings without flight clearance is identified within the geographical boundaries of the continental United States.⁶⁶

At the end of June 1951, ADC was in the process of revising the Interim Joint Plan. It was intended to eliminate the "interim" status of the plan, and in its place would be a plan of more permanent status based on recommended changes which have been submitted to USAF by other Air Force Commands, the Army, Navy and

---

64. ADC to CG SAC: "Movement Control of Aircraft During Military Emergency," 8 Mar 1951. (DOC 288)

65. ADC, "Interim Joint Plan for Movement Control of Military and Civil Aircraft Entering, Departing or Moving within the Continental United States," 1 Mar 1951.

66. TWX, ADC to EADF and CADF, 24 May 1951. (DOC 289)

CAA. In addition, it was intended to broaden the scope of the plan to include the control of electro-magnetic radiations. Procedures were to be established to shut down radio aids to air navigation in an emergency, in order to deny the use of such electro-magnetic radiations to the enemy. All civil and military navigation aids, including homing beacons, range stations and GSA, were to be controlled for purposes of security.

---

67. 1st Ind, ADC to EADF, 7 Jun 1951 to EADF to ADC: "Clarification of the Term 'White Alert,'" 26 May 1951. (DOC 290)

CHAPTER FIFTEEN

CANADA: TOWARDS A HEMISPHERIC DEFENSE

I

"If there is a third World War," said General H. H. "Hap" Arnold before he retired as head of the Army Air Forces, "its strategic center will be the North Pole." "Through the arctic," agreed General Carl A. "Tooey" Spaatz, former Chief of the Army Air Forces, "every industrialized country is within reach of our strategic air. America is similarly exposed. We are, in fact, wide open at the top."[1] These statements explain and dramatize the need for a defense against air attack from the polar regions.

Because both countries were "wide open at the top" and exposed to a common danger, the United States and Canada agreed that there had to be close coordination between their respective air defense systems. After the cessation of hostilities in World War II, the United States - Canadian Permanent Joint Board on Defense (PJBD) discussed the extent to which the wartime cooperation between the armed forces of the two countries should be maintained in the post-war period. Early in 1947, an agreement was reached. This agreement was in essence nothing more than a reiteration of the wartime principle that the PJBD was "to consider in the broad sense the defense of the northern half of the Western

---

1. New York Times, 13 February 1947.

Hemisphere."[2]

As a result of the agreement of 1947, joint planning continued for coordinating the air defense systems of Canada and the United States. Eventually, the joint planners envisaged a common set of policies on doctrine and procedure, common tactics and techniques, standardized equipment, and, in general, complete cooperation and coordination of all the components of an air defense system. The efforts of both countries to achieve a common air defense have gone far to erase the boundary which divides the two sovereign nations.

To be specific, the joint plans for mutual air defense operations included the following: (1) A Canadian - United States Emergency Air Defense Plan, (2) plans for radar extension into Canada, (3) agreements on air traffic control, (4) overfly agreements for purposes of interception, (5) communication requirements between the two air defense systems, (6) coordination on civil air defense programs, (7) joint use of IFF, (8) plans for joint training and operations in the field of electronic counter-measures, (9) cross-servicing of aircraft, and (10) exchange of information.

---

2. This principle of joint defense of the northern half of the Western Hemisphere was laid down by President Roosevelt and Prime Minister Mackenzie King when they established the PJBD in 1940. The PJBD was designed to work out ways and means for a mutual defense of the northern half of the western hemisphere. After plans had been made by the PJBD, its members coordinated the planning with their respective Joint Chiefs of Staff. If questions of sovereignty were involved the Joint Chiefs of Staff of both countries sought the approval of respective heads of government, i.e. the President and Prime Minister.

II

In the spring of 1949, the Joint Chiefs of Staff approved the Canada – United States Emergency Defense Plan. This plan designated the Commanding General, ConAC, as the United States planning agent to formulate, in conjunction with the Group Commander, Air Defense Group, RCAF, plans for the joint air defense of certain vitally important areas.[3] By mid-1950, the two planning agents had prepared the first Canada – United States Emergency Air Defense Plan (CANUSEADP).[4]

CANUSEADP set forth a policy for the operational integration of the air defense systems of Canada and the United States to go into effect in the event of an emergency or hostilities. The concept governing this mutual defense was the placing of emphasis of the integrated air defense effort on those important areas in the United States and Canada which were adjacent to the international boundary. Operational control of RCAF air defense forces was to pass to USAF air defense agencies, and operational control of USAF air defense forces was to pass to the RCAF ADCCs whenever the tactical situation so required.[5] The plan was also designed to

---

3. 2nd Ind ConAC to EADF, 22 Jun 1950, to ConAC to EADF and WADF: "Canada – U. S. Emergency Air Defense Plan," 1 Jun 1950.

4. Canada – U. S. Emergency Air Defense Plan, Jun 1950.

5. Ibid.

link the two national air defense systems by means of connecting communications facilities.

The original version of CANUSEADP calling for the operational integration of the two national air defense systems was never approved. A controversy arose between the Canadian and American planners with respect to certain terms employed in the plan. The RCAF Group Commander stated that his forces "must be integrated operationally into the U. S. System."[6] This viewpoint was based on his opinion that coordination between the two air defense systems would not prove effective during actual hostilities.

ADC, which succeeded ConAC as the planning agency, did not concur with the concept of operational integration. In view of the inherent rights of sovereignty of the respective governments, ADC specifically recommended that the two systems be coordinated.[7] In effect, the use of the term "coordinated" would still leave the two air defense systems in mutual support of each other, but would serve to curtail the respective responsibilities implied in the term "operational integration."

In order to cut the Gordian knot resulting from the divergence of opinion held by these two headquarters, ADC submitted this

---

6. ADC to DO/USAF: "Canada – U. S. Emergency Air Defense Plan 1-51," 2 Jun 1951. (DOC 291) Underlining added.

7. ADC to ADC of the RCAF: "Canada – United States Emergency Air Defense Plan," 10 Jul 1951. (DOC 292) Underlining added.

matter to higher headquarters for solution.[8] In August 1951, word was received from USAF that the RCAF Air Defense Command had accepted and unreservedly approved the ADC revision of the CANUSEADP.[9]

The new version of the plan was designated CANUSEADP 1/51 to distinguish it from the original plan. Apart from bringing the communication requirements up-to-date, the only major change from the original plan was the insertion of the term "coordinated Canada – U. S. air defense system," in lieu of "integrated Canada – U. S. air defense system."[10] The concept of concentrating the coordinated air defense effort of the two countries in the direction of those mutually important adjacent American and Canadian areas having the highest probability of attack remained the same. Thus, the principle of mutual support by the two air defense systems remained inviolate.

---

8. ADC to DO/USAF: "Canada – U. S. Emergency Air Defense Plan 1-51," 2 Jun 1951. (DOC 291)

9. Certain other changes not concerned with the integration-coordination controversy were to be made so final Canadian approval on the plan was forthcoming.

10. ADC to DO/USAF: "Canada – U. S. Emergency Air Defense Plan 1-51," 2 Jun 1951. (DOC 291)

11. Canada – U. S. Emergency Air Defense Plan 1-51 (Short title): CANUSEADP 1/51.

The most ambitious undertaking of the Canadian - U. S. air defense partnership has been the plan to extend the radar network from the United States into Canada. The joint radar extension plan was designed to stretch the early warning capabilities of the radar system of the continental United States, and at the same time provide Canada with a GCI and early warning capability.

During a conference at ConAC Headquarters in July 1950, a combined radar plan was drawn up by the Canadian and American air defense planners.[12] Relatively little difficulty was encountered in determining the radar sites for the Canadian radar net, because both countries had important population and industrial complexes adjacent to each other on the international border. The joint planning on the extension of the radar net was completed at the end of November, and was submitted to USAF.[13]

In the meantime, another important step had been taken towards the realization of the proposed Canadian radar network. In mid-July 1950, ConAC informed USAF that only one-half of the radar sites involved had been surveyed, and suggested that Ameri-

---

12. ConAC to C/S RCAF: "Expedition of Siting Surveys in Canada for Combined Radar Plan," 14 Jul 1950. (DOC 293)

13. ConAC Current Planning Activity Reports, 4 Dec 1950.

can survey parties be sent to aid the Canadians.   As a result, ConAC sent siting parties. Even with this American aid, the survey of the 35 sites in the proposed Canadian radar net was not completed until late July 1951.

The two nations agreed that of the 35 sites in the radar extension plan, twelve were to be built by the RCAF, and 22 were to be constructed with funds from the United States.[15] The cost of constructing the entire radar net (with a few exceptions) was to be shared on the basis of approximately two-thirds by the United States and one-third by Canada.[16] In-so-far as was practicable, the construction of the installations required for the Canadian radar net were to be carried out by Canadian agencies and contractors and with Canadian labor and materials.[17]

During the first six months of 1951, ADC assumed specific responsibilities in the joint radar extension net. ADC was to man, operate and give supply and logistical support to eight of the Canadian radar sites. In addition, ADC was also responsible

---

14. TWX, ConAC to DP/USAF, 20 Jul 1950. (DOC 294)

15. Minutes of the Meeting of the Sub-Committee on Supply, AFHQ Ottawa, 7-9 May 1951.

16. Ltr. Hume H. Wrong, Ambassador of Canada, to Dean Acheson, Secretary of State of the United States, 1 Aug 1951. (DOC 295)

17. Ibid.

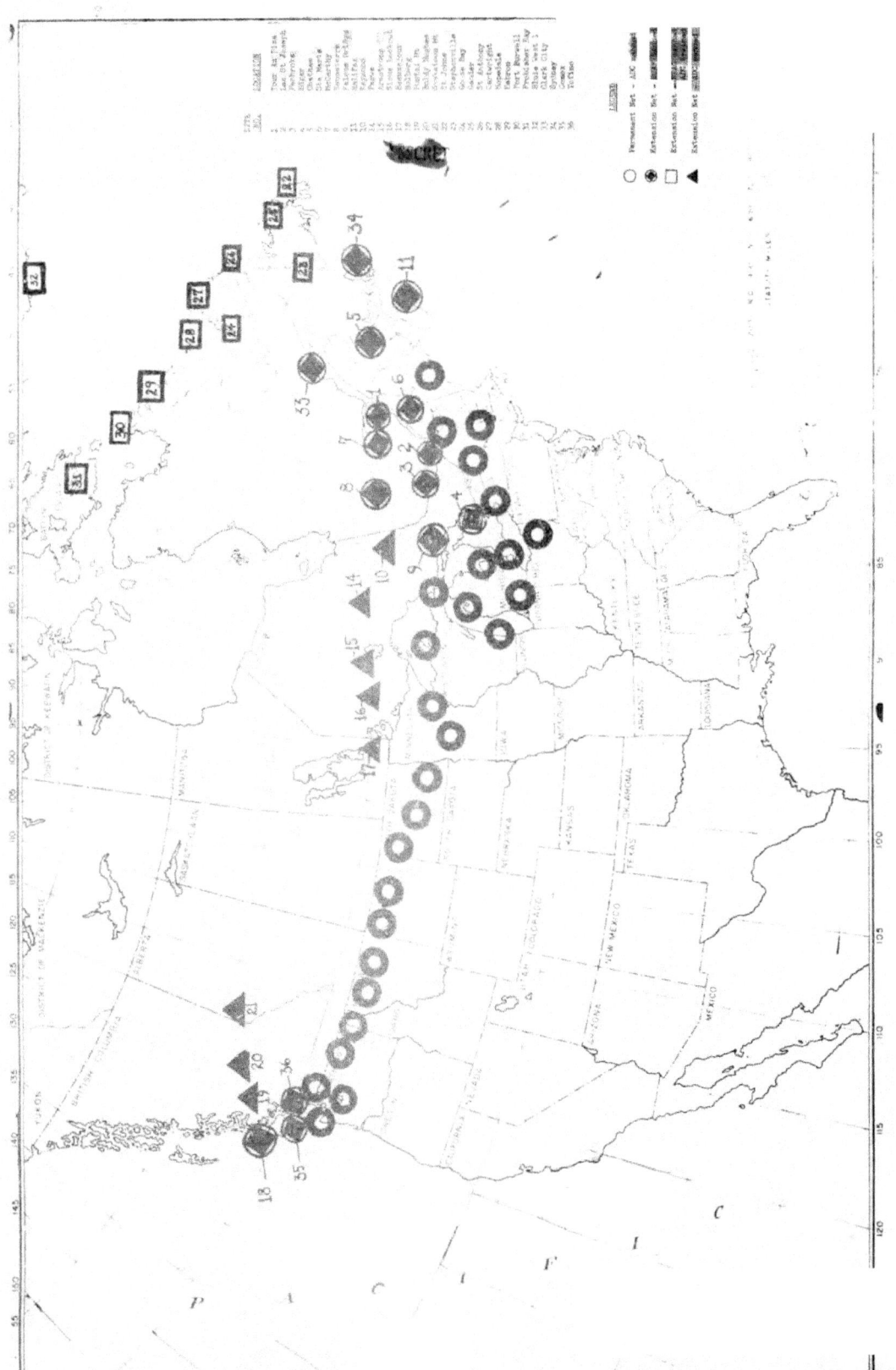

for the organization and training of certain AC&W personnel who were to be transferred to the Northeast Air Command for the purpose of manning ten radar stations included in the radar extension plan.[18] Plans were also made to determine the communication requirements for the joint radar net.[19]

In May 1951 a meeting was held to discuss the progress which had been made on the radar extension net. At that time it was noted that production problems had forced the RCAF to push back its target date six months on nine of the twelve radar sites for which the RCAF was responsible.[20] Three major factors were responsible for holding up the early completion of the initial nine radar stations: Scarcity of critical materials; design changes of equipment already in production; and the obtaining of security clearances for key Canadian personnel who were required to enter United States plants for consultation or production problems.[21] Steps were being taken to eliminate these bottlenecks.

In order to further expedite measures which had been taken to accomplish the radar extension plan, USAF and the RCAF decided

---

18. USAF to ADC: "Air Defense Command Responsibilities with Respect to the USAF World-Wide Radar Program," 10 Jul 1951. (DOC 296)

19. ADC, Current Planning Activities Report, 12 Mar 1951.

20. Minutes of the Meeting held in the Office of A. N. Zimmerman, Director of Electronics, Ottawa, 10 May 1951.

21. Ibid.

to form a Radar Extension Plan Operations Committee.[22] It was agreed that working groups would be appointed to this Committee from time to time to prepare material for the consideration of the Committee, and to perform specific tasks as directed by the Committee. Members of the ADC staff were designated to act as advisors to this Committee.[23]

The progress made on the radar extension plan by June 1951 has been noted in the chart on the following page. The chart represents more of a blueprint for future development of this project, than record of past achievements. It indicates, however, how closely the two nations have planned together to form a common radar defense.

IV

It was recognized from the outset that no attempt to institute controls over air traffic in this country could be successful unless air traffic entering the United States from Canada could be similarly controlled. When, in the spring of 1950, control of air traffic was inaugurated within certain areas

---

22. Minutes of the Meeting held at RCAF/AMC Ottawa, 21 Jun 1951. At a later meeting the name of this committee was changed to the Radar Extension Plan Steering Committee. This latter committee recommended that only one working group called the Commands Working Sub-Committee be formed to meet periodically.

23. Radar Extension Plan Operations Committee, Minutes of Meeting held at RCAF/AMC Ottawa, 23 Jul 1951.

A C & W Program Chart, June 1951 - Canadian Radar Sites.

SITE NO.	LOCATION	TYPE	TARGET BENEFICIAL OCCUPANCY	ESTIMATED TECHNICAL EQUIPAGE	LASH-UP LOCATION	LASH-UP EQUIPMENT	SITE CONSTR. STATUS	ADCC CONTROLLING	REMARKS
C 1	Tour Au Pica, P.Q.	GCI	1 Oct 51	1 May 52			50%	Lac St Joseph	RCAF manned
C 2	Lac St Joseph, P.Q.	GCI (ADCC)	1 Oct 51	1 May 52	St Hubert	Ames 11	50%	Lac St Joseph	RCAF manned
C 3	Pembroke (Foymount) Ont	GCI	1 Aug 51	1 Jan 52			65%	Edgar	RCAF manned
C 4	Edgar, Ont	GCI (ADCC)	1 Aug 51	1 Jan 52			65%	Edgar	RCAF manned
C 5	Chatham, N.B.	GCI (ADCC)	1 Aug 51	1 Jan 52	Chatham	Ames 11	65%	Chatham	RCAF manned
C 6	Ste Marie, P.Q.	GCI					Surveyed	Lac St Joseph	RCAF manned
C 7	McCarthy, P.Q.	EW	1 Nov 51	1 Jun 52			50%	Lac St Joseph	RCAF manned
C 8	Senneterre, P.Q.	EW	1 Nov 51	1 Jun 52			50%	Lac St Joseph	RCAF manned
C 9	Falconbridge, Ont	EW	1 Aug 51	1 Jan 52			65%	EDGAR	RCAF manned
C 10	Raymore, Ont	EW					Surveyed	Edgar	ADC manned initially
C 11	Halifax, N.S.	EW			Halifax	CHL	Surveyed	Chatham	RCAF manned
C 33	Clark City, P.Q.	EW			Summerside	Ames 11	Surveyed	Chatham	RCAF manned
C 34	Sydney, N.S.	EW					Surveyed	Chatham	RCAF manned
C 14	Pagwa, Ont	EW					Surveyed	Ft Snelling	ADC manned initially
C 15	Armstrong, Ont	EW					Surveyed	Ft Snelling	ADC manned initially
C 16	Sioux Lookout, Ont	EW					Surveyed	Ft Snelling	ADC manned initially
C 17	Beausejour, Man	EW					Surveyed	Ft Snelling	ADC manned initially
C 18	Cape Scott (Holberg) B.C.	EW	1 Nov 51	1 Jun 52			50%	Tofino	RCAF manned
C 35	Comox, B.C.	GCI	1 Nov 51	1 Jun 52			50%	Tofino	RCAF manned
C-36	Tofino, B.C.	GCI	1 Nov 51	1 Jun 52			50%	Tofino	Sites 35 & 36 are the height finders for site #18. RCAF manned
C 37	Vancouver, B.C.	ADCC					Surveyed	Vancouver	RCAF manned
C 19	Tatla Lake (Puntzi Mt) B.C.	EW					Surveyed	Tofino	ADC manned initially
C 20	Williams Lake (Baldy Hughes) B.C.	EW					Surveyed	Tofino	ADC manned initially
C 21	Tete Jaune (Saskatoon Mt) B.C.	EW					Surveyed	Tofino	ADC manned initially
C 22	St Johns Nfld	GCI					Surveyed	St Johns	NEC manned, Trained ADC
C 23	Stephenville, Nfld	GCI					Surveyed	St Johns	NEC manned, Trained ADC
C 24	Goose Bay, Lab	GCI (ADCC)					Surveyed	St Johns	NEC manned, Trained ADC
C 25	Gander, Nfld	EW					Surveyed	St Johns	NEC manned, Trained ADC
C 26	St Anthony, Nfle	EW					Surveyed	St Johns	NEC manned, Trained ADC
C 27	Cartwright, Lab	EW					Surveyed	Goose Bay	NEC manned initially, Trained ADC
C 28	Hopedale, Lab	EW					Surveyed	Goose Bay	NEC manned initially, Trained ADC
C 29	Hebron, Lab	EW					Surveyed	Goose Bay	NEC manned initially, Trained ADC
C 30	Port Burwell, Lab	EW					Surveyed	Goose Bay	NEC manned initially, Trained ADC
C 31	Frobisher Bay, N.W.T.	EW					Surveyed	Goose Bay	NEC manned initially, Trained ADC

of WADF without making provisions for flight plan information on aircraft coming down from Canada, it brought forth this warning:[24]

> ... the threat seaward is minimal and that there is a much greater danger of attack upon these areas a-cross the Canadian border and through the interior of the United States. /Underlining added by Historian/

This pointed up the need for an agreement on air traffic control with the Canadians.

The necessity for such an agreement was further revealed when USAF denied ConAC the authority to initiate interception operations in the entire Northwest area. Until negotiations could be completed between the CAA and the Canadians for the filing of flight plans for all aircraft penetrating this area from the Canadian side, USAF would not permit interceptions of unidentified aircraft.[25]

By the end of April 1950, some progress was reported on this problem. Agreements were underway with the Department of Transport of Canada for the transmission of flight plans of aircraft departing Canada for the United States.[26]

---

24. Col. Israel to Lt. Gen. Whitehead, 6 Apr 1950. (DOC 297)

25. USAF to ConAC: "Initiation of Active Recognition and Interception Operations in Air Defense of the United States," 7 Apr 1950 (cited in Identification Chapter). (DOC 311)

26. Col. Israel to Lt. Gen. Whitehead, 28 Apr 1950.

The consummation of these agreements by no means settled the problem of air traffic control between the two countries. Both countries were concerned in 1950 because the RCAF did not possess the power to make mandatory the filing of flight plans by Canadian civil aircraft. Frequently aircraft took off from Canada without filing flight plans, crossed the international border at some points, and landed again in Canadian territory. This situation was source of some concern to the American air defense units, stationed along the border, whose mission it was to intercept unidentified aircraft. In the spring of 1951, however, the RCAF representatives revealed that they had the authority to control Canadian civil air traffic through the Canadian Department of Transport.[27] Plans were being made by the RCAF to draw up civilian and military regulations similar to the American plans (CAR 620 and AFR 60-22) which would make mandatory the filing of flight plans by all air traffic. Thus, the promise of more effective measures for handling Canadian air traffic boded well for the air defense of the United States.[28]

---

27. ADC, Memorandum of Discussion at Meeting of Sub-Committee, U. S. - Canada PJBD, 27 Mar 1951. (DOC 298)

28. The RCAF was also working on plans for the control of air traffic during military emergency conditions and used the current ADC plan as a guide. See: ADC, Memorandum of Discussion at Meeting of Sub-Committee U. S. - Canada PJBD, 27 Mar 1951. (DOC 298).

A fundamental premise of international law is that every sovereign nation controls the air space above its territory, and aircraft operating in that air space do so at the pleasure of that nation. Most nations require governmental permission for *any* aircraft to fly in their air space. The flight of *military* aircraft of one nation over the territory of another is regarded with special caution, and specific permission for such flights is normally required. In view of the international law which normally prohibits the military aircraft of one nation to overfly the territory of another nation, the United States has found it necessary to persistently petition the Canadian government for the unrestricted privilege of sending interceptors over Canadian territory for air defense operations.

Because the vital cities and industrial areas in the Detroit-Niagara-Cleveland complex lie so close to the international border, relatively little protection can be afforded to these areas against an air attack unless interceptors can cross the international boundary. The city of Detroit is particularly vulnerable to attack through Canada, because enemy bombers could practically reach their bomb release line before penetrating territory of the United States.[29] What was sorely needed for this area was a defense in depth; this could be provided only if interceptors were to be allowed to operate over Canadian territory.

---

29. History of EADF, 1 Jan to 31

Both ConAC and its air defense forces waged a continuous campaign during 1950 to reach an agreement which would permit interceptors to overfly Canadian territory when conducting interceptions. In mid-March 1950, ConAC informed EADF that negotiations were being conducted with the Air Defense Group of the RCAF to effect such an agreement.[30] By the end of that month, ConAC was forced to admit that these negotiations had fallen through and directed EADF to suspend interceptions in the Canadian border area pending further instructions.[31] Authority to commence interceptions of unidentified aircraft on the American side of the international boundary was finally granted to EADF by the end of July 1950.[32] However, authority for American interceptors to cross the border into Canada to intercept and identify unknown flights was denied.[33]

---

30. ConAC to EADF: "Air Defense Operations in Canadian Territory," 16 Mar 1950. (DOC 299)

31. The History of the Eastern Air Defense Force, 1 Jan - 31 Dec 1950, p. 70.

32. ConAC to EADF: "Interception of Unidentified Aircraft," 29 Jul 1950. This letter firmed up the Canadian Boundary Identification Zone to a point 87°00' W longitude on the Canadian border and then eastward along the international boundary to the Atlantic Coast. (See DOC 325)

351

From March 1950 until the end of that year ConAC was unable to obtain from the Canadian government permission to overfly.[34] As a result of recommendations through channels, the PJBD was given this problem to study and to provide a solution acceptable to both Canada and the United States.

The PJBD soon recognized that the delay which would be encountered in obtaining governmental approval for a permanent agreement on this question would be so great that it would be advisable to attempt to reach a compromise or interim solution acceptable to both governments without delay. At the meeting of the PJBD in January 1951, the Canadian member offered a compromise solution. There was a major qualification in this interim solution. Interceptors would be permitted to cross the border; however, unless over their own national territory the interceptors would not be allowed to open fire on hostile aircraft.[35]

---

34. For a short time in the fall of 1950, EADF was under the assumption that the CANUSEADP was in effect. This plan included provisions permitting aircraft of either country to fly over the territory of the other in the event of war, but the original version of CANUSEADP specified that it was to be "effective for planning and training immediately." As a result, EADF interpreted the CANUSEADP to be a valid document which permitted training operations over Canada, and authorized fighters to disregard the border when engaged in the interception of unidentified aircraft. In a short time, however, the error was discovered and overflying by interceptors was again forbidden in this area. For a discussion of this episode, see History of EADF, 1 Jan to 31 Dec 1950, pp. 72-74.

35. USAF to ADC: "Interceptor Flights by RCAF and USAF," 7 Feb 1951. (DOC 300)

ADC's reaction to this proposal was that the Canadian suggestion, with a few minor changes, was acceptable as an <u>interim solution</u>. But ADC underscored the need that still existed for authority to permit USAF interceptors to intercept unidentified aircraft over Canadian territory, and if such aircraft were determined to be hostile, to be allowed unrestricted authority to destroy them. This, stated ADC, was the only solution it would regard as permanent; any other solution could only be regarded as a temporary measure.[36]

In April 1951, ADC reiterated the need for a permanent agreement to allow the free and unrestricted employment of interceptor aircraft, regardless of international boundaries.[37] It was pointed out that even the interim solution precluded defensive action against identified hostile aircraft over Canadian territory until bombs had been released on such border targets as Detroit, Sault Ste. Marie, Limestone Air Force Base, Buffalo, and Niagara Falls. Such a restriction, concluded ADC, neglected two basic principles of air defense: Defense in depth; and fighter aircraft mobility.[38] Accordingly ADC submitted a recommendation for a permanent agreement which would allow free and unrestricted use of interceptors.

---

36. ADC to USAF: "Interceptor Flights by RCAF and USAF," 5 Apr 1951. (DOC 301)

37. ADC to D/O USAF: "Interceptor Flights by RCAF and USAF," 26 Apr 1951. (DOC 302)

38. <u>Ibid</u>.

By the end of June 1951, little progress had been made with respect to overfly agreements with Canada. The interim solution suggested by the Canadians was still in the hands of the PJBD and did not receive approval by that body until the fall of 1951.[39] No progress had been made to obtain a __permanent__ agreement for unrestricted overfly and intercept rights which ADC felt were necessary.

As an outgrowth of the relatively unsuccessful attempts to obtain unrestricted authority for interception over Canadian territory, the Canadian Air Defense Command suggested an agreement which would provide for interceptions on a day-to-day routine training basis as well as for scheduled air defense training exercises. In May, ADC and the RCAF Air Defense Command came to an agreement which granted authority for overflying by RCAF and USAF aircraft __for training purposes only__.[40] USAF approved this

---

39. The interim proposal was labelled 51/4, and in September USAF advised that the PJBD had accepted 51/4 as an interim measure. As approved, this proposal had three main clauses: (a) That unidentified aircraft to be intercepted must show reasonable intention of crossing the Canada-United States border; (b) that close investigation would be performed solely on unidentified multi-engine aircraft; (c) that no attempt would be made to order an intercepted aircraft to land nor to open fire except when the intercepted aircraft was over the national territory of the aircraft performing the interception. The recommendation 51/4 was submitted by the Secretary of State to the President for approval. When approval was given, it was the intention of USAF and ADC to make recommendation to PJBD that further study be given to the unrestricted use of interceptors by both nations. /TWX, USAF to ADC, 25 Sep 1951. (DOC 303)/

40. TWX, RCAF Air Defense Command to ADC, 31 May 1951. (DOC 304)

agreement in June, and authority to implement it was dispatched to the air defense forces.[41] This was still a long way from the permanent agreement for unrestricted authority for across-the-border intercepts which was indispensable for a potent air defense in that area.

VI

At the close of June 1951, the communication facilities between the Canadian and American air defense systems were still in the formative stages. As early as June 1950, communications circuits linking ConAC, EADF and the RCAF Air Defense Group Headquarters were ordered.[42] At about the same time, voice circuits linking the St. Hubert, Quebec, GCI station with the early warning station at Fort Ethan Allen, Vermont, and linking the Chatham, New Brunswick, Control Center with the GCI at Dow Air Force Base were established.[43] Since the summer of 1950, the two air defense systems have been "wired" together more firmly, and realistic exercises in communications have been conducted to ascertain SOP's which would be mutually acceptable. The revised version of CANUSEADP contained plans for long line facilities which would link the national air defense systems even closer together in the event of hostilities.[44]

---

41. TWX, USAF to ADC, 16 Jun 1951. (DOC 305)

42. History of EADF, 1 Jan - 31 Dec 1950, p. 70.

43. Ibid.

44. Canada - U. S. Emergency Air Defense Plan, 1/51.

In addition, other communications plans were underway. The requirements between the Canadian and United States AC&W systems for overlap telling and communication were resolved at a meeting held at Headquarters USAF in March 1951.[45] There was an interchange of COI and other communications data between the two countries, and a standardization of techniques in communication procedures was envisaged.

VII

There were numerous other areas in which the two countries were making a mutual effort towards a common air defense system. These included civil air defense, Mark X IFF, electronic countermeasures, cross-servicing of aircraft, and exchange of vital information.

The Canadian program for civil air defense has followed a pattern of operations similar to that of its American counterpart. Efforts have been made to enlist the aid of the Canadian people in a ground observer corps, and steps have been taken to set up a civil organization to disseminate air raid warnings to communities. Agreements were being worked out in Canada between the Navy, Army and civilian authorities for the control of illumination, as well as for the control of radio and other electronic propagations. Finally, plans have been made to organize

---

45. ADC, Memorandum of Discussion at Meeting of Sub-Committee U. S. - Canada PJBD, 27 Mar 1951. (See DOC 298.)

an emergency air lift by Canadian civilian aircraft.[46]

Generally speaking, however, the Canadian civil air defense effort has lagged considerably behind that of the United States.

One aspect of the civil air defense program which was of great importance to the United States was the development of the Canadian long range early warning system. This system came into operation in October 1950, and was designed to provide early warning from the northern areas of Newfoundland, Labrador, British Columbia and other territories.[47] The agencies taking part in this early warning net consisted of the radio stations of the Armed Services, the Department of Transport, Hudson Bay Company, and the Royal Canadian Mounted Police. Since these agencies had outposts in the more isolated areas of northern Canada, they could perform a valuable early warning function. This long-range aircraft warning system was to report all four-engine aircraft movements in the northern areas of Canada to Canadian air defense authorities, and arrangements were made to pass pertinent information to the air defense system in the United States.[48]

Canada was engaged in the production and employment of

---

46. RCAF, Memorandum to Defense Council, "Relationship between the Civil Defense Organization and the RCAF," 13 Apr 1951.

47. ConAC to WADF: "Canadian Long Range Early Warning," 16 Oct 1950.

48. Ibid.

Mark X IFF along with the United States.[49] Since this equipment was to be operational within the RCAF at an early date, ADC has recommended that the new interim JANAP include operational procedures for joint use by Canada and the United States.[50] In the event of hostilities, this would permit friendly aircraft to identify themselves when flying over American or Canadian territory.

ADC was authorized to communicate directly with the RCAF Air Defense Command to establish a joint radar anti-jamming program.[51] Cognizant of the benefits that would be derived by the air defenses of the United States by such a joint program, ADC sent a few anti-jamming training teams from EADF to train Canadian AC&W units.[52] It was expected that with the anticipated expansion of our anti-jamming training capabilities, EADF would be able to devote more attention to the training of Canadian units.

In one area of planning between the two countries, the international boundary for all intents and purposes has been obliterated. An informal agreement for cross-servicing of interceptors has been reached between the 25th Air Division and the RCAF, which would permit interceptors of the United States to set down

---

49. ADC to Director of Communications, USAF: "Installation and Employment of IFF in Air Force Aircraft," 3 Apr 1951. (DOC 306)

50. Ibid.

51. 3rd Ind USAF to ADC, 10 Jan 1951, to RCAF to ADC: "Telecomm Training - Radio Warfare - ECM (Air)," 14 Nov 1950. (DOC 307)

52. ADC, Communications and Electronics Digest, May 1951. p. 24.

on certain RCAF air bases for servicing purposes.[53] Although this agreement had not been implemented, once in effect it was expected to prove invaluable for giving USAF interceptors greater range, prolonged combat time, more emergency landing strips and faster turn-around time in combat.[54]

Steps had been taken to facilitate the exchange of information between the two countries. Authorization was given for the free exchange of information on air defense matters between the American ADC and its Canadian counterpart.[55] There has been a constant exchange of pertinent regulations, COIs and SOPs between the two national air defense systems. The RCAF was to submit combat reports for the benefit of ADC, and there was an interchange of fighter and radar status reports between the EADF and Canadian air defense command units.[56]

Agreements were also made between the two countries for passing flash reports of intelligence having a bearing on the air

---

53. History of 25th Air Division, 1 Apr-30 Jun 1951, pp. 39-40.

54. Ibid.

55. ADC Regulation 205-1, 21 Apr 1951. The public relations policy governing publicity relating to joint Canadian-United States defense plans and operations has been outlined in ADC Regulation 190-6, 16 Jul 1951. See also Air Force Bulletin No. 15, 9 Apr 1951.

56. ADC, Memorandum of discussion at Meeting of Sub-Committee U. S. - Canada PJBD, 27 Mar 1951. (See DOC 298)

defense of the United States. In addition to the Canadian long range early warning system previously discussed, arrangements have been made with the RCAF intelligence component to relay operational intelligence to elements of the air defense system without delay.[57]

---

57. 1st Ind EADF to ADC, 5 Mar 1951, to ADC to EADF: "Agreements for Passing Intelligence Information Bearing on the Air Defense Mission," 6 Feb 1951. (DOC 308)

CHAPTER SIXTEEN

EARLY WARNING

I

It is a truism that all parts of our air defense system are necessary to the effective performance of the whole. In the work of air defense the most elaborate attempts to build a radar network and fighter system are valid only if the weapons employed can be utilized to achieve their primary mission – the successful detection, interception and destruction of the enemy.

The effective use of the intercepting aircraft depends on accurate and timely information of the whereabouts of the enemy. The supply of such pertinent data in the Battle of Britain was the difference between victory and defeat. In the air defense of the continental United States, the ability of our system to supply early warning of an impending attack may also mean the difference between defeat and victory, regardless of the impressive strength of our tactical weapons. A key to this problem is effective early warning.

The concept of early warning is a semantic nightmare in itself. Before a discussion of plans laid and measures taken in behalf of early warning can be undertaken, it is first necessary to discuss the question of what is being warned.

In the predicament of Great Britain in the early stages of World War II, the problem of early warning was relatively simple. In that case, the whole of the British Isles was a single, integrated, target complex and provision for early warning was effectively made by a perimeter detection system with greatest concentration on the frontier facing the probable direction of enemy attack. A radar defense in depth was necessary for backup of Britain's perimeter network and also for interceptor control purposes, but the most vital link in the British chain of defense was the network of ground radars on her western and southern coastal frontiers.

When the United States embarked on the creation of an air defense in being in 1948 the most important planning factor which confronted the United States Air Force was the question of *what* was to be defended. The relatively vast geographical extent of the continental United States, and its vulnerability to attack from the east, north and west, coupled with the inescapable fact that American defense resources were severely limited, prompted the decision that a defense of the whole was utterly impracticable for the immediate present and the near future. The decision was inevitably and painfully reached that of the vast resources of the country, the defense of only a few could be realistically attempted. Of these vital resources, the important industrial and population complex of the New York-Washington-Philadelphia area; the aircraft production, seaport and atomic installations of the Seattle-Hanford area; and the atomic plants in New Mexico received first priority. It was in these areas that USAF directed ADC to build the first air defense systems.¹ It was not until late 1949 and 1950 that this initial defense system was extended to include target complexes in California, Tennessee, and the Great Lakes area. By mid-1951, the interim air defense system was essentially not one, but five widely dispersed air defense systems. The provision of initial early warning, therefore, was a vital matter for each of these five "island" defense systems. As things stood under LASHUP, however, the thin distribution of ground radar in small clusters so widely separated removed the possibility of a defense in depth and rendered the time-interception problem one of staggering proportions.

When the United States Air Force announced its optimistic intentions to embark upon Plan SUPREMACY it appeared that the fondest desires of air defense-minded agencies would be answered. SUPREMACY made provisions for a vast network of ground radar along the entire perimeter of the continental United States and for a defense in depth of sizeable, though not of entirely ideal, proportions.² The Air Defense Command, however, was quick to point out a possible flaw in the plan, namely the absence of provision for extended early warning capabilities seaward, and in Canada.³

---

    1. See pp. 65-68 above, and Chap. IV.

    2. For SUPREMACY see pp. 55-58 above.

    3. 1st Ind, ADC to USAF, 8 Apr 1948, to USAF to ADC: "AC&W Plan for the United States," 19 Jan 1948. (DOC 19)

SUPREMACY, however, was an abortion. The next best thing which USAF was able to exact from Congress was authority to build 75 basic radar stations and eleven control centers. This Permanent System was to do for air defense what SUPREMACY tried to do - to distribute radar resources along the three vital frontiers susceptible to enemy attack, and to a limited extent provide for a defense in depth concentrated in the same five vital target complexes of the interim system. A feature of the planning for the Permanent System was the concurrent provision for a radar detection system for Alaska.[4] Provision for radar detection in Canada and seawards was a matter which was not wholly within the province of the United States Air Force, however. Tortuous negotiations were to be necessary before action could be begun in these directions.

Plans were laid for a campaign for Canadian participation in the defense of the Northern Hemisphere, and action was taken to obtain the aid of the Navy in the provision of a number of radar picket vessels to be stationed along the sea frontiers of the United States. In addition, USAF observed very closely the progress of Naval research on airborne early warning radar for possible use in air defense.

As LASHUP came into maturity and as active operations were begun in earnest, especially after the crisis engendered by Korean hostilities, the inadequacies of early warning became more and more

---

4. **Maj. Gen.** Gordon P. Saville, presentation to Secretary Forrestal on the Interim AC&W Program, 9 Sep 1948. (DOC 18)

critical. In repeated tests it was proven that in the extremely vulnerable Northwest and Northeast, existing early warning capabilities were insufficient to permit timely interception - even if the fighter system were ideally equipped and organized to supply that capability, which it was not.[5] The modification of LASHUP, however, was impossible; the whole system was destined to go. If any hope remained for early warning extension it rested on action taken to merge new capabilities with those of the proposed Permanent System. In this effort steps were taken toward: (1) the improvement of the ground radar early warning capability in the continental U. S.; (2) extension of the continental radar network into Canada, closer liaison with the Alaskan Air Command, and establishment of ground radar systems in the area of the Northeast Air Command; (3) integration of Naval early warning capability; (4) experimentation with airborne early warning; and (5) utilization of merchant shipping.

---

5. For discussion of the vulnerability of the Northwest and Northeast, see: History of the 25th Air Division, 1 Jan - 30 Jun 1951; and, History of the 26th Air Division, 1 Sep - 31 Dec 1950.

II

As has been frequently mentioned in this history, radar equipment employed in the temporary LASHUP system was limited in its capability by the arbitrary premises upon which its deployment was based. First and foremost of these premises was that of maximum economy. The result of adherence to this premise was a compromise with the most effective siting for the LASHUP radar, with a commensurate diminution of maximum early warning capability.

The problem of maximum continental early warning was tackled by USAF and ConAC in plans for the Permanent System. Although in this attempt the problem of economy was not so conspicuous as formerly, siting problems still continued to plague them. On our northern frontier the difficulties of geography frequently promised to deny maximum range capability to the new AN/FPS-3 and AN/CPS-6B radars destined to carry the burden. In the case of the CPS-6B radar, especially, the problem of making a choice between effective GCI coverage and maximum search range was troublesome, since that equipment as produced did not have the capability of both maximum GCI and EW simultaneously. Just how much more effective the new Permanent System would be over the old LASHUP system was entirely in the realm of conjecture. However, in many respects the new deployment promised considerable improvement over the old system.

A feature of research and development in the realm of early warning during 1950 was the announcement that a system of **passive** detection was on the drawing boards. Early in 1951 this new system had been integrated into a relatively simple device of which twelve sets were promised to the Air Defense Command in November 1951 for experimentation. Although originally designed for electronics countermeasures, passive detection promised to have considerable early warning advantages. Not only could it substitute for the prime search radar in case of breakdown of the latter, but its range was contemplated to be somewhat better than that of the radar. Another advantage was the fact that it was not subject to the vagaries of beam propagation and that it was not limited by the size of the invading aircraft. Although it was far too early during 1951 to judge of the benefits of the new device, it was greeted with optimism by the Air Defense Command, and provision was made for the addition of one such device for each of the stations in the Permanent System.[6]

A development which promised to have far greater results for early warning than any modification or improvement in continental U. S. ground radar in the near future was the extension of radar coverage into adjacent areas of Canada.[7] The fan-shaped configuration

---

6. USAF to ADC: "Passive Detection Systems and Equipment," 21 Jun 1951.

7. For a discussion of ADC's efforts to extend early warning into Canada see above chapter on Canada.

of the Northern Hemisphere which enabled Canada to extend eastwards and westwards beyond the land limits of the Continental United States was an eloquent advocate for inclusion of these strategic areas into an integrated ground radar system. Not only would additional areas be tapped for early warning possibilities in the regions of British Columbia in the West, and New Brunswick, Quebec, Nova Scotia, Newfoundland and Labrador in the East, but a defense in depth would be created along the northern periphery of the United States enabling the air defense system to predict with better certainty the direction and strength of the invader.

There were, of course, no limits to how far early warning could extend. From Canada to Alaska and Greenland was a logical step foreseen quite early in air defense planning. To this advance the Continental Air Command contributed greatly by manning and training the 531st Aircraft Control and Warning Group from ConAC's own resources. The establishment of the Northeast Air Command and the decision to create a radar chain in its area of cognizance in 1950 led to an additional contribution by the Continental Air Command. From out of ConAC's growing pool of personnel familiar with complex siting problems, teams were sent to those northern areas to locate the new radars destined for them, and for this purpose a continuing drain of experienced ConAC and ADC personnel was envisaged for the future.

By mid-1951, it is true, there were few concrete results to show in the effort to plug the northern early warning gaps, but the first and most important steps towards this end had been taken. The future promised to witness a continuous projection of the American air defense system ever northward to the very doorstep of Siberia.

III

In the matter of the extension of early warning capability seawards, Naval cooperation was the primary requirement. Naval combat operations had made valuable use of early warning for the defense of convoys and even of individual vessels. Since most, if not all, naval vessels were equipped with radar devices, the possibility of using some of these vessels to provide early warning to the continental United States was an early USAF consideration.

Although the use of radar picket vessels was a strategist's dream, the realities presented many obstacles. From time to time the Navy offered the use of one or more radar equipped destroyers for air defense maneuver purposes and their proven value was impressed upon the Air Force. Intermittent use of these facilities, however, served only to whet the appetite of the air defense commanders. What was required was a constant factor in seaward early warning for peace-time use as well as for exercises and war. As in so many other air defense considerations, there could be no finely drawn distinction between war and peace where intelligence was concerned.

Continuous use of naval picket vessels, however, was, under existing circumstances, not looked upon favorably by the Navy.[8] A constant naval surveillance of the Pacific and Atlantic coasts,

---

8. See chapter on the Navy's role.

would immobilize perhaps as many as twenty naval combat vessels at a time, and require the standby status of as many more. Furthermore, the expense of continuous naval patrol was deemed prohibitive. Although the Navy was obliged to provide for the air defense of the United States by formal JCS declaration, nevertheless by the same declaration their primary mission was the destruction of enemy resources on the seas. Although the matter of continuous use of naval picket ships was the subject of constant negotiation between the Air Force and the Navy, few concrete conclusions were reached up to mid-1951, though both services tried hard to resolve the dilemma to the common national advantage.

In another sphere of USAF-Navy relationships, greater advantage to air defense was achieved. Because of the concentrated nature of naval power on the high seas, the Navy had frequent recourse to airborne surveillance of wide territories for its own safety. It was inevitable, therefore, that the Navy take very seriously the possibility of using airborne radar for early warning purposes. In the post-war era the Navy embarked on an ambitious development and research program to develop airborne early warning equipment. In this project the United States Air Force was inevitably a most interested spectator, and contributed its own aid towards mutual success.[9] Reports on the promise of AEW poured in to both ConAC and ADC, and plans were laid to achieve fullest benefit of the device

---

9. *Ibid.*

when finally perfected.

How AEW was to be used posed difficult questions. A continuous air patrol of the sea frontiers of the continental United States promised to be even more prohibitive financially than the use of naval radar pickets in view of the limited airborne-time capabilities of aircraft (especially of the jet type), and of the rapid obsolescence of continuously-flown aircraft. The factor of cost, however, was deemed a secondary matter to the Air Defense Command. With the conviction that AEW was sufficiently advanced for use in the near future, ADC requested USAF to make provision for five squadrons of AEW aircraft for air defense.[10] The AEW problem, like that of the picket ships, promised to occupy much of ADC's attentions in 1952.

In its quest for a greater early warning capability on the high seas, USAF was bound inevitably to consider the American Merchant Marine and transoceanic airlines. Late in 1950, consequently, initial plans were made for utilizing these facilities for early warning and procedures for reporting were drawn up by ADC. As early trials proved, flash reports were not received from these highly desirable sources. ADC embarked on an aggressive campaign of education and training of merchant marine personnel in the importance of their contribution to air defense, as well as for more elaborate plans and procedures to integrate these facilities.[11]

---

10. *Ibid.*

11. ADC to USAF: "Extension of Air Early Warning by Ships and Aircraft Flash Reports," 11 May 1951. (DOC 309)

Thus, in the critical formative years of air defense operations, the vital importance of extensive early warning was clearly revealed to USAF, ConAC and ADC through the shortcomings of the Lashup system, and the prospective limitations of any future radar system based solely within the continental United States. The answer to this crucial problem was in the contiguous expansion of radar and visual detection constantly outwards from the shores and land frontiers of the United States. The importance of the project was well understood by ADC and the action taken was realistic, but the obstacles to immediate accomplishment were many. In this matter, as in so many other matters vital to air defense, only the future held the answer.

CHAPTER SEVENTEEN

IDENTIFICATION

I

One of the cardinal principles of an efficacious air defense system is prompt and accurate identification of all air traffic. The methods of identifying air traffic are (1) air traffic control, (2) interception by fighter aircraft, (3) IFF (Identification of Friend or Foe through use of electronic means), and (4) visual identification by ground observers.[1]

The obtaining of authority for the establishment of an air traffic control system was recorded in Chapter XIV. However, the actual functioning and operation of this pre-plot method of identification for air defense remains to be told in this chapter.

IFF, a system of identification by electronic means, and not discussed previously in the history, is designed to provide the means for identifying radar targets as either friendly or enemy. This is done by installing IFF equipment in an aircraft which enables it to identify itself automatically as friendly whenever it is challenged by properly equipped ground and airborne radars.

---

1. The story of the formation and operation of a Ground Observer Corps has been told in Chapter XII.

Interception by fighter aircraft is a method employed when identification by air traffic control, electronic means, and visual means have failed. Basic to the question of interception for identification has been the problem of getting authority for those agencies charged with the air defense mission to intercept unidentified aircraft. An account of this struggle to gain authority, as well as the operational aspects of the interception program, will be related in this chapter.

II

During the years 1946 and 1947, and most of 1948, practically no attempts were made to regulate air traffic for purposes of identification. In the fall of 1948, however, operations for air traffic control were inaugurated (the reader will recall)[2] in two active defense areas, the Seattle-Hanford area and the New York area. As previously related, all civilian and military aircraft entering these areas from the sea were requested to file flight plans by the first post-war ADC. From this pre-flight information the course and position of friendly aircraft could be plotted in advance and this information supplied the air defense system as a means of identification. No authority existed at this time to compel either civil or military aircraft to file these flight plans. It was on an entirely voluntary basis. The

---

2. See Chapter XIV.

end result was that the attempts at identification through this means proved relatively ineffective.

In December 1949 ConAC established an active air defense zone along the Eastern Coast. This zone ran along the coast line, roughly between Bangor, Maine and Norfolk, Virginia. All aircraft entering this zone from the sea were <u>requested</u> to file flight plans.[3] Once again, this system failed. It was quite evident by this time that if the filing of flight plans for control of air traffic for purposes of identification was to succeed it would have to be placed on a mandatory basis.

At about the same time that EADF was initiating the above procedures for air traffic control, WADF was conducting DRUMMER-BOY. One of the specific objectives of this training exercise was to test the effectiveness of plans for air traffic control in the Northwest area. At the conclusion of the exercise, Colonel Clinton D. Vincent, the commander of the 25th Air Division in whose area the maneuver was conducted, made the following observation:[4]

> In my opinion the single item requiring attention and emphasis at this time is the strengthening of the processes for control and identification of aircraft.

Headquarters WADF was in full agreement with the foregoing opinion, and stated the following in its own report on the exercise:[5]

---

3. EADF to ConAC: "Initiation of Active Air Defense for Vital Coastal Zone," 16 Nov 1949, and 1st Ind. (DOC 310)

4. 1st Ind, 25th Air Division to WADF, 2 Dec 1949, to I.G. Second Region to I.G. USAF: "Special Report on Observation of Exercise "Drummer Boy," 2 Dec 1949. (See DOC 55)

> This headquarters considers the problem of identification to be of first magnitude. The principal shortcoming is the lack of proper authority over civil and military aircraft. It is strongly recommended that higher authority secure the necessary legislation which will permit rigid enforcement of identification procedures on all air traffic. [Underlining added by the Historian.]

The experiences of EADF with air traffic control coupled with those of WADF in exercise DRUMMERBOY convinced USAF of the need for a more rigid control over civil air traffic. The Secretary of the Department of the United States Air Force requested the cooperation of various civil agencies engaged in flying. As told previously, a gentlemen's agreement was reached in February 1950 with these agencies and they agreed to file flight plans and conduct all flying in certain critical areas above 2000 feet and under IFR.[6]

About a month later a more dynamic step was taken to tighten controls over all air traffic in certain strategic areas. Two prohibited areas were established by Executive Order of the President in the WADF area. The filing of flight plans was required for all aircraft operating over Los Alamos, New Mexico and the Richland, Washington areas where atomic energy plants were located.[7] A short time later the same restrictions were authorized for the area surrounding the atomic plant in Oak Ridge, Tennessee.[8]

---

6. ConAC to USAF: "Identification of Federally Owned Aircraft by Air Defense System," 24 Feb 1950. (See DOC 267)

7. History of WADF, 1 Jan 50 - 30 Jun 1950, p. 50.

8. USAF to ConAC: "Initiation of Active Recognition and Interception Operations in Air Defense of the United States," 7 Apr 1950. (DOC 311)

Meanwhile, the policy of requesting flight plans from aircraft operating over certain areas continued. In April 1950 WADF published an SOP pertaining to the control and identification of civil and military air traffic.[9] The provisions of the SOP applied air traffic control procedures to all active air defense areas within the WADF area. The four active air defense areas designated at that time were: the Seattle-Hanford area, the San Francisco area, the Los Angeles area and the Albuquerque Air Defense area.[10]

---

9. <u>WADF SOP No. 13</u>, 10 Mar 1950.

10. See: <u>History of WADF, 1 Jan - 30 Jun 1950</u>, p. 52. It is interesting to note the reports on operations in some of these areas mentioned above, which were submitted just before the outbreak of the Korean war. The 25th Air Division and the Albuquerque Air Defense Area commanders were asked to report the number of flight plans received from the CAA and MFS, and the number of times GCI tracks were correlated with the flight plans submitted, for the period 12 May through 1 June 1950. In the Hanford area the 25th Air Division reported a total number of 7,678 flight plans had been received from the CAA, MFS, the Navy and Canadian air traffic control agencies during the period under consideration. Of these, 7,339, or about 95%, of the GCI tracks were correlated successfully with flight plans received. In the Albuquerque area, during the same period, 1,183 flight plans had been received, and only 141, or about 12%, were correlated with GCI tracks. This latter low percentage resulted from the relatively small radar coverage existing in the area at the time, the lack of modern equipment, the isolated position of the Los Alamos area, and the limited period during which the AC&W squadron in the area had been operating. In similar operations in the EADF area, approximately 90% of the GCI tracks had been correlated successfully with flight plans received. (For this information the historian is indebted to the <u>History of WADF, 1 Jan - 30 Jun 1950,</u> pp. 68-69.

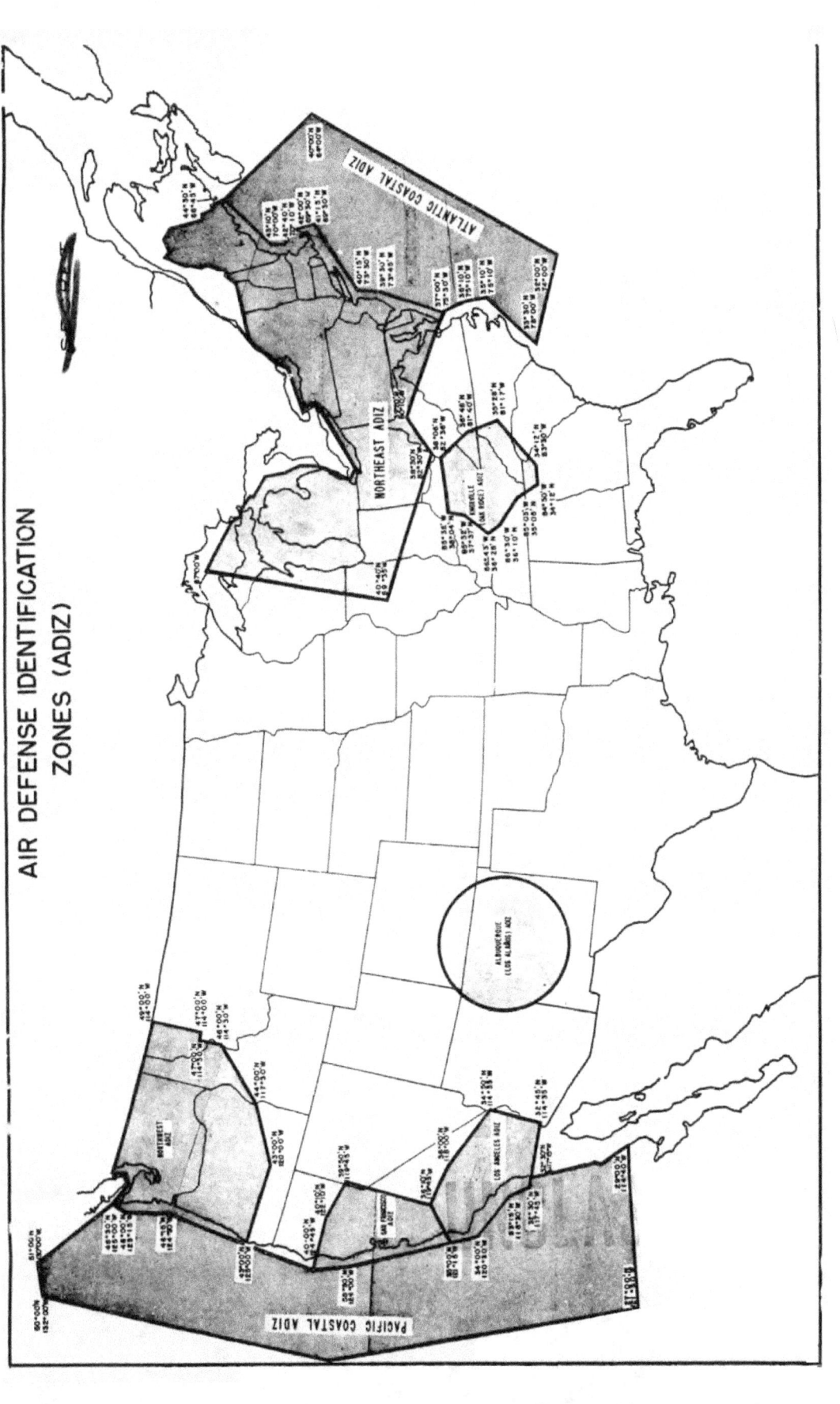

With the publication of the joint regulation AFR 60-22 in mid-July 1950, the procedures for air traffic control were more clearly defined.[11] The primary feature of this regulation was the creation of a number of air defense identification zones (ADIZ) in air spaces above specified geographical areas. Within these zones the recognition of aircraft was necessary for military purposes and procedures were set up to effect this recognition. The filing of flight plans was made mandatory for all military flights in ADIZs.[12] All civil aircraft operating within the ADIZs were requested to file flight plans. Three types of ADIZs were defined: domestic, coastal and international boundary. The domestic recognition zones were those ADIZs which lay primarily within the United States. The coastal recognition zones were ADIZs established along the Atlantic and Pacific coasts. The International boundary ADIZs were zones on or adjacent to the international boundaries of the United States. The boundaries of these ADIZs were to be subject to change as the capabilities of the air defense system expanded.[13]

---

11. AFR 60-22, 19 Jul 1950.

12. The only exception to this rule was local military flights. Procedures were worked out for easy recognition between the local agency having jurisdiction over the unit and the air division defense commander concerned.

13. All military aircraft entering or flying within domestic or international boundary ADIZs were required to file IFR or VFR plans as appropriate. In addition, position reports by radio were required before entering these ADIZs, and at periodic intervals while within the zone. For flights entering or flying within coastal ADIZs, provisions of the regulation included the filing of VFR or IFR flight plans, and the submission of position reports approximately ten minutes before entering the zone and every twenty minutes thereafter while within the zone.

The passage of Public Law 778 in the autumn of 1950 made possible more stringent regulations to control civil air traffic within the ADIZs mentioned above. Based on the authority given to it by Public Law 778, the CAA made mandatory the filing of flight plans and submission of position reports for all civil aircraft entering or flying in ADIZs.[14] Thus, the ineffective system of voluntary controls over civil aircraft which had inhibited the first postwar ADC and ConAC from promulgating an effective identification system through the means of air traffic control was overcome. The action taken by the CAA to make mandatory the filing of flight plans within ADIZs by civil aircraft coupled with the provisions of AFR 60-22 which made mandatory the filing of flight plans for military aircraft while operating within these zones, made it possible for ADC to extend controls over all air traffic within ADIZs during the first six months of 1951.

III

The refinement of procedures by which the air defense system was supplied with flight plan information provided an interesting story. In the spring of 1950, the order to facilitate the transmission of pre-flight information, the CAA had agreed to furnish security controllers who were to pass information from the CAA Air Route Traffic Control Centers (ARTCC) to the appropriate ADCC or GCI station. The Air Force for its part agreed to furnish all the

---

14. There were some exceptions to this rule. See chapter on Air Traffic Control.

communications needed between the CAA and the air defense system.[15] Later in the year, as civil air agencies voluntarily submitted flight plans in compliance with the gentlemen's agreement of February 1950, the procedural problem intensified. So assiduous was the CAA in its function of transmitting pre-flight information, that the air defense units found themselves unable to keep up their processing on the incoming mass of information for tracking and identification purposes.

In view of this new development, ConAC proposed that some type of movements section be established within the ARTCCs which would screen all flight plans and forward only pertinent information to the air defense system.[16] Under this plan all available flight plan and position information, both civil and military, would be screened at one central section within the ARTCC and then fed to the appropriate air defense units.[17] This would eliminate the screening of flight plan information at GCI stations which had limited facilities and personnel.

During the first six months of 1951, ADC authorized the establishment of Air Movement Identification Sections (AMIS) in the ARTCCs in Boston and Seattle. These AMISs were operated on an experimental basis along the lines proposed by ConAC for the trans-

---

15. Report of WADF CAA Conference, Kirtland AFB, 11 Jan 1950. (See DOC 266)

16. ConAC to EADF and WADF: "Routing of all Air Traffic Information into the AC&W System," 11 Aug 1950. (DOC 312)

mission of pertinent flight information. All flight plan information and position reports were routed through one source, the AMIS, and only pertinent information was forwarded to the air defense system.[18] By the end of June 1951, the AMIS experiment had not been evaluated, but an indication of its success was revealed in a statement by ADC that: "At this time, the establishment of the AMIS appears to be a desirable step and may be accepted as standard organization throughout the country."[19]

IV

IFF (Identification Friend or Foe) complements air traffic control in the identification of friendly aircraft. The IFF system utilizes two basic types of equipment. The interrogation or challenge of an unidentified aircraft is initiated by means of an electronic device known as the interrogator - responsor (IR). The reply by friendly aircraft to the challenge is produced by means of a transpondor. The IR consists of a transmitter and receiver which are arranged so that pulsations of radio-frequency energy are emitted by the transmitter and returning signals are picked up by the receiver. The transpondor also consists of a transmitter and receiver which are constructed so that a coded reply is automatically transmitted back to the IR whenever an IR transmission is received. By installing transpondors in friendly aircraft, and by equipping ground radar stations and airborne radars with IRs, a means for the

---

18. ADC, Headquarters Staff Briefing, 17 Mar 1951. (See DOC 282)

19. 1st and 2d Inds to 31st AD to CADF: "Circuit Requirements," 7 Jun 1951. (DOC 314)

identification of friendly aircraft is established.

The IFF system in use during the second World War was the Mark III. In October 1948, the Joint Chiefs of Staff decided to replace the Mark III system at the earliest practicable date by a new system known as Mark X.[20] There were urgent reasons for making this change in IFF systems as soon as possible, but it was not until 1 July 1951 that the Mark III system was officially discontinued throughout the air defense system.[21] During the interim period, the Mark III system continued to be used for training purposes.

One major reason behind the decision to change IFF systems was that the new Mark X system could perform certain functions which the Mark III system could not. In addition to its normal function as IFF, the new Mark X equipment could provide a beacon assist in the tracking and control of high speed aircraft. Many of our modern radars are not able to "see" jet fighters at great distances because of the small size of these aircraft, and so cannot control fighters to interceptions or navigate them in an overcast. Mark X equipment installed in aircraft was capable of emitting a beacon which registered on the PPI scope of a search radar set to distances up to 200 miles. This so-called beacon function of the Mark X system enabled the GCI operator to control and vector jet type interceptors which were out of range of the search radar set.[22] In accordance with the policy of the Joint

---

20. ADC to AFG: "Operational Suitability Test of the IFF Mark X Short Interval Identification System," 19 Apr 1951. (DOC 315)

21. ADC to EADF: "Mark III IFF Policy," 22 May 1951. (See DOC 127

22. 1st Ind, TAC to ConAC. 23 Sep 1950, to ConAC to TAC: "Mark X Utilization on AN/MSQ-1 Radar," 7 Sep 1950. (DOC 316)

Chiefs of Staff, the primary function of the Mark X system was to provide beacon assist.[23]

A second reason which prompted the decision of the Joint Chiefs of Staff to replace the Mark III as quickly as possible was that during World War II the USSR, as well as other foreign nations, and commercial carriers in the United States had been given Mark III equipment in quantity. Since the Russians had received over 500 Mark III transpondors, the security of the Mark III system was nil.[24]

The operational limitations to which the Mark III system was subject required its replacement by a better set. IFF information of the Mark III was not suitable for presentation on a PPI scope. Nor could the Mark III equipment match the range of the newer post-war radars. The Mark X system, however, could equal the range of the more recent radars and its information could be displayed on PPI scopes.[25]

From July through November 1949, ConAC conducted project "Rosebud," which had as its primary mission the testing of two radar

---

23. USAF to ConAC: "USAF Procurement Plan for IFF Beacons," 24 Jan 1950. (See DOC 121)

24. TWX, USAF to CG ConAC and other Commands, 27 Jul 1950.

25. The Mark X equipment had two other capabilities. It possessed the capability of sending emergency signals when an aircraft was in distress and required immediate assistance. By switching the Mark X equipment to the "Emergency" position, a special message of distress could be transmitted. It was also possible to use the Mark X IFF beacon for purposes of air traffic control. SAC was especially interested in this aspect of Mark X because it had established 200 miles as a minimum for identification of B-47s before these aircraft could be scheduled for automatic approach and landing.

assist beacons for the Mark X system. Of the two, the AN/APX-6 was selected, but not without misgivings. This beacon did not meet the required operational specifications, but the immediate need for such equipment for air defense purposes made it necessary to adopt the AN/APX-6.[26] A retrofit program for installing AN/APX-6s in aircraft was initiated, and production was also started for ground interrogators.

However, a bottleneck in the production and retrofitting of Mark X equipment quickly developed. In May 1950, General Whitehead asked General Benjamin W. Chidlaw, Commander of the Air Materiel Command, to bring pressure to bear on those responsible for the supply and retrofitting of Mark X equipment. General Whitehead said that this matter was of such a critical nature that "no stone should remain unturned in an effort to start retrofitting AN/APX-6s immediately and to speed up production of the necessary ground equipment."[27]

Two months later in a report to the Chief of Staff USAF, General Whitehead again stressed the seriousness of the Mark X supply problem. He stated that the existing delivery schedules for airborne beacons and ground interrogators presented such an unsatisfactory situation that "the development of an adequate capability for the air defense of the Continental United States [was] being

---

26. 1st Ind, ConAC to Dir. of Requirements, USAF, 2 Mar 1950, to USAF to ConAC: "USAF Procurement Plan for IFF Beacons," 24 Jan 1950. (See DOC 121)

27. Gen. Whitehead to Gen. Chidlaw, 9 May 1950. (See DOC 120)

seriously affected."[28]

Influenced, no doubt, by General Whitehead's admonitions, USAF took steps to set deadlines for the retrofitting and production programs of Mark X equipment. A deadline date of 31 December 1950 was set by USAF for the Air Materiel Command to completely retrofit all ConAC fighters.[29] USAF also furnished the Air Materiel Command with a deadline for the end of the year for the equipping of all Lashup III ground radar sets with Mark X ground equipment.

These deadlines were never met. By the end of the year, only the F-86s and F-94s were retrofitted with Mark X transpondors.[30] Of the 49 Lashup III sites which were to receive Mark X ground interrogators by the end of the year, only eight were supplied. Even these eight ground interrogators were not new equipment, but prototype Mark X equipment which had been modified to interrogate and receive replies from aircraft equipped with a Mark X airborne transpondor.[31]

---

28. ConAC to C/S, USAF: "Radar Equipment for Air Defense," 17 Jul 1950.

29. IRS, Dir of Comm. to O&T: "Mark X and SII System," 7 Oct 1950. (See DOC 125.)

30. See Part III, Chap. VII.

31 These ground interrogators were located in these strategic areas, as follows:

Neah Bay, Wash.	Santini, N. Y.
Larson AFB, Wash.	Twin Lights, N. J.
Selfridge, Mich.	Palermo, N. J.
Otis AFB, Mass.	Ft. Custis, Va.

During the first six months of 1951, ADC was forced to cope with this same supply problem. Despite voluminous correspondence which was written to prod the programs for retrofitting and supply, the situation in mid-1951 was still critical. Of the 850 fighter aircraft which were assigned to ADC at the end of June 1951, only about 350, or 41 per cent, were equipped with Mark X transpondors.[32] In other words, about 500 aircraft still required installation of this vital piece of equipment. The situation of the ground Mark X equipment was even worse. Not a single ground-interrogator was put into operation during the first six months of 1951, and ADC was forced to continue operating with the eight modified ground interrogators it had inherited from ConAC.

Despite the insufficient supply of Mark X equipment, ADC put to use the Mark X equipment it had during the first half of 1951. It should be emphasized that the Mark X system was used predominantly by ADC as a beacon assist to extend the radar range of fighter type aircraft; it was employed only to a limited degree in its identification function.[33] The reason for this was that the present Mark X IFF system could not provide sufficient security in identifying friendly aircraft. Although Mark X equipment could provide recognition of all aircraft with airborne Mark X IFF, the equipment was restricted to only four modes of recognition: general IFF, personal identity, flight leader identity and emergency.[34]

---

32. Memo, "Mark X IFF Program," C&E Supply and Maintenance Conference, 26-27 Jun 1951, ADC Hqs.

33. Ibid.

34. ADC COI 81-2, "Employment of Mark X, IFF"

These four modes of recognition did not allow enough variations in coded signals to provide genuine security in identification.

In order to correct this deficiency in the security of the Mark X IFF system, the Short Interval Identification System (SIIS) was developed. This equipment was designed to provide increased security and greater operational flexibility to the Mark X IFF by the use of faster coding techniques.[35] USAF directed the Air Proving Ground to evaluate the operational suitability of the SIIS, and a test of this equipment was scheduled to begin about 1 September 1951.[36]

Certain other measures were taken to insure the security of the Mark X IFF system. An IFF destructor, the XJ-3, was installed in most aircraft equipped with the Mark X IFF. USAF directed installation of destructors on all aircraft carrying Mark X AN/APX-6s. Permission for flying within the ZI in aircraft equipped with this Mark X equipment, but without the IFF destructor, was to be given only on the basis of an urgent operational requirement. Aircraft in flight equipped with the AN/APX-6 but without destructors were to be closely monitored, and operational orders to aircraft commanders were to include instructions on guarding the AN/APX-6 when landing at unauthorized bases.[37] Also, as a result of emergency landings by two fighter aircraft in Czechoslovakia, all aircraft were directed to operate destructors for IFF Mark X equipment in all cases where any

---

35. ADC, Communications and Electronics Digest, 6 Jul 1951, pp. 9-17.

36. ADC to APG: "Operational Suitability Test of the IFF Mark X Short Interval Identification System," 19 Apr 1951. (See DOC 315)

doubt existed as to whether a landing was being made in a friendly or unfriendly country.[38]

IFF Mark X equipment was also protected by special security policies when it was released for use to foreign countries other than the United Kingdom or Canada. If transpondors were installed in foreign aircraft other than aircraft belonging to the United Kingdom and Canada, the theater commander was to insure that the transpondor was not returned with the return of aircraft to the country concerned. The theater commander was also to make certain that individuals from these other foreign nations did not return to their countries with written Mark X procedures, specifications, or other pertinent literature.

Ambitious plans were made for an expanded use of Mark X equipment both as a means of identifying friendly aircraft, and as a beacon assist to reinforce the range of fighter aircraft. By the end of June 1951, only USAF and Navy aircraft were being equipped with Mark X IFF. Within the Air Force, the retrofit in all first-line bomber aircraft of the Strategic Air Command was to be completed by 1 July 1951, and the retrofit program for all first-line transport aircraft within the Military Air Transport Service was to be completed by 1 January 1952.[39] Provisions were being made by USAF to equip **all** types of military aircraft with Mark X equipment.[40] In addition

---

38. TWX, USAF to ADC and other Commands, 16 Jun 1951.

39. ADC to AFG: "Operational Suitability Test of IFF Mark X Short Interval Identification System," 19 Apr 1951. (See DOC 315)

40. TWX, ADC to EADF and WADF, 27 Jan 1951. The only exceptions were to be single engine propeller training aircraft and helicopters.

plans were made to install Group "A" parts of the Mark X IFF components in 500 four-engine commercial transports in order that these aircraft might be more readily equipped with a complete Mark X IFF set in the event of a national emergency. Finally, plans were laid for the joint utilization of Mark X IFF with the RCAF.[41]

V

When air traffic control and IFF fail to establish the identity of an aircraft within an active air defense area, interception by fighter aircraft for identification is made.

Identification by means of interception posed numerous difficulties for air defense planners. The primary problem was to gain authority to dispatch fighters to make intercept on unidentified aircraft within active air defense areas.

In November 1949 ConAC granted authority to its air defense forces to commence interceptions. In mid-January 1950, however, ConAC ordered that all interceptions of unidentified aircraft be suspended in both air defense force areas. Reasons for this were: (1) the need for developing a better means of coordination with the CAA on flight plan information in order to protect airlines and other civilian air traffic from interception by fighter aircraft, and (2) the necessity for more thorough training in the identification of

---

41. ADC to Dir. Comm., USAF: "Installation and Employment of IFF in Air Force Aircraft," 2 Apr 1951. (See DOC 306.)

multi-engine aircraft [42] and in interception procedures on the part of pilots and GCI controllers.

In the latter part of March, ConAC took steps to secure the approval of USAF to commence interceptions of unidentified aircraft over certain areas in the United States.[43] ConAC explained that action had been taken to correct deficiencies which had been evident in previous interception operations. By that time, the gentlemen's agreement had been consummated with the CAA whereby all civilian air traffic had been requested to file flight plans when operating in any of the active air defense zones. It was expected that this action would facilitate the process of recognition, and cut down the number of interceptions required since more aircraft would be identified by correlation of flight plans. In order to reduce the possibility of damaging friendly aircraft while intercepting for identification purposes, ConAC assured that interceptor pilots and GCI operators would be thoroughly briefed and indoctrinated in their respective duties and responsibilities.[44]

---

42. After the B-29 had been compromised in World War II, the Russians developed the T-U4 which had a remarkable resemblance to our B-29 and B-50 aircraft. This similarity in design has confused interceptor pilots.

43. ConAC to USAF: "Initiation of Active Recognition and Fighter Interception Operations in Air Defense of the United States," 27 Mar 1950. (DOC 318)

44. See the provisions of ConAC Regulation 55-6 (Tentative), 2 May 1950.

As a result, in early April 1950 USAF granted ConAC the authority to intercept and identify all aircraft entering the Richland, Washington and Oak Ridge, Tennessee airspace reservations. Provisions were also made for interception and identification of aircraft flying over the Los Alamos, New Mexico area, and specific areas along the Eastern Coast of the United States during certain hours.[45]

Authority for interception throughout the entire Northwestern area of the United States was not granted at this time. Unless agreements could be reached with Canadian flight agencies whereby the Canadians would supply necessary flight data on aircraft penetrating recognition zones from the Canadian side, any interception program in this area could not succeed.[46] The necessary agreements were reached in late May 1950, and authority for intercepts was granted for the Northwestern area of the United States, including the Hanford region.[47]

In June 1950, WADF received authority from ConAC to expand its area for interception of unidentified aircraft to include the Pacific Recognition Zone.[48] This authority was granted providing

---

45. See Memo of correspondence, USAF to ConAC: "Initiation of Active Recognition and Interception Operations in Air Defense of the United States," 7 Apr 1950. (See DOC 311)

46. TWX, WADF to 25th AD, 28th AD, Albuquerque Air Defense Area, and 4AF, 29 May 1950. (DOC 319)

47. ConAC to WADF: "Initiation of Active Recognition and Fighter Interceptor Operations in Northwestern United States," 27 May 1950. (DOC 320)

that coverage could be made by the AC&W units in that area, and that arrangements could be made with the CAA for the submission of flight plan information.

Thus, by the eve of the Korean war, progress had been made in the identification by interception program, although it was still inadequate in most respects. ConAC had defined the active air defense areas in which all unidentified aircraft were to be intercepted: the Pacific Ocean area, the Oak Ridge prohibited area, the Los Alamos air defense area, the Hanford-Seattle air defense area, and along the Atlantic Coast from Bangor, Maine to Norfolk, Virginia. In addition, ConAC regulations had been published which were to govern the methods of interception. ConAC Regulation 55-6 covered interceptor procedures and fighter rules of engagement in air defense operations.[49] ConAC Regulation 55-8 covered the recognition of aircraft.[50] Because these two regulations put a great burden of responsibility on the interceptor pilot, ConAC staff members had recommended that a comprehensive, thorough and realistic program of aircraft recognition be initiated.[51] In this program, emphasis was to be placed on distinguishing between the TU-4 and our B-29s and B-50s.

The glaring inadequacy in the interceptor program up to this

---

49. <u>ConAC Reg 55-6 (Tentative)</u>, 2 May 1950. See discussion following.

50. <u>ConAC Reg 55-8</u>, 29 Mar 1950.

51. IRS, O&T to Intelligence, and Training O&T: "Identification of Aircraft," 29 May 1950. (DOC 322)

time was the fact that interceptions for identification could not be made at night.[52] The reason for this was that ConAC had **never** possessed jet fighters equipped for night or all-weather operations. In view of the prevailing thesis that the enemy would strike with his bombers at night or during periods of inclement weather, the shortcomings of ConAC's interceptor capabilities were readily apparent.[53]

The outbreak of the Korean war had an electrifying effect upon ConAC's interception program. One of the initial steps taken by ConAC was the issuance of Operations Order 16-50, which deployed fighters to more advantageous locations for intercept operations.[54] The AC&W facilities were put on a 24-hour basis, and the air defense forces were directed to assume operational control of all combat-ready interceptor aircraft. All unidentified aircraft entering the United States from specified areas were to be intercepted: in the EADF area this order pertained to all unidentified aircraft entering the United States on a southerly course between 91 degrees and 269 degrees; and in the WADF area to all unidentified aircraft entering the United States from the north and from the ocean areas.[55]

---

52. TWX, ConAC to EADF and WADF, 8 May 1950. (DOC 323)
53. See Chapter VII.
54. Operations Order 16-50, ConAC, 25 Jun 1950.
55. Ibid.

Approximately a month later the policy with regard to the areas in which interceptions were authorized for identification purposes was firmed up. Joint Regulation AFR 60-22, dated 19 July 1950, listed the air defense identification zones (ADIZ) in the ZI and bordering ocean bodies. As previously told, all military aircraft operating in these ADIZs were <u>required</u> to file flight plans; however, civil air traffic operating in these zones could only be <u>requested</u> to file flight plans.[56] ConAC gave its air defense forces authority to conduct intercept operations against unidentified aircraft entering these zones.[57]

Shortly thereafter, ConAC specifically authorized intercepts to commence in two ADIZs, the San Francisco Identification Zone,[58] and the Canadian Boundary Identification Zone.[59] In the latter case, the Canadian - United States Emergency Air Defense Plan gave permission for aircraft of either country to fly over the territory

---

56. <u>AFR 60-22</u>, 19 Jul 1950.

57. ConAC, Air Defense Operations Division, History for Aug 1950. Coincident with the definition of ADIZs, ConAC issued a regulation designed to cover the rules of engagement for interceptors engaged against unidentified aircraft penetrating these identification zones. These new rules of engagement in <u>ConAC Reg. 55-6</u> were to apply prior to war, or to a state of emergency being declared. See: <u>ConAC Reg. 55-6</u>, 21 Jul 1950.

58. ConAC to WADF: "Interception of Unidentified Aircraft," 22 Jul 1950. (DOC 324)

59. ConAC to EADF: "Interception of Unidentified Aircraft," 29 Jul 1950. The problem remained of getting sufficient depth in the area of the Canadian Identification Zone which would permit successful interceptions of unidentified aircraft over the Detroit-Niagara sector. (DOC 325) See chapter on Canada for this story.

of the other in the event of war. Permission to overfly did not apply during peacetime, and consequently a request was made that the necessary agreements be made with the Canadian government to permit interceptors to cross the international border when engaged in intercepting unidentified aircraft.[60]

No sooner had the new ADIZs been put into effect than the problem of intercepting civil air carriers assumed major proportions. Upon the promulgation of the new ADIZs, civilian pilots had been encouraged to file flight plans when entering these zones and had been warned that they would be intercepted if they operated without flight plans or did not adhere to such plans. ConAC had requested that CAA contact the airline operators and show the need that existed for filing flight plans and to stress the necessity for intercepting those aircraft operating without flight plans. Apparently this information was slow in getting around, or else in many cases it went unheeded, for numerous reports of interceptions on civil aircraft were filed.[61] Before Public Law 778 ConAC had no legal authority to enforce the filing of flight plans; the only recourse possible to ConAC under these circumstances was to inaugurate a policy of intensive education of civilian pilots to impress them with the need

---

60. See chapter on Canada for the negotiations on overfly agreements.

61. ConAC, Air Defense Operations Division, History for Jul 1950.

for filing flight plans in order to avoid interception.[62] The passage of Public Law 778 in September 1950 empowered the government to regulate civilian air traffic in the interests of air traffic and identification. Based on this authority the CAA issued CAR 620, which made mandatory the filing of flight plans and submission of position reports for all civil aircraft operating in ADIZs. This had the effect of cutting down on the number of interceptions that had been made previously on civil aircraft classified as unidentified because they had not filed flight plans.

VI

During the first six months of 1951, ADC engaged in intercept operations within ADIZs. The publication of AFR 60-22 and the issuance of CAR 620 in 1950 had made it mandatory for military and civil aircraft operating in ADIZs to file flight plans. ADC's mission, therefore, was to make an effort to intercept all aircraft within ADIZs which could not be identified by means of correlating flight plans.

Although it was the aim of ADC to intercept all aircraft in ADIZs which could not be identified by flight plan correlation, in

---

62. EADF to ConAC: "Briefing of Civilian . . .," 21 Sep 1950. (See DOC 275) Civilian pilots had a bone of contention in that interceptors sometimes flew too close to civil air carriers, thus endangering civilian passengers. In response to these charges, ConAC warned its fighter units that any infraction of the rules of engagement which had been drawn up to prevent such close flying would not be condoned. See: ConAC, Air Defense Operations Division, History for Jul 1950.

reality, a relatively small number of interceptions could be attempted. For example, during January a total of 3,786 unidentified tracks were reported by all air divisions, and fighter interception was attempted only on 796 of these tracks.[63] This was a fairly representative preview of ADC's success with the interception for identification throughout the first half of 1951. The two major causes responsible for the failure to even attempt interception in so many instances were: (1) shortage of all-weather fighters, and (2) faded tracks.

As related in Chapter Seven, approximately 65% of the aircraft assigned the fighter interceptor units at this time were F-86s, which were not equipped to operate at night or under adverse weather conditions. The eventual assignment of F-94s, F-89s, and F-86Ds to the air defense system, all of which possessed night and all-weather interceptor capabilities, it was expected, would resolve the problem of the inability to effect night and adverse weather interception.

The problem of radar tracks fading from view on the radar screens was largely due to inadequate radar coverage resulting from arbitrarily sited Lashup III stations and from the use of inadequate radar equipment. As more strategically located permanent radar sites with new equipment replaced the temporary sites it was expected that this second problem of fading tracks would be considerably reduced.

Of the 796 actual interceptions attempted in January, 509, or approximately 64%, were successful.[64] This also was a fair repre-

---

63. ADC, Command Data

64. Ibid.

sentation of the ability of the fighter interceptors to make interception during the first half of 1951. The fading tracks from the radar screens was the principal reason for the non-successful attempts. It was expected that new radar equipment to be supplied the permanent aircraft control and warning system, and the acquisition of Mark X IFF equipment, which was designed to provide a beacon assist in the tracking and control of high speed aircraft, would substantially reduce the number of non-successful intercepts in the future.

One technique employed by ADC in the first six months of 1951 to ameliorate the difficulties encountered in its interception program was the establishment of "free areas" within ADIZs. In these areas all uncorrelated tracks of aircraft which originated in the ADIZs themselves were identified as friendly. This permitted scope operators to disregard numerous plots which appeared as the result of local flying, and had the effect of reducing the number of unidentified tracks for which interceptions were considered necessary.

VII

Thus far we have discussed interception by fighter aircraft without reference to two very important questions: (1) by what criteria could an aircraft be adjudged hostile, and (2) what measures were adopted within the interceptor program to offset a surprise enemy air attack?

On 7 April 1950, USAF gave ConAC authority to intercept and

identify aircraft trespassing prohibited areas and certain active air defense areas. ConAC was not caught unprepared. Anticipating USAF's move to authorize intercept operations, ConAC had been working on a plan concerned with interception procedures. This plan was first published in the form of a ConAC directive.[65] Shortly thereafter, its provisions were published in ConAC Regulation 55-6 (Tentative) and covered interceptor procedures and fighter rules of engagement.[66] The provisions of this Regulation were intended to apply only to peace-time operations.

The provisions of the Regulation required that pilots and GCI operators be thoroughly familiar with its contents. Each pilot and GCI operator participating in the interception program was required to pass a written examination on the provisions of the Regulation. The Regulation also stated that interceptor pilots would not participate in the interception program until they had proved beyond all doubt their capability to recognize all multi-engine aircraft instantly. No crews were to be released to intercept missions unless certified by air division commanders as having complete knowledge of 55-6.[67]

The provisions of 55-6 required that any aircraft approaching

---

65. <u>ConAC Operations Directive No. 50</u>.

66. <u>ConAC Reg. 55-6 (Tentative)</u>, 2 May 1950.

67. ConAC to Air Forces: "ConAC Regulation 55-6 (Tentative) Interceptor Procedures and Fighter Rules of Engagement," 26 Apr 1950. (DOC 326)

or entering an active air defense area which could not be recognized positively as friendly from the CAA and MFS plan data was to be considered unknown and therefore subject to interception. Recognition of such aircraft as friendly or enemy was to be made by one or more of the following means: recognition of the type of aircraft; recognition of distinctive marking and numbers; recognition based on behavior of aircraft when intercepted. Recognition of unknown aircraft as hostile was to be established by the following conditions: the position of an aircraft with its bomb-bay doors open when near a possible bombing target; bombs or paratroopers falling from the aircraft; machine gun and rocket fire emanating from the aircraft towards the ground or towards the interceptor.[68]

The limitations of this regulation were readily apparent. The interceptor could take action only if an aircraft opened its bomb-bay doors while in a straight and level flight on a probable bombing target, or if bombs and paratroopers were dropped from the aircraft, or if gun or rocket fire were directed from the aircraft towards a ground target or at the interceptor.[69] In other words, the interceptor, in most cases, could shoot an aircraft out of the skies only _after_ a hostile act had been committed.[70]

---

68. ConAC Regulation 55-6 (Tentative), 2 May 1950.

69. Ibid.

70. Another regulation affecting intercept operations at this time was ConAC Regulation 55-8, 29 Mar 1950, which established the general policy for the recognition of aircraft by the air defense system. This regulation was superseded by ConAC Regulation 55-8, 21 Jul 1950.

In July 1950, a new ConAC Regulation 55-6 was published replacing the previous regulation. However, this regulation in no way cleared up the limitations which restricted interceptors from taking action against unidentified aircraft until after a hostile act had been committed. The new regulation was designed primarily to provide the rules of engagement for interceptors engaged against unidentified aircraft penetrating the new ADIZs prescribed in AFR 60-22. These fighter rules of engagement, as in the previous regulation, were intended for conditions prior to war or to a state of emergency being declared.[71]

It was not until the fall of 1950 that a significant advance was made to free interceptors in taking action against unidentified aircraft before a hostile act had been committed. A policy statement by the President authorized the Commanding General, ConAC, to destroy aircraft in flight within the United States which had committed a hostile act, which were manifestly hostile in intent, or which bore the military insignia of the USSR (unless properly cleared or obviously in distress). This policy amplified the previous instructions issued in the ConAC Regulation 55-6 of July 1950, which had limited intercept operations to specific ADIZs and which had restricted the action that might be taken by interceptors. The purpose of this new policy was to arm the Commanding Generals of ConAC and the air defense forces with the authority to make an on-the-spot decision, thus making it possible to successfully cope

---

71. ConAC Regulation 55-6, 21 Jul 1950.

with a surprise air attack by hostile aircraft.[72]

ConAC proceeded to spell out an interpretation of the phrases contained in the President's policy statement. The phrase "manifestly hostile in intent" was to be determined on the basis of two broad conditions. If prior intelligence was received indicating that an airborne attack was likely to be launched or was actually airborne against the United States, a state of emergency was to be declared and the wartime rules of engagement and air traffic controls were to be applied, thus reducing to a degree the problem of determining which aircraft were hostile. Under the second condition, if no prior intelligence were available, the problem of determining intent before a hostile act had been committed would be difficult indeed. However, if the pattern or actions of an incoming unidentified aircraft indicated <u>beyond reasonable doubt</u> that a hostile raid was being attempted, action could be taken to destroy such aircraft. The decision to destroy aircraft under this second condition could be made only at defense force level or by higher headquarters.[73]

There was also a clarification of the term "obviously in distress" when applied to an aircraft bearing the military insignia of the USSR. This was interpreted by ConAC to mean that any USSR aircraft was "obviously in distress" when it was in such a condition that it was impossible for it to do other than crash or land. How-

---

72. TWX, C/S USAF to ConAC and other Commands, 1 Sep 1950. (DOC 327)

73. TWX, ConAC to EADF and WADF, 12 Sep 1950.

ever, it was added that as a general statement, any USSR aircraft was assumed to be hostile, regardless of its airworthy condition, if it were not properly cleared while flying over the United States.[74]

The President's policy statement was spelled out in even greater detail when ADC published ADC Regulation 55-10 covering interception procedures and rules of engagement which were to be applied prior to the declaration of a military emergency.[75] Included in this regulation was a working definition of what could be construed as a hostile act: any unidentified aircraft which engaged in minelaying operations, released parachutists or bombs, or which fired guns or rockets towards any target, was considered to have committed a hostile act. Unless the aircraft engaging in such operations was authorized to do so for training purposes, it was to be identified as a hostile aircraft and destroyed.

In addition, the regulation established other criteria by which an aircraft was to be judged as hostile. Aircraft bearing the markings of the USSR operating over the continental United States without proper flight clearance were to be declared hostile and destroyed. Any aircraft which did not meet the established standards for identification within an ADIZ could be declared hostile by the air defense division commander. Also, aircraft could be declared hostile by the air defense force commander when the pattern of actions

---

74. Ibid.

75. ADC Reg. 55-10, 12 Apr 1951.

of incoming unidentified aircraft indicated beyond reasonable doubt that they were "manifestly hostile in intent."[76]

These definitions of a "hostile act" and a "hostile aircraft" provided those engaged in intercept operations with a firm policy with which to carry out their mission of air defense.

The provisions of 55-10 also set down the intercept procedures and rules of engagement to be followed by air defense interceptors <u>before</u> the declaration of a military emergency. If an interceptor pilot was unable to identify an aircraft as friendly, he was to so notify the GCI controller and give all pertinent information of the intercepted aircraft. After doing so, there were two courses of action left open to the interceptor pilot. He was to engage the unidentified aircraft and destroy it if the intercepted aircraft committed a hostile act; if it was declared hostile by the air defense division commander or the air defense force commander, or if the intercepted aircraft bore the markings of the USSR and was not properly cleared. The other course of action was to maintain surveillance on the aircraft pending further instructions from the GCI controller.

Although the fighter rules of engagement and intercept procedures outlined in 55-10 were intended to cover most situations which might be encountered in peacetime intercept operations, in some cases they were inadequate. For example, small aircraft operating below 4000 feet in ADIZs were not required to file flight plans and

---

76. <u>Ibid.</u>

in most instances were not subject to interception. There were no provisions made in 55-10 to prevent such small aircraft from overflying critical restricted areas for sabotage purposes, or from taking pictures of vital installations. It was expected that action would be taken to correct this condition.

At the same time that ADC issued 55-10, Regulation 55-9 was also published to prescribe the interception procedures and fighter rules of engagement to be followed in air defense operations sub-sequent to the conditions of a military emergency.[77] As defined, a military emergency was to be constituted by any one of the following situations: a Presidential proclamation or Congressional declaration that a state of war exists, an enemy attack against targets within the continental United States, or under a tense military situation wherein the Commanding General, ADC, declared a state of military emergency.[78]

As far as interception procedures were concerned, the provisions of 55-9 followed closely those of 55-10. The definition of a "hostile act" was exactly the same for both regulations. The other criteria set down for identifying a hostile aircraft were the same for both regulations with a single exception. Whereas in 55-10 any aircraft bearing the markings of the USSR and operating over the United States was to be adjudged hostile, in 55-9 any aircraft bearing the markings of the nation or nations which had prompted the

---

77. Rules of engagement for fighter aircraft in time of war were first set down in the post-war period in ConAC Reg. 55-13, 20 Oct 1950.

78. ADC Reg. 55-9, 12

declaration of military emergency were to be declared hostile.[79]

The fighter rules of engagement prescribed by 55-9 permitted the interceptor pilot to destroy intercepted aircraft under the following circumstances: any aircraft bearing the markings of a known enemy nation which was observed within or approaching the United States, an intercepted aircraft which committed a hostile act, and any intercepted aircraft declared hostile by the air division defense commander or air defense force commander.[80]

In addition to firming policy by the publication of these two regulations, ADC took one more step in implementing measures for interception. In order to be prepared for a surprise enemy air attack, ADC took the precaution of prescribing various states of alert for interceptor aircraft employed in the air defense of the United States. The stages of alert prescribed in ADC 55-5 were designed to keep interceptor crews and aircraft poised to offset any surprise air attack on the United States.[81]

---

79. Ibid.

80. Ibid.

81. ADC Reg. 55-5, 6 Feb 1951. These states of alert were originally set down in ConAC Reg. 55-10 published 14 Jul 1950. States of alert prescribed in ADC 55-5 were as follows: a. Standby. Combat-ready crews and aircraft (fuel cells filled and guns loaded, "hot") positioned adjacent to the downwind end of the active runway with starting power units connected and with starting crews immediately available. Upon receipt of the scramble order, the crews will become airborne as soon as possible. b. Readiness. Combat-ready crews and aircraft (fuel cells filled and guns loaded, "hot") with a capability of becoming airborne in not more than five minutes after the receipt of a scramble order. c. Available. Combat-ready crews and aircraft in deferred states of preparedness with a capability of becoming airborne in fifteen minutes after receipt of a scramble order, with fuel cells filled and guns loaded, "hot." d. At Ease. Crews and aircraft in deferred states of preparedness with a capability of

becoming airborne ready for combat in not more than thirty minutes. Maintenance work may be accomplished providing aircraft can be prepared for take-off in thirty minutes. As a general rule, units "at ease" and "available" will be ordered to a higher state of alert before the scramble order is issued. e. <u>Released</u>. When a unit is released, the time at which it is to revert to alert status will be specified by the Air Defense Command air defense commander concerned.

CHAPTER EIGHTEEN

OPERATING THE INTERIM AIR DEFENSE SYSTEM

I

In the preceding chapters of this history an attempt has been made to describe the diverse efforts made toward the creation of an air defense for the continental United States. In these chapters the growth of each of the major elements in that system has been considered, but little or no attempt has been made to evaluate the achievements of ADC and its predecessors in the operation of these elements as part of an integrated air defense. It is the purpose of the present chapter to undertake such an analysis, confining discussion primarily to the operation of the radar and fighter aircraft elements in air defense.

Before embarking on such a presumptuous undertaking it is necessary to indulge in a few general considerations about the nature of the system which served as the nation's first line of air defense from 1948 to 1951. In Chapter IV it was shown that the temporary AC&W system known as LASHUP was a make-shift affair, born of immediate necessity and comprising old-model radars sited upon land which was either government-owned or else obtained at minimum cost. Mated to this LASHUP radar were whatever fighter aircraft resources USAF could garner for air defense purposes.

These fighter resources, which included obsolete World War II models as well as their newer jet-propelled counterparts, were not only insufficient in numbers and in ideal air defense capabilities, but were not deployed to maximum advantage. After the outbreak of Korean hostilities in mid-1950, this ill-mated assortment of weapons constituted the first line of defense against the threat of imminent air attack. ConAC and ADC had no other recourse but to do the very best they could to squeeze the maximum capability out of this arbitrarily created defense system. The existence of this interim air defense system with its inadequate and ill-arranged equipment in this period presents the major difficulty in any effort to evaluate the progress made towards a better operational capability in air defense. Indispensable to an accurate understanding of the Air Force predicament is the fact that extensive modification of the interim air defense system was not undertaken because of the urgent necessity of conserving funds, time, and effort towards the creation of the Permanent air defense system.

The discussion of the operation of the interim air defense system which follows will reveal the inescapable truth of the inadequacy of that system for the protection of the United States against air attack. As to how effectively the interim system could function, few persons if any, within ConAC and ADC had any illusions. From the beginning, explanations were issued before every maneuver to the effect that such operations were primarily designed for training and not as tests of the existing system. Inevitably, however, reports emanating from these exercises revealed the unpalatable fact that the interim system was a token defense and little more.

The purpose of the present chapter, therefore, will be two-fold: to indicate the shortcomings of the interim system as revealed by the exercises to mid-1951; and to indicate the progress made and problems encountered in gaining knowledge and experience in air defense tactics and operational procedures.

II

Almost as soon as the effort to assemble radar equipment for LASHUP began, exercises were scheduled for the new system. During 1949 three exercises were held, two in the Northeast (BLACKJACK and LOOKOUT) and one in the Northwest (DRUMMERBOY).[1] Critiques and reports emanating from these maneuvers were unanimous in their confirmation of ConAC's fears. The air defense systems established in the two most vital areas of the United States – the Northeast and Northwest – were proven to be nothing more than token systems. Reasons were not lacking for these evaluations:

----

1. See above chap. on LASHUP.

LASHUP equipment was inadequate; radar was not deployed to maximum advantage; and the aircraft available did not meet the requirements of air defense. These suspicions having been confirmed, other manifestations of the air defense effort were looked upon critically, with an eye to the ability of ConAC to operate these systems to the maximum capability of the equipment on hand. Even in this respect, however, balm was not forthcoming. "The sorry state of the logistic support and supply system, the personnel turnover, the meagerness of training" made any appraisal of the operating efficiency and progress of USAF's air defense agency most difficult. Expressions of approval such as "the outcome of the exercise was astonishingly good" represented subjective evaluations of the progress made. The realities of the situation did not escape even those given to wishful thinking. "Considering the outcome /of the exercise/ as against the need for real defense, it was not good."[2]

Only one major exercise was held during 1950. Between 18 and 24 June the Northwest defenses were subject to the exercise known as WHIPSTOCK.[3] The Northwestern AC&W system having been placed on a 24-hour, 7-day schedule in February, the increase in operating experience was well evidenced in the June exercise. In

---

2. USAF, Operations Analysis, Summary Report No. 9, 11 Apr 1950, pp. 75-94.

3. WADF Historical Monograph, "Operation WHIPSTOCK," 1950.

the "considerable increase" in combat effectiveness noted in
this maneuver by the Commanding General of the 25th Air Division,
much credit was given to the emphasis placed on stabilization of
duty and station assignment during the previous six-month period.[4]

Although for the most part WHIPSTOCK confirmed the general
inadequacy of existing fighter aircraft in performing all-weather
assignments and also verified the inability of the existing radars
to supply adequate early warning, procedural deficiencies not involving equipment performance were revealed. The inadequacy of
identification and reporting procedures, the insufficiency of
controller training, and the inadequacy of air defense organization
were emphasized.[5]

During the seven months following Operation WHIPSTOCK no
major exercise of the air defense system was held. To this, the
outbreak of war in Korea and the adjustments in fighter deployment
and command organization coincident with that event contributed.
System operation and training were not jeopardized by these events,
however, but on the contrary were greatly accelerated. Frequent
systems training was achieved under fairly realistic conditions
through the cooperation of SAC in supplying bomber penetration
flights, known as BIG PHOTO missions, into the air defenses. The

---

4. 25th AD Commander's Summary, Operation WHIPSTOCK, 18-24 Jun 1950.

5. Ibid.

expansion of air identification zones after Korea and the increase in active interceptions which followed also provided greater systems training opportunities.

Beginning in February 1951, large-scale training exercises were revived. In February and June 1951 exercises involving the entire air defense systems of EADF and WADF were held. In April 1951 exercises of specific defense sector systems were held in each air defense force area. In the general analysis of the accomplishments and shortcomings of the operation of the interim air defense systems which follows we shall draw from the reports, summaries, and critiques of these exercises held in 1951 as descriptive of the air defense practices and procedures at the end of the reporting period of this history.

III

Although the inherent limitations of the ground radar and aircraft equipment which made up the interim air defense system were fully realized at the start, the extent of these deficiencies was made progressively clearer as a result of the exercises.

How limited such radar equipment as the AN/CPS-1, AN/CPS-5, AN/TPS-1B, AN/CPS-4 and AN/TPS-10 were for early warning and control purposes was not revealed until they were harnessed to types of aircraft which required ideal radar performance to function adequately in air defense. For example, though AN/TPS-1B radars served as well as could be expected, their early warning capability, though perhaps adequate for a well-positioned jet fighter, was entirely inadequate to bring a reciprocal engine fighter such as the F-51 or F-47 into interception range.[6] In the relationship of the radar to the fighter, the close harmony necessary in deployment and operation was emphasized. Of what avail, for example, was a miraculous early warning detection capability when the fighter aircraft were not deployed so as to take advantage of the performance of the radar? Conversely, of what benefit was superb fighter capability and deployment when early warning was deficient?

A major deficiency of LASHUP radar which was repeatedly emphasized throughout 1949-1951 was the inadequacy of height-finding radar performance. "Ground radar equipment presently in use is such that GCI controllers rarely have sufficiently complete and accurate reading to insure tactical positioning for fighters. As a result many tally-hos were obtained from positions lacking tactical advantage."[7] In this deficiency of information, height-finding inadequacies were a most important factor. Reports from all components of the air defense system almost without exception commented upon the negative altitude information supplied to the interceptors. Differences in altitude between actual height and that reported to fighters varied as much as 20,000 feet. In one area during the April 1951 exercise, it was estimated that an additional 75 tracks

---

6. WADF, Operations Summary, 22-24 Jun 1951.

7. EADF, Report of Air Defense Exercise, 8-11 Feb 1951.

could have been intercepted had adequate height information been available.[8]

Especially annoying was the habit of many tracks fading from the radar scopes after having been detected. This was due to a variety of factors involving the predilection of radar to vary in search capability because of eccentric patterns of beam propagation or sensitivity to atmospheric conditions. Fading tracks were a frequent cause of interception failures and for loss of fighter control.[9]

It has been noted above that criticism was levied during operation DRUMMERBOY upon supply procedures. Throughout 1950-1951 the supply and maintenance of ground radar was a continuing problem, though in general radar maintenance was sufficient to permit continuous operation during the exercises. However, "the lack of new tubes and the age of the radar equipment utilized materially affected the ability of the equipment to detect aircraft to the theoretical and calibrated coverage of the equipment."[10] Although the radar-in-commission percentages were kept high during the 1951 maneuvers, this was frequently the result of the expenditure of much time and effort.

---

8. Ibid.
9. Ibid.
10. WADF, Operations Summary, 22-24 Jun 1951.

In spite of the inherent limitations of radar equipment revealed in air defense operations, the exercises noted an increasing competence in the handling of ground radar, born of familiarity and experience. As will be noted below, however, the factor of experience was a variable in the air defense equation.

Although LASHUP radar and deployment were generally condemned for the requirements of a national air defense, high expectations were placed upon the ability of the Permanent System to cancel out the shortcomings revealed in the interim system. The steps taken to prepare for the Permanent AC&W System and the plans made and measures taken to extend early warning into Canada and seawards have been discussed in earlier chapters.[11] Even in the case of the highly-touted Permanent System equipment there were misgivings, however, as painful experience with early delivery model of the AN/CPS-6B revealed.[12]

IV

So far as aircraft development was concerned, the post-war years 1945-1951 were a period of transition between types current in World War II and the jet-propelled aircraft produced after the war.[13] Both types were found in the interim air defense system.

---

11. See above chapters on the Permanent AC&W System, Canada and Early Warning.

12. History of the 25th Air Division, 1 Apr-30 Jun 1951.

13. See above chapter on Aircraft for Air Defense.

Although the flight characteristics of the newer jet fighters (the F-80, F-82, F-84, and F-86) were quite satisfactory for normal air battle requirements, the demands of air defense revealed great shortcomings in most of the fighters available. First and foremost of the air defense requirements was the need for an aircraft which possessed an all-weather and night-flying capability. Secondly, and almost as important, was the requirement for a combat potential which would permit a successful encounter with heavily-armed bombers.

As noted in Chapter VII, prior to the introduction of the F-94 jet fighter, no jet-propelled aircraft available to air defense possessed an all-weather capability; and as late as June 1951 there were insufficient numbers of even this aircraft to equip a sizeable portion of the fighter units. A compromise with ideal requirements was inevitable. Three different types of aircraft had to perform the work which under ideal conditions would have been performed by one; a day fighter; an all-weather fighter; and a night fighter. The first requirement was well-met by the F-86. The second was fulfilled to a limited degree by the F-94. The U.S. Navy was capable of providing numbers of night-flying aircraft of the F4U variety, but reliance upon the Navy to provide them was fraught with obstacles of a most troublesome kind to ADC. All three types of jet aircraft capabilities available were to a great

extent neutralized, however, by their deficiency of fire power.
As the Operational Readiness Test Report of the 26th Air Division testified in June 1951:[14]

> Another long-recognized deficiency is the capability of our fighters to destroy the enemy once the interception is effected. The present-day armament consists primarily of the 50 caliber machine gun, an obsolete weapon with a lethal potential too low for the rate of closure between fighter and target....Until such time as radar gunlaying equipment is installed in our fighters and the lethal potential of the armament used is substantially increased the kill potential of our fighter will remain unsatisfactory.

The necessity for more effective armament had indeed been long recognized before the above observation was made, but because of the time-factor involved retrofit of existing armament was perforce a matter for the future. Newer types of fighters such as the F-89 were to have vastly increased armament potential as compared with the previous types.

It has been mentioned that the existence of relatively large numbers of reciprocal engine fighters and the use of such aircraft by air defense units, particularly by the Air National Guard, posed many problems. Although even a small capability on hand was deemed better than none at all, the peculiarities of air defense operations indicated that very little of the potentialities of such old-type aircraft could be utilized. The vital importance

---

14. 26th Air Division, Operational Readiness Test Report, 22-27 Jun 1951.

of the time factor in interception, the rate of climb, speed, maneuverability, and fire-power, not to mention other requirements such as all-weather capability and armament, made such World War II models quite ineffectual. Although normally these aircraft might have served air defense well, their relation to the ground radar capability in existence under LASHUP negated even this slim promise. So long as early warning was inadequate, conventional fighter types could not hope to meet the urgent time element in interception. That this was more than academic belief was revealed in the maneuvers, where recourse to the use of these aircraft from an air alert or combat air patrol position, rather than from a ground alert status, was necessary.

In most instances "the location of fighter fields in relation to the effectiveness of performing interception from all patterns of approach was found adequate."[15] But there were important qualifications. Spokane, in Washington, an important industrial center and seat of a SAC bomber base, was almost entirely without early warning under LASHUP. Portland, on the other hand, though possessed of early warning coverage, was unprotected by fighters.[16]

It was noted that though USAF fighter bases were generally well-situated, naval fighter resources were not always so located. "In the future, consideration should be given to deployment of

---

15. WADF, Operations Summary, 22-24 Jun 1951.

16. History of the 25th Air Division, 1 Apr-30 Jun 1951.

fighters, both Navy and Air Force, during maneuvers to increase defense capability. The knowledge and experience gained would prove valuable during actual emergencies."[17]

The conversion of air defense units to newer-type jet fighters was a continuous process, but it brought problems to the fore which further complicated the air defense situation. Modern jets required longer runways than did conventional fighters. In some instances speedy extension of existing runways was mandatory, especially in areas which urgently required an all-weather defense. The painstaking engineering feats of extending runways at both McChord AFB and Paine AFB are cases in point.[18]

V

In the preceding sections of this chapter we have dealt generally with radar and aircraft equipment and deployment shortcomings of the interim air defense system. These deficiencies were beyond the power of ADC to modify in the time available and without detriment to the preparations being made for the future air defense system.

The harmonization of such a diverse group of elements required much more than ideal equipment and skilled technicians. Knowledge and experience as well as managerial skill were indispensable requirements to the effective operation of any air defense

---

17. WADF, Operations Summary, 22-24 Jun 1951.

18. History of the 25th Air Division, 1 Apr-30 Jun 1951.

system - no matter how well manned and equipped. In the acquisition of this knowledge and experience, unfortunately, there had been little or no opportunity presented prior to the emergence of the interim air defense system. If tactics and techniques were to be developed for the great tasks envisaged in the future, the interim system would have to create them.

The process of development of skilled operating personnel was inevitably a slow one. Whereas a radar operator or a fighter pilot could be reasonably well-trained under existing facilities, air defense posed requirements for more than just individual proficiency. The expression "systems training" which came into use during 1949 reflects this requirement. If air defense was to function effectively it would have to function as a synchronized unit and its leaders required to possess familiarity and experience in the management of a highly intricate enterprise composed of many diversely-functioning elements. Furthermore, any mistake in the air defense process might well result in incalculable detriment to an entire nation.

The position of the GCI controller best represented the requirement for knowledge of integrated operations. This person bore the responsibility for identifying aircraft, scrambling and deploying fighters to best advantage, vectoring fighters to best combat position, cross-telling pertinent information to neighboring defense sectors, and marshalling fighters. Not only was he required to have up to the minute information on the status of his ground radar equipment but his knowledge of fighter characteristics and tactical capabilities had to be equally thorough.

Such requirements posed novel demands upon controller personnel. If it was merely a matter of supplying such knowledge to the many capable ConAC and ADC officers the obstacle would have been relatively minor. But the obstacles were more formidable. Not only academic knowledge, but extensive experience was necessary to breed the conviction necessary to evoke proper command decisions. This experience was seldom presented, however. The demands of overseas theaters for capable fighter commanders (a prime requirement for good controllers) made for a continuous circulation of qualified personnel out of the command. The June exercise in the 25th Air Division disclosed that out of 51 controllers on duty during the exercise, 35 had less than six months controller training, and of these, fifteen had less than one month of on-the-job training.[19] In this exercise the Commanding General of the 25th Air Division noted that:[20]

> Controllers are new and in training, but they do not use tactical sense; they scramble too late; they do not take into consideration the time-distance factor; and it was obvious to me that they do not understand jet problems and tactics by the way they set the fighters up for the first pass at the bogey.

---

19. *Ibid.*

20. *Ibid.*

The following pages will discuss certain control and intercept processes in an effort to highlight the problems of operating the entire air defense system as a functioning unit for the primary purpose of destruction of an invading enemy aircraft.

VI

In the process of interception a host of complicated problems intervene to make decisive and timely action difficult. One of the most troublesome of these impediments is the factor of identification. In the chapter on identification procedures, the techniques employed have been discussed in some detail and the major problems presented.[21] Suffice it here to indicate the importance of the identification problem in the general interception picture. In the words of the inspecting team which performed the Operational Readiness Test of the 26th Air Division in June 1951:[22]

> Too much effort is required to identify incoming flights ....If flight plan correlation cannot be accomplished, a system of positive control and identification must be established farther out to intercept enemy penetrations effectively before targets are reached.

Unfortunately, the statistical summaries of both daily and maneuver operations are not valid enough as indices to permit an estimate of the damage which cumbersome identification procedures commit in air defense. Although ADC made it mandatory upon con-

---

21. See above chapter on Identification.

22. 26th Air Division, Operational Readiness Test Report, 22-27 Jun 1951.

trollers to identify all aircraft within one minute of detection, maneuver statistics indicated that this deadline was seldom adhered to. Of those tracks identified and intercepted in the WADF area during the June 1951 maneuver, the identification process consumed 1.8 minutes whereas the total time from detection to interception was 24.6 minutes.[23] An analysis of the interception-identification problem in the 34th Air Division area, performed by the ADC Operations Analysis Unit, showed that the average time required to identify aircraft as friendly in that area (from time of first plot to identification) was 3.3 minutes. The time required to identify as friendly varied from an average of 1.4 minutes during slack periods to 4.3 minutes during busy periods. Time required to identify aircraft as unknown averaged 4.4 minutes.[24]

The primary reason for the inordinate amount of time required to identify aircraft lay in the difficulty of identification in the confusing diversity of air traffic over vital defense areas. The story of the efforts to acquire authority to control civil air traffic has been told in Chapter XV and the practical problems of air traffic control in the identification process have been recounted in Chapter XVII.

---

23. WADF, Operations Summary, 22-24 Jun 1951.

24. ADC, Operations Analysis Report, "Albuquerque Air Traffic Control Test, 21 Jul 1951," 17 Sep 1951.

The operations summaries of the various maneuvers reveal the diversity of the reasons for the failure to attempt interceptions. Of a total of 488 tracks of unknown aircraft detected during the June 1951 maneuver in the WADF area, only 407 intercepts were even attempted. Eighty-one unidentified tracks were not challenged at all. A collation of the reasons for the failure to intercept these tracks revealed the following:[25]

Reasons for Non-Attempts

```
Fading tracks.....................35
Out of range......................22
Bad weather....................... 5
Identification before action...... 6
No aircraft available............. 1
Too low for intercept............. 2
Short track....................... 8
Controller error.................. 2
```

The statistics reveal even more discouraging details. Of the 407 intercepts actually attempted, only 251 were deemed to have been successful. One hundred and fifty-six got away! Reasons for the failure of these attempted interceptions were given by WADF as follows:[26]

---

25. WADF, Operations Summary, 22-24 Jun 1951.
26. Ibid.

Reasons for Unsuccessful Intercepts

    Track fade............................120
    Fighter fade.......................... 7
    Fighter equipment inadequate.......... 7
    Inadequate height finder.............. 1
    Identification before intercept....... 7
    Out of range.......................... 8
    Too low for intercept................. 1
    Abort................................. 1
    Weather............................... 3
    Other................................. 1

VII

The problems of getting a fighter into the air against a potential enemy have been generally indicated above. There were additional imponderables, however, not revealed in the statistics. Once the decision to intercept had been made, the scramble order was given. Actual scrambles as such presented few problems, except for bad weather and icy runways.[27] However, the lack of adequate communications between GCI stations and fighter units, especially when the latter were at a stand-by status, and the scrambling of aircraft at different states of readiness in order to operate as a single flight were factors which impeded timely scrambles.[28]

During the 1951 exercises many intercepts were undertaken from an air alert. Had direct scrambles been attempted the probability of interception would have been considerably reduced owing

---

27. EADF, Report of Air Defense Exercise, 8-11 Feb 1951.
28. Ibid.

to the aggressor track probably fading before interception was accomplished.[29] Although air alerts of the combat air patrols were inefficient with jet aircraft because of the high fuel consumption, in cases where the fighter base was located at some distance away from the GCI station and the source of approach of the enemy aircraft, the use of air alerts was deemed to provide the only solution.[30] The procedure of having the fighter aircraft fly until its jet fuel was exhausted before landing was made mandatory by ADC. Where the mission was a short one, the fighter was kept up in the air, thereby providing a jet combat patrol capability. For the most part, combat air patrols were flown by conventional type fighters, whose ability to become airborne and to intercept successfully from a ground position was slim. Where there were combat patrols in the skies, the inexperience of controllers sometimes led them to ignore the favorable position of the patrol and to scramble fighters on the ground.[31]

Important to the problem of timely scrambles was the matter of the shortage of combat ready crews.[32] The Operational Readiness Test of the 26th Air Division revealed that the number of such crews

---

29. Ibid.
30. Ibid.
31. History of the 25th Air Division, 1 Apr-30 Jun 1951.
32. See above chapter on Crews and their Training.

was insufficient for sustained operations. An 80-hour work week was estimated for the combat ready pilots assigned to the division. Such a situation was characterized as allowing the possibility for a "complete breakdown of the operations due to pilot fatigue."[33]

The 25th Air Division reported during the June 1951 exercise that the most unsatisfactory controller function was the "apparent inability to scramble fighters wisely."[34] It was found that the controllers not only did not have enough tactical experience to lead fighters well into the first pass at the enemy, but that they also were not scrambling from several bases for the same bogey.[35] In the event of a mass raid it was considered necessary to scramble fighters from several areas for the same target, but the controllers proved to be reticent in giving orders committing forces. In all fairness, however, it must be pointed out that as yet insufficient numbers of fighters were available to resort to this practice consistently.

The problem of sufficiency of numbers of fighters prompted ADC to take drastic action to make sure that every fighter capability was made available during an emergency. In the process of conversion and extensive retrofitting of fighter equipment, many aircraft had

---

33. 26th Air Division, Operational Readiness Test Report, 22-27 Jun 1951.

34. History of the 25th Air Division, 1 Jun-30 Jun 1951.

35. Ibid.

been grounded from time to time for equipment modifications. ADC took steps to insure the utilization of these aircraft by issuing a directive to the effect that aircraft grounded for equipment changes and factory modification would be flown in the event of an air defense emergency.[36]

VIII

Once the aircraft was scrambled and airborne, the element of GCI direction entered the operational scene. The basic principle of GCI being the vectoring of the fighter directly to the target, much depended upon the reliability of the information passed to the fighter. This reliability in turn hinged upon the adequacy of the ground radar equipment. It has been mentioned that height-finding equipment presented a major obstacle to effective GCI operation. Lack of height information resulted in a large number of intercept failures during the maneuvers, or in poor tactical positioning for the fighters in relation to the enemy, or in giving circuitous vectors which cut down the combat time of the jet aircraft.

Bearing directly upon the GCI function was the process of cross-telling pertinent information from sector to sector. Only too frequently it was observed that GCI controllers possessed a spirit of provincialism. Of vital importance to the air defense system was

---

36. Ibid.

the necessity of notifying a neighboring defense sector of the impending entry into its sphere of operation of friendly and enemy aircraft. Too frequently this important operation was ignored, with the attending inability of the neighboring GCI station to obtain the maximum advantage of scrambling and vectoring its aircraft to the scene of danger or in aid of an unguided friendly fighter. A basic premise of the continental air defense system was the concept of defense in depth. Unless the GCI operators were synchronized in their efforts and trained to work together, much of the value of the disposition of radars in depth would be negated.

According to the ORT team which surveyed the combat readiness of the 26th Air Division in June 1951, among the main reasons for the failure to cross-tell were:[37] (1) Divisions considered attacks only from their divisional viewpoint — not as overall action requiring cooperation in the exchange of intelligence and the use of forces; (2) Controllers appeared in some cases to be concerned with their areas alone; (3) Tellers were not passing all required information on, but were determining on their own what would and what would not be disseminated.

The necessity of conserving fighter resources was also vital. An overall knowledge of the tactical situation affecting all components was required to control the fighter attempting to return to base, or the fighter trying desperately to land on any safe base, or the fighter desiring to land where his equipment requirements

---

37. 26th Air Division, Operational Readiness Test Report, 22-27 Jun 1951.

could be most easily serviced. The controller, in other words, was responsible not only for the tactics of GCI, properly speaking, but also for aircraft-marshalling and management of the entire resources of a defense sector.

Corollary to the problem of marshalling of resources was the important factor of "turn-around" capability, i.e., the time for refueling, rearming and returning the fighter to alert status after the completion of a mission. This time varied considerably at different bases during the 1951 exercises.[38] From reports received in the EADF area, it was assessed that a normal ground crew complement, with refueling truck and ammunition easily accessible, was capable of turning around a flight of four aircraft in 20 to 30 minutes, regardless of type, but dependent upon weather conditions.[39] Here was a factor in the interception capability problem which, by continuous practice and preorganization, could lower the turn-around time rate to allow greater concentration of power in the air battle.

Of considerable aid to the conservation of fighter resources in the northern areas of the United States was an agreement reached by the 25th Air Division and the Canadian authorities to permit the cross servicing of various aircraft types on Canadian bases. Four

---

38. EADF, Report of Air Defense Exercise, 8-11 Feb 1951.
39. Ibid.

air bases were surveyed in British Columbia for this purpose during the June 1951 maneuver.[40]

IX

One of the greatest apparent weaknesses of the entire /air defense/ system is personnel error.[41]

The present radar net is inefficient, cumbersome, expensive, and easily overloaded, largely as a result of its overdependence on the human element.[42]

Methods now employed in transmission and display of information in our Aircraft Control and Warning nets are inadequate to use the full capabilities of our defensive radar and aircraft.[43]

The quotations cited above are representative of a chorus of opinion from responsible individuals with respect to one of the most troublesome factors in air defense — the difficulty of reporting information quickly and accurately through the air defense system. The possibility that the human element, through error, could destroy the painstaking effort of any element of the nationwide defense complex in the transmission of information had long been recognized by ConAC and ADC. The ORT team of the 26th Air Division was merely repeating an acknowledged observation when it recommended that

---

40. *History of the 25th Air Division, 1 Apr-30 Jun 1951*; see also above chapter on Canada.

41. 26th Air Division, Operational Readiness Test Report, 22-27 Jun 1951.

42. ADC, Operations Analysis Tech. Memo. No. 2, 24 Jun 1950.

43. ConAC to USAF; "Improv████████████████████ Information," 22 Jul 1950. (DOC 328)

"unit commanders take an active interest in impressing each individual connected with plotting, recording, and telling information with the importance of his role in the effective accomplishment of the air defense mission. No where in the entire air defense system is the necessity of team work so vital and could the laxness of one man be so catastrophic."[44]

The nature of the human element in air defense operations and the danger inherent in too great a reliance upon human uniformity of thought and action was well brought out in a report prepared by ADC's Operations Analysis Unit in June 1950. Pertinent extracts from that report follow.[45]

> The work of scope watching and reporting, plotting, telling, recording, and replotting in the radar net is characteristically exceedingly monotonous. During World War II when the voice and manual system originated, the large numbers of competent men required were available. Under the stress of war, monotony was at a premium, and the work was in fact, reasonably well done. The problem in peacetime is quite different. Monotony is the rule, good men able to stand it are scarce, and the work is ill done.
>
> The observing and reporting of aircraft movements on the radar reporter's scopes is a case in point. Careful selection of better, more responsible and higher ranking men....will, in the long run, increase both detection range in the radars and reliability and accuracy of the radar reporting. But the improvement at best can only be incremental and never certain to hold firm.

---

44. 26th Air Division, Operational Readiness Test Report, 22-27 Jun 1951.

45. ADC, Operations Analysis Tech. Memo. No. 2, 24 Jun 1950.

The work of the plotter behind the vertical plotting board to whom the radar reporter reports the position of his blips is even more monotonous. A phlegmatic disposition helps, but the man who is phlegmatic and who has at the same time a capacity for sudden alertness and keen sense of responsibility, both of which are necessary, is rare indeed. The result is that men not well suited to the job must be used, that few plotters can be kept long on the job, and that inaccurate and incomplete plotting is the rule rather than the exception. The plotter appears to be one of the slowest and weakest links in the long chain. Especially is he unreliable in the plotting of tracks received from adjacent radars.

Voice telling of aircraft track information from radar to radar and from radar to control center, introduces still further delay and error, calls for special and continuous training both of the tellers and plotters, and requires the recording of the message at the sending and often by men assigned to do nothing but recording. When air traffic is heavy, the communications become overloaded with the result that a portion of the track information fails to be passed through the radar net at all. The same happens when the teller or plotter dozes off, which no amount of training can altogether preclude.

A radar station is supposed to start overlap telling of track information to an adjacent station when the track reaches a defined overlap zone between the stations. Uncertainty exists occasionally as to which adjacent station should be told track information, stemming partly from the teller's doubts as to which way the aircraft will go. Decision must be made on each track as to when and to whom overlap telling should be started and as to how long it should continue. Because of the complexity of the air situation, the decision is often either a poor one, made too late, or not made at all.

The typical controller in a GCI station tends too often to scramble his fighter aircraft only when the bogey appears on his scope, often so late that his fighters cannot take off and climb to altitude in time to intercept. This reluctance to scramble on the basis of overlap track information comes partly from the controller's real knowledge of the unreliability of the overlap telling, but it seems also to arise from the fact that the controller, as an officer, instinctively distrusts the overlap telling information produced by a loose chain of men in an adjacent radar station whom he knows.... to be of doubtful preciseness and alertness.

Recognizing the urgency of removing the factor of human error from the intricate reporting network, ConAC, in July 1950, presented USAF with the requirement of an improved dissemination of information "through design and application of equipment which will comprise a partially automatic information handling system."[46] The automatic equipment was to perform the following functions:[47]

    a. Receive information from the GCI or early warning radar equipment.

    b. Provide convenient means of filtering such raw data, at the earliest feasible point in the system.

    c. Permit addition of other information into the system (e.g., height, identification, etc.)

    d. Transmission of filtered data, together with the added information to Control Centers, overlap GCI stations, or other required places.

    e. Provide means for combing information from two or more different GCI or other sources of information.

    f. Display the filtered information in appropriate form for use of the Fighter Controller, for the Duty Controller (for assignment of forces) and for the Air Defense Commander.

"The system should be designed and put into operation as soon as possible. This means crash programs, with intensive application and production programs. I consider the project to be exceedingly urgent...."[48] These words of Major General Charles T. Myers, Vice Commander of ConAC reflected the attitude towards this important

---

46. ConAC to USAF: "Improvement of Means of Handling AC&W Information," 22 Jul 1950. (DOC 328)

47. Ibid.

48. Ibid.

subject of the Continental Air Command. Unfortunately, progress on this important development project was extremely slow because of the complexity of the requirement. In late 1950, a semi-automatic plotting board, known as the Goodyear Evaluation Board, was developed, but met with cold reception by ConAC officials on the ground that it was no better than existing systems of manual recording.[49] By the end of June 1951 development on an automatic transmission system was proceeding, but little hope was afforded for initiation of the system actively until some time in 1953 at the earliest.

---

49. IRS, P&R to Comm, "Procurement of Goodyear Projection Board," 12 Aug 1950.

INDEX

A

A-1CM, gun-bomb-rocket sight, 149n
AAA, see Antiaircraft Artillery
AAF, see Army Air Forces
AAOC, see Antiaircraft Artillery
Acheson, Dean, 344
AC&W, see Aircraft Control and Warning; Radar
ADC, see Air Defense Command
ADCC, see Control Centers, Air Defense
ADIZ, see Air Defense Identification Zones
ADLG, see Air Defense Liaison Groups
AEC, see Atomic Energy Commission
AEW, see Airborne Early Warning
AGF, see Army Ground Forces
Airborne Early Warning, 237, 244, 248-50, 363, 364, 368, 369, 370
Airborne Instruments Laboratory, 109
Aircraft, (see also Fighter aircraft, Bomber aircraft)
  all-weather, 121, 141, 143, 154, 155, 157, 392, 411, 416
  armament, 175, 417
  conversion, chart p. 154, 154, 155, 158, 159, 192, 427
  construction, 135, 137-39, see ch. vi
  deployment, see Deployment
  grounded, use of, 428
  maintenance, 162-68
  marshalling, 429, 430
  number of, 152-53, 196, 427
  requirements for, 140-43, 175, 176, 177
  turn-around capability, 430
Aircraft Control and Warning System (AC&W), (see also Radar, ground)
  Alaska, 60
  Canada, see Canada
  Gap-filler program, 113-15
  LASHUP, see ch. iv, 73n, 74, 77, 95, 98, 102, 103, 104, 108, 111, 112, 200, 203, 210, 211, 212, 221, 362, 364, 371, 384, 407, 409, 413, 418
  L-P sites, 102
  logistics, 410, 444
  mobile radar program, 114
  New Mexico, 65, 67, 69n, 79, 81, 99, 362
  Northeast, 64, 65, 67, 68, 69, 77, 79, 108, 361, 364
  Northwest, 62, 63, 65, 67, 69, 79, 80, 81, 199, 364, 373, 376, 391, 410
  organization, 48, chart p. 214
  Permanent System, see ch. v., 73, 96, 97, 101, 102, 109, 113, 200, 211, 363, 415
  plans, 15, 18, 55, 56
  siting, 15, 19, 24, 60, 76, 96, 97, 100, 365, 367
  SUPREMACY, see Plans
  technical representatives, 85, 88
  training, 89, 90
  World War II, 19, 60, 103
Aircraft Warning Service in World War II, 251, 311
Air Defense Command
  sequence of commands bearing this name, 11n
  1940-41, 11
  1946-50, see ch. ii, ch ix (passim)
    abolition of, 212, 213
    activation, 31, 34
    and "unification," 53
    missions, see ch. ii
    organization of, 36, 53n, 197, 201
    Plan SUPREMACY, 56, 58, 362
    reorganization of, 54n, 201
  1951, 215-16
    reactivation, 215
Air Defense Forces, see Eastern, Western and Central Air Defense Forces
Air Defense Group, RCAF, see Canada
Air Defense Identification Zones, 320n, chart p. 376, 377, 390, 391, 393, 412
  coastal boundary, 329-330
  designation of, 324, 328
  free areas, 331-32
  local flying within, 329

position reporting in,
   chart p. 328, 328
requirements for flights in, 324
Air Defense Liaison Groups, 203
206
Air Districts, 13, 14
Air Divisions (Defense) 200, chart
   p. 214
  25th AD, 80, 123, 201, 203, 206,
    207, 208, 223, 224, 245, 357,
    376n, 421, 427, 430
  26th AD, 201, 203, 208, 247,
    248, 417, 431
  34th AD, 423
Air Forces, see by number, e.g.,
   Tenth Air Force
Air Force Combat Command (AFCC)
   18, 23
Airlines, 370
Air Materiel Command (AMC) 31, 81,
   92, 99, 100, 102, 106, 150, 165n,
   169, 170, 384
Air Movement Identification
   Section (AMIS) 5, 379, 380
Air National Guard,
  AC&W units, 58
  aircraft, 164, 417
  crews, 191
  expansion of, 107
  federalization of, 130-33
  fighter units, 126-37
  in air defense, 35, 47, 54
  pilot training, 191
  units assgd to ADC, 130-131
Air Proving Ground (APG) 388
Air Reserve, 35, 37, 269, 270,
   281
Air Route Traffic Control Centers
   (ARTCC) 378, 379
Air Traffic Control (see ch. xiv)
  agreements, 319-20, 323, 324
  Canada, 320n
  civil air traffic, 319, 325
  plans, 317, 318
  WWII, 311-13
Alaska, 22, 73, 86, 363
Alaskan Air Command, 136n, 364
Albuquerque, N. M., 376
  (see also New Mexico)
Albuquerque Air Defense Area,

207, 320, 324, (see also 34th
   Air Division)
Alerts, states of, 166n, 297, 405
Aleutian Island, 22
All-weather aircraft, see Aircraft
AMIS, see Air Movement Identification Section
Anderson, Maj. Gen. S. E., 321-22
Andrews AFB, Wash. D. C., 134, 136
ANG, see Air National Guard
Antiaircraft Artillery, (see ch. x)
  AAOC, 232, 233, 235
  air defense capability, 16, 217
  controversy with AAF, 28, 37, 40,
    44, 218, 219
  exercises 1951, 231-36
  Fifth Army, 222
  First Army, 222, 225, 226
  Fourth Air Force, 28, 33
  gun defended areas (GDAs) 224
  inner artillery zones (IAZ) 224,
    225, 226, 233
  interceptor commands, 19
  JCS, 220, 221, 222, 224
  joint agreements, 222, 223, 225
    226, 227, 228
  Key West Agreement, 220, 221
  organizational problems, 218-29
  procedures, 1948, 220, 221
  rules of engagement, 222-27, 234
  Sixth Army, 224
  Vandenberg-Collins Agreement, 228,
    229
  WWII, 218
Antigo, Wisc., 111
Arlington, Wash., 61, 62
Armament, see Aircraft
Army, military aviation in, 1935-
   41, 7-10
Army Air Forces, 218
  and ADC, 33
  and air defense, 23
  Continental Air Forces, 23
  organization, 8n, 18, 26
  relations with AGF, 26, 28, 29
    33, 40, 43, 45
  reorganization of 1946, 30
Army Antiaircraft Command (ARAACOM)
  establishment, 228-30

Army Ground Forces (AGF) 8n,
  air defense mission, 41, 42
    45, 220, 255
  control of AAA, 26, 27, 28,
    29, 33, 40, 43, 45
Army Service Forces (ASF) 8n,
  26
Arnold, Gen. Henry H., 10,
  11, 338
ARTCC, see Air Route Traffic
  Control Centers
Ashby, G. L. 86n
Assistant Sec. of War for Air,
  8n, 11
Atlantic Coastal Zone, 373, 374
Atlantic Coast in Air Defense,
  23, 24
Atolia, Calif., 108
Atomic Energy Commission, 121,
  307
ATRC, see Air Training Command
Automatic Transmission of Data
  in Air Defense, 434, 435
AWS, see Aircraft Warning Service

B

Baer Field, Ind., 131, 136
Baker Board Report, see Reports
Bangor, Me., 374, 391
Bartlesville, Okla., 108
Bases, Fighter, see under
  specific base
Bedford AFB, 136
Beebe, Col. R. E., 42
Bellefontaine, O., 111
Belleville, Ill., 111
Bellevue Hill, Vt., 107
Bendix Corporation, 109
Bermuda, 22
Berry Field, Tenn., 131
BIG PHOTO, see Exercises
Birch Bay, Wash., 108
BLACKJACK, see Exercises
Blackouts, WWII, 289, 312
Blue Knob Park, Pa., 111
Bohokus Peak, Wash., 111
Bomber aircraft
  B-26, 78

B-29, 91, 92, 389, 391
B-47, 382n
B-50, 148, 389n, 391
Bomber commands, 24
Bonneville, Wash., 66
Boston, Mass., 66, 379
Bradley Field, Conn., 131
Brainard Field, Conn., 131
Britain, Battle of, 11, 13,
  251, 360
British Columbia, Canada, 356
  367, 431
Brookfield, O., 111
Brunswick NAS, Me., 107
Buffalo, N. Y., 352
Bull Board Report, see Reports
Burlington Municipal Airport,
  Vt., 130, 134, 136

C

CAA, see Civil Aeronautics
  Authority
CAD, see Civil Air Defense
CADF, see Central Air Defense Force
Calibration, Radar, 78, 90-93, 113
California, air defense of, 81, 108,
  362
Cambria, Cal., 103, 111
Camera gunnery, 194
Camp Hero, N. Y., 102
Canada, (see ch. xv)
  Air Defense Group, RCAF, 340,
    341, 342, 350, 354
  air defense system, 364
  air traffic control agreements,
    320n, 339, 346-48
  Canada-U.S. Emergency Air Defense
    Plan (CANUSEADP) 339, 340, 341,
    351n, 354, 393
  civil air defense (GOC) 274-77,
    355, 356
  communications, 339
  cross-servicing of aircraft, 355,
    430
  early warning, 356, 362, 364,
    366
  electronics countermeasures,
    339, 355

exchange of information, 355, 358
IFF, 339, 355, 357
overfly agreements, 349-54
radar extension plan, 346, 346n
RCAF, 340, 344, 348, 357, 358, 388
SUPREMACY, 362
U.S.-Canadian Permanent Joint Board on Defense (PJBD) 338, 348, 351, 353, 358n

Canadian Radar Sites (see also AC&W)
extension plans, 343, 345
manning, chart p. 344
number of, chart p. 344, 344
siting, 100, 344, chart p. 344, chart p. 346

Caribbean Defense Command, 65
CARW, see Civil Air Raid Warning System
Cascade Mountains, 80
Caswell, Me., 103, 108
Central Air Defense Force, 215
Chaney, Brig. Gen. James E., 11n
Charleston, Me., 111
Chatham, New Brunswick, 354
Chidlaw, Lt. Gen. Benjamin W., 99n, 164n, 170, 170n, 383
Civil Aeronautics Authority, 314-15, 316, 317, chart p. 318, 319, 347, 378, 379, 389, CAR 620, 324-25, 395
  Joint CAA-USAF Air Defense Planning Board, 320, 323
Civil Air Defense,
  ADC Directorate of, 268
  civil air raid warning, see ch. xiii
  creation of agency for, 257
  formation of Civil Air Defense Section, 263
  GOC, see ch. xii
Civil Air Raid Warning, see ch. xiii, 260, 268
  alerts, 297, 302-303
  dissemination of, 289, 290, 291, 293

efficiency of, 295-96, 298n, 300
FCDA, 304-306
intertoll facilities, 298, 301
Key Points, 293, 295, 296, 298, 299, 300, 301, chart p. 302, 306
Multipoint Network, 298, 299, 300-301
organization, 292-94, 295
sequence list, 296
sub-audible frequencies, 292
SWKP, 293, 295, 300
telegraphic multipoint, 299, 300
WWII, 288-90

Civil Defense facilities, 294
Civilians in air defense in WWII, 251-54
Coast Guard, 245, 248, 272
Colville, Wash., 97, 102, 111
Combat air patrol, 425, 426
Combat crews, see Crews
Combat Crew Training School, see Schools
ConAC, see Continental Air Command
Condon, Ore., 103, 111
Congress, 57, 60, 71, 72, 73, 95, 96, 113, 363 (see also Public Laws)
Continental Air Command,
  activation, 117, 201
  air defense mission, ch. ix (passim)
  radar net, 96, 100
Control Centers, Air Defense, 97, 98
Controller,
  ACW functions, 420, 430, 433
  experience, 411, 427, 428
  responsibilities for AAA, 231-35
  training, 421
Controller schools, see Schools
Conversion of aircraft, see Aircraft
Conversion of radar, see Radar
Crews, (see also ch. viii)
  combat readiness, 426
  combat requirements, 178
  growth of, in numbers, 185, chart p. 186
  per aircraft, 177
  plans for manning, 177
  shortage of, 183, 186, 190
  training, 190-96

training directives, 191
training problems, 183
Cross Mt., Tenn., 108
Cross-telling, 428, 429, 432

D

Dalton, CWO R. W., 165n
Defense in depth, 363, 429
Defense Commands, 13, 15, 17, 22, 23, 24, 28, 29
Del Bonita, Mont., 111
Deployment, (see Radar, ch. vi, 210)
   23 squadron deployment plan, 125, 211
   other aircraft deployment plans, 125, 126
Detroit, Mich., 349, 352, 393n
Devers, Gen. Jacob L., 45
Dingledein, Capt. R., 182n
Douglass, Maj. Gen. R., 49n
Dover AFB, Del., 134, 136
Dow AFB, Me., 122, 130, 136, 354
Drum Board Report, see Reports
DRUMMERBOY, see Exercises
Duluth, Mun Arpt., Minn., 131, 134, 136
Duncansville, Tex., 108

E

E-1 Fire Control System, 149n
EADF, see Eastern Air Defense Force
Early Warning, see ch. xvi
East Farmington, Wisc., 107
Eastern Air Defense Force, see ch. ix
Eastern Sea Frontier, see ch. xi
Eastern Theatre of Operations, 32
Edwards, Lt. Gen. Idwal H., 93
Edwards AFB, Cal., 156
Eleventh Air Force, 31
El Vado, N. M., 99, 103
Elkhorn, Wisc., 102, 107

Ellington, Tex., 108
Empire, Mich., 107
Engel, Maj. G. W., 193n
England, see Great Britain
Exercises,
   1951, 234, 286, 412-31
   BIG PHOTO, 243, 249, 411
   BLACKJACK, 78, 244, 318, 409
   DRUMMERBOY, 80, 150, 207, 248, 374, 375, 409, 414
   Korea and, 411
   LOOKOUT, 79, 150, 258, 275, 291, 292, 295, 318, 409
   Northeast 1948, 69
   Northwest 1948, 64, 116, 121, 199, 313
   NOVFLEXPAC 1948, 238
   TUNA, 247
   WHIPSTOCK, 81, 213n, 244, 245, 411

F

Fairchild, Gen. Muir S., 177n
Far East Air Forces (FEAF) 85, 160, 162
FCDA, see Federal Civil Defense Administration
FEAF, see Far East Air Forces
Federal Civil Defense Administration (FCDA) 280, 303, 304-306
Federal Forest Service, 272
Field Artillery, 9n
Field Manuals,
   FM 1-15, 25, 28, 33
   FM 100-20, 26, 27, 28, 30-31, 33
Fighter Aircraft
   F4U, 416
   F-47, 47n, 144, 153, 154, 165, 185, 413
   F-51, 62, 63, 145, 153, 154, 165, 185, 413
   F-61, 47n, 62, 144, 145, 148
   F-80, 145, 146, 147, 149n, 153, 165n, 172, 173, 185, 416
   F-82, 148, 151, 152, 153, 416
   F-84, 133, 144, 146, 147, 152, 153, 161, 162, 165n, 168n, 172, 173, 174, 185, 416

F-86, 147, 152, 153, 155n, 157, 159, 160, 168n, 174, 183, 185, 191, 384, 396, 416
F-86D, 153, 154, 155, 156, 157, 158, 162, 181, 182, 396, 416
F-89, 153, 154, 155, 156, 158, 162, 179, 181, 182, 396, 417
F-94, 148, 149, 150, 151, 152, 153, 154, 158, 166, 167, 169, 170, 174, 179, 181, 182, 183n, 185, 192, 384, 396, 416
Fighter Rules of Engagement, see ch. xvii, 397, 406
Filter Centers,
 functions, chart p. 260, chart p. 262, 261-62
 location, 263, 264, 278, 286
 personnel, 262, 265, 269-71, 279, 280, 282
 problems, 268-69, 283
 WWII, 19-20, 252, 254
Finland, Minn., 102
Finlay, N. D., 111
First Air Force, 22, 23, 24, 31, 69, 77, 201, 203, 206, 209
FIRST AUGMENTATION, see Plans
Flash reports, 370
FM, see Field Manuals
Fordland, Mo., 111
Forrestal, James, 56n, 70, 104n
Fort Austin, Mich., 103
Fort Custer, Mich., 103, 111
Fort Custis, Va., 102, 111, 384n
Fort Ethan Allen, Vt., 354
Fort Knox, Ky., 111
Fort MacArthur, Cal., 81, 294n
Fort Meade, Md., 84
Fort Monmouth, N. J., 10
Fortuna, N. D., 111

Fourth Antiaircraft Command, 24, 29

G

GCI, see Ground Controlled Interception
Geiger Field, Wash., 130, 131, 134, 136
General Electric Co., 104, 105
General Headquarters Air Force, 3, 8, 9, 10n, 11, 13, 14, 15, 16, 17, 33
Gen. Mitchell Fld., Minn., 131
George AFB, Cal., 134, 136
GHQ Air Force, see General Headquarters Air Force
GOC, see Ground Observer Corps
Gonzales, N. M., 103
Goodyear Evaluation Board, 435
Grandview, Mo., 136
Great Britain, 12, 20, 68, 361
Great Lakes, air defense of, 362
Greater Pittsburgh Arpt, Pa., 134, 136
Grenier AFB, N. H., 78, 79, 130, 136
Griffiss AFB, N. Y., 91, 134, 136
Ground Controlled Interception, (see ch. xviii)
 communications, 425
 in Great Britain, 20
 marshalling, 429, 430
 principles, 105
 vectoring, 428
Ground Observer Corps, (see ch. xii)
 alerting of, 273
 Canada, 273-77
 coordinators, 282
 cost of, 258
 formation of, 259, 260
 function of, 257-58, 261-62
 in Exercise LOOKOUT, 79, 258-59
 observers in WWII, 19, 251-54
 personnel, 261, 265
 posts, 252, 254, chart p. 260,

Groups AC&W (see chart p. 214)
   503d, 86, 200
   505th, 48n, 61, 86, 200
   531st, 86, 367
Groups, Fighter, see Wings
Guided Missiles, 46
Gunnery training, 192, 194
Guthrie, W. Va., 111

H

Half Moon Bay, Cal., 61, 80
Hamilton AFB, Cal., 62, 91, 122, 134, 136, 156, 294n
Hanford, Wash., see Seattle-Hanford area
Hanna City, Ill., 111
Hanscom AFB, Mass., 134
Hartford, Conn., 66
Hazeltine Corporation, 112
Height-finders, (see Radar, equipment) 82, 84, 111, 112, 413
Hensley NAS, Texas, 134, 136n
Hill Peak Road, Cal., 102
Holman Fld., Minn., 131
Hood, Maj. Gen., R. C., 53n
Hood Committee, 53n
Hopley Report, see Reports
House of Representatives, Committee on Armed Services, 72n 113n
Hutchinson NAS, Kans., 108

I

Identification (see ch. xvii)
  air traffic control as a means of, 372, 373-80
  effect on interception, 422, 423
  GOC, as a means of, 372
  IFF, as a means of, 372
  interception, as a means of, 372, 373
IFF,
  adoption of, 12
  Beacon assist, 170-75, 381, 383
  compromise of, 314, 382

  ground interrogators, 171, 173, 380, 383, 385
  Group "A" parts, 388
  Mark III, 172, 173, 174, 175, 381, 382
  Mark X, 171, 172, 174, 175, 381-388, 396
  plans with Canada, see Canada
  WWII, 20, 312n
IFR, see Instrument Flight Rules
Instrument Flight Rules, 318, 320, 327, 328
Interception, see ch. xvii, 388-406
Interceptor Commands, 19, 20, 24, 25
Interim AC&W System (LASHUP), see AC&W (see also ch. iv)
Israel, Col. Robert S., Jr., 320n, 321, 347n

J

JCS, see Joint Chiefs of Staff
Joint Board of Army and Navy, 6, 13
Joint Chiefs of Staff (JCS)(see also Antiaircraft Artillery, Navy)
  Air Defense policy, 38, 40, 52, 72, 96, 369
Joint Defense Planning Committee, 225

K

Kansas City, Mo., 216
Keesler AFB, Miss., 183
Kellogg Fld., Mich., 131
Keweenaw, Mich., 103
Key West Conference, see Antiaircraft Artillery; Navy, 53, 65, 239
King, MacKenzie, W. L., 339n
Kinross AFB, Mich., 134, 136
Kirtland AFB, N. M., 66, 81, 123, 131, 134, 136

identification, 42
interceptor program, 126-29, 157, 175, 392
LASHUP, 86, 363, 408
number of crews in ADC, 186, 187
number of radar personnel, 214

L

Labrador, 356, 367
Lackland AFB, Texas, 111
Langley AFB, Va., 134, 136
Larson AFB, Wash., (Moses Lake) 80, 122, 123, 134, 136, 150, 384n
LASHUP, see AC&W
Leaf River, Minn., 111
Lee, Col. Joseph D., 222
Limestone AFB, Me., 352
Lockbourne AFB, Ohio, 130, 136
Lockheed Aircraft Corp., 148
Long Beach, Calif., 136
LOOKOUT, see Exercises
Los Alamos, N. M., 58, 66, 81, 325n, 375, 390, 391
Los Angeles Air Defense Area, 376
Los Angeles, Calif., 320, 321, 322
Luftwaffe, 12

M

MacArthur, Gen. Douglas, 3n
Madera, Calif., 102, 111
Maneuvers, see Exercises
Marines, see Navy
Mather AFB, Calif., 108
McChord AFB, Wash., 47, 62, 80, 107, 124, 134, 136, 150, 419
McClellan AFB, Calif., 62
McGhee-Tyson AFB, Tenn., 81, 134, 136
McGuire AFB, N. J., 66, 134, 136
McNitt, Col. J. R., 96
Merchant Marine, 364, 370
MFS, see Military Flight Service
Microwave, radar, 10n

Military Air Raid Warning, 260, 288, 387
  military key point, 307-10, 310n, chart p. 310
  multipoint private line, 309-310
  principles of operation, 307-308
  types of alert, 308-309
Military Air Transport Service, 330, 387
Military Flight Service, 314-15
Minty, Brig. Gen. Russell J., 248
Mitchel AFB, N. Y., 11n, 31, 47, 77, 91, 122, 123
Mobile Training Detachments, 194-195
Montauk, N. Y., 68, 69, 77, 111, 247
Moriarty N. M., 102
Moses Lake AFB, see Larson AFB
Moulton, Minn., 111
Mount Bonaparte, Wash., 103, 111
Mount Laguna, Calif., 111
Mount Tamalpais, Calif., 81, 103
Moving Target Indicator (MTI) 97, 98, 99, 103, 105, 109
MTD, see Mobile Training Detachment
MTI, see Moving Target Indicator
Mud Pond, Pa., 107
Muroc AFB, Calif., 81
Myers, Maj. Gen. Chas. T., 164n, 213n, 434

N

Naselle, Wash., 111
Nashville, Tenn., 136
Navesink, N. J., 102, 107
Navy, (see ch. xi; also, Picket vessels)
  airborne early warning, see AEW
  aircraft, 217, 237, 238, 416, 418
  and air defense, 369
  antiaircraft, 217, 237

exercises, 244-50
Joint Chiefs of Staff, 238, 239, 240, 246, 340, 381
Joint Operations Center (JOC) 238, 239
Key West, 239
Marines, 242, 243
Mark X IFF, 387
NOVFLEXPAC, 238
radar, 111, 115, 217, 238
TUNA, 247
USAF policy on doctrine and procedures, 240
Neah Bay, Wash., 62, 80, 98, 384n
Neal, Col. Haskell E., 99n, 107n, 113n
New Brunswick, Canada, 367
New Castle AFB, Del., 130, 134, 136
Newfoundland, 22, 356, 367
New Mexico, see AC&W; Albuquerque
New York, N. Y., 22, 66
Niagara Falls, N. Y., 66, 131, 134, 136, 352, 393n
Norfolk, Va., 374, 391
Norstad, Maj. Gen. Lauris, 42, 43, 69
Northeast Air Command, 345, 364, 367
North Truro, Mass., 107
Northwest Air Defense Wing (Provisional) 199
Northwest Maneuver 1948, see Exercises
Nova Scotia, 367
NOVFLEXPAC, see Exercises
Nyrop, Donald W., 323

O

Oakridge, Tenn., 375, 390, 391
Office of Chief of Engineers (OCE) 99, 100, 101
Office of Civil Defense, 19, 258
Office of Civil Defense Liaison, 263, 267, 278
Offutt AFB, Neb., 134, 136
O'Hare AFB, Ill., 134, 136
Olathe NAS, Kan., 111
Olympia, Wash., 80

Omaha, Neb., 211
Operational Readiness Test of 26th AD, 417, 422, 426, 429, 431
Operations, see ch. xviii
Operations Analysis Unit, ADC, 423, 432
Ophiem, Mont., 111
Orlando, Fla., 89
Oscoda AFB, Mich., 134, 136
Otis AFB, Mass., 134, 136, 384n
Oxnard AFB, Calif., 134, 136

P

Pacific Beach, Wash., 80, 245
Package Plan, 126, 128, 133, 137
Paine AFB, Wash., 80, 134, 136, 245, 419
Palermo, N. J., 69, 77, 102, 111, 247, 384n
Panama, 10n
Pasco, Wash., 61, 80
Passive detection, 366
Personnel error in AC&W System, 431, 432
Philadelphia, Pa., 66
Philco Corp., 86
Picket vessels, 237, 244, 245, 246, 247, 248, 363, 368, 369
Pine Camp, N. Y., 78, 79
PJBD, see U.S.-Canadian Permanent Joint Board
Plan Position Indicator (PPI) 382
Plans, air defense (see Deployment; SUPREMACY)
23 squadron plan, 125, 211
1933, 3
95 wing, 126
ADC 1946, 36, 47, 48-52, 197, 198
FIRST AUGMENTATION, 72, 73n, 95, 104
Package Plan, 126, 128, 133, 137
SEEDCORN, 133
Point Arena, Calif., 111
Port Austin, Mich., 111
Portland, Ore., 62, 131, 134, 136,

Pre-plotting system, 311, 314
Presque Isle, Me., 130, 134, 136
Price, Col. James H., 322
Prohibited flying areas, 324-25
  in WWII, 312-13
Public Laws,
  Public Law 30, 72
  Public Law 778, 324-25, 378, 394, 395
  Public Law 920, 303, 305, 306

Q

Quantico, Va., 111
Quebec, 367

R

Radar, airborne,
  AN/APX-6, 170-75, 383, 388
Radar, ground,
  AN/CPS-1, 82, 83, 93, 98, 412
  AN/CPS-4, 82, 83, 84, 94, 112, 412
  AN/CPS-5, 61, 69, 78, 82, 83, 93, 107, 108, 109, 110, 412
  AN/CPS-6, 68, 69, 78, 82, 84, 103
  AN/CPS-6B, 57, 71, 72, 83, 103, 104, 106, 108, 109, 110, 365, 415
  AN/CPS-6B (M) 106
  AN/FPS-3, 57, 71, 93, 94, 106, 108, 109, 110, 111, 112, 115, 365
  AN/FPS-6, 110, 111, 112, 113, 115
  AN/FPS-10, 106, 107
  AN/MPS-4, 112, 113, 115
  AN/MPS-7, 115
  AN/TPS-1B, 62, 69, 82, 83, 84, 93, 412
  AN/TPS-1D, 107, 110, 115
  AN/TPS-10A, 82, 84, 85, 94, 112, 412
  AN/TPS-10D, 107, 110, 112
  delivery of, 106, 109

Research, 6, 10, 10n, 82, 103
Radar Observers,
  operations, 156
  procurement, 182, 184, 185
  school, see Schools
  training, 182, 188
Radio Corporation of America, 87
Rapid City, Iowa, 134, 136
RCAF, see Royal Canadian Air Force
Reading AFB, Pa., 130
Reedsport, Ore., 111
Renton, Wash., 66
Reporting, 431 ff.
  (see also Automatic transmission of data and Cross-telling)
Reports,
  Baker Board, 4-5, 8n
  Bull Board, 254
  Drum Board, 4
  Hopley Report, 254
  USAF Policy Panel, 219, 244
Richland, Wash., 325n, 375, 390
  (see also Hanford)
Roosevelt, F. D., 339n
ROSEBUD, project, 382
Roslyn, N. Y., 69, 77, 78, 79, 294n
Roswell, N. M., 81
Royal Canadian Air Force, see Canada
Rush, Maj. Gen. Hugo P., 320n

S

SAC, see Strategic Air Command
Saddle Mt., Wash., 102, 111
San Clemente I., Calif., 111
San Francisco, Calif., 22, 57, 376
San Francisco Identification Zone, 320, 321, 322, 393
Santa Rosa Isle, Calif., 108
Santini, N. Y., 247, 384n
Sault Ste Marie, Mich., 102, 111, 352
Saville, Maj. Gen. Gordon P., 15n, 21, 56n, 70, 71, 84, 104n, 113, 202n, 208n
Schlatter, Maj. Gen. David M., 146n

combat crew training, 168n, 178, 179 (see also ch. viii)
controller, 189
loss of pilots to, 187, 188
radar observer, 182, 183, 184, 188
Schuylerville, N. Y., 111
Scott Field, Ill., 134, 136
Scrambles, 425, 427
Seaside, Ore., 62, 80
Seattle, Wash., 57, 61, 63, 66, 108, 315, 361
Seattle-Hanford area, 62, 66, 199, 315, 316, 320, 326, 373, 376, 391
Second Air Force, 22, 23, 31
Secretary of Defense, 84
Secretary of War, 16
SEEDCORN, 133
Selfridge AFB, Mich., 78, 102, 103, 134, 136, 294n, 384n
Sequim, Wash., 80
Shawnee, N. Y., 103
Short Interval Identification System (SIIS) 386
SIIS, see Short Interval Identification System
Simpson, Mont., 111
Sioux Falls Mun. Arpt., S. D., 136
Smith, Maj. Gen. F. H. Jr., 106, 213n
Spaatz, Lt. Gen. Carl, 46n, 338
Spokane, Wash., 62, 80, 418
Squadrons, see chart p. 214
State Wide Key Point, see Civil Air Raid Warning
St. Hubert, Que., 354
Stone, Maj. Gen. Charles B., 35n
Stout Field, Ind., 131
Strategic Air Command, 31, 34, 40, 54n, 62, 78, 89, 113, 114, 117, 119, 120n, 140, 192, 330, 382n, 387, 411, 418
Stratemeyer, Lt. Gen. George E., 31, 32, 35, 37, 39, 45, 49n, 64, 69, 117, 199, 238, 255, 256, 316
Sublette, Mo., 108
Suffolk Cy Arpt, N. Y., 134, 136
SUPREMACY, Plan, 56-60, 64, 67, 69, 70, 95, 362, 363

SWKP, see State Wide Key Point
Syracuse, N. Y., 105
Systems Training, 411, 420

T

T-33 aircraft, 148, 167-68, 192 (see also F-94)
TAC, see Tactical Air Command
Tacoma, Wash., 66
Tactical Air Command, 31, 33, 40, 54n, 91, 92, 117, 118, 120n, 192, 201, 204, 212, 215
Taft, Calif., 81
Tamalpais Mt., Calif., 107
Tennessee, 362
Tenth Air Force, 31
Thatcher, Brig. Gen. H. B., 127, 127n, 140n
Third Air Force, 22, 23
Tinker AFB, Okla., 108
Transmission of information, see Automatic transmission of data; Reporting
Travis AFB, Calif., 134, 136
Truax Field, Wisc., 130, 134, 136
T-U4, 389n
TUNA, see Exercises
Twelfth Air Force, 207
Twin Lights, N. J., 68, 77, 78, 84, 384n
Tyndall AFB, Fla., 180

U

Upston, Maj. Gen. John E., 145, 207n, 209n
U.S.-Canadian Permanent Joint Board on Defense, see Canada
USN, see Navy

V

Vampire aircraft, 68
Vancouver, B. C., 80
Vandenberg, Gen. Hoyt, 138, 139,

VHF, see Very High Frequency
Vincent, Brig. Gen. Clinton D., 411, 421
Visual Flight Rules, 327, 328

W

WADF, see Western Air Defense Force
Walker AFB, N. M., 66
Walla Walla, Wash., 62
War Assets Administration, 60n
War Department, 9, 10
  Aircraft Warning Service, 12
  air defense system, 15, 20
  assignment of responsibility, 46
  Circular No. 138, 43, 44, 65
  creation of four defense commands, 13
  directive of Mar 1941, 16, 28, 33
  directive of 8 Apr 1946, 41, 42
  General Staff, 2
  recruits civilians as ground observers WWII, 18
  reorganization of Mar 1942, 26
  reorganization of 1946, 30, 41
  research in 1936, 6, 9
  reunites OCAC and GHQ, 17
Washington, D. C., 66, 78
Watertown, N. Y., 111
Watson-Watt, R. A., 18n, 20, 21, 252
Waverley, Iowa, 108
WD, see War Department
Webster, Maj. Gen. Robert M., 124, 208
Western Air Defense Force, see ch. ix
Western Sea Frontier, 249
Westover AFB, Mass., 66, 134, 136
Whidbey Island, Wash., 79, 80
Whitehead, Lt. Gen. Ennis C., 92, 93, 101, 143n, 145n, 170, 173, 173n, 177, 178, 207, 208n, 210, 321, 322n, 347n, 383,
Wichita AFB, Kans., 134
Wings, Fighter-Interceptor
  composition of, 118
  1st, 119, 120, 129, 145
  4th, 119, 124, 128, 129, 159
  14th, 47n, 118, 120, 122, 144
  20th, 119, 162
  23d, 130
  27th, 144
  31st, 119
  33d, 119, 129, 151, 158, 166
  52d, 47n, 122, 129, 144, 148, 151, 165, 183
  56th, 119, 129, 151, 158, 166
  78th, 47n
  81st, 120, 123, 129, 174
  82d, 120
  325th, 47n, 62, 63, 118, 121, 122, 124, 129, 144, 145, 148, 150, 151
  449th, 136n
Wold-Chamberlain AFB, Minn., 134, 136
Wright-Patterson AFB, Ohio, 134, 136
Wrong, Hume M., 344

X
(No Entries)

Y

Yaak, Mont., 111
Yeager, Col. Hobart R., 60n, 86
Youngstown AFB, Ohio, 134, 136

Z
(No Entries)